THE SENTENCE

Y0-BVF-504

THE
CENTURY COLLEGIATE HANDBOOK

THE
CENTURY
COLLEGIATE
HANDBOOK

Garland Greever
Easley S. Jones
Agnes Law Jones

THIRD EDITION

New York

APPLETON-CENTURY-CROFTS, INC.

PREFACE TO THE THIRD EDITION

The Century Collegiate Handbook, Third Edition, is a manual for the use of college and university students of writing. Part One treats essential matters of sentence structure, grammar, diction, spelling, and punctuation. Part Two treats the form and organization of the theme as a whole and of the paragraph, the large topics of logic and style, and the habits and procedures which students of writing do well to cultivate.

In large plan this book is like its predecessors. In nearly every other respect it is markedly different.

Within many articles and blocks of five articles the order of presentation is changed. A large amount of fresh illustrative material is supplied. Structure is tightened to facilitate reference. The exercises throughout are new.

Certain innovations call for brief mention:

1. Two devices help the student to focus on a definite purpose. (*a*) Each article conspicuously bears, just before the detailed treatment, the subcaption *How to Correct* or *How to Achieve*. (*b*) Instead of broad labels for examples—*Weak* or *Wrong* and *Improved* or *Right*—this revision provides a condemnatory label which indicates the explicit fault and a corrective label which, as a complete sentence, tells the student exactly how to proceed.

2. Besides the usual front chart of article titles, the revision has at the back an analytical chart for referring to subdivisions. By jotting *3a* or *36b* in the margin of a theme the teacher can direct the student to the treatment of a specific difficulty. By jotting *X-3a* or *X-36b* he can further instruct the student to write out the exercise which accompanies the treatment.

The Third Edition was prepared by Garland Greever and Agnes Law Jones, widow of Dr. Easley S. Jones. Each collaborator has criticized and assisted the work of the other. Mr. Greever, however, assumes full responsibility for the first twenty-four articles; Mrs. Jones for Articles 25-55.

G. G.

A. L. J.

CONTENTS

Part One

THE SENTENCE AND ITS PARTS

THE COMPLETE SENTENCE

CONTENTS

CONTENTS

Part Two

LARGER ELEMENTS AND PROBLEMS

THE WHOLE COMPOSITION

CONTENTS

CLEAR THINKING

STYLE

CONTENTS

LETTERS AND MANUSCRIPT

KEY TO YOUR INSTRUCTOR'S MARKS OF CORRECTION
ON THEMES

2   = Study Article 2.

2a   = Study Subdivision 2a.

X-2 = Study Article 2; write all the exercises which follow it.

X-2a = Study Subdivision 2a; write the exercise for it.

X-2c = Study Subdivision 2c; on finding that its exercise is combined with the one for 2d, write the combined exercise (it is labeled X-2c,d).

PART ONE

THE SENTENCE AND ITS PARTS

The Complete Sentence

FRAGMENTS WRONGLY USED AS SENTENCES

I. Do not write a subordinate part of a sentence as if it were a whole sentence.

HOW TO TEST FOR SENTENCE WHOLENESS

Ia. **The Complete Statement Test** Does the group of words express a complete thought? If it does, it forms a sentence. If it does not, it forms only a fragment of a sentence.

Fragment: Behind the manager's desk sat a redheaded secretary. Ripping open envelopes and tossing them into a wastebasket. [The second group of words does not in itself convey a complete meaning. It must be joined to the first.]

Complete statement: Behind the manager's desk sat a redheaded secretary, ripping open envelopes and tossing them into a wastebasket.

Fragment: What do you think of our chances? If Jim is out of the game. [The second group of words conveys only a part of a thought. It should not be allowed to pose as the expression of a full meaning.]

Complete statement: What do you think of our chances if Jim is out of the game?

The complete statement test depends wholly on thought. It may be made by a person who is ignorant of grammar. But you as a student should be able to test the completeness of a sentence grammatically.

1b. The Grammar Test for Wholeness Does the group of words contain at least one subject and one finite verb? Does it have these in a main (independent) clause? If it fails on either count it is only a fragment of a sentence.

(1) Learning to distinguish between finite verbs and verbals

A **finite verb** is a word or a group of words used to assert (or ask) something.

The baby now walks. [The word *walks* makes an assertion about the baby; it tells what the baby does. It is a finite verb.]

Snow has been falling since midnight. [The words *has been falling*, taken as a group, tell what the snow has done. They form a finite verb.]

A **verbal** is a word or group of words formed from a verb but used mainly as a noun or a modifier. It does not, like the finite verb, assert something. There are three types of verbals: infinitives, participles, and gerunds.

An *infinitive* is a verbal used as a noun or a modifier (adjective or adverb). Ordinarily it is introduced by *to*, the sign of the infinitive.

Infinitive as noun: *To have been defeated* is his misfortune. [An ordinary noun would have the same force as the infinitive: Past *defeat* is his misfortune.]

Infinitive as adjective: Her ability *to sing* was soon discovered. [Ordinary adjective: Her *vocal* ability was soon discovered.]

A *participle* is a verbal used as an adjective. It may either precede or follow the noun it modifies.

Participle: *Standing*, a person seems tall. [Regular adjective: An *erect* person seems tall.]

Participle: Isabel, *musing*, did not reply. [Regular adjective: Isabel, *pensive*, did not reply.]

Participle: At last the ship had become a hulk, *battered* by a thousand storms. [Regular adjective: The ship had become a hulk, *helpless* after a thousand storms.]

4

A *gerund* is a verbal used as a noun. It contains the ending *ing*.

Gerund: *Seeing* is *believing*. [Ordinary nouns: *Sight* is *belief*.]

Gerund: For *having answered* correctly you receive the prize. [Ordinary noun: For correct *answers* you receive the prize.]*

(2) Learning to distinguish between main and subordinate clauses

A *main (independent) clause* is a group of words which contains a subject and a finite verb (not just a verbal) and which is not introduced by a subordinating word.

Single main clause: Wolves howl. [The clause contains but two words, a subject *wolves* and a finite verb *howl*.]

Single main clause: The unrest has increased alarmingly. [The clause contains a subject *unrest*, a verb *has increased*, and other words besides.]

Two main clauses: Lola sings and Tim plays. [Neither clause is subordinated to the other; the word *and* joins equals.]

A *subordinate (dependent) clause* is a group of words which contains a subject and a finite verb but which is linked to a main clause by a word showing its dependence. It cannot stand alone as a sentence; it does the work of a single part of speech—adjective, adverb, or noun. The word which introduces it must be either

a relative } who, which, that, whom, whose, whoever, whatever, pronoun } (by) whom, (during) which, etc.

or a subordinating } when, where, if, while, though, unless, conjunction } because, as, that, so that, etc.†

* For a further study of verbals see 14.

† Note, however, that some of the words listed as subordinating conjunctions or as relative pronouns may be used as other parts of speech, in which case they may belong to main clauses, that is, to complete sentences. Examples: *When* do you go? *Where* is your shawl? *Who* is the first? *That* is his room. *That* bucket leaks. *Whose* hat is *that*? She stayed for a *while*. They worked *as* laborers. By *whom* was it written? *Which* dog is yours?

Subordinate clause as adverb: They will come *where we are.*
[The sentence could read: They will come *here.*]

Subordinate clause as adjective: The runner *who wins* is wildly
applauded. [The sentence could read: The *successful* runner
is wildly applauded.]

Subordinate clause as noun (subject): *Whatever you ask* shall
be granted. [The sentence could read: Your *requests* shall be
granted.]

Subordinate clause as noun (object): He will choose *whoever
is best qualified.* [The sentence could read: He will choose
the best qualified *person.*]

Subordinate clause as predicate noun: This is *what we want.*
[The sentence could read: This is our *desire.*]

HOW TO CORRECT THE FRAGMENTARY SENTENCE

Fragmentary sentences may be corrected (1) by attaching
the fragment to a main clause, or (2) by supplying the elements necessary to make the fragment into a main clause
or a complete sentence.

I c. **Phrases and Clauses as Fragments** A common error in
student writing is the detached phrase or clause following a main statement. The writer is able to identify the
main statement as a complete grammatical unit which can be
set off by a period. But he has not paused to ask whether
the succeeding part can likewise stand alone. Test each statement to make sure that it is complete *without the aid of the
preceding sentence.*

Prepositional phrase detached: * Such students work hard.
From the very shortness of their hours or with an eye to
Phi Beta Kappa.

* A phrase is a group of words which does not contain a subject
and a finite verb. It is used as a single part of speech. A prepositional
phrase is "introduced" by a preposition: *of, in, with, by, for, like, to,
at, down, from, over, under, through, between, among, above, below,
except,* etc. The introducing preposition does not always come first.
Example: Which address did you write *to?*

Combine in one sentence: Such students work hard, from the very shortness of their hours or with an eye to Phi Beta Kappa.

Subordinate (adverb) clause detached: We must send social workers into the homes. If we would learn what the living conditions are.

Make the *if* clause modify *must send*: We must send social workers into the homes if we would learn what the living conditions are.

Subordinate (adjective) clause detached: The teamsters drive out these men. Who have come among them as stool pigeons.

Make the *who* clause modify *men*: The teamsters drive out these men, who have come among them as stool pigeons.

Verbal (participial) phrase detached: The tires are worn thin. Having been used for twenty thousand miles.

Join the phrase to the main clause: The tires are worn thin, having been used for twenty thousand miles. [Or give the detached element a subject and verb and express the idea independently.] The tires are worn thin. They have been used for twenty thousand miles.

Verbal (infinitive) phrase detached: Thousands of men have been at work. To check the spread of blister rust and beetles through the pine forests of the South and West.

Join the phrase to the main clause: Thousands of men have been at work to check the spread of blister rust and beetles through the pine forests of the South and West.

Verbal (gerund) phrase detached: Do you know you make yourself a lawbreaker? By parking in front of driveways.

Join the phrase to the main clause: Do you know you make yourself a lawbreaker by parking in front of driveways?

1d. Other Types of Wrongly Used Fragments

Detached member of a compound predicate: Nowadays we erect very tall buildings. But make them secure from earthquakes.

Combine the elements: Nowadays we erect very tall buildings but make them secure from earthquakes. [Or expand the fragment into an independent sentence.] Nowadays we erect very tall buildings. But we make them secure from earth-quakes.

Detached appositive: * At Jamestown stands a ruined tower. A memorial of the historic first settlement.

Join the phrase to the main clause: At Jamestown stands a ruined tower, a memorial of the historic first settlement.

Detached repetitions of a grammatical construction: It is a land of desert stretches. A land of distant mountains. A land of sparse population.

Join the elements with commas: It is a land of desert stretches, a land of distant mountains, a land of sparse population. [Or use dashes.] It is a land of desert stretches—a land of distant mountains—a land of sparse population.

Detached items of a series: We may name the chief parts of a fountain pen: first, the point. This does the writing. Second, the barrel. This holds the ink. Third, the cap. This protects the pen when it is carried in the pocket.

Assemble the detached items into complete sentences: We may name the chief parts of a fountain pen: the point, the barrel, and the cap. The first does the writing. The second holds the ink. The third protects the pen when it is carried in the pocket. [Or do not group the items but make all statements complete.] We may name the chief parts of a fountain pen. The first is the point; this does the writing. The second is the barrel; this holds the ink. The third is the cap; this protects the pen when it is carried in the pocket.

I e. Permissible Fragments Modern authors sometimes write fragmentary sentences for special literary effects.

Permissible use of fragments for emphasis: The little boy, from the top of his ladder, looked down at Renfrew. And stuck out his tongue. And winked. And gloated.

Permissible use of fragments to suggest stream of consciousness: A woman in a fawn-colored suit came through the doorway.

---

* An appositive accompanies a grammatically equal element and qualifies or explains it. Example: Elmquist, *the secretary*, replied.

For Linstowe the sight of her annihilated thirty years. A dingy station. A crowd. The approach of a train. Bells. Steam. A grinding stop. Hurry and confusion. Passengers alighting. A girl in a fawn-colored suit. A girl or an angel from heaven? The meeting of eyes. Radiant recognition. "Oh, you're Archie Linstowe."

Such writing is justified when it is used purposely for effects which cannot be achieved otherwise. But until you have established yourself as an expert you should prove by marginal notes on your theme that each use of a fragment is stylistic rather than careless.

EXERCISE

X-1a. Complete Statement Test

Write each statement, at need combining it with another statement or adding words, to give any incomplete sentence completeness. Two items are correct already; simply copy these.

1. Crowds attend the auctions. Often without thought of buying anything.
2. They canvassed the poorer districts, seeking the source of infection.
3. Democracy will survive. Wherever the people have a free choice of candidates.
4. The tests may be positive. Indicating a need for further treatment.
5. Cotton production anywhere depends on a plentiful labor supply.
6. Eager to set a new speed record for jet planes.
7. He was fascinated by the Italian paintings. Especially the murals of Michelangelo.
8. The men talk about international problems. Each supporting the views of his own party.
9. The city editor of the paper he worked for being an impatient man.
10. She rose to challenge the speaker. Even before he finished his lecture.

9

X-1b. Grammar Test

(1) Verbs and Verbals

Copy the finite verbs. Underline each with a straight line. Copy the verbals. Indicate whether each is a participle, infinitive, or gerund.

1. To the police, hammering at the door, the silence was ominous.
2. They radioed the incoming plane, hoping to avert a crash.
3. To create a new design is a task requiring several hundred engineers.
4. Sowing must be done before the first rain.
5. Determined to win the race, the crew unfurled all sails.
6. Having been approved for membership, he could attend the meeting.
7. To have lived under a dictator is something which makes a person suspicious of everybody.
8. He hoped that, having paid his debts, he would be immune from prosecution.
9. Broken in spirit, the infantrymen surrendered without fighting.
10. The business was operating at a loss when he offered to buy it.

(2) Main and Subordinate Clauses

Copy each subordinate clause. Underline the subordinating word which introduces it. Indicate whether the clause is used as noun, adjective, or adverb. (A clause that modifies anything other than a noun or pronoun is an adverb clause.)

1. If there had been no pact with Russia, the Germans might not have started World War II.
2. In that age a Hindu woman committed suttee when her husband died.
3. Whoever runs for public office must be prepared to suffer slander and abuse.
4. Each year a Pulitzer prize is awarded the American novel which is judged best.
5. Long before the enemy flight appeared, the radar operator warned us that planes were approaching.

6. Tuberculosis can be cured provided treatment begins early.
7. However hard they rowed, they could make no headway against the tide.
8. Without additional information he refused to predict whether the storm would strike before morning.
9. Billy Mitchell was one of the few men who foresaw the rôle of the airplane in war.
10. They asked what his political opinions were.

X-1c, d. Sentence Fragments

Label each fragment with whichever (one or more) of the following terms you think applicable: (1) subordinate clause, (2) participial phrase, (3) prepositional phrase, (4) infinitive phrase, (5) gerund phrase, (6) member of a compound predicate, (7) appositive, (8) item of a series. Then correct the fragment by attaching it to the main sentence or by recasting to enable it to stand alone.

1. The editor gave the order. To spare no one involved in the scandal.
2. He refused the commission. And returned our check.
3. News of the armistice came too late. After the company had been wiped out.
4. This girl was a senior. The president of her sorority.
5. Alexander was a skillful general and administrator. But a poor self-disciplinarian.
6. The police captured the thief before he could escape from the building. Cornering him at the end of a hallway.
7. Franklin D. Roosevelt died in April. A few months before the Japanese surrendered.
8. The delegates were dressed alike. Wearing swallowtail coats. And striped trousers. And tall silk hats.
9. Panchromatic film must be developed in complete darkness. Since it is sensitive to light of any color.
10. A new building must pass rigid inspections. To insure safety of the structure.
11. Our timber supply is dwindling. First because of the increased demand for lumber. Second because of careless logging. Last because trees are not replanted.
12. Tradition says the crowd cheered. Every time Casey came to bat.

13. The sport was forbidden because the birds were becoming rare. That is, shooting pheasants.
14. He was ready to take over the job. Being well instructed in his duties.
15. We got ready to bail out. Both engines having failed.

OMISSION OF NECESSARY WORDS

2. Insert all the words needed to express your thought clearly and completely.*

HOW TO CORRECT ERRORS OF OMISSION

2a. Illogical Constructions (General) †

Verb omitted: At taps all lights must go out. A cessation of noise and the soldier's day ends. [*A cessation of noise* is grammatically incomplete.]

Make a complete clause: At taps all lights must go out. Noise ceases and the soldier's day ends. [Or complete and rearrange the thought.] At taps all lights must go out and noise must cease. Thus the soldier's day ends.

Main clause omitted: With the knowledge that, although you cannot use the document itself, you can procure a photostat. [The writer, beginning with a subordinate construction, forgets that it is subordinate.]

Supply a main clause (including subject and verb): You know that, although you cannot see the document itself, you can procure a photostat.

Verb omitted from a subordinate clause: He was a young man who, coming from the country with ignorance of city ways, but with plenty of determination to succeed. [The writer, taking up a subordinate construction, loses himself in still further subordination.]

* The omission of essential words or phrases may also destroy parallelism. See **8d**.
† For other illogical constructions see **41a, b**.

Replace one prepositional phrase with a verb: He was a young man who, coming from the country with ignorance of city ways, nevertheless had plenty of determination to succeed. [Or replace two phrases with verbs.] He was a young man who, coming from the country, was ignorant of city ways but had plenty of determination to succeed.

Completing word omitted: Your finger prints will identify you in any situation you may find yourself. [The writer, mindful of having used *in*, fails to see that a second *in* is needed to round out the thought.]

Supply the completing word: Your finger prints will identify you in any situation you may find yourself in. [Or better] Your finger prints will identify you in any situation in which you may find yourself.

Idea left uncompleted: From the window of the train I perceived one of those unsightly structures. [The writer implies that he will tell us more about the structures, but fails to do so.]

Express the idea completely: From the window of the train I perceived one of those unsightly structures which are always to be seen near a station. [Or strike out both the idea and the suggesting word] From the window of the train I perceived an unsightly structure.

Comparison not completed: Injun Joe's elixir is better. [Better than what?]

Supply a completing comparison: Injun Joe's elixir is better than the costlier patent medicines.

Thought not completed: I was so thrilled. [*So, such, too*, etc., used as intensives, logically require a completing clause. See Intensives, 19.]

Supply a completing clause: I was so thrilled that I could not sleep for two nights.

Thought not completed: Our new car is too beautiful.

Substitute an adverb which does not suggest a comparison: Our new car is extremely beautiful.

2b. **Illogical Constructions (Double Capacity)** Often the omission of an essential element forces upon another element an awkward or ungrammatical use.

Infinitive phrase omitted: This is a note to tell you that I arrived safely, and whether I left a roll of film at your house. [The writer tries to make one infinitive carry the meanings for two.]

Supply the second phrase: This is a note to tell you that I arrived safely, and to inquire whether I left a roll of film a your house.

Preposition omitted: Are you fond and diligent in work? [The single preposition is forced, unnaturally, to do the work of the omitted word.]

Supply a second preposition and reconstruct the sentence: Are you fond of work and diligent in it?

Conjunction wrongly omitted: He was as old, if not older, than any other man in the community. [... *as old ... than*]

Supply the conjunction and reconstruct the sentence: He was as old as any other man in the community, if not older.

Double use of noun form (as singular and plural): He is one of the most skillful, if not the most skillful, tennis players in the state.

Reconstruct the sentence: He is one of the most skillful tennis players in the state, if not the most skillful. [Double capacity is especially awkward when the first element is suspended while the second is being introduced. If the first element is completed before the second is mentioned, an omission from the second can usually be supplied by the reader.* Thus it is unnecessary to write *player* at the end of the sentence here revised.]

Double use of main verb (in past perfect and future tenses): He has and will prosecute trespassers.

* But sometimes the omission is grossly awkward. Example: We always have done it and are. [Add *doing it now.*]

Repeat the main verb form and add a pronoun: He has prosecuted trespassers and will prosecute them. [Or use the main verb in the first element and repeat the subject] He has prosecuted trespassers and he will.

Awkward double use of the verb *to be* (as a main verb and as an auxiliary): Herman is a good workman but kept poor by sickness.

Repeat the verb (preceding it with a pronoun): Herman is a good workman, but he is kept poor by sickness.

2c. Misleading Constructions

Subject and verb omitted: When one year old, my mother died. [The omission from the *when* clause gives the sentence a meaning which is not intended.]

Supply the missing elements: When I was one year old, my mother died.

Subject and verb omitted: My parents moved to New York at the age of nine.

Supply the missing elements: My parents moved to New York when I was nine years old.

Definite article omitted: We talked with the president and general manager. [Did we talk with one man or two?]

Supply the words necessary for clearness: We talked with the president and the general manager. [Or] We talked with the officer who was both president and general manager.

Conjunction omitted from a series: * We need food, shelter, medicine, and depend upon the Red Cross to supply them. [The reader might at first suppose that *depend* continues the series.]

Make the end of the series clear: We need food, shelter, and medicine, and depend upon the Red Cross to supply them. [Or] We need food, shelter, and medicine; we depend upon the Red Cross to supply them.

* When no confusion can arise, the end of a series need not be formally indicated by a conjunction. Examples: Buy stocks, bonds, mortgages.

Faulty omission of subordinating conjunction: I saw the whole audience was against him.

Supply the conjunction: I saw that the whole audience was against him. [*That* may be omitted in informal writing when there is no possibility of misreading. Example: He said he was not going.]

Misleading omission of relative pronoun: At such hours there are people ringing bells disturb.

Supply the pronoun: At such hours there are people whom ringing bells disturb.

2d. Faulty Idiom *

Preposition wrongly omitted: He ran the engine double the speed permitted.

Supply the preposition required by usage: He ran the engine at double the speed permitted.

Preposition wrongly omitted: Some colleges all sports are intramural.

Supply the preposition required by idiomatic usage: In some colleges all sports are intramural.

Preposition wrongly omitted: They lived in the city Toledo.

Supply the preposition required by usage: They lived in the city of Toledo.

Part of formal title omitted: Our pastor, Reverend Hopkins, served as chairman.

Supply the full title required by usage: Our pastor, the Reverend Mr. Hopkins, served as chairman. [Or supply the full name] Our pastor, the Reverend William R. Hopkins, served as chairman.

2e. Permissible Incomplete Constructions Words may be omitted from a sentence if they can be supplied instantly by the reader and if the tone of the sentence is in keeping with the context.†

* For other examples of omissions which violate idiom see "Idiomatic use of articles," 18c(3).

† For the use of fragmentary sentences for literary effects see 1e.

Permissible omissions from informal speech or writing: What next? [question]—Never! [exclamation]—Hurry! Tell them to stay out. Please close the door. [request or command]—If only I were there! [wish]—The twelfth? Yes. The eleventh if you prefer. [conversation]—A spoonful of lard and a pinch of salt. [thinking aloud]—Now for the last point. [transition] —Not a living thing in sight! [emphasis].

Permissible in headlines: U.S., British Policies Economic. [For] U.S. and British Policies Are Based on Economics.

Deliberate telegraphic style: Don't come if not convenient, but would enjoy seeing you. [Telegraphic style, if clear, is permissible in informal personal letters. But it should be avoided in business letters and in formal writing.]

EXERCISE

X-2a. Illogical Constructions (General)

In each item decide whether the need is to supply omitted elements or to change the construction. Then write the item as a clear and complete sentence.

1. The new constitution which provided for direct election of the mayor.
2. Early immunization now prescribed by doctors to prevent many common diseases of children.
3. Streamlining is not new, but its application to many products.
4. One clue was missing—the one which they hoped to solve the mystery.
5. Brisky's Breakfast Food is better.
6. Modern farmers who, taking advantage of the latest scientific discoveries, analyze their soil before planting crops.
7. Whenever the gun is fired while the battleship is moving.
8. Gouache painting is not the same though it is done with opaque water colors.
9. Although his intentions being good, he lacked perseverance to carry through.
10. Because their late arrival delayed the opening of the meeting.

X-2b. Illogical Constructions (Double Capacity)

In each item write and underscore the word (or word group) which is used in a double capacity. Then recast the sentence in correctly written form.

1. The old lady wants a companion with whom she can travel and treat like a daughter.
2. Sponsors of the United Nations hoped to prevent wars in the future and world security.
3. He asked Bartley to check the layout for the new advertisement and whether the correct type sizes were called for.
4. The book was open at another page than that which it had been opened when I left.
5. A seeing-eye dog will disobey his master when ordered to do something dangerous and refuse to move.
6. Photo-lithography is the cheapest printing process and best adapted to reproducing exact copies of documents.
7. The governor is elected by voters of all parties, but expected to show appreciation to no one except his party machine.
8. The senator found himself in a position no politician wants to be.
9. Burroughs was as good a mechanic if not better than any one else in the shop.
10. English is a Teutonic, but has borrowed words from various Romance, languages.

X-2c, d. Misleading Constructions and Faulty Idiom

Decide what words are omitted or what idioms are faulty. Then write each sentence in correct form.

1. The detectives made a thorough search in the vicinity the post office.
2. While duck hunting the boat sprang a leak.
3. Paris is at once mentioned when speaking of France.
4. George Bernard Shaw writes plays, novels, criticisms, and satirizes society in all his works.
5. I see the newspapers are campaigning for tax reduction.
6. The Liberal Party advocated municipal ownership of the electric power plant and busses.

7. The United States exports grain, potatoes, vegetable oils, and imports beef and bananas.
8. Henry Clay was a man, when he talked, people listened to.
9. We're deciding a question which your opinion will be helpful.
10. Edna Millay's "Renascence" was written while an undergraduate.

THE RUN-TOGETHER SENTENCE

Just as a sentence may contain too little (see Articles **1** and **2**), it also may contain too much. Articles **3** and **4** are concerned with flagrant aspects of this fault. Article **3** treats ungrammatical combinations. Article **4** treats combinations which, though grammatical, are too inclusive for effective communication.

3. **Avoid running main clauses together with only a comma or no mark between them.*** (The joining of sentences by means of a comma is sometimes called "the comma splice." Sentences joined together without any punctuation whatever may be called "telescoped sentences.")

HOW TO CORRECT RUN-TOGETHER SENTENCES

3a. Comma Splice

Comma splice: The town has three railroads, it was founded when oil was discovered. [Is one statement made, or are two? Is each statement, if taken alone, complete?]

Show separation of thought by using a period: The town has three railroads. It was founded when oil was discovered.

---

* For a treatment of punctuation of main clauses see "Main Clauses," **25a.** For additional information see "The Semicolon," **29b.**

Comma splice: The speed of the car seemed slower than it really was, this was due, no doubt, to the absence of noise. [Here are three commas. The reader cannot quickly discover which one marks the larger division of thought.]

Show separation of thought by using a period: The speed of the car seemed slower than it really was. This was due, no doubt, to the absence of noise.

Comma splice with a conjunctive adverb: He spoke at every opportunity, thus he became a skillful debater. [A conjunctive adverb (*then, so, however, thus, therefore*, etc.) or a transitional expression such as *in fact, on the other hand* must not be confused with a coördinating conjunction. Such an adverb or expression when used between main clauses must be preceded by a semicolon or a period.]

Show partial connection in thought by using a semicolon: He spoke at every opportunity; thus he became a skillful debater.

Comma splice in a quotation: "They're on the mark," the broadcaster cried, "now we'll hear the starting gun."

Show partial connection in thought by using a semicolon (it follows the explanatory phrase): "They are on the mark," the broadcaster cried; "now we'll hear the starting gun."

Comma splice: The tire was flat, we had no spare.

Show close connection in thought by using a comma and a coördinating conjunction: The tire was flat, and we had no spare.*

Comma splice: The winters are long and cold, nothing can live without shelter.

Show subordination of one thought by employing a phrase: The winters are too long and cold for anything to live without shelter. [Or]

Express the minor thought in a subordinate clause: The winters are so long and cold that nothing can live without shelter.

---

* When three or more short coördinate clauses are closely related in thought the conjunction may be omitted. Permissible: All was excitement. The ducks quacked, the pigs squealed, the dogs barked.

3b. Telescoped Sentences

Telescoped sentences: Next we stroll past the exhibits these are roped off. [Here are two statements, each grammatically able to stand as a sentence. By fusing the two the writer denies the grammatical independence of one or the other.]

Separate the independent thoughts by a period: Next we stroll past the exhibits. These are roped off.

Telescoped sentences: The crowd surged into the auditorium everyone hoped to get a front seat.

Show partial connection in thought by using a semicolon: The crowd surged into the auditorium; everyone hoped to get a front seat.

Telescoped sentences: You may drive the car downtown park it on a side street.

Show close connection in thought by using a comma and a coördinating conjunction: You may drive the car downtown, but park it on a side street.

Telescoped sentences: Henry sprained his ankle he limped across the finish line in third place.

Show the subordination of one thought by employing a phrase: Despite a sprained ankle Henry limped across the finish line in third place. [Or]

Express the minor thought in a subordinate clause: Although he sprained his ankle Henry limped across the finish line in third place.

EXERCISE

X-3a. Comma Splice

Rewrite, correcting each comma splice in the way you consider best: (1) by making two sentences, (2) by using a semicolon, (3) by inserting a coördinating conjunction after the comma, or (4) by subordinating one thought.

1. Whistler, the painter, attended West Point, there he failed in chemistry and was dismissed.

2. The citizens held a meeting, Napoleon's army was reported approaching.

3. Supply and demand determines the value of a rare stamp, therefore collectors prize misprints.

4. "The policy provides full coverage," he said, "it protects you against fire, theft, and damage."

5. Water freezes and expands in very small holes or crevices, this finally causes the rock to crack.

6. DDT does not kill flies immediately, it paralyzes them by affecting their nervous systems.

7. Fossils are not necessarily bones, often they are merely imprints in a rock.

8. The tourist trade must be considered one of Canada's biggest businesses, it brings millions of dollars to the country every year.

9. Shape the bowl by hammering, then antique it by using an acid bath.

10. The government subsidy was insufficient, so the farmers ignored the request to plant fewer potatoes.

11. Porter is the only candidate with experience, that is why he is favored to win.

12. The boat docks at Plymouth, from there you take the train to London.

13. Some banks will lend sixty per cent of the land's value, their evaluation of the property, however, is far below the market price.

14. Many students are handicapped by reading difficulties, often poor vision is the cause.

15. Inexperienced fishermen sometimes snap their lines, this happens when they reel in too fast.

X-3b. Telescoped Sentences

Rewrite, correcting by the method you think best: (1) separate independent thoughts by using (a) a period, (b) a semicolon, or (c) a comma and a coördinating conjunction; or (2) recast the sentence, making one thought a subordinate clause or a phrase.

1. The school board rejected the request of the teachers for higher salaries they declared that sufficient money was not available.

2. Geologists are pessimistic about our oil supply present resources are being depleted rapidly.

3. Doctors recognize a child's need for affection they say that unless a baby is held and fondled it may grow sick and even die.

4. Alfred T. Mahan is called the prophet of Manifest Destiny he publicized the need for American control of the Caribbean.

5. The wealthy sugar and pineapple corporations of Hawaii were established many years ago by American missionaries these early churchmen obtained land cheaply from the native rulers.

6. "Don't throw away your old dresses" Jim advised her "they will be stylish again in another ten years."

7. A college student can earn spending money by baby-sitting he must know how to care for children.

8. Basketball is gaining popularity with sport fans more athletes are showing interest in the game.

9. Parking meters provide an easy means of controlling parking many motorists object to paying for use of the public streets.

10. Where malaria is common mosquito abatement crews should be employed such crews eliminate insect breeding places.

11. Advertising rates of national magazines are higher than those of local publications charges are based mainly on circulation and of course are likely to change as this goes up or down.

12. Often traffic problems can be solved only by the construction of freeways this is especially true when a city grows rapidly.

13. The Dewey decimal system is a method of classifying books it is used by most libraries in the United States.

14. Bret Harte is credited with popularizing the local color story his writings were first published before the gold mining days were over.

15. Roger Williams left the Plymouth Colony and went to Rhode Island he wanted to establish a church free from Puritan control.

THE TACKED-TOGETHER SENTENCE

4. Guard against the habit of thoughtlessly piecing two or more statements together with the connective *and, so,* or *but.* A sentence of this type is needed occasionally. But when it is written merely from habit it often contains too many thoughts. A series of such sentences becomes monotonous.

HOW TO CORRECT TACKED-TOGETHER SENTENCES

Separate the independent statements with periods or semi-colons. If some of the statements are of minor importance subordinate them.*

Thoughtless repetition of *and*: Jones sat on the bench, and he was cold and the wind whipped through his thin coat, and he thought of the warm fire he had left.

Separate the independent statements: Jones sat on the bench. He was cold, and the wind whipped through his thin coat. He thought of the warm fire he had left.

Thoughtless repetition of *and*: The second speaker had sat quietly waiting, and he was a man of a different type, and he began calmly, and the audience paid little heed to him, and after a while he became more earnest.

Separate the main statements and subordinate the lesser ones: The second speaker, who had sat quietly waiting, was a man of a different type. He began so calmly that the audience paid little heed to him. After a while he became more earnest.

"Rocking-horse" sentences: Carl wished to play the organ and he was willing to practice hard. There are many stops on the instrument and these control the tones of the pipes. Carl had to learn how to use them and this took a great deal of time.

Condense and rearrange (subordinating minor statements): Carl, eager to play the organ, was willing to practice hard. But learning to use the many stops which control the tones of the pipes took a great deal of time.

* Many sentences primarily involve problems of subordination. For the treatment of such sentences see **43b** and **48a.**

Thoughtless repetition of *so*: Reynard wished to catch Chanticleer, so he flattered the cock and got him to sing with his
eyes shut and seized him, so there the story might have ended,
but Chanticleer persuaded his captor to brag, and the fox
opened his mouth, and so Chanticleer escaped.

Condense and rearrange (subordinating minor statements): Reynard, wishing to catch Chanticleer, flattered the cock into
singing with his eyes shut; then he seized him. There the story
might have ended, but Chanticleer persuaded his captor to
brag. When the fox opened his mouth Chanticleer escaped.

Thoughtless repetition of *but*: He was undoubtedly a brave
man, but now he was somewhat alarmed, but he would not
turn back. [The sentence changes its course twice. Many good
writers refuse to begin two successive sentences or clauses
with *but*.] *

Condense and rearrange (subordinating one minor statement):
He was undoubtedly a brave man. Though he was now somewhat alarmed, he would not turn back.

EXERCISE

X-4. The Tacked-Together Sentence

Rewrite to eliminate the tacking together of independent
thoughts. Separate main statements; subordinate lesser ones.

1. The graduates filed into the auditorium and mounted the
   stage and sat there until they received their diplomas, and
   then they marched out.
2. Mark Twain's writings were profitable, but he was always
   interested in get-rich-quick schemes, but he lost money in
   his business ventures.
3. Brown crossed the country in a covered wagon and he
   built a home on the desolate prairie. He worked hard
   through the years and he and his family turned the waste
   land into productive fields. He lived to see his children
   grow rich and they added new land to the homestead.
4. The epidemic was spreading, and the two doctors could not
   treat all the sick in private homes, so they set up a clinic,

* For the use of *but* in prolonged comparisons see the example in **43a**.

and they called for volunteers to help, and they taught the volunteers how to give injections, but the townspeople were afraid, and they refused to go to the clinic for treatment.

5. He had no matches, so he tried to build a fire by rubbing sticks together Indian fashion, but he was unsuccessful, so he struck two stones together to make sparks, but that did not work either, so he ate a cold supper and rolled up in his blankets to keep warm.

6. The linotyper sets the type and the make-up man puts it in the form and then the stereotype operators make mats and mold plates for the press.

7. Airline travel is cheap, but private flying is costly, but it is an exciting sport.

8. Expose the enlarging paper and develop it at least three minutes. Then put the paper in an acid short stop and leave it for two minutes. Next, put it in the fixing bath and leave it for fifteen minutes. Finally, put the print in running water and wash it thoroughly.

9. The storm diminished, so they decided to cross the river, so Henry untied the boat and jumped in. But the swift current drew the boat away from the shore so that Dale could not reach it, so Henry tried to row against the flood, but he could make no headway, so Dale plunged in and swam for the boat.

10. The first speaker drew his question and began preparing his topic, but before he was ready time was called, so he had to begin talking before he was fully prepared. But as he talked he warmed to his subject, and ideas came to him, so his lack of preparation was not evident to the judges.

The Clear Sentence

REFERENCE OF PRONOUNS

5. Make every pronoun refer unmistakably to a definite antecedent. If the antecedent (the noun or noun equivalent to which the pronoun refers and for which it stands) is not clear and definite, the pronoun may appear to refer to the *wrong* word or to hang in the air and refer to *no* word.*

HOW TO CORRECT FAULTY REFERENCE

5a. No Antecedent Provide each pronoun with a specific and expressed antecedent, or replace the pronoun with a noun.

Antecedent missing: If you smoke constantly, do not give them up all at once.
Supply the antecedent: If you smoke cigarettes constantly, do not give them up all at once.

Antecedent missing: All he has to do is that of heating the rooms properly.
Recast the sentence to supply an antecedent: His only task is that of heating the room properly.

Antecedent missing: The wind blew his hat off, leaving it bare.
Replace the pronoun with a noun: The wind blew his hat off, leaving his head bare.

* For errors resulting from unnecessary shifts in the number and person of pronouns see 7a and f.

27

Antecedent missing: Mark Twain fell in love with a picture and afterward married her.

Replace the pronoun with a noun: Mark Twain fell in love with a picture and afterward married the girl shown in it.

Vague impersonal construction: It says in the paper that fifty men were laid off. [Avoid the unnecessary use of the indefinite *it, you,* or *they*.] *

Replace the pronoun with a noun: The newspaper says that fifty men were laid off.

Vague impersonal construction: They are noted for their tact in France.

Replace the pronoun with a noun: The French are noted for their tact.

5b. False or Feeble Antecedent Make sure that the antecedent is a noun (or the equivalent †) to which the pronoun refers naturally and grammatically. Do not let the antecedent be an adjective, a possessive, or a clause not used as a noun; do not let it be a noun that is obscured or only half expressed.

Adjective wrongly used as an antecedent: The Mayan system of numbering is now understood. Their writing is known to be hieroglyphic.

Replace the pronominal adjective with a definite article: The Mayan system of numbering is now understood. The writing is known to be hieroglyphic. [Or provide a proper antecedent] The system of numbering used by the Mayans is now understood. Their writing is known to be hieroglyphic.

* Sometimes the impersonal construction is permitted or even required.

Correct: It is raining. [No antecedent is called for.]

Offensively personal: You aren't hanged nowadays for stealing.

Use the impersonal pronoun: No one is hanged nowadays for stealing.

† A gerund or an infinitive may be an antecedent since either serves as a noun. Gerund: *Sailing,* which he as a boy had engaged in, was still his favorite sport. Infinitive: *To philosophize* is usually enjoyable, but it is seldom profitable.

Compound adjective wrongly used as an antecedent: Cat-skin coats are warm if they are killed in winter.

Replace the pronoun with a noun: Cat-skin coats are warm if the cats are killed in winter. [Or] Cat skins make a warm fur coat if the cats are killed in winter.

Antecedent in the possessive case: He threw a stone at the wasps' nest, which flew out angrily and stung him.

Recast the sentence to omit the pronoun: He threw a stone at the nest, and the wasps flew out angrily and stung him.

Broad reference to a clause: The tapper strikes a gong, which continues as long as the push button is pressed. [The writer intends that *which* shall refer to the entire preceding clause, but the reader naturally relates it to the specific noun *gong*.]

Supply a specific antecedent: The tapper strikes a gong, a process which continues as long as the push button is pressed. [Or abandon the pronoun] The tapper strikes the gong as long as the push button is pressed.*

Part of a compound noun wrongly used as an antecedent: Fashion makers change them to obtain new sales.

Replace the pronoun with a noun: Fashion makers change the fashions to obtain new sales.

5c. Ambiguous Reference When a pronoun may refer to two or more words (or word groups) of which only one is its proper antecedent, reconstruct the passage to insure reference to the true antecedent, or replace the pronoun with a noun.

Ambiguous reference of *they*: As the riders were leaving, one of the men tossed some coins on the grass. A few minutes later they disappeared over the edge of the mountain. [Who disappeared? The men? The coins?]

---

* It cannot be maintained that a pronoun must *always* have a definite word for its antecedent. Occasionally the best authors use a pronoun to refer to a clause. But the reference must always be clear.

Clear use of broad reference: He pays us whatever our products will sell for in the market. This seems fair enough.

Repeat the noun: As the riders were leaving, one of the men tossed some coins on the grass. A few minutes later the riders disappeared over the edge of the mountain.

Ambiguous reference of *it*: If you want to make a good speech take your hands out of your pockets, open your mouth wide, and throw yourself into it.

Replace the pronoun with a noun clause: If you want to make a good speech take your hands out of your pockets, open your mouth wide, and throw yourself into what you are saying.

Ambiguous reference of *which*: He dropped the bundle in the mud which he was carrying to his mother.

Bring the pronoun near its proper antecedent: He dropped in the mud the bundle which he was carrying to his mother.

Ambiguous reference of *this*: My failure in mathematics was serious. My grades in English, history, and Latin were good enough. But this brought down my average. [What *this*? Five nouns intrude between the pronoun and its antecedent.]

Bring the pronoun near its proper antecedent: In English, history, and Latin I received fairly good grades. But in mathematics I received a failure. This brought down my average.

Ambiguous reference of *he*: Gordon told Tom that if he did not pay his dues he would be dropped from the club. [Who owed dues? Who would be dropped?]

Recast the sentence to make the antecedents clear: If Tom did not pay his dues he would be dropped from the club, Gordon told him. [Or use a direct quotation] Gordon said, "Tom, if you do not pay your dues you will be dropped from the club."

Double reference of pronouns: The feet of Chinese girls were bandaged so tightly when they were babies that they could not grow. [*They* refers successively to *girls* and *feet*, whereas it should refer unmistakably to one antecedent only.]

Recast the sentence and change the number of one noun: In China the feet of a girl baby were bandaged so tightly that they could not grow.

Double reference of pronouns: As long as the sun shines it is warm, but as soon as it goes behind a cloud, it is cold. [One use of *it* is specific; one is impersonal. This fact makes the double reference especially confusing.]

Replace two pronouns with nouns and repeat one noun: As long as the sun shines the weather is warm, but it turns cold as soon as the sun goes behind a cloud.

EXERCISE

X-5a. Pronouns Without Antecedents

Rewrite, supplying definite antecedents, or change the pronouns to nouns (or their equivalents). If necessary recast the sentence.

1. At that time there was little emphasis on football. They encouraged only those with good grades to try for the team.

2. Our trip to the reservation was difficult to make in an old car. Their roads are in poor condition, and they have no service stations.

3. To establish a nation's foreign policy requires extensive knowledge of history, economics, and political science. He must also understand human nature.

4. Aphids are persistent pests, and the farmers have to spray frequently in order to save it.

5. The influence of the Communist Manifesto has been far-reaching in the hundred years since he issued it.

6. In badminton you must learn to use a wrist stroke. You cannot return it to the back court by using a full-arm swing.

7. What the deep sea diver has to venture is that of salvaging sunken ships.

8. The FBI employs only college graduates. The standards are so high that it is seldom granted.

9. Racial prejudice is unjustified according to scientific studies which indicate that their so-called inferiorities are not matters of race, but of environment.

10. The lie detector records respiration and blood pressure while they ask questions.

X-5b. Pronouns with False or Feeble Antecedents

Rewrite, supplying noun (or equivalent) antecedents to which the pronoun refers naturally and grammatically.

1. Even the squalid sections of a city are somewhat beautiful. But it is not noticed by most people, who see only the dirt and ugliness.
2. The original design was May's, who developed it in secret.
3. The city was demolished. It left only a few well enough to care for the injured.
4. Labor leaders declare that its only bargaining weapon is the strike.
5. To get at the meaning in modern art you must be familiar with their symbolism.
6. Truthful advertisements are rare, which few readers are aware of.
7. The land was theirs who could first stake out a claim and file papers with the government agent.
8. In speaking of jazz he said that, though the vogue of this kind of rhythm is recent, they appear as syncopation in Beethoven and other classical masters.
9. The air flows over the wing more rapidly, which reduces the pressure above, causing the airplane to rise.
10. Juvenile delinquency cannot be solved by the schools alone. Their parents must also coöperate in developing a community-wide program.

X-5c. Ambiguous Reference of Pronouns

Clarify the ambiguous reference of each pronoun by reconstructing the sentence or by replacing the pronoun with a noun (or its equivalent).

1. The men empty their nets of fish. Then they store them on the deck.
2. Some cosmetic manufacturers use chemical dyes in making face powder, to which many women are allergic.
3. According to feudal custom vassals pledged oaths of fealty to their lords. These promised to protect the vassals.
4. The joint families of India have been affected by the growth of factories. Their influence has increased in recent years.

5. Marvin told Gilbert that he could not get there in time unless he flew.
6. Dora gave the dresses to the church bazaar that she didn't like.
7. The Indians resented the presence of the white men, who long had hunted there with bow and arrow.
8. After the sheriff locked up the prisoner he disappeared.
9. Slavery was characteristic of Byzantine life. Among its features was the right of a slave to marry a freeman.
10. When the light is placed in position on the stand it must be fastened tightly.

DANGLING MODIFIERS

6. **Make certain that each participle, phrase, or elliptical subordinate clause has a word to modify and is linked closely in position with that word.** Otherwise it may appear to hang in the air or "dangle." It may even attach itself to the wrong word.

Dangling participial phrase: Coming in on the train, the high school building is seen. [Is the building coming in? If not, who is? *Coming* implies a special actor, but the use of the passive voice prevents that actor from being named and made the subject.]

Make the actor the subject and discard the passive voice: Coming in on the train, one sees the high school building. [Or change the phrase to a subordinate clause] As one comes in on the train he sees the high school building.

HOW TO CORRECT DANGLING MODIFIERS

In general, use common sense in making the modifier relate unmistakably to the proper word.

6a. **Modifier Beginning a Sentence** Supply the sentence with a subject to which the modifier will clearly and properly refer. Or, if the modifier is a phrase, change the phrase to a subordinate clause.

Dangling infinitive phrase: To run efficiently, a competent mechanic should check your car every thousand miles or so. [What is to run? The mechanic? The car?]

Make *car* the subject of the sentence: To run efficiently, your car should be checked by a competent mechanic every thousand miles or so. [Or change the phrase to a subordinate clause] If your car is to run efficiently, a competent mechanic should check it every thousand miles or so.

Dangling participial phrase: Having taken our seats, the umpire announced the batteries. [Who took the seats? Was it the umpire or we?]

Make the actor in the phrase the subject: Having taken our seats, we heard the umpire announce the batteries. [Or change the phrase to a subordinate clause] When we had taken our seats, the umpire announced the batteries.

Dangling phrase containing a gerund: On tasting the gooseberry pie, his frown grew deeper.

Supply a subject that can be logically referred to: On tasting the gooseberry pie, he frowned deeply. [Or change the phrase to a clause] When he tasted the gooseberry pie, his frown grew deeper.

Dangling phrase containing a gerund: In talking to Phelps he told me that you intend to buy a car.

Provide a logical subject: In talking to Phelps I learned that you intend to buy a car. [Or change the phrase to a clause] When I talked to Phelps he told me that you intend to buy a car.

Dangling elliptical clause: While eating dinner, Wilson arrived. [The subordinate clause appears to modify *Wilson*.] *

Supply a subject in the subordinate clause: While I was eating dinner, Wilson arrived.

6b. Modifier Ending a Sentence A modifier at the end of a sentence does not necessarily refer to the subject of the sentence. The only possible test of its reference is one of

_____

* For other examples of dangling constructions resulting from the omission of necessary words see 2, especially 2c.

common-sense logic. To correct any fault in reference make sure that the word to be modified is present in the sentence and as close as possible to the modifying phrase, or change the construction of the sentence.

Dangling gerund phrase: The address was concluded by reciting a passage from Wordsworth. [Who did the reciting?]

Make the implied actor the subject: The speaker concluded his address by reciting a passage from Wordsworth. [Or replace the gerund with a noun] The address was concluded by the recitation of a passage from Wordsworth.

Dangling participial phrase: The horse had only one good eye, caused by an encounter with a wire fence. [The good eye was not caused by the encounter.]

Recast the sentence: One eye of the horse was blind from an encounter with a wire fence.

Uncertain participial phrase: At once the coach rebuked the runner, angered by this conduct.

Place the phrase near the word it modifies: At once the coach, angered by this conduct, rebuked the runner.

Dangling elliptical clause: My shoestring broke when hurrying to the office at eight o'clock.

Fill out the subordinate clause: My shoestring broke when I was hurrying to the office at eight o'clock.

6c. **Permissible Modifiers of the Whole Sentence** Modifiers that do not imply a special actor qualify the sentence as a whole. They need not be attached to single, particular words.

Participle used in a directive expression (to summarize, abate, etc.): Taking everything into consideration, the investment is a good one.

Participle used in a directive expression: Generally speaking, women live longer than men do.

Gerund phrase indicating general action: In gardening, common sense is the first requirement.

EXERCISE

X-6a. Dangling Modifier Beginning a Sentence

Rewrite and correct all sentences containing dangling modifiers. Two items contain permissible modifiers of the whole sentence.

1. To sell vacuum cleaners, the housewife must be convinced that her work will be lightened.
2. Having passed the test, the examining board admitted him to the university.
3. For performing the operation, Newell received an exorbitant bill from his doctor.
4. While reading the newspaper in the garden the thief entered through a front window.
5. Considering the poor condition of the car, it is no bargain.
6. To be a presidential nominee a man's political party must select him at its convention.
7. While marching along the muddy road the airplanes dived.
8. On entering the gallery Van Gogh's "Bridge at Arles" was hanging near the door.
9. Being eighteen, Marilyn's mother allowed her to apply for a driver's license.
10. In public speaking clear enunciation is necessary.

X-6b. Dangling Modifier Ending a Sentence

Rewrite, correcting each dangling modifier. Recast the sentence or supply words as required. One item contains a permissible modifier of the whole sentence.

1. The fire started by throwing a lighted cigarette from a car.
2. The airplane was lost, caused by faulty navigation.
3. An embargo was imposed on American films, intended to eliminate competition from Hollywood.
4. Newspapers are responsible for much ill-feeling between nations, publishing half-truths and suppressing facts.
5. The telephone line was cut while not on guard.
6. Sulfa powder is sprinkled on the wound before being bandaged.
7. Every car on the road passed us, caused by the faulty carburetor.

8. Doctors recommend meat for young babies when needing a high protein diet.
9. American jazz grew out of Negro music when playing at funerals.
10. Restrictive labor laws are considered good or bad, depending on one's attitude toward unions.

UNNECESSARY SHIFT

7. Do not needlessly shift the construction of sentence elements. Keep one point of view until there is reason for change.

HOW TO CORRECT ERRORS OF SHIFT

7a. Shift of Number

Crude shift of number: Everyone should save their money.

Make the pronoun agree in number with its antecedent: Everyone should save his money. [Or change the antecedent to a plural noun] People should save their money.

Crude shift of number: Pioneer women often served as a plow horse.

Make the two nouns agree in number: Pioneer woman often served as a plow horse.

Crude shift of number: Take your umbrella with you. They will be needed today.

Make the pronoun and its antecedent agree in number: Take your umbrella with you. It will be needed today. [Or] Take your umbrella with you. You will need it today.

7b. Shift of Tense

Crude shift from past to present tense: When he heard the news he hurries down town and buys a paper.

Put all verbs in the past tense: When he heard the news he hurried down town and bought a paper.

Crude shift from present to past tense: Freedom means that men may conduct their affairs as they please so long as nobody injured anybody else.

Put all verbs in the present tense: Freedom means that men may conduct their affairs as they please so long as nobody injures anybody else.*

7c. Shift of Subject

Unnecessary shift of subject: Mark Twain was born in the West, but the East was his home in later years.

Make the subject of one verb the subject of both verbs: Mark Twain was born in the West, but lived in the East in later years. [Or recast the sentence to provide subjects parallel in idea] The West was the birthplace of Mark Twain, but the East was his home in later years.

7d. Shift of Voice †

Faulty shift from active to passive voice: A careful driver can go fifteen miles on a gallon of gasoline, and at the same time very little lubricating oil is used.

Put both verbs in the active voice: A careful driver can go fifteen miles on a gallon of gasoline and at the same time use very little lubricating oil.

7e. Shift of Mood **

Faulty shift from indicative mood to subjunctive mood: By making every letter from our office courteous and correct we obtain the respect of our associates and would be in a position to receive whatever business they had. [*Obtain* is in the indicative mood, while *would be* and *had* are in the subjunctive.]

---

* A change of tense within a sentence is desirable and necessary in certain instances; see How to Express Time Relations, pages 82 ff.

† Voice refers to the change in verb form that indicates whether the subject acts (active voice) or is acted upon (passive voice). For further definition see 14; for voice as a factor in emphasis see 48d.

** For a definition of mood (sometimes called "mode") see Verb, 14.

Put all verbs in the indicative mood: By making every letter
from our office courteous and correct we obtain the respect
of our associates and are in a position to receive whatever
business they have. [Or make all verbs consistently subjunc-
tive] By making every letter from our office courteous and
correct we would obtain the respect of our associates and be
in a position to receive whatever business they had.

Faulty shift from potential to indicative: An automobile
should be kept in good working order so that its life is
lengthened.

Put both verbs in the potential: An automobile should be kept
in good working order so that its life may be lengthened.
[Or put both verbs in the indicative] If an automobile is kept
in good working order its life will be lengthened.

Faulty shift from imperative to potential: Open the door and
then you should turn to the right.

Make both verbs imperative: Open the door and then turn to
the right.

7f. Shift in Point of View Shifts in point of view often involve other types of faulty shifts, particularly of person, tense, and mood.

Confusing shift in point of view: As you stand on the sandstone
cliffs, a small valley lies below them.

Give both clauses the same subject: As you stand on the sandstone cliffs, you look down upon a small valley. [Or recast
the sentence] Below the sandstone cliffs lies a small valley.

Faulty shift of person, tense, mood, and construction:

How to Drive a Car

   I. In teaching people to drive I first explained the controls....
  II. Next you must.... [Shifts from the first person to the
second, from the past tense to the present, and from the
indicative mood to the imperative.]
 III. The third step is.... [Shifts from personal to impersonal
construction.]

In telling how to do or make something, definitely assume one of these three points of view and keep it consistently:

1. Personal—Tell what you did (past tense) or what you customarily do (present tense), using the pronoun *I*: "First I take ... Next I prepare ... Finally I. ..."
2. Imperative—Instruct someone, using no pronoun: "First take ... Then prepare ... Finally do this. ..."
3. Impersonal—Explain what is to be done, what should be done, or what one should do: "The first thing to do is to take ... The next thing is to prepare ... The last thing is to...."

7g. Shift in General Sentence Plan (Mixed Construction)

Faulty shift in thought of the sentence: A fountain pen, unless you keep other people from using it, you will soon find it is ruined. [The writer starts to make *a fountain pen* the subject of the sentence, but abruptly turns to another construction, leaving the three words suspended.]

Make *fountain pen* the subject of the sentence: A fountain pen will soon be ruined if many people use it. [Or adopt the alternate plan for the sentence throughout] You must keep other people from using your fountain pen, or they will ruin it.

Faulty shift in thought of the sentence: Take for instance the Gettysburg Address contained only a few hundred words.

Choose a single subject for use throughout the sentence: The Gettysburg Address, for instance, contained only a few hundred words.

EXERCISE

X-7a, b, c. Unnecessary Shift in Number, Tense, and Subject

For each item list the errors of shift in number, tense, and subject. Rewrite each sentence to eliminate all such errors.

1. Once a person has been rejected the army would not again consider their application.
2. The train had arrived late. They were delayed by flash floods which washed out several bridges.
3. She liked the new style so much that she buys a complete new wardrobe.

4. Carnivals appeared exciting and glamorous to us as children, but when you grow up most people see only its shoddiness.

5. Jane Addams wrote of her experiences in *Twenty Years at Hull House*. The settlement where she worked had been in Chicago's slums.

6. The committee reconsidered its motion; then they adjourned.

7. Before going into business a young man should consider how much capital they require.

8. The mosquitoes were thick. The marsh lands provide ideal conditions for it to breed.

9. Seward's critics called Alaska "Seward's Folly." Later when the value of the territory had become evident, Seward wins praise from these same men for his foresight.

10. Graduation from college does not guarantee one a good job, but you will have a better chance than the high school graduates.

X-7d, e. Unnecessary Shift in Voice and Mood

For each item list the errors involving shift of voice or mood. Rewrite each sentence to correct the errors.

1. Andrew Carnegie retired at the age of sixty-four. Before his death $350,000,000 was given away by him.

2. Many citizens vote blindly, the qualifications of the candidates not being made known to them.

3. Before planning an advertising campaign, make a careful survey of the market; then you should direct your appeal to potential customers.

4. Whenever the rat made a wrong turn in the maze it received an electric shock in order that the proper path for it to follow might be learned.

5. If a coach hopes to develop a winning team the respect of his men must first be gained.

6. To put the overdrive into operation, release the throttle for a moment. When you advance it again the overdrive is engaged.

7. Scientists watching the explosion saw the flash, and almost immediately the force of the blast could be felt.

8. Title insurance provides protection against loss from a defective land title, but do not assume that a clear title is guaranteed you.
9. Were I intending to become a radio announcer, voice and diction would be studied by me.
10. Make sure the landing gear is in down-locked position; then you should lower your flaps.

X-7f, g. Unnecessary Shift in Point of View and General Sentence Plan

Rewrite each item, correcting all errors of unnecessary shift.

1. As you step into the new cars the seats are built close to the ground to provide a low center of gravity.
2. Turn on the white footlights before raising the curtain. After the curtain is up I dim the footlights, and at the same time the anteproscenium floodlights are brought full up.
3. Before cutting a stencil I always clean the typewriter type thoroughly. It is also important to strike the keys with a firm, even touch. If you make an error, put the correction fluid on the stencil and let it dry before any correction can be made.
4. Modern air conditioning units, now available for homes, there is no need to swelter in the summer.
5. Cinco de Mayo, the Mexican Independence Day, the defeat of the French by General Zaragoza's troops is celebrated.
6. When you look through the microscope the paramecium divides, forming two organisms.
7. The pronunciation is always difficult when studying a foreign language.
8. Combustible materials soaked with vegetable or animal oil you must never store them away where they might create a fire hazard.
9. Consider for a moment high-frequency sound waves are now used to sterilize foods.
10. John Marshall, when news of the battle of Lexington reached his father's farm, both he and his father joined the militia.

PARALLELISM

8. **Make sentence elements which are parallel in thought parellel in form** If ideas are coördinate (for example, if they are properly linked by *and*, *or*, or *but*) they should not be unnecessarily different in structure. A change in construction ordinarily suggests a change in thought.

HOW TO CORRECT FAULTS IN PARALLELISM

8a. **Shift in Part of Speech (or Kind of Verbal)** Express parallel ideas in words of the same kind or form: two (or more) nouns, two adjectives, two gerunds, two infinitives, and so on.

Awkward shift from noun to adjective: His qualities were thrift, energy, and persistent.

Use nouns throughout: His qualities were thrift, energy, and persistence.

Awkward shift from gerund to infinitive: Riding is sometimes better exercise than to walk. [Though both gerunds and infinitives are used as nouns, they are not parallel in construction.]

Use two gerunds: Riding is sometimes better exercise than walking. [Or]

Use two infinitives: To ride is sometimes better exercise than to walk.

8b. **Shift Involving Larger Sentence Elements** To express parallel thoughts match words with words, phrases with phrases, clauses with clauses, or topics with topics. Do not match an element with a larger or structurally different element.*

* For securing emphasis through parallelism in larger elements see 48d.

Faulty shift from phrase to clause: Frazier had two desires—first, for money [phrase]; in the second place, he wanted fame [clause].

Use two phrases: Frazier had two desires—first, for money and second, for fame. [Or]

Use two clauses: Frazier had two desires: in the first place he wanted money; in the second, fame. [In the last clause *he wanted* is understood.]

Faulty shift from clause to phrase: When you have mastered the operation of shifting gears [clause] and after a little practice [phrase] you will be a good driver.

Use a compound predicate (a shortened form of the use of two clauses): When you have mastered the operation of shifting gears and [when you] have had a little practice you will be a good driver. [Or]

Use two phrases: After mastering the shifting of gears and practicing a little you will be a good driver.

Awkward shift from adjective to compound predicate: He was red-faced, awkward, and had a disposition to eat everything on the table. [The third element is like the others in thought and should have the same form.]

Use adjectives throughout: He was red-faced, awkward, and voracious. [Or]

Use nouns (with modifiers) throughout: He had a red face, an awkward manner, and a disposition to eat everything on the table.

Inconsistent shift from phrase to clause to topic:

These are the duties of the president:

    (*a*) To preside at regular meetings [phrase]
    (*b*) He calls special meetings [clause]
    (*c*) Appointment of committees [topic]

Use all phrases:

These are the duties of the president:

    (*a*) To preside at regular meetings
    (*b*) To call special meetings
    (*c*) To appoint committees [Or]

Use all clauses:

These are the duties of the president:

    (*a*) He presides at regular meetings
    (*b*) He calls special meetings
    (*c*) He appoints committees

Faulty shift from prepositional phrase (adverbial) to plain adverb: He spoke with candor, with force, yet gently.

Use phrases throughout: He spoke with candor, with force, yet with gentleness. [Or]

Use plain adverbs throughout: He spoke candidly, forcefully, yet gently.

8c. Careless Use of Correlatives After correlatives (conjunctions used in pairs: *both ... and; either ... or; neither ... nor; whether ... or; not only ... but; not only ... but also*) use elements which are parallel in form.

Faulty position of correlatives: He was not only courteous to rich customers but also to poor ones. [The phrases intended to be balanced against each other are *to rich customers* and *to poor ones*. As the sentence stands it is the word *courteous* that is balanced against *to poor ones*.]

Place the correlatives before like elements: He was courteous not only to rich customers but also to poor ones.

Faulty position of correlatives: I talked both with Miller and Brown. [One conjunction is followed by a preposition and the other by a noun.]

Place the correlatives before like elements: I talked with both Miller and Brown. [Or] I talked both with Miller and with Brown.

8d. Failure to Repeat Necessary Words Repeat a subject (noun or pronoun), an article, a conjunction, a preposition, the sign of the infinitive, an auxiliary verb, or the introductory words of a phrase or clause when repetition is needed to make a parallel consistent and clear.

Preposition not repeated: He was regarded as a hero by all who had known him, and especially his old schoolmates.

Repeat the preposition: He was regarded as a hero by all who had known him, and especially by his old schoolmates.

Sign of the infinitive not repeated: He wishes to join with those who love freedom and justice, and end needless suffering.

Repeat the sign of the infinitive: He wishes to join with those who love freedom and justice, and to end needless suffering.

Conjunction not repeated and pronoun confusingly omitted: He explained that the strikers asked only a fair hearing, since their contentions were misunderstood; were by no means in favor of the violent measures to which the public had grown accustomed; and had no desire to resort to bloodshed and the destruction of property.

Repeat the conjunction and insert the necessary pronoun: He explained that the strikers asked only a fair hearing, since their contentions were misunderstood; that they were by no means in favor of the violent measures to which the public had grown accustomed; and that they had no desire to resort to bloodshed and the destruction of property.

Article wrongly omitted: She belongs not only to the Baptist Church but also to the Woman's Club, Teachers' Club, and the Welfare Council.

Repeat the article before each item: She belongs not only to the Baptist Church but also to the Woman's Club, the Teachers' Club, and the Welfare Council. [Or]

Let the first article serve for all items in the series: She belongs not only to the Baptist Church but also to the Woman's Club, Teachers' Club, and Welfare Council.

Subject of a clause wrongly omitted: We knew they suffered from this charge and tried to disprove it.

Repeat the subject: We knew they suffered from this charge and we tried to disprove it. [Or] We knew that they suffered from this charge and that they tried to disprove it.

8e. Misuse of Parallelism Avoid giving parallel form to thoughts which are not parallel.

Misleading parallel structure: He was admired for his knowledge of science, and for his taste in art, and for this I too honor him. [The last *for* gives a false parallelism to unlike thoughts.]

Place the unlike thought in a separate sentence: He was admired for his knowledge of science and for his taste in art. I honor him for both these qualities.

Misleading parallel structure: The program is given at two o'clock, and at four o'clock, and at six o'clock the doors are closed.

Show the change of direction in the unlike thought: The program is given at two o'clock and at four o'clock, but at six o'clock the doors are closed.

Detailed parallelism is not always possible. A lack of parallelism is preferable to awkward, unclear, or unidiomatic constructions.

Permissible lack of parallelism: He always walked slowly and with a limp. [*Limpingly* would not be idiomatic.] You may answer either orally or in writing. We shall die ashore, aboard ship, or wherever the heavens decree. In the party were a Congressman, a justice of the Supreme Court, and a man whom I did not know. We arrived very dirty and covered with mosquito bites.

EXERCISE

X-8a. Faulty Shift in Part of Speech (or Kind of Verbal)

Rewrite, using words of the same kind or form to express parallel ideas.

1. To provide wholesome recreation for children is as important as giving them nourishing food.

2. When the Haitian dances he shuffles his feet, twisting his body, and his arms waving.
3. Before permitting a doctor to perform a major operation, some hospitals require him to hold a surgical diploma or having three years of special training in surgery.
4. The ghost of Drury Lane is said to be of medium height and dresses well.
5. He began pacing up and down and to scowl angrily.

X-8b. Faulty Shift in Large Sentence Elements

Recast each sentence, giving parallel elements parallel form.

1. An ostrich has two means of defence—it is a powerful kicker, and pecking with its sharp bill.
2. The critic insists that many movies are poor because often producers are business men, not artists, and because of misjudgment about the wishes of movie-goers.
3. The use of modern mine machinery in the United States has resulted in keeping coal prices low and wages are higher than those of English miners.
4. Irving Berlin's early life was one of hardship, deprivation, and he was often hungry.
5. Weaving a Navajo rug involves four steps:

   (1) Choosing a design
   (2) The frame is then made
   (3) Placing the warp on the frame
   (4) Weaving

X-8c. Careless Use of Correlatives

Recast, giving parallel form to elements which follow the correlatives.

1. Authors of children's stories must not only write vividly but also accurately.
2. The Supreme Court found the corporation guilty of both monopoly and of conspiracy.
3. An experienced stage crew can both shift scenery quietly and quickly.
4. Often allergies are caused by neither pollen nor by food.
5. Emerson neither took part in the reforms of his day nor did he think he should.

X-8d. Failure to Repeat Necessary Words

Add the words necessary to make the parallel thoughts consistent and clear.

1. The university was filled with young people who had wealthy parents, particularly foreign students.
2. He pooled his talents with those of engineers who believed it possible to span the bay and other public-spirited citizens.
3. The report pointed out that the United States uses half the radios and three-fourths of the automobiles produced in the world, and we purchase a third of the world's wool.
4. His eagerness for a career in law and hard work began to attract notice.
5. The occidental mind cannot easily understand the Chinese, the Japanese, or Russians.

SENTENCE COHERENCE

9. **Keep related sentence elements together; keep elements not related apart.** To cohere means to stick or hold firmly together. A sentence has coherence when the relative position of its parts clearly indicates the relationship of the thoughts they express.

HOW TO CORRECT FAULTY COHERENCE

9a. Related Elements Not Kept Together

Illogically placed adverb: I only need a few dollars. [The faulty position of *only* makes the sentence appear to mean "I do not want money; I only need it." *Only* should refer to *few*.]

Put the adverb near the word it modifies: I need only a few dollars.

Illogically placed adverb: I don't ever intend to go there again.

Put the adverb near the words it modifies: I don't intend ever to go there again. [Or] I intend never to go there again.

Illogically placed adverb: She has the sweetest voice I nearly ever heard. [The faulty arrangement makes *nearly* modify *ever* rather than *sweetest*.]

Put the adverb near the word it modifies: She has nearly [or *almost*] the sweetest voice I ever heard.

Split comparison: * She is as old if not older than he. [The construction *as old . . . than he* is illogical.]

Put the related elements together: She is as old as he, if not older.

Related modifiers needlessly separated: If both of us can go we'll have some grand skating if the weather clears.

Put the related modifiers together: If the weather clears and both of us can go, we'll have some grand skating.

9b. Unrelated Elements Joined

Squinting construction: I told him when the time came I would do it. [*When the time came* is said to "squint" because the reader cannot tell whether it looks forward to the end of the sentence or backward to the beginning.]

Separate the unrelated elements: When the time came I told him I would do it. [Or] I told him I would do it when the time came.

Faulty coördination: She looked up as he approached and smoothed her hair. [Which two words does *and* connect? Does the writer mean *He approached and smoothed* or *she looked* (as he approached) *and smoothed*?]

Separate the unrelated elements: She looked up and smoothed her hair as he approached. [Or] As he approached she looked up and smoothed her hair.

* A split infinitive, though it does not violate logic, separates the parts of a construction and appears to many readers, including thousands of non-academic ones, a fault.
Split infinitive: to immediately go . . . to carefully observe. . . .
Put the infinitive and its sign (*to*) together: to go immediately . . . to observe carefully. . . .
But a split infinitive is preferable to the artificial construction which too consciously avoids it.

9c. Straggling Modifiers Distribute unrelated modifiers instead of letting them pile up and cause confusion at the end of a sentence.

Unrelated modifiers bunched: I found a heap of snow on my bed in the morning which had drifted in through the window. [Subject—verb—object—place—time—explanation.]

Distribute the unrelated modifiers: In the morning I found on my bed a heap of snow which had drifted in through the window. [Time—subject—verb—place—object—explanation. An adjectival modifier must cling close to the word it modifies. The relative clause *which had drifted in through the window* is adjectival. It must follow closely after the noun *snow*.]

Unrelated modifiers bunched: He went to meet the train with his sister whenever it was scheduled to arrive. [Subject—verb—infinitive phrase—manner—time.]

Distribute the unrelated modifiers: Whenever the train was scheduled to arrive he went with his sister to meet it. [Time—subject—verb—manner—infinitive phrase. An adverbial modifier of time or place need not always cling close to the verb. When it refers to the main verb it may usually be placed first in the sentence.] *

EXERCISE

X-9a. Related Elements Not Kept Together

Rewrite, placing related elements together.

1. In the Presidential primary a voter only can vote for convention delegates of his own party.
2. Simpson testified that he had nearly paid double the value of the land.
3. Playing the rôle of valet, if he were less outspoken he would be more convincing while shaving his master.
4. At Thebes archeologists have found elaborately decorated Egyptian burial chambers in the valleys of the tombs.

* Elsewhere in this book you are urged to place adverbial modifiers first in the sentence, both to overcome the lazy human tendency to "tack on" details at the end and to secure a variety in style. See 48c(2) and 49a.

5. College preparatory students attend modern high schools, and students who will not go to college, both.
6. His wife had only been dead two months.
7. The government prosecutor insists that to under such circumstances give rebates is a restraint of trade.
8. On the second night the crowd was as big, but not as responsive, as the first-night audience.
9. The Audubon Society sends bird counters out into the country before the first snow to determine how many birds winter in certain areas of the North and what kinds.
10. The labor-management delegates continued long into the night to confer.

X-9b. Unrelated Elements Joined

Rewrite to bring related elements together.

1. He polished the new convertible which his father had bought him with tender care.
2. The manager dictated letters into a wire recorder while his secretary ate her lunch and then spent the afternoon playing golf.
3. The doctor instructed him while in the hospital to take light exercise every day.
4. A broken wheel on the locomotive near the crossing caused the train to jump the track.
5. Oklahoma was opened to settlers in 1899, although it had been previously set aside as an Indian reservation, and was immediately overrun.

X-9c. Straggling Modifiers

Recast, properly distributing the modifiers.

1. Do not try to study while listening to the radio after a long day at school.
2. Motion picture studios employ some of the country's finest musicians to play for films requiring background music at great expense.
3. Judge Rasdell pronounced the sentence in a dramatic manner before a packed courtroom of silent spectators after the jury had announced its verdict of guilty.

4. The crew took off before daylight in the rain and sleet for their record cross country non-stop flight from Washington, D. C., to Los Angeles in the new jet bomber reported to be capable of more than seven hundred miles per hour.

5. The U.S.S. *Oregon* steamed 13,000 miles at full speed from San Francisco to Santiago, Cuba, around the tip of South America in 1898 under Captain Charles Clark to take active part in the sea battle with the Spanish fleet.

Grammar

Grammar * has to do with the functions and relations of words in a sentence. You need not memorize complicated rules in order to grasp the essentials of grammar. You need have only a knowledge of the basic elements of a sentence and an understanding of the logical relationships between them.

CASE

10. Give to each noun or pronoun the case form required to show its function in the sentence. In English there are only three cases: (1) nominative—that of the subject; (2) objective—that of the object; (3) possessive—that of a possessor.

All nouns and a few pronouns (such as *it, you, which*) have the same form for subject and object. Most pronouns have separate forms for subject and object (*I, me; they, them*). Some pronouns have two forms as possessors (*my, mine; their, theirs; your, yours*); a few have no possessive form (*this, these, which*).

Pronouns, being much more fully inflected than nouns, are more frequently misused as to case.

HOW TO CORRECT ERRORS OF CASE

10a. **Nominative Case** Put both the subject of a finite verb and the predicate noun in the nominative case.

* For an explanation of the terms of grammar see **14.**

(I) Subjects of main clauses

Subject given the wrong case form: Dave and me heard him.
[Is the pronoun one of the subjects of the verb *heard*? Yes.
But *me* is the objective case form. Take the two subjects sepa-
rately: *Dave* heard him; *I* heard him.]
Put the subject in the nominative case: Dave and I heard him.

Subject in appositional construction given the wrong case form:
Us boys formed a club. [The pronoun is the subject of the
sentence, but this fact is overlooked because of the appositive
boys.]
Put the subject in the nominative case: We boys formed a club.

Subject of a main clause given the wrong case form: Whom
do you suppose made us a visit? [A parenthetical expression
like *you suppose, they believe, he says, we think* does not
affect the case of the preceding pronoun. The pronoun takes
the same case as if the expression were omitted. Here the pronoun is the subject of *made.*]
Put the subject in the nominative case (disregarding the parenthetical expression): Who do you suppose made us a visit?

(2) Subjects of subordinate clauses

Subject of a subordinate clause given the wrong case form:
Punish whomever is guilty. [The pronoun is the subject of *is*.
The object of *punish* is the entire subordinate clause.]
Put the subject of a subordinate clause in the nominative case:
[You] punish whoever is guilty.

Subject of a subordinate clause given the wrong case form: The
mystery as to whom had rendered him this service remained.
[The pronoun is the subject of *had rendered*. The object of
the preposition *to* is the entire subordinate clause.]
Put the subject of a subordinate clause in the nominative case
(even though the clause is the object of a preposition): The
mystery as to who had rendered him this service remained.

Subject of a subordinate clause wrongly made the object of a
parenthetical expression: The man whom they believed was
the cause of the trouble left the country. [The first pronoun
is the subject of *was.*]

Put the subject of a subordinate clause in the nominative case (disregarding the parenthetical expression): The man who they believed was the cause of the trouble left the country.

Subject of an elliptical clause given the wrong case form: The boys in Grade B are as old as us. [Is *us* the subject of a finite verb? Apparently not; but part of the sentence is implied rather than expressed. The pronoun is the subject of an uncompleted clause.]

Put the subject of the uncompleted clause in the nominative case: The boys in Grade B are as old as we [are old].

Subject of an elliptical clause given the wrong case form: Loren is taller than her.

Put the subject of the uncompleted clause in the nominative case: Loren is taller than she. [The use of the conjunction *than* or *as* does not affect the form of the following pronoun, which is determined by the function of the pronoun in the uncompleted clause. For examples of the objective case following *than* or *as* see **10b.**]

(3) Appositives and predicate nouns

Appositives given the wrong case form: The whole party—him, her, and us—have bought tickets. [Appositives take the same case as the substantive with which they are in apposition. Here the pronouns are in apposition with the subject *party*. For examples of appositives in the objective case see **10b.**]

Put appositives of the subject in the nominative case: The whole party—he, she, and we—have bought tickets.

Predicate noun (or equivalent) given the wrong case form: Was it her? Was it them? It is him. The only contributors have been him and his mother. [The verb *to be* (in any of its finite forms) does not express action or take an object. A noun or pronoun completing this verb agrees in case with the subject.]

Put predicate nouns in the nominative case: Was it she? Was it they? It is he. The only contributors have been he and his mother.

10b. **Objective Case.** Put the object of a finite verb or of a preposition in the objective case. Put the assumed subject of an infinitive in the objective case.

(1) Objects of verbs (expressed or implied)

Object of a verb given the wrong case form: Such conduct disgusts you and I. [When both pronouns are subjects, follow *you and* with *I*. But here the pronouns are objects of the verb *disgusts*.]

Put both elements of the compound object in the objective case: Such conduct disgusts you and me. [Disgusts *you*. Disgusts *me*.]

Object of an unexpressed verb given the wrong case form: He trusts you as much as [he trusts] I. [*I* is the object of the unexpressed verb *trusts*, but it is in the wrong case.]

Put the object of a verb in the objective case (even though the verb is unexpressed): He trusts you as much as [he trusts] me.

Object of an unexpressed verb given the wrong case form: I like his brother better than [I like] he. [*He* is the object of the unexpressed verb *like*, but it is in the wrong case.]

Put the object of an unexpressed verb in the objective case: I like his brother better than [I like] him.

Object in an interrogative sentence given the wrong case form: Who shall we nominate as president? [*Who* is the object of *shall nominate*. *We* is the subject of the sentence.]

Put the object in an interrogative sentence in the objective case: Whom shall we nominate as president? [In speech or informal writing the interrogative pronoun *who* is often used to begin a sentence when strict grammar requires *whom*. Informal, but allowable: Who did you see?]

Object in a subordinate clause given the wrong case form: The doctor who he most respected had retired. [*Who he most respected* is a subordinate clause in which the relative pronoun *who* is the object of the verb *respected*. But its case form is that of the subject.]

Put the object in a subordinate clause in the objective case: The doctor whom he most respected had retired.

(2) Appositives and objects of prepositions

Appositive given the wrong case form: They want us—you and I. [*You* and *I*, as appositives of *us*, must agree with it in case.]

Put appositives of an object in the objective case: They want us—you and me.

Object of a preposition given the wrong case form: Who have you been looking for?

Put the object of a preposition in the objective case: Whom have you been looking for? [*Who* would be allowable in informal writing.] [Or]

For whom have you been looking?

Second object of a preposition given the wrong case form: That seems incredible to you and I. [The pronouns are objects of the preposition *to*.]

Put both objects of the preposition in the objective case: That seems incredible to you and me.

Object of a preposition in an appositional construction given the wrong case form: Some of we fellows went fishing. [The pronoun is the object of *of*, but this fact is overlooked because of the appositive *fellows*. The subject of the sentence is *some*, modified by the prepositional phrase.]

Put the object of the preposition in the objective case: Some of us fellows went fishing.

(3) Assumed subjects of infinitives

Assumed subject of an infinite given the wrong case form: Who do you wish to be your leader? [An infinitive cannot assert action and hence cannot take a true subject. But it implies that something is at least capable of action and hence it often has a latent or assumed subject. This assumed subject is put in the objective case. Here *who* is the assumed subject of *to be*, but it is improperly in the nominative case.]

Put the assumed subject of an infinitive in the objective case: Whom do you wish to be your leader? [*Who* would be allowable in informal writing.]

10c. Possessive Case *

Somewhat illogical use of the possessive: The pole's top is gilded. [Do not, ordinarily, make an inanimate object a possessor.]

Use an *of*-phrase: The top of the pole is gilded.†

Illogical use of the possessive: The man's denunciation was uncalled for. [Do not let the receiver of an action appear to be the actor.]

Use an *of*-phrase: The denunciation of the man was uncalled for.**

Failure to use the possessive with a gerund: Is there any criticism of Arthur going? [The criticism is of the *going*, not of *Arthur*. Hence the object of *of* is *going* (a gerund). *Arthur* modifies *going*.]

Put the noun modifier of the gerund in the possessive case: Is there any criticism of Arthur's going? ††

Failure to use the possessive with a gerund: We regret you being sick. [What is regretted? Not you, but the sickness. *Being sick* is a gerund—the object of the verb.]

Put the pronoun modifier of the gerund in the possessive case: We regret your being sick.

---

* For writing the possessive form see **27b** and **27c.**

† But possessives may be used in idioms expressing time (*the day's work, two months' wages, a month's notice*), measure (*a dollar's worth, two dollars' worth, a cable's length*), or personification (*for mercy's sake, the heart's desire, the world's progress*).

** Compare the use of the possessive for the actor himself. Correct: The man's denunciation of his enemies was venomous.

†† But if attention is focused on the actor rather than the act, make the verbal the modifier.

Wrong use of the possessive with a verbal: After a long search for Edzell, I caught sight of his buying a shotgun. [The pronoun, not the verbal, is the object of *of*. *Buying* is a participle modifying the pronoun.]

Put the pronoun object of the preposition in the objective case: After a long search for Edzell, I caught sight of him buying a shotgun.

EXERCISE

X-10a, b. Use of the Nominative and Objective Cases

Decide which word in each pair of parentheses shows the right case. Then copy the sentence in correct form, underscoring each pronoun you have retained.

1. The invitation was sent to you and (me, I).
2. They had a better infield than (we, us), but we had better batters than (them, they).
3. Ralph and (him, he) took business administration courses, intending to enter partnership with the Clarks and (we, us).
4. Soon after Eli Whitney demonstrated his cotton gin it was stolen, possibly by someone (who, whom) had witnessed the demonstration.
5. When the girl turned he decided it was really (she, her).
6. It seemed to us—(he, him) and (me, I)—that we should sign the petition.
7. (Whom, Who) will be appointed Secretary of State?
8. The coach wants the entire team—you as well as (they, them)—to be dressed a half hour before the game begins.
9. Sample ballots are mailed to only (us, we) voters (who, whom) are registered.
10. Gordon and (him, he) together developed a new process for photographing fingerprints.
11. (Us, We) three pooled our money to buy the car.
12. She was as tall as (I, me), but I looked larger than (her, she).
13. (They, Them) are the same men (whom, who) we saw buying up tickets to last year's big game.
14. Policies of the company are dictated by (whomever, whoever) controls fifty-one per cent of the stock.
15. "Was it (they, them)?" he asked.
16. The boat belongs as much to you as to (he, him).
17. By a compromise the first prize was awarded to an artist (who, whom) none of the judges considered most worthy.
18. The Social Security Law applies to you, but not to (me, I).
19. If the members will tell the committee (whom, who) they want nominated, we will draw up a list of candidates.
20. You and (I, me) are the only sorority members (who, whom) were chosen to work on the newspaper staff.

X-10c. Use of the Possessive Case

Decide which word or word group in parentheses shows the right case. Then copy the sentence in correct form, underscoring the word or words chosen.

1. The (car's color, color of the car) made it easily identifiable.
2. Their commanding officer did not object to (their, them) using free hours for target practice.
3. Detectives proved him guilty by taking motion pictures of (him, his) etching the plates and printing the money.
4. Traffic laws prohibit (children, children's) driving without their parents' consent.
5. The army objected to the (public, public's) seeing the new plane before the flight tests.
6. The (criticism of the editor, editor's criticism) forced him to reply through (the paper's columns, the columns of the paper).
7. The (door's handle, handle of the door) is of brass.
8. The (negotiator's rejection, rejection of the negotiator) by the strikers delayed settlement of the strike.
9. (The use of gasoline, Gasoline's use) for cleaning clothes is dangerous.
10. It was (the man whom I saw's watch, the watch of the man whom I saw).

AGREEMENT IN
NUMBER, GENDER, AND PERSON

11. **Make a verb agree with its subject in number and person.**
Make a pronoun agree with its antecedent in number, gender, and person.

You will have few problems of agreement in person or gender, many in number. When confronted with a choice as to number, you must hold to either the singular or the plural throughout, not switch illogically from one to the other.

HOW TO CORRECT ERRORS OF AGREEMENT

11a. Subject and Verb A verb agrees with its subject in person as well as number, but agreement in person offers little difficulty. Few people are so illiterate as to say *you am* or *he walk*. The errors pointed out in this section are limited to those of agreement in number.

(1) Simple agreement

Gross disregard of agreement in number: He don't get up early on Sunday morning. [*Don't* equals *do not*.]

Use a singular verb with a singular subject: He doesn't get up early on Sunday morning.

Faulty use of a singular verb with a plural subject: More attends than used to. [*All, more, some,* and *such* may be either singular or plural. *None* (from *no one*), though singular in origin, is now more often plural in use. Correct: All is well. All are excited. Some is just where we placed it. Some have sought relief.] *

Use a plural verb with a subject clearly plural: More attend than used to.

(2) Agreement with compound or alternate subject

Faulty agreement with a compound subject: A man and his wife has to be patient with each other. [Singular nouns or pronouns joined by *and* are a plural subject.] †

Use a plural verb with a compound subject: A man and his wife have to be patient with each other.

---

* The noun or pronoun of an expression like *none of, some of, most of, half of, two thirds of, a part of,* or *the remainder of* may be singular or plural. It takes its number from the word following *of,* and this number determines the number of the verb.

Right: Some of it *was* lost. [*Was* agrees with *some,* which is singular because *it* is singular.] Some of the cattle *were* sold. Three fourths of that wire *has* been insulated. Three fourths of the musicians *have* resigned.

† Singular nouns or pronouns joined by *and* are used as a singular subject when they name the same person or thing ("His friend

Faulty agreement with alternate subjects: A book or a speaker
are often influential in changing the course of a life. [Singular
nouns or pronouns joined by *or* or *nor* are considered a
singular subject.] *

Use a singular verb with singular alternate subjects: A book or
a speaker is often influential in changing the course of a life.

(3) Agreement with subject following the verb Make the verb
agree with the subject, but not with a predicate noun.

Faulty agreement with subject following the verb: From such
rigid training develops good athletes.

Find the real subject (with which to make the verb agree):
From such rigid training develop good athletes. [The subject
of the sentence is *athletes,* not *training.*]

Faulty agreement with subject following the verb: There was
three men in the room.

Find the real subject (with which to make the verb agree):
There were three men in the room. [The subject of the sentence is *men.*]

Predicate noun mistaken for the subject: The weak point in
the team were the fielders.

Find the real subject (with which to make the verb agree): The
weak point in the team was the fielders. [*Point* is the subject
of the sentence.]

Predicate noun mistaken for the subject: Laziness and dissipation is the cause of his failure.

Find the real subject (with which to make the verb agree):
Laziness and dissipation are the cause of his failure.

---

and patron visits him often"), when they form a logical unit ("Our
end and aim is just this"), or when they are modified by a preceding
each, every, no, or *many a* ("Each boy and girl is responsible for his
own chores"). For additional illustrations see 11b(1), note.

* When one of the subjects joined by *or* or *nor* is singular and the
other plural the verb agrees with the nearer ("Neither the drum nor
the brasses are loud enough"). Usually, however, it is better to recast
the sentence to make the subject clearly plural ("Both the drum and
the brasses are too soft"). For additional examples see 11b(1), note.

(4) Agreement of subject and verb separated by intervening words

Intervening noun mistaken for the subject: The greater length of the levers we are using increase our lifting power. [Nouns or pronouns which come between the subject and the verb do not affect the number of the verb. Such nouns or pronouns are usually introduced by *of, with, together with, as well as, no less than,* or the like.]

Find the real subject (with which to make the verb agree): The greater length of the levers we are using increases our lifting power. [The subject is *length*, not *levers*.]

Intervening noun mistaken for the subject: The size of the plantations vary.

Find the real subject (with which to make the verb agree): The size of the plantations varies. [Or] The plantations vary in size.

Intervening pronoun mistaken for the subject: Each of us expect to make a fortune.

Find the real subject (with which to make the verb agree): Each of us expects to make a fortune.

Intervening noun in parenthetical phrase mistaken for the subject: The mayor of the city, as well as several aldermen, have investigated the charges. [The expression *as well as* shows that the *aldermen* are brought in only parenthetically.]

Find the real subject (with which to make the verb agree): The mayor of the city, as well as several aldermen, has investigated the charges.

Intervening noun in parenthetical phrase mistaken for the subject: He, and not the others, deserve the credit for originating the process.

Find the real subject (with which to make the verb agree): He, and not the others, deserves the credit for originating the process.

(5) Agreement of subject and verb in who constructions The verb agrees in number with *who*. Since the form *who*

does not show number, the problem is to determine whether *who* is singular or plural. Find the word to which *who* refers; give *who* the number of that word.

Correct use of number in a *who* construction: Pratt is the man who takes your ticket. [*Who* is singular because it refers to *man*, a singular. *Takes* agrees with *who*.]

Correct use of number in a *who* construction: Tell the news to all who are there. [*Are* agrees with *who*, which is plural because *all* is plural.]

Faulty use of number in a *who* construction: There are people who never attends religious services.

Give the verb of a *who* clause the same number the antecedent of *who* has: There are people who never attend religious services.

Faulty agreement in a *one of* . . . [plural term] *who* construction: Mrs. Blodgett is one of those women who pushes market baskets around. [Who refers to *women*, not to *Mrs. Blodgett*.]

In a *one of* . . . [plural term] *who* construction treat *who* and its verb as plurals: Mrs. Blodgett is one of those women who push market baskets around.*

Faulty agreement in an *it is* . . . *who* construction: It is we who has to clean up the mess. [*Who* refers to *we*, not to *it*.]

In an *it is* . . . *who* construction give *who* and its verb the number of the noun or pronoun completing *is*: It is we who have to clean up the mess.

Faulty agreement in an (*is, are*) (*the one, the person*) *who* construction: You are the one who hear the gossip soonest. [*Who* refers to *one*, not to *you*.]

In an (*is, are*) (*the one, the person*) *who* construction give *who* and its verb the number of the noun or pronoun completing (*is, are*): You are the one who hears the gossip soonest.

* But in such a construction *only* before *one* causes *who* to refer to *one* and therefore to be singular: He is the only one of the players who bats [not *bat*] above three hundred.

(6) Agreement of verb and pronoun with a collective noun

Inconsistent use of verb and pronoun with a collective noun: The committee has disbanded and gone to their homes. [Collective nouns may be used as singular or plural, the choice depending on whether the individual members are referred to or the group is considered as a unit.* But in this example *committee* is used both as a singular and as a plural. As a subject it is given a singular verb; as an antecedent it is linked to a plural pronoun.]

Be consistent in making verbs and pronouns agree with a collective noun: The committee have disbanded and gone to their homes. [The expressed idea of committee members having gone to their homes requires that *committee* be treated as a plural.]

(7) Agreement with plural-looking singular nouns

Faulty agreement with a singular noun which is plural in form: Mathematics are a bugbear to many students.

Use a singular verb with a noun which is plural in form but singular in meaning: Mathematics is a bugbear to many students. [*Economics, measles,* and *news* are other examples of plural forms which take singular verbs. Some nouns, such as *athletics* and *politics,* are either singular or plural.]

Faulty agreement with a noun which is singular in thought but plural in form: † *Jungle Tales* are an interesting collection of stories.

Use a singular verb with a subject which is singular in thought: *Jungle Tales* is an interesting collection of stories.

* Correct use of a collective noun as a singular subject: The crowd is waiting. As a plural subject: The crowd are of various moods. For additional examples see 11b(1).

† A title of a book (*Jungle Tales*), a plural form ("*They* is a pronoun"), any group of words ("'Honesty is the best policy' is an excellent motto"), or any designation of a quantity or sum ("Five dollars is the amount I owe you"), when considered in itself or as a single thing, is singular.

I I b. Pronoun and Antecedent

(I) Agreement in number

Faulty agreement with a grammatically singular antecedent: Nobody did their best. [*Each, every, every one, everybody, anybody, either, neither,* * *no one, nobody,* and similar words
are singular. Pronouns referring to them must be singular.] †

Make the pronoun singular (to agree with its antecedent):
Nobody did his best.

Faulty agreement with a compound antecedent: A car and a
plane are a convenience to its owner. [Singular nouns or pronouns joined by *and* are considered a plural antecedent.] **

Make the pronoun plural when it refers to singular compound
antecedents: A car and a plane are a convenience to their
owner.

* The words *either* and *neither*, when used as conjunctions (*either
...or, neither...nor*), do not in themselves have number. Number is
shown by the nouns or pronouns which the conjunctions connect.
Examples: Either Lucy or Harriet has my handbag. Neither they nor
the critics are mistaken.

† Careful writers use them as singulars. Speakers, however, often use
them as plurals.
Colloquially allowable: Everybody crowded about the hostess and
assured her they had had a good time.
Formally correct: Everybody crowded about the hostess and assured
her he had had a good time.
More natural: All the guests crowded about the hostess and assured
her they had had a good time. [Usually the best way to avoid awkwardness is to replace the first pronoun in such sentences with an
unquestionably plural noun.]

** Singular nouns or pronouns joined by *and* are used as a singular
antecedent when they name the same person or thing ("My friend
and colleague sends you his good wishes"), when they form a logical
unit ("The long and short of the matter is that it means higher
wages"), or when they are modified by a preceding *each, every, no,*
or *many a* ("Many a soldier and sailor learns to mend his own
clothes").

Faulty agreement with alternate antecedents: A car or a plane are a convenience to their owner. [Singular nouns or pronouns joined by *or* or *nor* are considered a singular antecedent.] *

Make a pronoun singular when it refers to singular alternate antecedents: A car or a plane is a convenience to its owner.

Faulty agreement with a collective noun: The crowd is waiting for their tickets. [When a collective noun (one referring to several persons or things) is thought of as referring to the group as a unit it is singular; when it is thought of as referring to the individuals of the group it is plural. The use of a singular verb in this example indicates that *crowd* is being used in a singular sense.]

Use a singular pronoun to refer to a collective noun treated as a singular: The crowd is waiting for its tickets. [Or, if the noun is to be treated as a plural, change the number of the verb] The crowd are waiting for their tickets.

Crude use of a pronominal adjective: I never did like these sort of post cards. [Although in *these sort* or *those kind* the pronominal adjectives *these* and *those* agree in thought with a plural noun (expressed or unexpressed) which follows, they modify the singular nouns *sort* and *kind*.]

Make the pronominal adjective agree in number with the noun it modifies: I never did like this sort of post cards. [Or, better] I never did like post cards of this sort.

(2) Agreement in person and gender

Faulty agreement in person: One can't let them out of your sight. [Idiom treats the impersonal pronoun *one* as a third person pronoun.]

Put the pronoun in the same person as its antecedent: One can't let them out of his [or very formally, *one's*] sight. [Or] You can't let them out of your sight.

* When one of the alternate antecedents is singular and the other plural the pronoun agrees with the nearer ("He or his partners must have their way in the matter"). Usually, however, it is better to recast the sentence ("He must have his way in the matter, or his partners must have theirs").

Awkward use of alternate antecedents differing in person: You or she comes every day on her errand of mercy. [When alternate antecedents differ in person the pronoun agrees with the nearer. Although grammatically correct, such awkward sentences should be avoided.]

Recast the sentence, eliminating the final pronoun: Every day you come, or she does, on an errand of mercy.

Awkward use of alternate antecedents differing in gender: There are men and deeds which we cannot forget. [When compound antecedents differ in gender the pronoun agrees with the nearer. Such awkwardness, however, can usually be avoided.]

Use a pronoun which can refer to both antecedents: There are men and deeds that we cannot forget. [Or, as is often possible, strike out the pronoun] There are men and deeds we cannot forget.

Awkward use of alternate antecedents differing in gender: A man or woman must make his choice. [The subject emphasizes two genders.]

Recast the sentence, providing a single antecedent: A human being—man or woman—must make his choice. [The correct but awkward "A man or woman must make his or her choice" is usually limited to legal documents.]

Awkward use of two pronouns to refer to an antecedent of common gender: A human being must make his or her choice.

Use a masculine pronoun to refer to an antecedent of common gender: A human being must make his choice.

EXERCISE

X-11a. Agreement of Subject and Verb

Copy, writing the correct form of each subject and verb. Two items need no revision.

1. An artist don't have to paint what he sees; he may paint what he feels.

2. Among busy men to whom time is valuable, a bus or a train offer little competition to the airliner.

3. Many social workers feel that sympathy and benevolence is insufficient help for the needy.

4. Each of them consider psychological adjustment important in marriage.

5. The membership is given an opportunity to buy their tickets at reduced rates.

6. Ten tons are the load limit for trucks crossing the bridge.

7. Spraying to kill undesirable insects has destroyed many beneficial bugs as well.

8. In local elections a very small proportion of eligible citizens bothers to cast votes.

9. More than one child in every classroom needs individual attention.

10. Taxes and insurance has to be added to the sales price of a car.

11. Through careful experimentation by such men as Pasteur has come our most important medical discoveries.

12. A more efficient method of irrigation, along with the late rains, were what prevented a drought.

13. The number of pages are planned to permit sixteen to be printed in one press run.

14. The new homes, unlike the earlier style, are built primarily for comfort and utility.

15. The cause of the weakness of the administration are the factions that split the cabinet.

X-11b. Agreement of Pronoun and Antecedent

Copy the sentences, using the correct form of each incorrect pronoun or verb. Recast any awkward sentence. Two items need no correction.

1. Anyone flying in a modern transport plane loses all sense of how fast you are traveling.

2. The men and the cattle who had taken the longer trail arrived late at night.

3. In some states the driver of a car involved in a major accident loses his or her driving license if they cannot post a bond with the court.

70

4. A standard model differs from a deluxe in the amount of chrome and the number of extra gadgets they have.

5. The audience was enthusiastic; they remained in their seats, applauding, for ten minutes after the concluding number.

6. These kinds of paper, which are porous, are suitable for mimeographing.

7. You and they must inquire at the health office for your medical reports.

8. A man or woman cannot hope to succeed in a new business unless they have sufficient capital to operate at a loss for the first year.

9. The Palau father supports their families well.

10. When all are working, a cotton picker and his family earn living wages; but he works only a few months of the year.

11. Each trip is carefully planned so that they will include visits to historical sites.

12. If they are to succeed, a new product or a new business needs an effective advertising campaign.

13. The student body are determined that they will make the election truly representative.

14. These sort of articles in our newspapers give Europeans a wrong opinion of American life.

15. Everybody who has visited a veterans' hospital is determined they will do all they can to prevent another war.

TONE AND TIME
(Mood and Tense)

12. Use the mood and the tense which express the exact tone and time of an assertion. Since the tone and the time of successive statements may vary subtly, make all necessary adjustments; but do not change the mood or the tense needlessly.

Your difficulties in using mood and tense with reasonable correctness are probably not many. Most of them are covered in 7b, 7e, and 14 (the item on Principal Parts, with its list of troublesome verbs). When you have become somewhat familiar with the present article you will find the examples at the end of 12f(5), 12g(2), 12h(2), 12i(2), and 12j(4) helpful in meeting further problems of correctness.

. Article 12, however, differs from nearly all the rest of the handbook in not having correctness as its chief objective. Its purpose is to awaken you to the possibilities of using tone (mood) and time (tense) to make distinctions and express relationships in thought. Most people regard mood and tense as restrictive, as confining us to narrow and inflexible rules. Actually nothing shows more impressively the richness and resourcefulness of English. New ways of indicating tone and time are being constantly introduced. The process tends to break down formal grammatical patterns; also it adds color and variety to the language, and the challenge of unexplored opportunities to speaker and writer.

TONE

What tone an assertion has—whether of affirming, commanding, or supposing—is indicated by the mood (also called the "mode") of the verb.

HOW TO EXPRESS TONE EFFECTIVELY

12a. Expression of Tone by the Indicative and Imperative Moods

(1) The indicative mood states, questions, or denies.

> Dogs *bark*.
> *Are* you *crying?*
> My words *were* not *heard*.

This mood is expressed by the form the verb regularly takes in the tense you are using.

Faulty change of moods (potential to indicative): In times of difficulty people may grow discontented, and they blame their troubles on a racial or religious minority.

Use the indicative mood throughout: In times of difficulty people grow discontented, and they blame their troubles on a racial or religious minority. [Or use the potential throughout] ... may grow discontented and may blame....

(2) The imperative mood urges or commands. This mood is expressed by the form of the second person singular present indicative of the verb, with the subject usually omitted. "[You] *Hurry! Eat* that spinach!"

Faulty change of moods (imperative to potential): Shift gears; then you should let the clutch out slowly.

Use the imperative mood throughout: Shift gears; then let the clutch out slowly. [Or use the potential throughout] You should shift the gears; then you should let the clutch out slowly.

12b. Expression of Tone by the Subjunctive Mood

(1) Uses of the subjunctive In informal and colloquial use the subjunctive has largely faded from the language. In formal use it is still sometimes employed to express the following:

A supposition or assumption (especially one contrary to fact): If I *were* [informal *was*] seven feet tall I could see over these heads. He tries to act as if he *were* [informal *was*] young again.

A wish: If only I *were* [informal *was*] as lucky as she!

A necessity, recommendation, demand, etc. (in *that*-clauses): It is imperative that he *have* your support. We suggest that she *receive* special treatment. The committee demands that he *make* an investigation. The court commanded that the document *be produced.*

A parliamentary motion or resolution: I move that the claim *be allowed. Be it resolved* that the convention *endorse* William Pond for county supervisor.

73

The subjunctive is used only occasionally to express a doubt or uncertainty.

If this *be* [informal *is*] yours I congratulate you.
The child looks as if she *were* [informal *is*] undernourished.

(2) Subjunctive forms In grammatical form the subjunctive has largely ceased to be distinctive. The only place in which it shows in all verbs is in the third person singular of the present tense, where it takes the form of the third person plural ("It is necessary that he *learn* the rules"). The subjunctive of the verb *to be* has two forms, *be* and *were*,* which are used throughout the present tense, singular and plural ("If help *be required* we will telephone," "Unless I *were facing* destitution I should not accept the job"). Elsewhere the subjunctive uses indicative forms, though perhaps to express time different from that of the indicative; see 12i(3).

In current practice even the few distinctive forms are being dropped or displaced by equivalent indicative expressions, especially in informal and colloquial use.

Subjunctive form: A demand was made that his life *be spared*.
Subjunctive replaced by indicative phrase: A demand was made to spare his life. [Or] . . . for his life to be spared.

Subjunctive form: What would you do if he *were* here?
Subjunctive replaced by indicative: What would you do if he *was* here?

12c. **Expression of Tone by Modal Auxiliaries (Potential Mood)**
By using such auxiliaries as *may, might, can, could, must, should, would, may be, could have been* you can build up various modal forms or modal aspects. These are sometimes called collectively the potential mood.

* These two forms are probably used as frequently as all other distinctive forms (from all other verbs) combined.

(I) Use of shall **and** will **in expressing tone** * In formal use, determination or emphatic assurance is expressed by *will* in the first person (both singular and plural) and by *shall* in the second and third persons.

I will; I tell you I will.	We will not be excluded.
You shall do what I bid.	You shall not delay us.
He shall obey me.	They shall pay tribute.

Informal practice varies; some writers use *shall* throughout, and others use *will* in all persons. Determination or emphasis is expressed in speech by stressing either word.

(2) Use of should **and** would **in expressing tone** In addition to their functions in indicating time, *should* and *would* are used in expressing the following modal aspects: †

Possibility: He *should* be out of debt by the first of the year.

Uncertainty: *Should* I go? I *should* [or *would*] be glad to go [meaning that I have the desire, but do not think I shall have the chance or the ability]. Compare: I shall be glad to go [meaning that I expect to go].

Polite or emphatic request: *Would* you return my book when you go to the library?

Something only supposed: Do that? You *wouldn't*.

Wish: If the nights *would* only turn cool!

Sense of obligation (weaker than *ought*): Since he knows we expect him, he *should* make an effort to attend.

(3) Use of auxiliary do **in expressing tone** Emphatic constructions are often built by using forms of the auxiliary *do* (*does, did*).

I *do* study hard.	She *did* wait for me.
He *does* deserve the award.	*Do* write as soon as you arrive.

* For their ordinary use, that of expressing time, see 12e(2).
† In informal and colloquial use *should* is mainly limited to the expression of tone.

TIME

Do not confuse *tense* and *time*. *Tense* applies to the grammatical form of the verb; *time* is the temporal idea expressed by that verb form. In general, tense and time coincide. For example, present time is expressed by the present tense. But usage shows a strong tendency to set aside rigid tense-time association. Example: I sail tomorrow [present tense, future time].

TENSES AND THEIR FORMATION

12d. **The Six Tenses** Formal grammar recognizes six tenses, of which one, the future perfect, is seldom used:

(1) Present (He *watches* now)
(2) Past (He *watched* yesterday)
(3) Future (He *will watch* tomorrow)
(4) Present perfect (He *has watched* all week)
(5) Past perfect (He *had watched* until yesterday)
(6) Future perfect (By eleven o'clock he *will have watched* for an hour)

12e. **Formation of Tenses** Only the present and past tenses indicate time by means of the main verb alone ("He *runs*," "He *ran*"). All other tenses are formed with the help of auxiliary ("aiding") verbs.*

For nearly every verb the forms of all tenses are based on its three principal parts: the first person singular present indicative, the past, and the past participle.

(I) Formation of the past tense and past participle

Regular verbs Regular verbs form the past tense and past participle by adding *d*, *ed*, or *t* to the present. Hence the past tense and past participle are alike.

---

* Even the present and past tenses require auxiliaries in questions and in negative statements: *Is* he driving? She *did* not go.

Present: I *watch*; I *burn* (now)
Past: I *watched*; I *burned.* [or *burnt*] (yesterday)
Past participle: I have *watched*; I have *burned* [or have *burnt*]
(on former occasions)

Irregular verbs Irregular verbs do not form the past tense and past participle by adding *d, ed*, or *t* to the present. Often they change the vowel of the main stem (*swim, swam, swum*). Sometimes they show the change of tense through irregularity in endings (*forget, forgot, forgotten*). In these verbs the past tense and past participle are often not alike; you must be constantly on guard against using one form for another.*

(2) Formation of the future tense The simple future tense is formed by use of the auxiliaries *shall* or *will* with the present (infinitive) form of the main verb ("I *shall* [*will*] *need* to work hard").

Formal use of shall **and** will Formal practice differentiates between the uses of *shall* and *will*. Some writers and editors still insist upon this formal usage because it makes possible important distinctions in thought. For expressing simple futurity or mere expectation formal grammar uses *shall* in the first person (both singular and plural) and *will* in the second and third persons.

I shall be nineteen.	We shall have rain.
You will play.	You will hear.
He will sing.	They will reply.

Formal usage requires that in questions the form be used that is expected in the answer.

Question: Shall you be hungry after your walk?
Answer: Yes, I shall. [Or] No, I shall not.

* For a list of verbs with troublesome forms, see **Principal Parts, 14**. For verbs with principal parts often confused, see **Lie-lay** and **Sit-set, 19**.

Grammatically *should* and *would* are the past forms of *shall* and *will*. But present-day usage (both formal and informal) tends to use *would* for all persons in the expression of time.*

Old grammatical usage (statement of fact): I realized that I *should* never see them again.

Current usage: I realized that I *would* never see them again.

Informal use of shall **and** will. In expressing simple futurity or mere expectation the prevailing informal and colloquial practice is to use *will* in all persons.

I will be taller next year.	We will see strange faces.
You will meet him.	You will eat together.
He will come.	They will decide.

Informal usage in questions is divided, but there is considerable tendency to use *shall* in the first and *will* in the second and third persons. In negative questions *won't* (*will not*) is commonly used. ("*Won't* I be able to get in?" "*Won't* you give me the book?").

(3) Formation of the perfect tenses The present, past, and future perfect tenses are formed by the use of auxiliary verbs with the past participle.

The present perfect uses *have* or *has* with the past participle ("I *have moved* three times during the year," "She *has succeeded* without help from anyone").

The past perfect combines *had* with the past participle ("He *had received* three warning notices").

The future perfect uses *shall* or *will* with *have* and the past participle ("I *shall* [*will*] *have finished* my work before

* For uses of *shall* and *will*, *should* and *would* in expressing tone, see 12c(1) and (2).

vacation time," "By spring they *will have saved* enough for their trip").*

(4) Progressive verb forms All of the six regular tenses indicate an action (or state of being) as taking place (or existing) at a definite point in time or with reference to such a point. In order to show an action in process, English uses a progressive form. It is made in the same manner for all tenses, that is, by combining a form of the verb *to be* with the present participle of the main verb.

> Present progressive: He is watching.
> Past progressive: He was watching.
> Future progressive: He will be watching.
> Present perfect progressive: He has been watching.
> Past perfect progressive: He had been watching.
> Future perfect progressive: He will have been watching.

HOW TO EXPRESS SIMPLE TIME

The expression of simple time (not related to other times) poses few problems. You will avoid the most common errors if you do not make careless shifts in tense.

12f. Expression of Simple Time There are three simple times: the present, the past, and the future.

(1) Simple present time is expressed by

PRESENT TENSE

> He *owns* the fastest car in town.
> You *depend* upon him too much.†

---

* Formal and informal usage of *shall* and *will* is the same in the future perfect tense as in the simple future tense. See **12e(2)** above.
† All examples in this section are simple sentences. A compound sentence may express two or more simple times, each independent of the other. Example:
Hogan *failed* his chemistry examination [simple past time], but the professor *will give* him another chance [simple future time].

PRESENT PROGRESSIVE

> I *am running* a temperature.
> *Is* the boat *leaking?*

In many expressions we ordinarily use the present progressive rather than the simple present tense, especially when the action is a continuing one. We say "What *are* you *doing?*" instead of "What *do* you *do?*" and "I *am eating* dinner" rather than "I *eat* dinner." Use of the progressive is increasing.

AUXILIARY (*do*) WITH THE PRESENT (in questions and negative sentences)

> *Do* they *sleep* late?
> We *do* not *remember.*

Such constructions as "I *like* him not," used in older English, are no longer current. Modern idiom requires use of the auxiliary ("I *do* not *like* him").

(2) Simple past time (indicating an action completed in the past) is expressed by

PAST TENSE

> He *asked* for the report.
> She *dived* into the water.

PAST PROGRESSIVE

> He was *driving* the car.
> They *were shouting* for help.

PAST AUXILIARY (*did*) WITH THE PRESENT TENSE FORM (in questions and negative sentences)

> *Did* they *go?*
> She *did* not *reply.*

(3) Simple future time (time extending from the present or falling after it) is expressed by

FUTURE TENSE

He *will arrive* on time.
They *will pay* their bills.

FUTURE PROGRESSIVE

She *will be wearing* a green dress.
He *will be studying* geometry.

Simple future time may also be shown by

PRESENT TENSE (usually with a time modifier implied or expressed)

I *am* a dead man. [That is, I cannot live long.]
Are you *attending* the reception [on Friday afternoon]?
I *go* next Thursday.

(4) Timeless general statements are expressed by the present tense (regardless of the tense of any verb with which they are used).

Grapes *grow* well in sandy soil.
He said that Venus is a planet. [But] The ancients believed the earth *was* flat. [This opinion is no longer considered true.]

(5) Habitual actions are expressed by

PRESENT TENSE (for present habitual actions)

They *go* to the mountains for their vacations.

PAST TENSE (for actions no longer continuing)

They *went* to the mountains for their vacations [before they moved to the country].
They *used to go* to the mountains for their vacations. [This form suggests discontinuance of the habitual action more strongly than does the simple past.]
They *would play* ball as long as there was daylight.

81

EXAMPLES OF FAULTY EXPRESSION OF SIMPLE TIME

Faulty expression of simple past time by the present progressive: We are left sitting there for half an hour.

Use the past tense: We were left sitting there for half an hour.

Faulty use of past tense for a timeless general statement: *Dodsworth* was a novel. [It still is.]

Use the present tense: *Dodsworth* is a novel.

HOW TO EXPRESS TIME RELATIONS

Not only must you be able to express simple present, past, or future time, but also you must be able to express clearly the relationship of one time to other times.

USING TIME MODIFIERS Often you must use time (adverbial) modifiers in making time relations clear.

They have worked hard *until this week*. He mailed the check *after the first of last month*. She will complete her novel *before next June*. He comes *at two o'clock*. They are *about* to begin the race.

Having discontinued the cattle business *long ago*, he is running a dude ranch. [Omission of the time modifier would make the time relation ambiguous.]

From a geologist I learned about formations in southern Idaho. *Millions of years ago* the entire country was covered by a vast flow of lava. *Afterward* a crust hardened and caverns were left underneath. [Note that the tense of the verbs is the same throughout.]

USING TENSE ALONE WITH REFERENCE TO A BASIC TIME More often (and more importantly) you must rely upon the existence of a basic time. In presenting a series of circumstances you will perceive that not all are simultaneous. For every such series therefore you must establish clearly in mind one of the three simple times as a point of reference; this will be the basic time. Having it, you must then use tense intelligently in expressing other times in relation to it. (Time modifiers, at your convenience, may be inserted; but you can make distinctions accurately without them.)

Consider this example:

The Confederates hit upon the idea of using an ironclad ship. The Union forces sank the *Merrimac* on abandoning the Norfolk navy yard. The Southerners decided to raise this vessel.

Here manifestly is a failure to show time relations clearly. The basic time is the past. But not all the times involved are precisely concurrent with that basic past time. You may assume that the sinking took place before the idea was hit upon or the decision made to raise the ship.

To express these time relations accurately you must make the simple past your basic time and adopt for the other times the tenses which will place them in proper relation to it, thus:

The Confederates *hit* [basic past time] upon the idea of using an ironclad ship. The Union forces *had sunk* [prior past time] the *Merrimac* on abandoning the Norfolk navy yard. The Southerners *decided* [time concurrent with basic past] *to raise* [subsequent to basic past] this vessel.

The basic time, as has been indicated, may be present, past, or future. Whichever it is, three times (present, past, and future) may be expressed with reference to it. (The *Merrimac* example expresses the three with reference to a basic past.)

A basic time may be implied rather than expressed.

Implied basic present: They have finished tallying the votes. [*Have finished* expresses a time prior to the time the statement is made—the implied basic present.]

Implied basic past: He had hunted big game in Africa. [The past perfect expresses a time prior to some past point of time reference—the implied basic past.]

Implied basic future: She will have lived there for three weeks. [The future perfect expresses a time prior to some future point of time reference—the implied basic future.]

You now have the broad principle of adapting tense to a basic time. The following sections apply the principle in further detail to the expression of time relations. Because such expression may become very intricate, only the more ordinary forms are shown.

12g. Expression of Time with Reference to a Basic Present Time

(1) Using finite verbs

Time concurrent with a present time: He BELIEVES * that our advertising *is* * effective. [The basic time is that of the verb *believes*—the present. With reference to the basic time the time of *is* is also present: he believes now; advertising is effective now.]

Time prior to a present time: He BELIEVES that our advertising *paid*. [The past tense indicates an action completed at a definite past time. He believes now; our advertising paid last month.] [Or]

He BELIEVES that our advertising *has paid*. [The present perfect tense indicates a past action completed by a present time or continuing into it.]

Time subsequent to a present time: He BELIEVES that our advertising *will pay*.

(2) Using verbals (infinitives, participles, gerunds)

INFINITIVES

Time concurrent with a present time: They USE postcards *to advertise* their business.

* The basic-time verb is printed in small capitals; the verb expressing time with reference to the basic time is in italics.

84

Time prior to a present time: They ARE sorry *to have spent* so little on advertising. [Note that the *perfect* infinitive expresses prior time.]

Time subsequent to a present time: They PLAN *to advertise* with postcards. [Note that the *present* infinitive is used to express future time.]

PARTICIPLES

Time concurrent with a present time: *Advertising* with postcards, they CONCENTRATE on a select group of prospective buyers.

Time prior to a present time: *Having advertised* over the radio, they ARE widely known.

Time subsequent to a present time: [The participle is not used to express this time relationship.]

GERUNDS

Time concurrent with a present time: *Advertising* with postcards PAYS them well.

Time prior to a present time: They ATTRIBUTE their success to *having advertised* with postcards.

Time subsequent to a present time: They PLAN a campaign of *advertising* by billboards.

EXAMPLES OF FAULTY EXPRESSION OF TIME WITH REFERENCE TO A BASIC PRESENT

Faulty use of the past perfect tense to express time prior to a basic present: She thinks we had taken the key.

Use the past tense: She thinks we took the key. [Or use the present perfect to indicate that the key is still missing] She thinks we have taken the key.*

Faulty use of the present participle to express time prior to a basic present: Dressing, he goes out to the theater.

Use the perfect participle: Having dressed, he goes out to the theater.

* The original sentence is correct if the basic time to be understood is the past: Yesterday the key was missing. She thinks [now] we had taken it [prior to yesterday].

12h. Expression of Time with Reference to a Basic Past Time

(1) Using finite verbs

Time concurrent with a past time: Swimming WAS * good when ships *avoided* * the channel. [The tense of *avoided* is past, but the time it expresses is present with reference to the time of the basic verb *was.*]

Time prior to a past time: Swimming WAS good where the channel *had been dredged.* [Where no ambiguity will result, common usage often employs the past tense instead of the past perfect: He INVESTED the money which he *inherited.*]

Time subsequent to a past time: The boys HOPED the swimming *would be* good. [Where no ambiguity will result, the past tense may be used in both verbs, even if the time of the second verb is subsequent: He INHERITED the money that he *lost* in bad investments.]

(2) Using verbals (infinitives, participles, gerunds)

INFINITIVES

Time concurrent with a past time: She TRIED *to understand* the explanation.

Time prior to a past time: They WERE happy *to have arrived* in time to fish.

Time subsequent to a past time: They MADE plans *to climb* to the top of the falls.

PARTICIPLES

Time concurrent with a past time: *Flying,* he WAS able to study the terrain.

Time prior to a past time: *Having flown,* he ARRIVED in Washington before the office opened.

Time subsequent to a past time: [The participle is not used to express this relationship.]

GERUNDS

Time concurrent with a past time: Through careful *driving* he AVOIDED accidents.

* The basic-time verb is printed in small capitals; the verb expressing time with reference to the basic time is in italics.

Time prior to a past time: Through *having driven* carefully he WON a safety award. [Where no ambiguity will result, the present gerund is often used: Through careful *driving* he WON a safety award.]

Time subsequent to a past time: He ADVOCATED continued careful *driving*.

EXAMPLES OF FAULTY EXPRESSION OF TIME WITH REFERENCE TO A BASIC PAST

Faulty use of the present tense to express time concurrent with a basic past: As soon as he arrived he begins to talk.

Use the past tense: As soon as he arrived he began to talk.

Faulty use of the present perfect auxiliary to express time subsequent to a basic past: We hoped that you would have come to the party.

Use the past auxiliary: We hoped that you would come to the party.

Ambiguous use of the past tense to express time prior to a basic past: A monument was erected where the house stood.

Use the past perfect tense: A monument was erected where the house had stood.

Faulty use of the perfect infinitive to express time subsequent to a basic past: I intended to have gone.

Use the present infinitive: I intended to go.

Faulty use of the perfect infinitive to express time subsequent to a basic past: I should have liked to have seen him.

Use the present infinitive: I should have liked to see him.*

Faulty use of the perfect participle to express time concurrent with a basic past: Having been hungry, he ate a hearty meal.

Use the present participle: Being hungry, he ate a hearty meal.

---

* If, however, the intention is to express time prior to a basic present, the sentence may read: I should like [now] to have seen him [yesterday]. [But the normal construction would be: I wish I had seen him.]

Faulty use of the present participle to express time prior to a basic past: *Wasting* his savings, he had no reserves when hard times came.

Use the perfect participle: *Having wasted* his savings, he had no reserves when hard times came.

12i. Expression of Time with Reference to a Basic Future Time

(1) Using finite verbs

Time concurrent with a future time: He WILL MAKE * certain that the business *pays.** [The present tense *pays* may convey either a concurrent or a subsequent time. The context must determine which.]

Time prior to a future time: He WILL REMAIN in business when other stores *will have failed*. [More common usage: . . . when other stores *have failed*.]

Time subsequent to a future time: He WILL INTRODUCE methods which *will make* the business pay.

(2) Using verbals (infinitives, participles, gerunds)

INFINITIVES

Time concurrent with a future time: They WILL BE glad *to attend*.

Time prior to a future time: They WILL BE glad *to have attended*.

Time subsequent to a future time: They WILL DECIDE *to attend*.

PARTICIPLES

Time concurrent with a future time: *Living* outdoors, they WILL GROW healthy.

Time prior to a future time: *Having lived* outdoors, they WILL BE familiar with the woods.

Time subsequent to a future time: [The participle is not used to express this time relationship.]

---

* The basic-time verb is printed in small capitals; the verb expressing time with reference to the basic time is in italics.

GERUNDS

Time concurrent with a future time: *Dancing* WILL BE their entertainment.

Time prior to a future time: *Having danced* WILL MAKE them eager for refreshments.

Time subsequent to a future time: They WILL RESERVE the room for *dancing*.

EXAMPLES OF FAULTY EXPRESSION OF TIME WITH REFERENCE TO A BASIC FUTURE

Faulty use of the present tense to express time subsequent to a basic future: She will prepare an advertisement which sells our furniture.

Use the future tense: She will prepare an advertisement which will sell our furniture.

Faulty use of the present tense to express time prior to a basic future: He will still be writing after everyone else finishes. [But acceptable in informal writing]

Use the present perfect: He will still be writing after everyone else has finished.

SUMMARY OF ORDINARY FORMS FOR EXPRESSING TIME RELATIONS

BASIC PRESENT   With reference to a basic present time, use the following forms to express

CONCURRENT TIME:	PRIOR TIME:	SUBSEQUENT TIME:
Pres. tense (*run*, *runs*)	Past tense (*ran*)	Future tense (*shall* [*will*] *run*)
Pres. infinitive (*to run*)	Pres. perf. tense (*have* [*has*] *run*)	Pres. infinitive (*to run*)
Pres. participle (*running*)	Perfect infinitive (*to have run*)	Pres. gerund (*running*)
Pres. gerund (*running*)	Perf. participle (*having run*)	
	Perf. gerund (*having run*)	

BASIC PAST With reference to a basic past time, use the following forms to express

CONCURRENT TIME:	PRIOR TIME:	SUBSEQUENT TIME:
Past tense (*ran*)	Past perf. tense (*had run*)	Past auxiliary (*would run*)
Pres. infinitive (*to run*)	Past tense (*ran*) *	Past tense (*ran*) *
Pres. participle (*running*)	Perf. infinitive (*to have run*)	Pres. infinitive (*to run*)
Pres. gerund (*running*)	Perf. participle (*having run*)	Pres. gerund (*running*)
	Perf. gerund (*having run*)	
	Pres. gerund (*running*) *	

BASIC FUTURE With reference to a basic future time, use the following forms to express

CONCURRENT TIME:	PRIOR TIME:	SUBSEQUENT TIME:
Pres. tense (*run, runs*)	Fut. perf. tense (*shall [will] have run*)	Future tense (*shall [will] run*)
Pres. infinitive (*to run*)	Pres. perf. tense (*have [has] run*) †	Pres. infinitive (*to run*)
Pres. participle (*running*)	Perf. infinitive (*to have run*)	Pres. gerund (*running*)
Pres. gerund (*running*)	Perf. participle (*having run*)	
	Perf. gerund (*having run*)	

12j. **Use of Progressive Forms, Modal Auxiliaries, the Sub-junctive Mood, and the Passive Voice in the Expression of Time Relations** Time relationships (12g-12i) have been presented with reference to simple basic times only—to simple

---

* May be used only when no ambiguity will result.
† Less consciously formal usage than future perfect tense.

present, simple past, and simple future in the indicative mood and the active voice.

The present section considers important problems of time expression in other verb forms. The following examples show only a few of the distinctions in time which your writing may employ.

(1) Progressive forms You can make most constructions progressive by combining the present participle with the appropriate tense form of the verb *to be*. But take care not to complicate your expression by unwieldy verb phrases. Do not say "He will be having" when "He will have" expresses the thought intended.

EXAMPLES OF POSSIBLE PROGRESSIVE FORMATIONS

Time prior to a basic progressive present: He IS ASKING * for the job he *has applied* * for before.

Progressive time prior to a basic progressive present: He IS ASKING for the job he *has been applying* for since the beginning of last winter.

Progressive time prior to a basic progressive past: He WAS ASKING for the job he *had been applying* for steadily.

Progressive time prior to a basic progressive future: He WILL BE ASKING again for the job that by May Day he *will have been seeking* for two years.

(2) Modal auxiliaries have but three tense forms: present, past, and present perfect. Some, however (such as *should* and *would*) have no simple past tense.† Because of this irregu-

* The basic-time verb is printed in small capitals; the verb expressing time with reference to the basic time is in italics.

† *Should* and *would* are grammatically the past tenses of *shall* and *will*. But as modal auxiliaries both have acquired new meanings, and these past forms are now used as present tenses (often grammarians call such forms preterit presents). The modal *should* ordinarily signifies obligation ("I know I *should* eat, but I am not hungry"). The modal *would*, in one sense, suggests probability ("I think he *would* do it this way"). Both verbs express present time in these uses.

larity it is impossible to establish a time-tense pattern for all modal auxiliaries. They may, nevertheless, be divided into two general classes.

(*a*) With modal auxiliaries whose present, past, and present perfect forms have similar meanings (as *can, could, could have*—signifying ability) the tenses are used as follows:

PRESENT TENSE EXPRESSES

Simple present time: I *can* hardly *see* with these glasses.

Simple future time: *Can* you *be* there early?

Time concurrent with a present time: He IS OFFERING * what he *can*not * rightfully *give.*

Time subsequent to a present time: You ARE TAKING something he *can* never *replace.*

Time prior to a future time: She WILL GET the money if he *can borrow* it.

Time subsequent to a future time: If he WILL GIVE it to me, I *can carry* it in my car.

PAST TENSE EXPRESSES

Simple past time: They *could* not *manage* the horse.

Time prior to a present time: He SAYS he *could* not *endure* it [yesterday]. [In proper context the same construction may also indicate time subsequent to a basic present.]

Time concurrent with a past time: He SAID he *could see* the fire.†

Time subsequent to a past time: I DEMANDED more than he *could* ever *earn.*

PRESENT PERFECT TENSE EXPRESSES

Time prior to a past time: I BLAMED him for something he *could* not *have done.*

* The basic-time verb is printed in small capitals; the verb expressing time with reference to the basic time is in italics.

† In contrary to fact statements the past tense is also used to express concurrent present and concurrent future time. Examples:
Concurrent present: If he were here [now], he *could tell* us the truth.
Concurrent future: If he were to be here [tomorrow], he *could tell* us the truth.

(*b*) With modal auxiliaries whose original past forms have become present tenses (as *should*—expressing obligation) the tenses are used as follows:

PRESENT TENSE EXPRESSES

Simple present time: I *should study* for the examination. [To avoid ambiguity the progressive form is often used to express present time] I *should be studying* [at this moment] for the examination.

Simple future time: To save time we *should fly*. [A time modifier may be required to prevent ambiguity.]

Time concurrent with a present time: I AM TAKING what I *should leave*.

Time subsequent to a present time: I AM TELLING her what road she *should take*.

Time concurrent with a past time: He GAVE what he felt he *should give*.

Time subsequent to a past time: She SAID that I *should call* again.

Time concurrent with a future time: He WILL TAKE whatever steps he *should* [*take*].

Time subsequent to a future time: She WILL TELL them what they *should do*.

PRESENT PERFECT TENSE EXPRESSES

Simple past time: He *should have* resisted.

Time prior to a present time: I AM DOING what he *should have done*.

Time prior to a past time: We REFINISHED the table as you *should have done* in the beginning.

Time prior to a future time: When she ARRIVES, he *should have completed* the job.

(3) Subjunctive mood Time in the subjunctive is often expressed by the same tenses as time in the indicative. The following, however, are a few special usages in the subjunctive:

Present time may be expressed by the past subjunctive.

If he *were* you, he would refuse the offer.

You *had* better take his advice.

Past time may be expressed by the past perfect subjunctive.

If Hargrave *had been* our attorney, we would have won the case.

Had she *insisted*, we would have granted her request.

Future time may be expressed by the past subjunctive.

If he *got* the option soon he would make a profit.

Even if the train *were* five minutes late, we could not catch it.

(4) Passive voice To show tense in the passive voice, the appropriate indicative tense form of the verb *to be* is used with the past participle of the main verb. Examples:

Simple present time: We *are watched* constantly.

Simple past time: He *was taken* prisoner early in the war.

Simple future time: They *will be counted* as they enter the room.

(For other passive forms see "Conjugation of the verb *see*" under Verb, **14.**)

EXAMPLES OF FAULTY TIME EXPRESSION IN THE
POTENTIAL AND SUBJUNCTIVE MOODS

Faulty use of the present modal auxiliary to express completed time subsequent to a basic past: I told him to call whenever he can.

Use the past tense: I told him to call whenever he could. [But if the time is not completed, *can* is correct.]

Wrong use of *would* to express prior past time in the potential: If he would have been vaccinated he wouldn't have caught smallpox.

Use the past perfect subjunctive in the conditional clause: If he had been vaccinated he wouldn't have caught smallpox.

Wrong expression of past perfect form in the subjunctive: If he
had have [or *had of*] read the book he could have passed the
examination.

Use the correct tense form: If he had read the book he could
have passed the examination.

12k. Anomalies in the Expression of Time Relationships English as actually spoken and written expresses time
relationships in ways far more varied than is ordinarily
understood. In the proper context, tenses may indicate times
wholly different from those which the grammatical forms
suggest. The following are a few of the countless examples:

It is certain that if you tell him you will regret that you said
anything.

Analysis of time relations in foregoing sentence: It is certain
[basic present] that if you tell him [present tense, future
time] you will regret [basic future subsequent to previous
future] that you said anything [past tense, time prior to the
basic future time].

I repeated that if they didn't advertise they would wish they
had.

Analysis of time relations in foregoing sentence: I repeated
[basic past time] that if they didn't advertise [past tense, time
subsequent to basic past] they would wish [past auxiliary,
basic future time—possibly prior to an implied present time]
they had [elliptical past perfect tense, time prior to basic
future time].

The conquests Napoleon made were long to be remembered.

Analysis of time relations in foregoing sentence: The conquests
Napoleon made [past tense, time prior to a basic past] were
[basic past time] long to be remembered [present infinitive,
time subsequent to a basic past].

I must answer all who have applied.

Analysis of time relations in foregoing sentence: I must answer
[present tense, time subsequent to an implied basic present]
all who have applied [perfect tense, time prior to the implied
basic present].

If he exercised he would feel invigorated. [This innocent-looking, seven-word sentence contains many possibilities of interpretation, some of them involving tone as well as time.]

Analyses of time relations (and mood) in foregoing sentence:

(1) If he exercised [past tense, past time or habitual past time (indicative mood if the statement is of fact, subjunctive mood if the statement is of condition contrary to fact)] he would feel [past auxiliary, present time (potential mood) or habitual past time] invigorated.

(2) If he exercised [past tense, present time or habitual present time (subjunctive mood—condition contrary to fact)] he would feel [past auxiliary, present time or habitual present time (potential mood)] invigorated.

(3) If he exercised [past tense, future time or habitual future time (subjuncture mood—doubt or supposition)] he would feel [past auxiliary, future time or habitual future time (potential mood)] invigorated.

EXERCISE

X-12a, b, c. Expression of Tone

Rewrite, correcting errors of form and mood.

1. Cast your line; then you will have to wait patiently until you get a bite.
2. Many diseases could be wiped out if a concerted nation-wide campaign of prevention and cure be launched.
3. He shall come if he believes you shall be there.
4. I make the motion that the resolution should be returned to committee for further study.
5. The board insists that he applies in person.

X-12d, e. Tenses and Their Formation

Use each of the six tense forms in every one of the following sentences.

1. I reply.
2. He goes.
3. They rent.
4. You read.
5. We swim.

X-12f. Expression of Simple Time

Compose sentences expressing the following simple times.

1. Present
2. Present progressive
3. Past
4. Past progressive
5. Past negative statement
6. Future
7. Future progressive
8. Present habitual action
9. Past habitual action in form of a question
10. Timeless general statement

X-12g. Expression of Time with Reference to a Basic Present Time

Copy, choosing from the parentheses the correct verb or verb phrase. Doubly underscore the basic-time verb or time modifier. Indicate the time relationship in each sentence (as "time prior to a basic present," etc.).

1. They continue to supervise his work until he (proves, has proved) himself a capable journeyman.
2. (To sing, to have sung) with the choir is her immediate goal.
3. While I am drilling the holes he (measured, measures) the bars and (cut, cuts) them.
4. (Having been, being) the daughter of an architect, she is interested in home designing.
5. He wants his views (to have been, to be) considered before action is taken.

X-12h. Expression of Time with Reference to a Basic Past Time

Copy, choosing from the parentheses the correct verb or verb phrase. Doubly underscore the basic-time verb or time modifier. Indicate the time relationship in each sentence (as "time subsequent to a basic past," etc.).

1. The reforms he (advocated, had advocated) fifty years before were instituted after his death.
2. The delegates were confident that, regardless of whom they chose, their nominee (will be, would be) the next President.
3. Rats which for weeks past (were, had been) denied vitamin C developed eye inflammations.
4. (To be, to have been) a member of the Rainbow division was an honor of which he was always proud.
5. The patient had been growing steadily worse for several days before help (had been, was) called.

X-12i. Expression of Time with Reference to a Basic Future Time

Copy, choosing from the parentheses the correct verb or verb phrase. Doubly underscore the basic-time verb or time modifier. Indicate the time relationship in each sentence (as "time concurrent with a basic future," etc.).

1. The new rate (will have been, will be) in effect three months before taxes are calculated.
2. The ranch hands (will have been, will be) branding cattle all next week.
3. She is (to have appeared, to appear) in the contest finals next Tuesday.
4. Unless he (will have changed, changes) his mind, the manager will send Boyd to Argentina next month.
5. Shirley will rejoin her family in New Orleans next March. She (will have been, will be) separated from them for two years.

X-12j. Progressive Forms, Modal Auxiliaries, the Subjunctive Mood, and the Passive Voice in the Expression of Time Relations

Compose sentences using the forms called for and expressing the time relations indicated. Label each sentence.

1. Progressive time prior to a basic progressive past.
2. Modal auxiliary expressing time subsequent to a basic present.
3. Modal auxiliary expressing time concurrent with a basic future.
4. Future time in the subjunctive mood.
5. Time prior to a basic past (using the passive voice).

SUBSTITUTED FORMS AND ELEMENTS

13. Do not improperly substitute one part of speech for another.* Particularly avoid using an adverb as an adjective, or an adjective as an adverb. Choose the part of speech according to its function in the sentence. (A part of speech

* It cannot be said that one part of speech can never be substituted for another. For the more common substitutions regarded as acceptable see Noun and Verbal, 14.

may consist of a word or a word group, such as a phrase or a clause.)

HOW TO CORRECT ERRORS OF SUBSTITUTION

FORMS OF ADVERBS The faulty interchange of adjectives and adverbs is the most common error of substituted forms. Familiarity with the distinctive forms of adverbs will help you to avoid such errors.

Most adverbs end in *ly* (*surely*, *rapidly*, *strictly*, etc.)
Some do not (*far*, *ill*, *much*, *well*, etc.)

A few adverbs have two forms, with and without the *ly* ending (*slow*, *slowly; quick*, *quickly; cheap*, *cheaply; clear*, *clearly; sharp*, *sharply;* etc.)

The short form is normally used in brief imperative sentences ("Jump *quick!*" "Buy *cheap*," "Hold *tight*," "Stand *clear*," "Look *sharp* now").

The longer form is used (1) to modify an adjective ("A *quickly* confirmed rumor," "A *cheaply* wrought device," "*Tightly* wound bandages," "A *clearly* evasive answer"); or (2) in a formal declarative or interrogative sentence ("They seal the documents *quickly*," "He will secure the equipment as *cheaply* as he can," "She binds the package *tightly* with string," "Does he look *sharply* for errors in the figures?").

13a. Adjectives (and Adjective Phrases) Misused as Adverbs

To modify a verb, an adjective, or an adverb use, not an adjective, but an adverb (word, phrase, or clause).

(1) Adjectives wrongly used to modify verbs

Gross misuse of adjectives to modify the verb: He spoke slow and careful. [The modifiers refer to the manner of speaking—that is, to the verb, not the noun.]

Use adverbs to modify the verb: He spoke slowly and carefully.

Gross misuse of adjectives to modify the verb: He sure does good in his classes.

Use adverbs to modify the verb: He surely does well in his classes.

Adjectives wrongly used as modifiers of verbs: He protested loud. He scowls angry. They persist obstinate. She has acted intelligent in the matter. Cuff his ears sound. [The reference in each case should be clearly made to the verb.]

Use an adverb to modify each verb: He protested loudly. He scowls angrily. They persist obstinately. She has acted intelligently in the matter. Cuff his ears soundly.

Adjective phrase incorrectly used to modify a verb: The pipes froze, caused by the cold weather. [*Caused by* is adjectival. But it is here used to refer to the verb *froze*.]

Use an adverbial phrase to modify the verb: The pipes froze because of the cold weather. [Or recast the sentence] The freezing of the pipes was caused by the cold weather.

Adjective followed by a phrase and wrongly used to modify a verb: Agreeable to this understanding the ship steams into port. [The fact that a modifier introduces a phrase does not affect its status as an adjective or adverb. Here the agreeableness does not pertain to the ship, but to the action taken—that is, to steaming into port.]

Use an adverb to modify the verb (even though the modifier introduces a phrase): Agreeably to [or *In consequence of*] this understanding the ship steams into port.

(2) Adjectives wrongly used to modify adjectives

Colloquial misuse of an adjective to modify adjective: A terrible strong wind was blowing.

Use an adverb to modify an adjective: A terribly strong wind was blowing.

Adjective wrongly used to modify an adjective: The new painted house attracted much attention.

Use an adverb to modify an adjective: The newly painted house attracted much attention.

Colloquial misuse of an adjective to modify a predicate adjective: The train is some later than we thought.

Use an adverb to modify a predicate adjective: The train is somewhat later than we thought.

Crude use of an adjective to modify a predicate adjective: I was that tired.

Use an adverb to modify an adjective: I was extremely [or *very*] tired.

Colloquial misuse of an adjective to modify a predicate adjective: We were most dead from weariness.

Use an adverb to modify an adjective: We were almost dead from weariness.

(3) Adjectives wrongly used to modify adverbs

Crude use of an adjective to modify an adverb: It is a real elegantly cut dress.

Use an adverb to modify another adverb: It is a really [or *very*] elegantly cut dress.

Adjective wrongly used to modify an adverb: A lumberjack had sawed the limb most through.

Use an adverb to modify another adverb: A lumberjack had sawed the limb almost through.

Crude use of adjective to modify an adverb: After this rebuff the banished prince went around awful shabbily dressed.

Use an adverb to modify another adverb: After this rebuff the banished prince went around very shabbily dressed.

13b. Adverbs Misused as Adjectives To modify a noun or pronoun use an adjective (word, phrase, or clause). Pay particular attention to modifiers after sensory verbs (such as *look, sound, taste, smell,* and *feel*). If the modifiers denote a quality of the subject they are predicate adjectives ("She looks *weary*," "The dinner bell sounds *inviting*"). But if they refer clearly to the verb they are adverbs ("She looks *wearily* at the crowd," "He sounds the gong *invitingly*").

Adverb wrongly used as a predicate adjective: My food tastes badly. [*Badly* is intended to describe the food.]
Use an adjective after a sensory verb: My food tastes bad.

Adverb colloquially misused as a predicate adjective: I feel badly.
Use an adjective after a sensory verb: * I feel bad.

Adverb colloquially misused as a predicate adjective: Mother is poorly. [The modifier, though following the verb, refers to the subject.]
Use an adjective or adjective phrase to modify the subject: Mother is ill. [Or] Mother is not well. [Or] Mother's health is poor. [Or] Mother is in poor health.

Adverbs wrongly used as predicate adjectives: He becomes angrily. They remain obstinately. Your argument appears soundly. [In each case the reference should be clearly made to the subject, not to the verb.]
Use an adjective to modify the subject of each sentence: He becomes angry. They remain obstinate. Your argument appears sound. [In some sentences the modifier may correctly be either an adjective or an adverb, according to the meaning intended. Adjective describing the subject: *We stood firm.* Adverb emphasizing the manner of standing: *We stood firmly.* Adjective emphasizing the appearance of the subject: *The alfalfa is sown thick in the field.* Adverb emphasizing the manner in which the alfalfa is sown: *The alfalfa is sown thickly in the field.*]

13c. Other Forms and Elements Wrongly Substituted

Pronoun illiterately used as an expletive: They was a dog on the porch.
Use the expletive *there*: There was a dog on the porch.

Colloquial substitution of a verb for a noun: She gave me an invite to her party.
Use a noun as the object of the verb: She gave me an invitation to her party. [Or recast the sentence] She invited me to her party.

* Note the difference between "I feel *strong*" (adj.) and "I feel *strongly* about this injustice" (adv.).

Adjective phrase wrongly used as a subject: Born in a log cabin gave him a poor start in life.

Supply a proper subject: Born in a log cabin, he had a poor start in life. [Or change the phrase to a clause] The fact that he was born in a log cabin gave him a poor start in life. [Or change the adjective phrase to a gerund phrase] Being born in a log cabin gave him a poor start in life.

Adverbial clause wrongly used as a subject: Because color photography was not used makes the scarf look black instead of red.

Make the adverbial clause clearly a modifier: Because color photography was not used the scarf looks black instead of red. [Or change the clause to a noun phrase] The failure to use color photography makes the scarf look black instead of red.

Adverbial clause used illiterately as a predicate noun: A car hop is where somebody brings food from a lunch room to customers in their cars. [A car hop is not *where*.]

Use a predicate noun (modified by an adjective clause) after the verb: A car hop is a waitress who brings food from a lunch room to customers in their cars.

Like colloquially used as a conjunction: He walks like a sailor does. [The use of *like* as a conjunction to join two clauses is gaining some popularity, but careful writers avoid it.]

Use a conjunction to join the clauses: He walks as a sailor does. [Or use an elliptical phrase] He walks [in] the way a sailor does. [Or change the second clause to an adverbial phrase] He walks like a sailor.

Like colloquially used as a conjunction: He talked like he had mashed potato in his mouth.

Use a conjunction to join the clauses: He talked as if he had mashed potato in his mouth.

Like colloquially used as a conjunction: They didn't have books then like we have now.

Use a conjunction to join the clauses: They didn't have books then such as we have now.

Predication misused as a noun: I stayed away on account of I was sick.

Replace the predication with a noun [or noun equivalent]: I stayed away on account of sickness [or *of being sick*].

Clumsy use of nouns as adjectives (modifying other nouns): A Baltimore automobile accident; trust positions; a socialism outline; a colds crusade.*

Use prepositional phrases: An automobile accident in Baltimore; positions of trust; an outline of socialism; a crusade against colds.

EXERCISE

X-13a, b. Misuse of Adjectives and Adverbs

Rewrite, correctly using all adjectives and adverbs.

1. The car ran good on level roads, but was particular slow on hills.
2. Trains were delayed five hours caused by the extreme heavy snowfall.
3. Medical authorities disagree some concerning the effects of cigarette smoking.
4. The dam was most completed when the flood hit.
5. She looks beautifully in satin.
6. They were so hungry that anything edible would have tasted well.
7. He argued strong for repeal of the zoning ordinance.
8. She sealed the jar quick, but not tight enough.
9. Philosophy sure is heavy reading when the terms are new.
10. He was now wealthy due to the death of his rich uncle.
11. Hot contested elections were held throughout western Europe after World War II.

* Though "newspaper heading adjectives" (as such nouns may be called) are often objectionable, the genius of the language sanctions them when they are skillfully and sparingly employed. *Queen Anne furniture* is more concise than *furniture belonging to the period of Queen Anne. An art gallery* is more natural than *a gallery for the exhibition of paintings.* Note too how easily this use of nouns enables us to draw such distinctions as that between *a player piano* and *a piano player.*

12. A real well educated man is not afraid to admit he doesn't know everything.
13. The steam shovel tore a terrible big hole in the wall.
14. It is good that he didn't let the insurance policy lapse.
15. The speaker was illy prepared; consequently his arguments were poor.

X-13c. Miscellaneous Forms and Elements Wrongly Substituted

Rewrite, correcting all errors of substituted forms and elements.

1. They only hope was to find some trail that was not blocked by the landslide.
2. Ridiculed as a child gave him a feeling of inferiority.
3. The bow of the boat dipped like it was shipping water.
4. An *aside* is where the actor speaks directly to the audience.
5. The reason for the high infant mortality rate was because of the unsanitary water supply.
6. The victory hope was based on the inability of the enemy to supply its troops.
7. She cooked a good feed for the guests.
8. Because he refused to stay on a diet was why he became sick so often.
9. Diathermy is effective in treating some internal disorders on account of the heat rays penetrate.
10. They ate like they were starving.

THE TERMS OF GRAMMAR

14. Acquire practical knowledge of the terms of grammar listed in this article. Be able to explain the construction of any part of an ordinary sentence.*

The most useful terms of grammar are those which name

the large elements ⎰subject, predicate, complement,
of the sentence ⎱modifier, phrase, clause.

* For a simple introduction to the parts of a sentence see the item on Construction in this article.

$$\text{and the parts of speech} \begin{cases} \text{verb,} & \\ \text{noun, pronoun,} & [\; = \text{substantives}] \\ \text{adjective, adverb,} & [\; = \text{modifiers}] \\ \text{preposition, conjunction,} & [\; = \text{connectives}] \\ \text{interjection.} & \end{cases}$$

You will know nine tenths of all that is important in grammar when you are able to recognize these elements in an ordinary sentence.

Absolute expression. See **Independent element.**

Active voice. See **Verb.**

Adjective (one of the eight parts of speech). An adjective is a word used to modify a noun or pronoun. It describes (*gay* colors, airplanes are *noisy*), points out without describing (*a* girl, *the* boy, *first* page), or tells how many (*ten* men, *dozen* eggs).

Pronominal adjectives are a special kind of adjective. When not used as modifiers, the words become pronouns (sometimes with a change in form). Pronominal adjectives fall into five classes:

Possessives: *my* dog, *his* problems, *her* name, *our* school, *your* car, *their* hopes.

Demonstratives: *this* day, *that* page, *these* nuts, *those* pies.

Interrogatives: *whose* cat? *which* key? *what* street?

Relatives: one *whose* name I forgot, during *which* time.

Indefinites: *each* man, *any* minute, *some* friends, *no* doorstep.

See **Clause, Comparison, Predicate Adjective,** and **Pronoun.**

Adverb (one of the eight parts of speech). An adverb is a word used to modify a verb or a modifier. Adverbs answer the questions *When? Where? How? How Much?*

Adverb modifying a verb: played *well, almost* won.

Adverb modifying an adjective: *too* clever, *unusually* handsome.

Adverb modifying another adverb: *very* sternly, *too* eagerly, fast *enough*.

More rarely, an adverb may modify a verbal (*Walking fast* is good for the health), or a phrase (The ship drifted *almost* into the breakers), or a subordinate clause (The messenger came *just* when we were starting), or a substantive (*Approximately* half of his wages went for food; *Nearly* all were customers).

See **Clause, Comparison,** and **Conjunctive adverb.**

Antecedent. An antecedent is a noun (or pronoun) to which a pronoun refers.

> The *man* who hesitates is lost; the *woman* who hesitates is won. [*Man* is the antecedent of *who. Woman* is the antecedent of the second *who.*]
>
> Literally, *antecedent* means *that which goes before;* but sometimes the antecedent follows the dependent word.

Appositive. An appositive is a noun (or its equivalent), often with modifiers, set alongside another noun as a substitute name or equivalent expression. The second name is said to be in apposition with the first.

> Noun as appositive: Ronald Custis, *a hard-riding polo player,* bought my father's favorite horse, *Morning Star.* [*Player,* with its modifiers, is in apposition with *Ronald Custis,* and *Morning Star* is in apposition with *horse.*]
>
> Noun phrase as appositive: The first rule, *to come promptly,* is a good one.
>
> Noun clause as appositive: This rule, *that he who would not work should not eat,* Smith at once put into effect.

> For "merged" appositives, and for the punctuation of appositives, see **26a.**

Article. *A* and *an* are indefinite articles. *The* is a definite article. All three articles function as adjectives.

Auxiliary. *Be, have, do, shall, will, ought, may, can, must, might, could, would, should,* etc., when used as helpers with other verbs, are called *auxiliaries.* A verb often consists of one or two words, but may consist of three or four: *sing, has sung, had been singing, should have been sung. Should* and the various forms of *have* and *be* are here the "helping verbs" or auxiliaries. *Be* in its several forms (*is, are, was, were,* etc.) is used as an auxiliary oftener than any other verb.

Case. Case is the relation of a substantive to other words in the sentence as shown by inflectional form or position.

The **Nominative** is the case of a subject of a verb, or of a predicate noun or pronoun after a finite form of the verb *to be.*

The **Objective** is the case of an object of a verb or preposition, or the "assumed subject" of an infinitive.

The **Possessive** is the case of a noun or pronoun which denotes possession.

Clause. A clause is any part of a sentence which contains a subject and verb, perhaps with modifiers.

Main (independent) clause (one which expresses a complete thought and is capable of standing alone as a sentence):

She is a rosy Irish girl.
The sun tries to shine.

Subordinate (dependent) clause (one which does not express a complete thought and which must be joined to a main clause):

who makes good cherry pies
after the rain is ended

A subordinate clause functions as a single part of speech (noun, adjective, adverb).

Noun clause: *Whoever comes first* will receive the largest share.

Adjective clause: We visited the family *which had moved in next door.*

Adverbial clause: The thieves ran *when the watchman turned on the light.*

Comparison. Comparison of an adjective or an adverb is the indication, by inflection or otherwise, of degrees of quality, quantity, or manner. There are three degrees of comparison:

	POSITIVE	COMPARATIVE	SUPERLATIVE
adjectives {	old	older	oldest
	beautiful	more beautiful	most beautiful
adverbs {	hard	harder	hardest
	rapidly	less rapidly	least rapidly

Ordinarily *er* or *r* is added to the positive to form the comparative, and *est* or *st* to the positive to form the superlative (*brave, braver, bravest*). But many words of two or more syllables are compared by placing *more* or *less* before the positive stem for the comparative and *most* or *least* for the superlative. Some adjectives and adverbs express qualities that do not permit comparison (*dead, four-sided, unique, original*).

Complement (also called **completer**). A complement is a word or word group in the predicate which completes the essential meaning of the verb. There are three kinds of complements:

Object: Trees mark the *course* of the river. (See **Object.**)

Predicate noun: My sister is a *teacher*. (The term is also applied to pronouns: John admitted it was *he*.)

Predicate adjective: The program was *jolly*.

Conjugation. Conjugation is a series of inflectional changes in the verb to indicate person, number, tense, voice, mood. See pp. 123-124.

Conjunction (one of the eight parts of speech). A conjunction is a word used to join elements of a sentence and to show the relations between them.

Coördinating conjunction: joins elements of equal rank (words, phrases, or clauses). Examples: *and, or, but, for, yet.*

See **Conjunctive adverb.**

Subordinating conjunction: joins a subordinate clause to some other word in the sentence. Examples (introducing adverb clauses): *after, as, before, since, till, until, when, whenever, while, where, wherever, because, why, if, unless, than, although, though, that, so that.*

Conjunctive adverb. An adverb which introduces a coördinate clause is sometimes called a conjunctive adverb. Examples: *then, besides, too, also, moreover, further, indeed, in fact, nevertheless, however, still, only, otherwise, therefore, thus, hence, consequently, accordingly, as a result.*

Sales fell off; therefore profits declined.

For punctuating sentences with conjunctive adverbs see **3a.**

Construction (also called **syntax**). Construction is the grammatical relation between words, phrases, and clauses in a sentence. Always ask, "What work does this word or word group do in the sentence?" The answer is its construction or syntax.

Example: When fools make mistakes, my boy, they lay the blame on Providence.

What is the construction

of *they?*	It is the subject of *lay.*
of *lay?*	It is the predicate of *they.*
of *blame?*	It is a completer after *lay.*
of *on Providence?*	It is a modifier of *lay.*
of *When fools make mistakes?*	It is a modifier of *lay.*
of *my boy?*	It is an independent element.

Any word or word group in any sentence must do one of these six kinds of work:

MAIN KINDS OF WORK

It may name the SUBJECT.

It may assert—be a PREDICATE (say *verb* if you prefer).

It may name the COMPLEMENT or COMPLETER of a verb or of a preposition.

It may serve as a MODIFIER (adjective, adverb).

MINOR KINDS OF WORK

It may serve as a CONNECTIVE (*and, or, but, to, with, by*).

It may serve as an INDEPENDENT ELEMENT (interjection, etc.).

Thus a knowledge of six constructions will enable you to explain any ordinary sentence, provided you box off each phrase or subordinate clause and treat it as if it were a single big word (it will always do the work of a single part of speech). This is the "first stage of grammatical knowledge," when you do not attempt to explain what is inside a phrase or clause but take each as a unit.

Afterward you learn to *go inside* the phrase or clause and to explain the construction of all the words within it. This is the "second stage of grammatical knowledge." To attain it you need a knowledge of all of the parts of speech.

Coördinate. As an adjective *coördinate* means *equal in rank;* as a noun it means *an equal in rank*. The term may be used of any sentence element.

Coördinate nouns: *Tom* and *Jerry.*

Coördinate verbs: *hop, skip,* and *jump.*

Coördinate adverbs: *quarterly* or *semiannually.*

Coördinate phrases: *before dawn* and *after sunset.*

Coördinate clauses (main): *Demand ceases* and *prices decline.*

Coördinate clauses (subordinate): *If the report was sent* and *if we received it,* why is it not in our files?

Copula. See **Linking verb.**

Declension. In earlier English, declension was a series of changes in the inflectional form of a noun, pronoun, or adjective to show person, number, gender, and case. Subsequently the language lost most of these inflections except from the pronoun. In modern English we do not change the form of the adjective except in comparison; we do not change that of the noun except to show the possessive case, number, and in rare instances gender (*alumna, actress*). To indicate that a noun or adjective is in the nominative or objective case we employ, not inflectional form, but position in the sentence.

Dependent clause. See **Clause.**

Direct address or **vocative.** A "word in direct address" is a noun or pronoun used parenthetically (set off by commas) to show who is spoken to: *George*, will you hand me the soup ladle, please? [Do not confuse *direct address* with *direct quotation*, the exact words of another.]

Element. An element is any word or word group which has a separate grammatical function in a sentence. *Sentence element* is a convenient general term because it spares us the necessity of repeating the awkward series "word, phrase, clause, or other word group" when we are discussing punctuation or grammar.

Ellipsis, elliptical expression. An ellipsis is an expression logically incomplete, so that words have to be understood to round out the meaning. An idea or relation corresponding to the omitted words is present, at least vaguely, in the mind of the speaker. Elliptical sentences are usually justifiable except when the reader cannot instantly supply the understood words.

I will go if you will [go]. You are as lazy as I [am lazy].
Is your sister coming? I think [my sister is] not [coming].

Finite. See **Verb.**

Gerund. A gerund is a verbal in *ing* used as a noun. See **Verbal.**

I do not object to your *telling.*

His *having deserted* us made little difference.

Independent clause. See **Clause.**

Independent element (also called **interrupter**). An independent element is a word or word group which has no construction—no grammatical connection with other words in the sentence.

Interjection: *Ah*, I have found it at last.

Noun in direct address: *Sister*, stop talking.

Directive expression: Her family, *they say*, is wealthy.

Absolute expression: *The wind having died down*, we took to the oars. [An absolute expression is regularly built upon a noun and a participle. Sometimes it has almost the meaning of an adverb clause (when the wind had died down).]

Infinitive. An infinitive is a verbal regularly introduced by *to* and used as a noun or a modifier. See **Verbal.**

Infinitive used as a noun: *To err* is human. I like *to eat. To have offended* him is a thing I regret.

Infinitive used as an adjective: A car *to borrow* was not to be found.

Infinitive used as an adverb: ready *to go,* dressed *to attract* attention.

After certain verbs (*bid, dare, help, make, need*) the sign *to* is omitted. Do you dare *go?* Please help *peel* potatoes.

Inflection. Inflection is a series of changes in the form of a word to show a modification or shade of meaning. Once our language offered a separate form for nearly every modification. Though separate forms are now less numerous, *inflection* is still a convenient general term to include the declension of nouns, the comparison of adjectives and adverbs, and the conjugation of verbs.

Interjection (one of the eight parts of speech). An interjection is a word *thrown into* speech to express emotion. It has no grammatical connection with other words.

Oh, is that it? *Well,* I'll do it.

Linking verb (also called **copula**). A linking verb is a verb used to express the relation between the subject and a predicate noun or adjective. Linking verbs include *be* (*is, are, was, were, has been, had been, will have been,* etc.), *become, seem,* etc., and sometimes *feel, smell, sound, taste.*

Main clause. See **Clause.**

Modal aspects. See **Modal auxiliaries** under **Verb.**

Mode (also called **Mood**). See **Mood** under **Verb.**

Modifier. A modifier is a word or expression used to describe or limit the meaning of another word. *Fried rabbit* means something different from *rabbit;* hence *fried* is said to modify or limit *rabbit. Women in politics* means something different from *women;* hence the phrase *in politics* is said to modify or limit *women.*

To modify is to be grammatically dependent; hence in *the girl I like* both *the* and *[that] I like* are dependent upon *girl.* In *a very intelligent girl* the adjectives *a* and *intelligent* modify *girl,* and *very* modifies *intelligent.*

Modifiers may be words, phrases, or clauses. They may be **adjectival modifiers** (modifying a noun) or **adverbial modifiers** (modifying a verb, an adjective, or an adverb).

ADJECTIVAL MODIFIER | ADVERBIAL MODIFIER

Clause · children { *who are healthy*
Phrase · children { *in good health*

come { *when you've eaten*
come { *after dinner*

Word *healthy* children

{ come *afterward* (modifies a verb)
extremely good (modifies an adjective)
very soon (modifies an adverb)

Noun (one of the eight parts of speech). A noun is a name. The uses of a noun are these four:

Subject of a verb: The *bank* will close at one o'clock.

Object
> of a verb: He closed the *banks* for a week.
> of a preposition: I am going to the *bank* at noon.
> of a verbal: Closing the *bank* at noon inconveniences many working people.

Predicate noun: This building is the *First National Bank*.

Appositive: He has an account at the County National, the leading *bank* of the town.

By a change of force a word which ordinarily does the work of a noun may be made to do the work of an adjective (the *brick* sidewalk, *Joseph's* coat), or an adverb (John went *home*), or an independent element (*Jehoshaphat*, what an idea!).

Classification. A noun may be **proper** (*Philip Watkins*), or **common**. Common nouns may be CONCRETE (perceptible through the senses: *man, windmill*), or ABSTRACT (not perceptible through the senses: *gratitude, nearness*). A noun applied to a group is said to be COLLECTIVE (*family, race*).

Object. An object is a noun (or the equivalent) which completes the meaning of a preposition or a transitive verb.

Object of a preposition: through the *house*, between *her* and *me*.

Object of a verb: broke a *window*, presented a new *play*.

Indirect object is the term sometimes used to describe a noun or pronoun that comes before the direct object (such a construction is sometimes explained as an elliptical phrase from which the preposition *to* or *for* has been omitted): The cook baked *me* a gooseberry pie. [Here *me* is the indirect object, and *pie* is the direct object. The direct object receives the verb act, and the indirect object receives the object.]

Special constructions:

(1) Objective complement: Jim made his front room an *office*.

(2) Retained object: We are given the *bank* as a reference.

Participle. A verbal in *ing* (and a past form ending in *ed, t, en,* or the like) when used as an adjective is called a participle.

Señora Garcia, *wearing* the pearls, came to the footlights.

Having emptied the fish basket, he returned to the wharf.

See **Verbal.**

Passive Voice. See **Verb.**

Phrase. In loose usage a phrase is any group of words. In strict grammatical usage it is a word group which functions as a single part of speech and is not built around a subject and verb.

A prepositional phrase is built around a preposition: *With a whistle and a roar* the train arrived.

A verbal phrase is built around a participle, gerund, or infinitive: Jack and Jill went up the hill *to fetch a pail of water* [infinitive phrase].

Predicate. A predicate is a word or word group which makes an assertion about the subject. We may use *predicate, predicate verb,* or *simple predicate* to mean the verb alone. We may use *predicate* or (more accurately) *complete predicate* to mean the verb assertion expanded by modifiers or complements. Two or more verbs which are governed by the same subject form a *compound predicate*:

Jerry can't float, but he *swims* and *dives* expertly.

Predicate adjective. A predicate adjective is an adjective in the predicate which points back to the subject, describing it or limiting it. A predicate adjective occurs only after *be* (*is, are, was, were, has been,* etc.), some other no-action verb like *become, appear, seem,* or a verb which pertains to the senses:

> She is *redheaded* and *Irish.* She appears *clever.* This milk smells *sour.* His playing sounds *terrible.*

Predicate complement (also called **subjective complement**). A general term referring both to predicate adjectives and to predicate nouns.

Predicate noun (also called **predicate nominative**). A predicate noun is a noun (or pronoun) in the predicate which points back to the subject, classifying it or explaining it. A predicate noun occurs only after *be* (*is, are, was, were, has been,* etc.) or some other linking, no-action verb.

> John is *halfback.* They became *neighbors.*

Predication. A predication is a related word group containing a subject and a predicate. A simple sentence is a predication. A clause is a predication, but may be dependent.

Preposition (one of the eight parts of speech, literally *pre* = before + *positus* = placed). A preposition is a connective which takes hold of a substantive and forms with it a modifying phrase. There are about seventy prepositions in the language. Here are the common ones:

of	to	in	through	since	across	during
with	at	into	between	about	beneath	concerning
by	on	from	among	until	beyond	owing to
for	up	over	above	after	beside	because of
like	down	under	below	before	except	in spite of

A **prepositional phrase** (a preposition plus its object, sometimes with modifiers) normally does the work of an adjective or an adverb:

a man	*without fear*	⎫ prepositional phrase
differences	*between you and me*	⎬ used as an adjective
runs	*toward the enemy*	⎫ prepositional phrase
works	*for him and her*	⎬ used as an adverb

In exceptional instances a prepositional phrase is used as a noun:

Over the fence is out.

Principal parts. The principal parts of a verb are the present tense, the past tense, and the past participle (*help, helped, helped*). The principal parts of the following verbs are often troublesome. In not all do the past tense and the past participle actually differ, but in most the two forms may cause uncertainty.

PRESENT TENSE	PAST TENSE	PAST PARTICIPLE	PRESENT TENSE	PAST TENSE	PAST PARTICIPLE
am	was	been	deal	dealt	dealt
attack	attacked	attacked	dig	dug	dug
awake	awoke	awaked		digged	digged
	awaked	awoke	dive	dived	dived
bear	bore	borne		dove *	
		born	do	did	done
begin	began	begun	drag	dragged	dragged
bend	bent	bent	draw	drew	drawn
bid (order)	bade	bidden	dream	dreamed	dreamed
	bid	bid		dreamt	dreamt
bid (offer money)	bid	bid	drink	drank	drunk
			drive	drove	driven
bite	bit	bitten	drown	drowned	drowned
		bit *	dwell	dwelt	dwelt
bleed	bled	bled		dwelled	dwelled
blow	blew	blown	eat	ate	eaten
break	broke	broken	fall	fell	fallen
broadcast	broadcast	broadcast	fight	fought	fought
	broadcasted †	broadcasted †	flee	fled	fled
burn	burned	burned	flow	flowed	flowed
	burnt	burnt	fly	flew	flown
burst	burst	burst	forget	forgot	forgotten
catch	caught	caught			forgot
choose	chose	chosen	freeze	froze	frozen
climb	climbed	climbed	get	got	got
come	came	come			gotten

* Colloquial.
† Has some standing in radio use.

NOTE: Verbs whose forms are often confused are *lie-lay* and *sit-set*. See these items in Article 19.

PRESENT TENSE	PAST TENSE	PAST PARTICIPLE	PRESENT TENSE	PAST TENSE	PAST PARTICIPLE
go	went	gone	shrink	shrank	shrunk
grow	grew	grown		shrunk	
hang	hung	hung	sing	sang	sung
hang (execute)	hanged	hanged		sung	
			sit	sat	sat
hold	held	held	smite	smote	smitten
kneel	knelt	knelt			smit
	kneeled	kneeled			smote
know	knew	known	sow	sowed	sown
lay	laid	laid			sowed
lead	led	led	speak	spoke	spoken
lean	leaned	leaned	spit	spat	spat
	leant	leant		spit	spit
lend	lent	lent	spring	sprang	sprung
lie (recline)	lay	lain		sprung	
light	lighted	lighted	steal	stole	stolen
	lit	lit	strike	struck	struck
loose	loosed	loosed			stricken
lose	lost	lost	strive	strove	striven
mean	meant	meant		strived	strived
prove	proved	proved	swear	swore	sworn
read	read	read	sweat	sweat	sweat
ride	rode	ridden		sweated	sweated
ring	rang	rung	swim	swam	swum
	rung		take	took	taken
rise	rose	risen	tear	tore	torn
run	ran	run	thrive	throve	thrived
say	said	said		thrived	thriven
see	saw	seen	throw	threw	thrown
set	set	set	tread	trod	trodden
sew	sewed	sewed			trod
		sewn	wake	waked	waked
shake	shook	shaken		woke	
shine	shone	shone	wear	wore	worn
show	showed	shown	weave	wove	woven
		showed		weaved	wove
			write	wrote	written

Pronominal adjective. See **Adjective.**

Pronoun (one of the eight parts of speech). A pronoun is a substitute for a noun. A noun for which a pronoun stands is called the *antecedent.*

Politicians promise much, but *they* accomplish little. [*Politicians* is the antecedent of *they*.]

Personal pronouns: *I, you, he, she, it, we, they.*

Relative pronouns: *who, which, that.*

Interrogative pronouns: *who, which, what.*

Demonstrative pronouns: *this, that, these, those.*

Indefinite pronouns: *some, any, one, each, either, few, all, both,* etc.

Reflexive or intensive pronouns: I blamed *myself.* You *yourself* are at fault.

The uses of pronouns are in general the same as those of nouns. In addition, relatives serve as connectives (the man *who* spoke), interrogatives ask questions (*Who* is the man?), and demonstratives point out (*That* is Van Lehr's secretary).

DECLENSION OF PERSONAL PRONOUNS

	Singular			Plural		
Person	Nominative	Possessive	Objective	Nominative	Possessive	Objective
1.	I	my, mine	me	we	our, ours	us
2.	you	your, yours	you	you	your, yours	you
3.	he, she it	his, her, hers its	him, her it	they	their, theirs	them

Sentence. A sentence is a group of words which contains a verb and its subject and whatever else is necessary to complete the thought. A part of a sentence built around a subject and a verb is called a **clause.**

A **main clause** (also called an **independent clause**) is an independent statement; it could stand alone and form a sentence by itself.

A **subordinate clause** (also called **dependent clause**) is one which does the work of a single part of speech (adjective, adverb, or noun).

Two main clauses: *The dog barked,* and *the thief ran.*

Subordinate clause: The thief runs *when the dogs bark.*

A sentence of one independent statement is called **simple**.

Simple sentence
: The dogs barked at the thief.
: Thieves and tramps fear dogs. [Compound subject]
: Dogs bark and howl at night. [Compound predicate]

A sentence of two or more independent statements (two or more *main clauses*) is called **compound**.

Compound sentence
: The thieves ran, and the dogs followed.
: Dogs barked; thieves ran; excitement reigned.

A sentence containing a subordinate clause is called **complex**.

Complex sentence
: *When the dogs barked* the thieves ran.
: The night is cold, and the dogs bark *when the wind blows.* [This sentence is both complex and compound; it may be called a compound-complex sentence.]

Subordinate clause. See **Clause.**

Subordinate (subordinating). See **Clause** and **Conjunction.**

Substantive. Substantive is an inclusive term for a noun or a word or word group which stands in the place of a noun (pronoun, clause, infinitive, gerund).

A substantive phrase is a phrase used as a noun: *From Dan to Beersheba* is a term for the whole of Israel.

A substantive clause is a clause used as a noun: *That he owed the money* is certain.

Syntax. See **Construction.**

Tense. See **Verb.**

Verb (one of the eight parts of speech). A verb is a word or word group which makes an assertion or asks a question. It usually expresses action (Winds *blow*), but it may express state of being (*Is* it true? She *sleeps*).

121

Ordinarily the term *verb* refers to a *finite verb*, that is, to one which asserts or asks. A finite verb is contrasted with a verbal, which names or implies action or being but cannot assert or ask either. See **Verbal**.

A **transitive verb** is one which requires a receiver of the act (*trans* means "across"; hence *transitive* means "action carried across"): Our car *outruns* the train.

An **intransitive verb** is one which does not require a complement: The streamliner *is whistling* for the signal.

The full meaning of a verb depends on the inflectional forms which show voice, mood, and tense (and in some instances number: *is, are; has been, have been;* etc.).

Voice shows whether the subject performs or receives the action expressed by the verb.

The active voice shows the subject as actor: Carter *loaded* the truck.

The passive voice shows the subject as acted upon: The truck *was loaded* before daybreak.

Modal auxiliaries (*may, can, must, might, could, would, should,* etc.) are used with other verbs to form **modal aspects** of the verb for the purpose of expressing ability, possibility, obligation, etc. There are as many different aspects as there are auxiliaries. Aspects are sometimes spoken of as separate moods or called collectively the "potential mood."

Mood (also called **mode**) indicates the mood or manner in which the speaker views the action of the verb.

The indicative mood states or questions a fact: She *does* not dance. *Has* he *gone?*

The subjunctive mood expresses a wish or a condition contrary to fact: Would that I *were* there! If I *were* older, I'd be wiser.

The imperative mood expresses a command or an urgent request: *Take* notes. *Save* all your papers. *Let* us pray.

Tense expresses the time of the action or state of being. The tenses are the **present, the past, the future** (employing the auxiliaries *shall* and *will*), the **present perfect** (employing *has* or *have*), the **past perfect** (employing *had*), and the **future perfect** (employing *shall have* and *will have*).

CONJUGATION OF THE VERB *SEE*

INDICATIVE MOOD

ACTIVE VOICE   PASSIVE VOICE

PRESENT TENSE

	Singular	*Plural*		*Singular*	*Plural*
1.	I see	we see	I am seen	we are seen
2.	you see	you see	you are seen	you are seen
3.	he sees	they see	he is seen	they are seen

PAST TENSE

1.	I saw	we saw	I was seen	we were seen
2.	you saw	you saw	you were seen	you were seen
3.	he saw	they saw	he was seen	they were seen

FUTURE TENSE

1.	I shall see	we shall see	I shall be seen	we shall be seen
2.	you will see	you will see	you will be seen	you will be seen
3.	he will see	they will see	he will be seen	they will be seen

PRESENT PERFECT TENSE

1.	I have seen	we have seen	I have been seen	we have been seen
2.	you have seen	you have seen	you have been seen	you have been seen
3.	he has seen	they have seen	he has been seen	they have been seen

PAST PERFECT TENSE

1.	I had seen	we had seen	I had been seen	we had been seen
2.	you had seen	you had seen	you had been seen	you had been seen
3.	he had seen	they had seen	he had been seen	they had been seen

FUTURE PERFECT TENSE (SELDOM USED)

1.	I shall have seen	we shall have seen	I shall have been seen	we shall have been seen
2.	you will have seen	you will have seen	you will have been seen	you will have been seen
3.	he will have seen	they will have seen	he will have been seen	they will have been seen

SUBJUNCTIVE MOOD

| ACTIVE VOICE | PASSIVE VOICE |

PRESENT TENSE

if I, you, he see   if I, you, he be seen
if we, you, they see   if we, you, they be seen

PAST TENSE

if I, you, he saw   if I, you, he were seen
if we, you, they saw   if we, you, they were seen

PRESENT PERFECT

if I, you, he have seen   if I, you, he have been seen
if we, you, they have seen   if we, you, they have been seen

IMPERATIVE MOOD

PRESENT TENSE

See!

Principal parts. For formation of principal parts see 12e(1). For a list of verbs with troublesome forms see **Principal parts** (in this article).

Verbal. A verbal is a form derived from a verb but used as a noun or a modifier.

A PARTICIPLE does the work of an adjective: See the *drifting* snow. The tree, *having fallen*, supplied them with fuel.

A GERUND does the work of a noun: *Drifting* with the current is pleasant. His *having failed* dismays us.

An INFINITIVE does the work of a noun or a modifier: *To drift* is pleasant. *To have failed* brings regret. Work *to do*. Good enough *to eat*.

A verbal is not a main verb; it cannot take a subject or be used alone as a predicate in forming a sentence. It does, however, retain some of the functions of a verb:

124

it may take an object or be modified by an adverb. Hence it is no one part of speech but an "in between." Below are examples of verbals which have objects or adverbial modifiers:

object   adverb

Infinitive: *To shoe* a horse well requires skill. [*To shoe a horse well* is an infinitive phrase.]

object

Gerund: In *shoeing* a horse, trim the hoof carefully. [*In shoeing a horse* is a gerund phrase.]

adverb   object

Participle: The old gray, continually *stamping* his feet, is hard to handle. [*Continually stamping his feet* is a participial phrase.]

SUMMARY OF VERBAL FORMS

		Present	*Past*
Infinitive	{ Active:	*to give*	to have given
	{ Passive:	to be given	to have been given
Participle	{ Active:	*giving*	having given
and	{		having been given
Gerund	{ Passive:	being given	*given* (short form, participle only)

Participle and gerund are identical in form (except that the short past passive is used as a participle only). Some grammarians do not use the term *gerund*.

Voice. See Verb.

Diction

WORDS AS SYMBOLS   Words are verbal symbols which may or may not have referents. That is, they may or may not symbolize or refer to objects, relationships, and experiences which we can observe or verify in real life. Blackboards are tangible objects. The word *blackboard* represents something actual; it has a referent. The word *leprechaun* has no referent. Similarly the terms *labor, capital, general intelligence, public opinion,* etc., when used in a broad, collective sense, have no referents. There are only individual workmen, capitalists, and persons with varying intelligence and differing opinions.

WORDS WITHOUT REFERENTS   Few persons are likely to write of a leprechaun as if he really existed. But many write seriously of equally intangible objects and conditions. Such statements as this are common: "Modern American youth is pampered, undisciplined, and irresponsible." It is an apparently meaningful sentence. But exactly what does it mean? Who is this "American youth?" Johnny Jones? But the statement isn't true of him. Mary Smith? Pampered, yes; but not the rest. Willie Jackson? Perhaps he used to be undisciplined, but the army took care of that. Undoubtedly the statement may apply to some young people. But certainly not to all; and to few in the same degree. The truth is, this "American youth" who is uniformly pampered, undisciplined, and irresponsible does not exist. The term is a symbol without referent.

Such terms without referents are often dangerous because they obscure the facts needed for calm judgment and intelligent action. To statements employing such terms people can respond with their emotions only—with an undirected sense of annoyance, fear, or indignation. Base your thinking on verifiable facts. Whenever possible communicate your thoughts in words with referents—words and examples that clearly indicate realities which your reader can evaluate intellectually and objectively.

WORDS WITH AMBIGUOUS REFERENTS Even when words have identifiable referents the problem of effective communication is not solved. In themselves words are meaningless. They derive significance only from the way we use them—from the meanings we assign to them. Because our backgrounds, and our experiences with particular words, vary, the referent in the writer's mind is not necessarily that in the mind of the reader.

Such uncertainty of meaning is particularly likely with general and abstract words (words of broad meaning and those referring to an idea or concept rather than a particular object). By the term *asset* one person may mean *stocks* and *bonds;* another may primarily associate the word with *oil wells;* a third may relate the term to *bank credit* or definite amounts of *paper money.*

If such a discrepancy in understanding does not obscure your intended meaning, you may safely use a general or abstract term. But ordinarily it is essential to convey more definite concepts, to recreate in the mind of your reader objects and experiences nearly identical with those in your own mind. This you can do by using specific terms (terms which have definite referents) and concrete terms (terms which call to mind particular sights, sounds, feelings, tastes, and smells). The word *asset* may be made specific by substituting or by adding as a definition the term *one thousand dollars in currency*. It may be made concrete by the phrase *a stack of two hundred crisp, smooth five-dollar bills.*

Observe carefully; keep your thinking close to the objects and experiences of life. Then make your writing accurate and forceful by using terms which are specific and concrete.*

CONCISENESS

15. Be concise. Keep superfluous words and irrelevant ideas out of your writing.

HOW TO GAIN CONCISENESS

15a. **Deadwood and Circumlocution** A term or a phrase which adds nothing to the essential thought is deadwood. Strike it out. An expression needlessly drawn out is a circumlocution. Replace it with a direct expression.

* The student interested in how words get their meanings (the study called *semantics*) and why our use of words involves important problems of communication will find the following books significant and stimulating.

Advanced treatments of the subject:

> C. K. Ogden and I. A. Richards, *The Meaning of Meaning* (New York, Harcourt, Brace & Co., 1938. 6th ed., 1944).
>
> Alfred Korzybski, *Science and Sanity: An Introduction to Non-Aristotelian Systems and General Semantics* (Lancaster, Pa., The Science Press Printing Co., 1941).
>
> Charles Morris, *Signs, Language, and Behavior* (New York, Prentice-Hall, Inc., 1946).

Introductory treatments of the subject:

> *a.* Deriving from *The Meaning of Meaning*
>> Hugh R. Walpole, *Semantics: The Nature of Words and Their Meanings* (New York, W. W. Norton & Co., Inc., 1941).
>> F. A. Philbrick, *Understanding English* (New York, The Macmillan Co., 1942).
>
> *b.* Deriving from *Science and Sanity*
>> S. I. Hayakawa, *Language in Action* (New York, Harcourt, Brace & Co., 1941. Revised as *Language in Thought and Action*, 1949).
>> Irving J. Lee, *Language Habits in Human Affairs* (New York, Harper & Bros., 1941).

Wordy construction: An hour's hike brought us to the place where the monument stood. [12 words]

Strike out the deadwood: An hour's hike brought us to the monument. [8 words]

Terms that add no meaning: They all agreed on the idea that cramming for an examination is useless. [13 words]

Strike out the deadwood: They agreed that cramming for an examination is useless. [9 words]

Wordy expression: In very few cases do men approve of women's hats. [10 words]

Replace the circumlocution with a single word: Men seldom approve of women's hats. [6 words]

Roundabout expression: He liked every student he came in contact with. [9 words]

Replace the circumlocution with one word: He liked every student he met. [6 words]

Wordy construction: While they were waiting for him to arrive, they passed the time away playing the ancient game of chess. [19 words]

Strike out the needless words and the irrelevant idea: While waiting for him they played chess. [7 words]

Roundabout expression: During the time that he was in the Navy he made only one sea voyage. [15 words]

Replace the circumlocution with one word: While in the Navy he made only one sea voyage. [10 words]

Wordy construction: It happened to be raining at the time, and we couldn't go. [The wordy construction obscures the causal relation of the first clause to the second.] [12 words]

Strike out the unnecessary words and make clear the relationship of thoughts: Because it was raining we couldn't go. [7 words]

Needless piling up of clauses: Next morning a thin layer of snow covered the ground, and this made tracking easy. [15 words]

Combine the clauses: Next morning a thin layer of snow made tracking easy. [10 words]

Needless piling up of short sentences: The new farm buildings are of white stucco. They have red tile roofs. The colors of the buildings attract attention. [20 words]

Combine the sentences, eliminating the connectives: The new farm buildings stand out in white stucco with red tile roofs. [13 words]

Wordiness for humorous effect: The canine quadruped was under suspicion of having obliterated by a process of mastication that article of sustenance which men transport from the butcher shop to the culinary section of their domiciles. [Even as a humorous device such wordiness, when long sustained, repels modern readers.]

Use straightforward expression in ordinary writing: The dog was suspected of having eaten the meat.

15b. **Impersonal Constructions**   Impersonal constructions (*there are, it is,* etc.) often add needless words to the sentence and may make the structure involved.

Roundabout impersonal construction: There were three of us that had cars. [8 words]

Strike out the useless impersonal and connective words: Three of us had cars. [5 words]

Roundabout impersonal construction: There was a feeling among the members that they had not been given all the facts. [16 words]

Strike out the useless impersonal and connective words: The members felt they had not been given all the facts. [11 words]

Roundabout impersonal construction: It is a superstition held by many people that to break a mirror brings bad luck. [16 words]

Revise to make the statement direct: Many superstitious people believe that to break a mirror brings bad luck. [12 words]

15c. **Passive Construction** The passive voice is occasionally necessary (see Verb, 14). But used without purpose it is awkward and wordy.

Wordy passive construction: The play was enjoyed by all. [6 words]
Use the active voice: Everybody enjoyed the play. [4 words]

Wordy passive construction: The football team was cheered by us in defeat as in victory. [12 words]
Use the active voice: We cheered the football team in defeat as in victory. [10 words]

EXERCISE

X-15a. Deadwood and Circumlocution

Rewrite these sentences, ridding them of deadwood and substituting direct terms for circumlocutions.

1. In only a few instances did the men fear their leaders.
2. Science majors were required to take additional courses in the humanities, and, as a result of this change in the curriculum, they were expected to develop broader cultural interests.
3. The original idea behind the beginning of the UN was to create an assembly of nations for the purpose of promoting peaceful relations and preventing war.
4. In only a very few instances are people who buy cosmetics aware of what materials are used to make the various and sundry beauty aids.
5. After thinking the matter over, Greenough concluded that it would be unwise to leave town so soon.
6. When the curtain rose and the play began a good many of the audience had not yet arrived and taken their seats.
7. The members of the grand jury all agreed that an indictment should be issued naming each of the officers of the organization and charging them all with illegal conspiracy.
8. Sometime or other almost every motion picture writer seems, for one reason or another, to have an impulse to write a satire on Hollywood.

9. After arriving at the top of the building they found that the view of the city from there was, for the most part, obscured by the fog which lay below them.

10. When you are in Canada you can see old, flooded silver mines, deserted by the men who originally dug them. These mines are now being reclaimed. That is, the water is being pumped out of them, and when they become dry enough to permit they are again being worked.

11. From the very beginning of his life he had been forced to live in the midst of all sorts of personal conflicts.

12. As a reviewer he gained something of a reputation by vigorously attacking in his writings all of the performances which he himself felt were not quite sincere.

13. Even though the wreckage of the derailed train was cleared off the tracks in the shortest possible time, setting a new record for the salvage crew, nevertheless the Limited was delayed some ten minutes because of waiting for the damaged track to be put back into good shape.

14. While digging in an old gravel pit not very far from Cambridge, Nebraska, scientists found there the fossilized bones of a saber-toothed tiger.

15. For the purpose of gaining more time in which to prepare the evidence which they had, the prosecutor made a request to the court that the case be postponed.

X-15b. Weak Impersonal Constructions

Rewrite, making each statement direct and forceful.

1. Carelessness, it is reported by traffic officers, is the most frequent cause of automobile accidents.

2. It is the opinion of many economists that the American economy cannot survive if isolationist policies are adopted.

3. There was strong support among welfare workers for a social security program which would apply to all employees.

4. It has been pointed out by medical researchers that vitamin A is especially important to good eyesight.

5. There is much doubt among sociologists as to the wisdom of sending first offenders to prison.

X-15c. Feeble Passive Constructions

Rewrite, substituting direct, active constructions.

1. Peanuts have been made a valuable crop as a result of Dr. George Washington Carver's research.
2. Even before he was old enough to read he was driven to petty theft by the poverty of his family.
3. Use of a gasoline-powered crane makes it possible for the truck to be loaded by two men in half an hour.
4. The prize-winning model plane was built by him in his spare time.
5. By the use of walkie-talkie radios, traffic throughout the city can be coördinated by one man.

REPETITION

16. Do not repeat a word, a phrase, or an idea needlessly. But do not hesitate to repeat when repetition is necessary for clearness.*

16a. Ungrammatical Repetition

Pronoun repeated ungrammatically: Let's us take a holiday. [Omit *us*.]

Preposition and pronoun ungrammatically repeated: It was an agreement to which all of them were parties to it. [Omit *to it*.]

Conjunction repeated ungrammatically: He resolved that when he could that he would. [Omit the second *that*.]

Object repeated ungrammatically: Whatever she sings, she sings it well. [Omit *it*.]

Double negative: The pilot couldn't hardly see. [Omit either *n't* or *hardly*. The second term of a double negative not only repeats the first, but logically cancels it.]

---

* For the needless repetition of an entire idea see 42c. For faulty repetition in defining terms see 41c. For unpleasant repetition of a sound or an inflectional form see 47c. For slovenly or confusing repetition of *and, so,* or *but* see 4. For repetition as a means of emphasis see 48e.

16b. **Tautology** Tautology is a needless repetition of meaning; it is like saying *black blackbird*. To avoid it think what your words really mean.

Strike the unnecessary words (here italicized) from black blackbird expressions such as these:

return *back*	total effect *of all this*
ascend *up*	connect *up*
repeat *again*	meet *up with*
biography *of his life*	combine *together*
good benefits	*final* outcome
fellow playmates	*more* unique
perfectly all right	*strictly* accurate
utter absence of	*absolutely* annihilated
quite round	*still* continue to
circular *in form*	*absolutely* new creation
big *in size*	*one evening* about 8 p.m.
many *in number*	the *two* twins
Halloween *evening*	*in* back of
important essentials	*new* recruit
endorse *on the back*	*end* result
necessary requisite	*fundamental* basis

Double subject: George Landon he marched in front. [Omit *he*.] *

Hand me that there coat hanger. [Omit *there*.]

This here fishing rod is my favorite. [Omit *here*.]

He wouldn't tell me where it was at. [Omit *at*.]

They both look alike. [Omit *both*.]

Their numbers were very numerous. [Omit *numbers* and change the pronominal adjective to a pronoun] They were numerous. [Or] Their numbers were great.

By waiting I got it free gratis for nothing. [Omit any two of the three equivalents: *free, gratis, for nothing*.]

---

* An appositive, however, may accompany a noun: *George Landon, the parade marshal*, marched in front.

The 1½ cent stamp is brown in color. [The 1½ cent stamp is brown.]

After a moment of brief silence Greta spoke. [Omit *brief*.]

In your opinion do you think the method safe? [Omit *in your opinion*.]

The reason for the failure in crops was caused by the scanty rainfall. [Omit either *the reason for* or *caused by*.]

Though the revenue from the oil fields goes to the owners, the workmen's pay, however, benefits the merchants. [Omit *though* or *however*. If you omit *though* replace the first comma with a semicolon.]

He had an entire monopoly of the whole fruit trade. [Omit *entire* and *whole*.]

16c. **Awkward or Needless Repetition** Except to gain force or clearness, do not repeat a word or phrase. Get rid of recurring expressions (1) by substituting equivalent expressions, (2) by using pronouns, or (3) by pruning or rearranging the sentence to say only once what has been awkwardly said twice.

Awkward repetition of words: *Just as* we were half way down the lake, *just off* Milwaukee, we *began* to feel a slight motion of the ship and the wind *began* to freshen.

Recast to avoid repetition: Half way down the lake, *opposite* Milwaukee, we *felt* the wind freshen and the boat *begin* to rock.

Monotonous repetition: The *Law Building*, the *Commerce Building*, and the *Science Building* are close together. The *Commerce Building* is south of the *Law Building*, and the *Science Building* is south of the *Commerce Building*. The *Law Building* is the oldest of the three *buildings*. The *Commerce Building* is the newest.

Strike out words, combine ideas, and use pronouns in place of nouns: The *Law*, *Commerce*, and *Science Buildings* are close together in a row. *The first of these* is the northernmost and the oldest. South of *it* stands the *Commerce Building*, which is the newest.

Awkward repetition: The *autumn* is my favorite of all the *seasons*. While *autumn* in the *city* is not such a pleasant *season* as *autumn* in the country, yet even in the *city* my preference will always be for *autumn*.

Rearrange and condense the sentences: My favorite *season* is *autumn*. I like *it* best in the country, but even in the *city it* is the most pleasant *time of the year*.

Careless repetition: The *average* record with music on both sides retails, on the *average*, for more than a dollar. [Omit *on the average*. Also omit the first *average* unless you are stressing the idea that the record is representative.]

Careless repetition: On a *winter morning* I like to walk briskly and breathe the cool air of the *winter morning*. [Omit *of the winter morning*.]

Correct but needless repetition of pronoun: Shall we inspect his cattle and his hogs? [Neither awkwardness nor obscurity would result from omitting the second *his*.]

Correct but needless repetition of subject and verb: At the Friday matinee the attendance is five hundred; at the Saturday matinee it is a thousand. [The second clause may omit *it is*.]

16d. **Necessary Repetition** Repeat any words needed to make a statement natural and clear.*

Obvious strain for a synonym: For days elephants had filled the child's dreams, and now the largest of quadrupeds stood before him.

Repeat the noun: For days elephants had filled the child's dreams, and now the elephants stood before him.

Ambiguity from failure to repeat the pronoun: This is a trend in painting about which people grow angry and denounce. [Because *which* is not repeated *about which* seems to accompany *denounce*.]

---

* For errors resulting from the omission of necessary words see **2**. For errors in parallelism resulting from the omission of essential elements see **8d**.

Repeat the pronoun and adjust the remainder of the sentence: This is a trend in painting about which people grow angry and which they denounce. [Or modify the phrasing] This is a trend in painting which people resent and denounce.

Awkward and illogical double capacity: There were thirty singers in the choir and dressed exactly alike. [Because *were* is not repeated it is used in a double capacity—as a main verb before *singers* and as an auxiliary before *dressed.*]

Repeat *were* and fill out the second clause: There were thirty singers in the choir, and they were dressed exactly alike. [Or use a single predication] In the choir were thirty singers dressed exactly alike.

Momentary doubt whether the last noun is a subject or an object: Habit grips a person in much the same way as an octopus. [As habit grips an octopus?]

Repeat the verb idea for clearness: Habit grips a person in much the same way as an octopus does.

Ambiguity from failure to repeat a preposition and an article: After the death of the vice-president and cashier, the depositors became alarmed. [Did one man die, or did two?]

Repeat the necessary elements: After the death of the vice-president and of the cashier, the depositors became alarmed. [Or use a clearly explanatory adjective clause] After the death of the vice-president, who was also the cashier, the depositors became alarmed.

Ambiguity from failure to repeat a preposition: He was greeted warmly by all the delegates except those who opposed his candidacy, and especially the members of his own party.

Repeat the preposition for clearness: He was greeted warmly by all the delegates except those who opposed his candidacy, and especially by the members of his own party.

Ambiguity from failure to repeat the sign of the infinitive: He had only two wishes, to join a fraternity and get straight A's.

Repeat the sign of the infinitive for clearness: He had only two wishes, to join a fraternity and to get straight A's.

Ambiguity from failure to repeat a conjunction: Mr. Trent insists that the ink is diluted, and the Lightning-Dry Company should be prosecuted.

Repeat the conjunction: Mr. Trent insists that the ink is diluted, and that the Lightning-Dry Company should be prosecuted.

EXERCISE

X-16a. Ungrammatical Repetition

Rewrite to prevent elements from being ungrammatically repeated.

1. Paul Gauguin, he first worked in a bank before becoming a painter.
2. My favorite flower is those there Talisman roses.
3. The intelligence officer reported where the enemy submarines were based at.
4. Let's us take the night train so that we will arrive in the morning.
5. Of the five who went fishing, only two of them caught anything.
6. Home gardening doesn't hardly pay when you consider the time spent in cultivating and watering.
7. This here Syrian coin is unique.
8. Margaret promised that if Jimmie arrived in time for the meeting that she would bring him.
9. Water, as it flows over the plowed ground, it carries the rich topsoil with it.
10. Whatever they earn they earn it by hard work.

X-16b. Tautology

Rewrite, eliminating all tautology.

1. Marlow climbed up to the second floor.
2. The complete absence of life gave the island an appearance of utter desolation.
3. John's life as a homeless transient made him appreciate the pleasant joys of the family he had deserted.
4. When you are flying, the distance from San Francisco to New York does not seem far.
5. His new policy called for regular monthly payments.

X-16c. Awkward or Needless Repetition

Rewrite, eliminating awkward or needless repetition.

1. When the referee blew his whistle when the game was about to start, the captain of each team signaled to the referee that his team was ready to start the game. Then the referee blew his whistle again and the game started.

2. His first semester in college was most difficult. Even though he earned higher grades in his second semester, he studied less than he had the first semester.

3. They counted on the income from their stocks and their bonds.

4. The building was constructed in a triangular shape, with the center of the triangle planted in grass and shrubs. In each corner of the center triangle was a bench constructed to fit the shape of the building.

5. The weather seldom varies. In the morning it is always foggy and cold; in the afternoon it is sunny and warm.

X-16d. Necessary Repetition

Rewrite, repeating words or rephrasing to make each statement natural and clear.

1. A bright red car led the parade. Then came a second motor-driven vehicle.

2. He had more love for money than his family.

3. She was an experienced singer, and never afraid of a first night audience.

4. He would not publish the article until he could confer with the publisher and editor-in-chief.

5. The doctor testified that the old woman had died through neglect, but he was not responsible.

6. Mathematics is a subject for which he shows special aptitude and enjoys.

7. The police kept their car close behind, and the siren shrieking.

8. Dale is as much an authority on the Renaissance as a historian.

9. They plan to hire three new salesgirls and build an addition to the store.

10. He took his complaint directly to the president and general manager.

EXACTNESS

17. Seek the exact word. Do not clothe in ready-made phrases what you have seen and thought for yourself.

English is rich in expressive words and phrases. Extend your command of the language by studying synonyms (words of similar meaning). Your dictionary can be of only limited help; wide reading, careful listening, and persistent practice in writing are the quickest means to an expressive vocabulary.

HOW TO EXPRESS YOURSELF MORE EXACTLY*

17a. Misused Specific Terms Do not use specific terms inaccurately. Make sure that the word you use conveys the meaning intended.

Inaccurate: Football squads are expensive *items.* [An *item* is one article of a list.]

Better: Football squads are expensive organizations. [Or] Football squads are expensive.

Inaccurate: Reed's intentions are an unknown *quantity.* [*A quantity* is an *amount* or *portion.*]

Better: Reed's intentions are unpredictable. [Or] No one can make out Reed's intentions.

Ludicrously inaccurate: He *literally* hit the ceiling. [*Literally* is here misused for its opposite, *figuratively.*]

Better: He became very angry. [Or] He hit the ceiling.

17b. Trite or Hackneyed Expressions Avoid outworn tags from everyday speech ("the worse for wear," "had the time of my life"), stale phrases from newspapers ("taken into custody"), forced humorous substitutions ("paternal

---

* For errors resulting from the confusion of words similar in spelling or meaning see **19**. For errors resulting from similarity in the sound of words see **20c(5)**.

ancestor"), forced synonyms ("gridiron heroes"), conventional fine writing ("reigns supreme"), oft-repeated euphemisms ("pass away" for "die"), and overworked quotations from literature ("footprints on the sands of time").

EXAMPLES OF TRITE EXPRESSIONS

along these lines
meets the eye
feathered songsters
a long-felt want
the last sad rites
doomed to disappointment
at one fell swoop
trees stood like sentinels
method in his madness
tired but happy
hoping you are the same
nipped in the bud
seething mass of humanity
specimen of humanity
with bated breath
green with envy
too full for utterance
conspicuous by its absence
sadder but wiser

last but not least
a goodly number
budding genius
the plot thickens
beggars description
a dull thud
silence broken only by
wended their way
abreast of the times
with whom they come in contact
exception proves the rule
as luck would have it
more easily imagined than described
the proud possessor
a pugilistic encounter
all nature seemed to

17c. **General Terms** General terms (terms of broad meaning) are necessary and useful. But some such terms are vague; others are subject to misinterpretation unless used thoughtfully.

(1) Indefinite statements Vague, indefinite terms fail to pin ideas down.

Indefinite statement: It was learned who was there. [Learned by whom? Often the use of the passive voice prevents the naming of the agent.]

Be specific: The police took the name and address of each person there.

141

Vague "gossip": They say Mr. Brass was forced to resign.

Be specific: Miss Wimple told her bridge club that Mr. Brass was forced to resign.

Indefinite word: They saw a vehicle approaching.

Be specific: They saw a gray Ford sedan approaching.

(2) Omnibus expressions Certain terms have become vague through misuse. By meaning almost anything they mean nothing; their careless use is a mark of fuzzy thinking. Substitute clear, specific expressions.

Examples of terms whose meanings have become vague through overuse and misuse: thing, line, factor, proposition, lots, fun, funny, keen, cute, dumb, grand, swell, rotten, perfectly, absolutely, awfully, get, fix, claimed.

Vague overused term: An army pilot has to be good.

Be specific: An army pilot must have an alert mind, good co-ordination, and trained reactions.

Vague misused term of approval: a nice suit, a nice dinner, a nice time, nice people, nice treatment, a nice job, nice word, a nice idea.

Be specific: A well-cut suit, an appetizing dinner, a pleasant time, well-bred people, friendly treatment, a desirable job, a proper word, an appealing idea.

(3) Unsupported judgments Support your judgments by citing specific evidence. Or, better, present your evidence and let the reader make his own judgment.

Unsupported judgment: The book is interesting.

Give specific evidence: The book accurately pictures life in the Bahamas.

Unsupported judgment: The dance was a failure.

Give specific facts: Only ten couples came to the dance.

Unsupported judgment: Of the three candidates Hammond is the best.

Cite specific evidence: Of the three candidates Hammond has had most experience in public office.

Unsupported judgment: The judge was obviously prejudiced against the defendant.

Give specific evidence: The judge denied the defendant's motion to postpone the case until two of his witnesses could be found.

(4) Undefined general terms Certain useful general terms have specific reference for the writer, but they require definition if that reference is to be clear to his reader. Define your terms by using more specific—not more general—expressions. For example, do not define *edifice* as *a structure*, but rather as *a large or massive building such as a church or palace.*

Undefined general terms: Our nation produces many politicians, but few statesmen. [In what respects does a statesman differ from a politician?]

Define the general terms: Our nation produces many politicians (men able to win elections), but few statesmen (men wise and competent in directing affairs of the state).*

Undefined general terms: Progressive education emphasizes development of the whole child. [Many different educational theories and practices are called "progressive." To which does the writer refer? What is meant by "the whole child"?]

Define the general terms: Progressive education, those educational programs which stress social and psychological adjustment, emphasizes development of the whole child. That is, progressive education is concerned with developing emotional stability and social responsibility as well as with imparting information and teaching skills.

Undefined general terms: The twentieth-century American novel is better than its eighteenth-century predecessor. [Does the writer refer to all novels of each period? What qualities make a novel better?]

* Your definition need not be identical with that of your reader. A definition is neither true nor false. It is only useful or not useful. A definition is useful when it conveys accurately the writer's use of the term.

Define the general terms or substitute more precise expressions: Many of the twentieth-century American novels are closer to everyday life and are simpler in style than their eighteenth-century predecessors. [When a writer defines his terms he often sees that his original statement is inaccurate and must be modified.]

17d. Abstract Terms * Most writing involves some use of abstract terms (terms which refer to no material object or actual experience). But overuse of abstract terms makes communication remote and writing colorless. To say "A consciousness that the scene was a busy one penetrated my senses" does not bring the scene alive. See the picture yourself. Then, by using concrete terms and illustrations, make your reader see, hear, smell, and taste.

Vague abstract terms: She was a faithful mother, always considerate of her children.

Be concrete: She spent long hours washing and cooking for her children and nursing them when they were sick, but she was never too busy to romp with them or to take them walking in the park.

Vague abstract expression: They found numerous means of amusement.

Be concrete: They spent the day skiing and skating; then they eased their weary muscles in big chairs before the fire, and, coffee cups in hand, planned sleigh rides for the next day.

Vague abstract terms: Our fathers held loyally to their ideals of freedom and service.

Be concrete: Our fathers fought for the right to speak freely and to elect their own rulers. They would leave their own affairs to clear the forest, hew the trees, and build a house for a neighbor.

___

* For a treatment of the use of concrete terms, examples, and analogies in longer passages see 46b.

17e. **Faulty Connotation** * In addition to their literal meanings (denotations) words have suggestive powers (connotations). They arouse feelings and emotions and express ideas beyond their simple dictionary definitions. For example, *Christmas* calls to mind more strong and varied feelings than *December 25* does. Choose your words carefully, not only for their denotations, but also for their connotations.

(1) Weak connotation

Weak connotation: After a twenty-year absence he returned to his residence.

Use words with stronger associations: After twenty years of wandering he returned home.

Weak connotation: He remembered the congested streets where he had found amusement in his earlier years.

Use more suggestive terms: He remembered the dirty, crowded streets where he had played as a child.

Weak connotation: The soldiers sat close together to keep warm.

Use a more suggestive word: The soldiers huddled together to keep warm.

(2) Inappropriate connotation

Ludicrous suggestion: She lifted the glass in her thin digits.

Use words suited to the picture you are drawing: She lifted the glass in her slender fingers.

Undignified expression: The governor was bumped off.

Use words suited to the subject: The governor was assassinated.

Clashing imagery: They launched the meeting by singing the *Star Spangled Banner*.

Use words suited to one figure or to none: They began the meeting by singing the *Star Spangled Banner*.

* For a treatment of the sustained use of connotation see 45b.

Startling change of tone: Scientists and government men had been developing the atomic bomb. They brought it to completion secretly. At Hiroshima the first bomb went off with a bang.

Use words suited to the context: Scientists and government men had been developing the atomic bomb. They brought it to completion secretly. At Hiroshima the first bomb exploded with devastating might.

(3) Loaded connotation

Biased phrasing: The Sewall nine met the roughnecks from Ralston. [In which town does the writer live?]

Give your opponents compositional fair play: The Sewall nine met the team from Ralston.

Verdict in advance: Let's study the Republican machine and the Democratic organization.

Avoid prejudgment: Let's study the Republican and Democratic organizations.

Slanted expressions: The leaders of industry and the labor bosses met in an effort to settle the strike.

Avoid prejudicing labels: The leaders of industry and of labor met in an effort to settle the strike. [Or] The leaders of industry and the union officers met in an effort to settle the strike.

Advertising patter: Try our lanolin shampoo. [It may be asking too much to suggest that the advertiser substitute *wool fat* for *lanolin*.]

17f. Faulty Expression of Relationship Use the correct conjunctions and prepositions to express the relationships intended.

Wrong conjunction: He lost all his money, *and* he was unconcerned about it.

Use a conjunction expressing opposition or contrast: He lost all his money, *but* he was unconcerned about it. [Or] *Although* he lost all his money he was unconcerned about it.

Wrong preposition: He dived *in* shallow water.

Use a preposition expressing motion: He dived *into* the shallow water [from the outside].

Ambiguous preposition: He was wounded while fighting *with* the Indians.

Use a preposition expressing opposition: He was wounded while fighting *against* the Indians.

Ambiguous subordinating conjunction: *Since* we won the election they have become very friendly.

Use a more precise connective: *After* we won the election they became very friendly. [Or] *Because* we won the election they have become very friendly.

Ambiguous subordinating conjunction: *While* he isn't in college he has a good mind.

Use a more exact conjunction: *Although* he isn't in college he has a good mind.

EXERCISE

X-17a. Misused Specific Terms

Copy each sentence, replacing misused terms with accurate expressions.

1. Her hat is decorated with several unique feathers, all alike.
2. With his vocal equipment he should be a successful radio singer.
3. Since Joe installed a down-draft carburetor, his car is a superb apparatus.
4. Any salesman who develops an efficient technique for dispensing vacuum cleaners can earn large commissions.
5. Synthetic rubber has longer-wearing faculties than natural rubber.

X-17b. Trite or Hackneyed Expressions

Rewrite, substituting fresh terms for the trite or hackneyed expressions.

1. Take along only tried and true companions when you go on such a dangerous mission.

2. The proud father passed out cigars to celebrate the blessed event.
3. The intrepid detective burned the midnight oil, seeking a clue to the perpetrator of the dastardly crime.
4. The milling crowd grew quiet and stood spellbound as the silver-tongued orator spoke.
5. Her eyes welled with tears as she bade them a fond farewell.

X-17c. General Terms

Rewrite to eliminate vagueness and ambiguity: (1) substitute specific terms for indefinite and omnibus expressions, (2) cite evidence for judgments, and (3) define useful but ambiguous general terms.

1. It has been reliably reported that Congress will be called into special session.
2. A swell fellow, a swell car, a swell dinner, a swell afternoon, a swell party, a swell library, a swell record collection.
3. The referee was obviously unfair in his decisions.
4. Our representative in the legislature was wonderful.
5. A feature of American journalism is sensationalism.
6. There is reason to believe that the prices of certain commodities will rise.
7. Joe is a terrific guy. He drives a nifty car, wears sharp clothes, has a cute laugh, and is anything but dumb.
8. Martin spoke very poorly.
9. I understand a drive against speeders is being launched.
10. Many Americans believe strongly in individual enterprise.

X-17d. Abstract Terms

Rewrite, substituting concrete expressions for abstract terms or defining the abstract terms by means of concrete examples.

1. Dillon was the most unreliable student in the dormitory.
2. His unselfishness inspired many of the neighbors to generosity.
3. Everyone can achieve success, regardless of his social or economic position.
4. The animal gave signs of being in excruciating pain.
5. Her devotion to her parents was manifested in many ways.
6. Modern music is often loud, but seldom beautiful.

7. Every citizen is expected to support the American way of life.
8. The excitement of the crowd was unrestrained as Sanders tallied another score.
9. She demanded more liberty in conducting her business affairs.
10. They moved to an unpleasant part of town.

X-17e. Faulty Connotation

Rewrite, improving the connotation (1) by using words of stronger suggestive power, (2) by substituting terms more appropriate to the context, or (3) by replacing biased terms with expressions not "slanted."

1. Their close association, begun when they were young, continued until they were advanced in age.
2. The former Miss Nancy Briggs snapped the shackles on Mr. Doyle Paddleworth in a formal ceremony at St. Mark's Cathedral Wednesday afternoon.
3. Chief Donovan's flatfeet of the traffic squad are still fumbling around for a solution to the traffic problem.
4. The view of the harbor filled with numerous vessels held our attention for a long time.
5. You must read the book of life carefully if you want to succeed in your career. Otherwise it may end on the rocks.
6. He would never forget the circus with its sounds and odors, its spirit of celebration.
7. Dr. Woody, our new college president, stood at the door and gave the glad hand to each guest as he entered.
8. America's statesman, casually dressed Secretary Bailey, met England's baggy-suited socialist minister, James Cox, to discuss the United States' ten billion dollar handout.
9. Professor Nottingham delivered a darling lecture on the military implications of atomic energy.
10. Easy-off shave cream makes life worth living.

X-17f. Faulty Expression of Relationship

Copy the following sentences, choosing the correct connectives to express the relationships intended.

1. They bought a new house (and, but) were not satisfied with it.

2. She returned home (after, for) the book he had forgotten.
3. He stood (by, with) his father throughout the old man's troubles.
4. They argued (with, against) their former friends.
5. (While, Although) I agree with him (in, on) most points, there are some questions (in, on) which we do not see eye to eye.
6. Mogul's new film is an original comedy (but, and) it is not very humorous.
7. He lowered the boat (in, into) the water.
8. (Because, Since) he became sick he was unable to continue his painting.
9. The swimmers were saved (with, by means of) the life-jackets.
10. He soon joined (into, in) the fun.

GOOD USE

18. Choose words and idioms which are appropriate and in general and approved use.* If your knowledge of an individual word is uncertain consult a good dictionary.

HOW TO USE A DICTIONARY

18a. Selecting a Dictionary The value of a dictionary depends on its completeness and on the care with which it is edited. The most comprehensive dictionaries (listed in **50b**) are available in libraries. For your own desk you should buy a good abridged volume, such as *Webster's New Collegiate Dictionary* (see **18b**), *Webster's Secondary School Dictionary*, Harper & Brothers' *The American College Dictionary*, *Funk and Wagnalls New College Standard Dictionary* or *The Desk Standard Dictionary*, Macmillan's *Modern Dictionary*, Scott, Foresman's *Thorndike Century Senior Dictionary*, the *Winston Simplified Dictionary* (College Edi-

---

* For stylistic principles governing the choice of words see **45** and **46**.

tion), Grosset & Dunlap's *Words: The New Dictionary*, or the *Oxford Concise Dictionary*.

18b. Finding Information in a Dictionary Dictionaries differ in their methods of presenting information about a word. Familiarize yourself with the arrangement of material and the system of notations in your dictionary by studying the explanatory notes in the introductory pages.

The following instructions on the use of a dictionary are based on the entries **crack** and **nice** in *Webster's New Collegiate Dictionary* (1949), published by G. & C. Merriam Company.

(1) Note the part of speech The part of speech is shown by an abbreviation immediately following the phonetic spelling of the word:

> **crack** (krăk), *v.i.* ...

If the word may be used as several parts of speech, each is treated separately, and each use after the first is indicated by a dash and the appropriate abbreviation. Note that *crack* may be an intransitive verb (*"v.i."*), a transitive verb (*"—v.t."*), a noun (*"—n."*), an adverb (*"—adv."*), or an adjective (*"—adj."*).

(2) Refer to the etymology for the origin of a word (but not for its present meaning). The origin and evolution of a word form are shown in brackets:

> **nice** ... [OF., ignorant, fool, fr. L. *nescius* ignorant, fr. *nescire* to be ignorant, fr. *ne-* not + *scire* to know.]

The bracketed matter tells us that *nice* was taken from the Old French word of the same spelling (meaning "ignorant, fool"), which was derived from the Latin word *nescius* (meaning "ignorant"), which still earlier developed from the verb *nescire* ("to be ignorant"), a combining form of *ne-* ("not") plus *scire* ("to know").

(3) Note carefully any limitation on the use of a particular definition Restricted or special meanings are indicated by labels preceding the definitions: *

> **nice** . . . **1.** *Obs.* **a** Foolish; silly. **b** Lewd; wanton. **2.** *Archaic.* Affecting coy reserve; shy. . . .
>
> **crack** . . . **2. a** *Now Dial.* To brag; to boast. **b** *Scot. & N. of Eng.* To chat; to gossip . . . **4. a** *Slang.* To hit; slap. . . . **7.** *Colloq.* To cry up; to extol; to praise;—usually with *up*. . . .

(4) Seek the definition preferred for general (unrestricted) use Any definition not labeled as limited may be accepted as approved for general use. But many words have a number of general meanings which vary in the degree of their acceptability. Some dictionaries (such as *The Desk Standard Dictionary* and *The American College Dictionary*) list the meanings in the order of frequency of current use. Others (such as *Webster's New Collegiate Dictionary*) list them in the order of their historical development. Webster's gives the following generally approved definitions for *nice:*

> **nice** . . . **3.** Fastidious; hence, finical; also refined; discriminating. **4.** Demanding close discrimination, delicate handling, or the like. **5.** Displaying, or characterized by, close discrimination, delicate treatment, etc.; subtle; . . . **6.** Susceptible to fine distinctions, or able to make them; delicately discriminative; hence, of instruments, methods, etc., minutely accurate. **7.** Scrupulous; punctilious. **8.** Pleasing; agreeable. **9.** Properly modest; well-mannered. . . .

* Among the more common labels indicating restricted usage are the following: *Obs.* (obsolete—no longer used), *Archaic* (used only in such writings as Biblical works and poetry), *Dial.* (dialectal—limited to certain geographical areas), *Coll.* or *Colloq.* (colloquial—used in talk rather than in writing; hence informal), *Slang.* If other usage labels in your dictionary are too shortened for the meaning to be clear see the volume's list of abbreviations.

Sometimes you may obtain a clue as to which meanings are preferred by studying the synonyms at the end of an entry. The synonyms for *nice* in *Webster's New Collegiate Dictionary* ("dainty, fastidious, ... squeamish") indicate that the closely related definitions **3, 4, 5,** and **6** are preferred. Definitions which are not suggested by the synonyms (in this instance **8** and **9**) are less likely to be preferred.

HOW TO CORRECT ERRORS OF USE

18c. Faulty Idioms An idiom is a combination of words favored by usage but not easily explained by the usual rules or by the separate meanings of the words. "I enjoy to read" is wrong, not because the words offend logic or grammar, but merely because people do not conventionally make that combination of words. "I like to read" and "I enjoy reading" are good idioms.

Alert reading is the easiest road to a natural use of idiom.

FAULTY IDIOMS	CORRECT IDIOMS
in the year of 1950	in the year 1950
I hope you a good time	I wish you a good time
stay to home	stay at home
different than	different from
independent from	independent of
in search for	in search of
enamored with	enamored of
listen at	listen to
comply to	comply with
win out	win
possessed with ability	possessed of ability

(I) Idioms involving prepositions Make sure that the right preposition accompanies other words. Study the following list of correct idioms:

accord with (a person)	accused by (a person)
according to (rules)	accused of (a theft)

agree to (a proposal)
agree with (a person)
agreeable to

angry at (a condition)
angry with (a person)

careful about (an affair)
careful of (one's money)

convenient for (a purpose)
convenient to (a person)

correspond to (things)
correspond with (persons)

part from (a person)
part with (a thing)

wait for (a person or thing)
wait on (a customer)

(2) Mixed idioms Avoid a compromise between two idioms. That is, do not begin one idiom and shift to a second before the first is completed.

Careless shift from one idiom to another: Hitler had no *hesitation to use* force.
Use only one idiom: Hitler had no *hesitation in using* force. [Or] Hitler did not *hesitate to use* force.

Careless shift from one idiom to another: Marvin asked for the *privilege to take* a make-up examination.
Use only one idiom: Marvin asked for the *privilege of taking* a make-up examination. [Or] Marvin asked for *permission to take* a make-up examination.*

(3) Idiomatic use of articles

Unidiomatic omission of articles: Many political refugees came to United States in nineteenth century.
Supply the articles required by idiomatic usage: Many political refugees came to *the* United States in *the* nineteenth century.†

Unidiomatic inclusion of articles: Any such *a* person ... That kind of *a* man ... A half *an* hour....
Omit the articles not required by idiom: Any such person ... That kind of man ... A half hour. [*or*] Half an hour....

* For additional examples of faulty shift in idiom see **7g**.
† See **2d** for other errors of idiom resulting from the omission of necessary words.

18d. Technical Words and Jargon When writing for the general reader avoid technical terms which might not be readily understood. Words or meanings commonly restricted to a single profession or technical field are so labeled in dictionaries.

Unnecessarily technical for general writing: Alarmed at the *loss ratio*, the company's officers voted to raise the rates for all automobile insurance.

Translate the technical term: Alarmed that losses were increasing out of proportion to the premiums collected, the company's officers voted to raise the rates for all automobile insurance.

Unnecessary use of technical jargon: A pilot always *revs up* his engines before take-off. [Although *take-off*, as here used, is also to an extent a technical term, it is readily understood.]

Substitute a generally understood term: A pilot always races his engines before take-off. [Or]

Explain the technical term used: A pilot always revs up his engines (runs them at high speed) before take-off.

Educational jargon: The motivated low I.Q. sections fell into the third quartile.

In general writing clarify the technical terms: Members of the low intelligence groups who were given some incentive achieved scores which put them in the third quarter of those tested.

Journalese: The Tivoli's double bill offers this week's paying customers ample thrills and chills.

Avoid strain for novelty: The Tivoli's double feature program offers this week's patrons excitement and mystery.

18e. Colloquial Terms *Colloquial* means used in colloquy or speech, especially informal conversation. You may appropriately use many colloquial words in informal writing, especially in personal letters. But in writing formal papers be on your guard. Use colloquial terms only where they will not strike discords.

LOW COLLOQUIALISMS

| cussed | contraption | a swig | tuckered out |
| plumb crazy | a sight of | tote | gumption |

Inappropriately mixed colloquial and formal terms: Our first fund-raising drive was a flop, but we won much good will which should come in handy whenever we decide to renew our efforts.

Use formal terms throughout (in formal writing): Our first fund-raising drive was unsuccessful, but we won much good will which should be advantageous whenever we decide to renew our efforts. [Or]

Use colloquial terms consistently (in informal writing): Our drive for funds was a flop, but we won a lot of good will which should come in handy if we elect to try the thing again.

18f. **Slang** Slang is a language which comprises certain widely current terms having a forced, fantastic, or grotesque meaning, or exhibiting eccentric humor or fancy. Though a slang term sometimes satisfies a need and becomes established in a language, in most instances it is short-lived. The least desirable types of slang are these:

Expressions of vulgar origin (from criminal classes, the prize ring, cheap radio programs, etc.): dope, ten grand, down for the count, take it on the lam, hep, rod [*for* gun], hood [*for* gangster], picklepuss.

Language strained or distorted for novel effect: He bingled a tall drive that sent the horsehide rambling out into center garden.

Blanket expressions used as substitutes for thinking: swell, lousy, awful [for *very*], terrific, nuts, it's a honey.

18g. **Illiterate or Ungrammatical Forms** Avoid words and expressions which the dictionary does not print. Avoid words which the dictionary labels *illiterate, vulgar, low,* or the like. (See the Glossary of Faulty Diction in the next article.)

18h. **Euphemisms and Genteelisms** In impersonal writing avoid euphemisms (softened expressions for something unpleasant or not quite proper) and genteelisms (elegant terms, especially those intended to suggest high social standing).

EXAMPLES OF EUPHEMISMS	EXAMPLES OF GENTEELISMS
passed away, is among the departed, etc., for *died*	*saleslady* for *saleswoman*
blessed event for *birth*	*laundress* for *washerwoman*
elderly for *old*	*custodian* for *janitor*
recreation center for *pool hall*	*sanitary engineer* for *street cleaner*
perspire for *sweat*	*serviceman* for *repairman*
story or *fib* for *lie*	*attorney-at-law* for *lawyer*
expectorate for *spit*	*realtor* for *real estate agent*
limb for *leg*	*public relations counselor* for *publicity agent*
lingerie for *underwear*	*modiste* for *dressmaker*
cocktail lounge for *bar*	*officer of the law* for *policeman*
intoxicated for *drunk*	*riding academy* for *livery stable*

EXERCISE

X-18b. Finding Information in a Dictionary

Note on your paper the name of the dictionary you use in completing the following exercise. (Use one of those mentioned in Article 18a or 50b.)

1. The following words may be used as what parts of speech? List the words and after each indicate the parts of speech.

   a. contract   *c.* eccentric   *e.* much
   b. brood   *d.* incommensurable

2. Give the etymology of the following words. Write the explanation in full; do not merely copy the signs and abbreviations from the dictionary.

    a. sophomore   *c.* chief   *e.* interfere
    b. bridegroom   *d.* descend

3. List the following words and indicate what restricted, special, or technical meanings each has (such as *slang, colloquial, archaic, law,* etc.)

    a. cut   *c.* sharp   *e.* attaint
    b. section   *d.* dope

4. Study the explanatory notes of the dictionary you ordinarily use. Write a statement telling whether your dictionary lists definitions in the order of their historical development or in the order of their most common current use.

5. For each of the following words (1) copy the preferred general meaning(s) of the word, (2) give one closely allied synonym, and (3) give one antonym if your dictionary lists one.

    a. declare   *c.* termination   *e.* suggestion
    b. charge (v.t.)   *d.* awkward

X-18c. Faulty Idioms

Copy the following sentences, selecting from the parentheses the proper word for idiomatic use.

1. They decided to stay (to, at) home.
2. The course provides knowledge (of, in) personal hygiene and creates interest (of, in) it.
3. The children compare the customs of the United States (to, with) those of foreign countries.
4. She was enamored (to, with, of) herself in the role of Juliet.
5. At an early age he learned obedience (to, for) his parents and respect (for, to) them.

X-18d. Technical Words and Jargon

Write five sentences using technical terms or jargon common to vocations or fields with which you are familiar. Then rewrite the sentences, substituting commonly understood expressions or explaining the technical words.

X-18e, f, g. Colloquial Terms and Slang

Rewrite items 1-5, using correct informal diction and constructions and omitting slang. Rewrite items 6-10 in consistently formal language.

1. He hasn't got nobody to go his bail, so I guess he'll cool in the jug for a spell.
2. When it comes to hot rods, he's hep.
3. If you get a yen for some ham-and, you will discover the ingredients arrayed in the refrigerator.
4. They got no call to shove off the blame onto me.
5. She's a dumb doll, but she has lots of poise.
6. The offer sounds swell to us. Are you absolutely sure there's no catch to it?
7. Am I going? Natch! If pater comes through with the shekels for some new rags.
8. Millie blew her top when I informed her we were broke and wouldn't be able to make the shindig.
9. There ain't hardly any use in us studying. We're cinches to flunk out irregardless.
10. Considering what a big wheel he is, he sure hasn't got much know-how.

X-18h. Euphemisms and Genteelisms

Copy, replacing the euphemisms and genteelisms with ordinary, direct terms.

1. John has told me one prevarication, and I'll not believe him again.
2. The old gentleman was laid to rest in the new cemetery.
3. Put your soiled garments here. The washlady will come this morning.
4. William expects to be a mortician.
5. Horace insisted that he was only slightly inebriated, but the judge took his driver's license for six months.

GLOSSARY OF FAULTY DICTION

19. Use only such terms and forms as are employed by careful writers. Do not confuse expressions similar in spelling or sound.

Accept and **except.** *Accept* means *to receive; except* as a verb means *to exclude* and as a preposition means *with the exception of.* "He accepts the nomination." "The army accepts [takes in] the fit, but excepts [leaves out] the unfit." "All were present except Susan."

Affect and **effect.** *Affect* is not used as a noun (except in a specialized psychological sense); *effect* as a noun means *result.* As verbs, *affect* means *to influence in part; effect* means *to accomplish totally.* "His story affected me deeply." "The Russians effected a revolution." *Affect* also has a special meaning, *to feign.* "She has an affected manner."

Ain't. Never correct. Say *I'm not, you [we, they] aren't, he [she, it] isn't.*

All the farther, all the faster. Dialectal. Use *as far as, as fast as* in such sentences as "This is all the farther I can go."

Allusion and **illusion.** *Allusion* means a *reference; illusion* means a *deceptive appearance.* "A Biblical allusion." "An optical illusion."

Already and **all ready.** *Already* means *by this time* or *beforehand; all ready* means *wholly ready* or *every one ready.* "I have already invited him." "Dinner is all ready." "We are all ready for dinner."

Alright. Not in good use. Use *all right.*

Altogether *and* **all together.** *Altogether* means *wholly, entirely; all together* means *collectively, in a group.* "He is altogether honest." "The King sent the people all together into exile."

And which. Often involves a conflict between coördination and subordination. Wrong: This is a vital problem *and which* we cannot study too closely. Right: This is a vital problem, *which* we cannot study too closely. Also right: This is a problem *which* is vital *and which* we cannot study too closely.

A good rule of thumb is, "Do not use *and which* unless you have already used *which* in the sentence." But an exception must be made for sentences like the following: "He told me what countries he had visited, and which ones he liked most."

Anxious and **eager.** *Anxious* means *disquieted* or *concerned.* *Eager* means *keenly desirous* or *spirited.*

Any place, anyplace. *Any place* is colloquial when used for the adverb *anywhere* or the adverbial phrase *in any place.* *Anyplace* is not an accepted form.

As. (*a*) Incorrect in the sense of *that* or *whether.* Wrong: "I don't know *as* I can tell you [Use *whether*]." "Not *as* I know [Use *that*]." (*b*) *As . . . as* are correlatives. *Than* must not replace the second *as.* Right but awkward: "As good as or better than his neighbors." Improved: "As good as his neighbors, or better [than they]." See **Like.**

Auto. An abbreviation not desirable in formal writing.

Awful. Means *filling with awe* or *filled with awe.* *Awful* is slang when used in the sense of *uncivil, serious,* or *ludicrous,* or (in the adverbial form) in the sense of *very, extremely.*

Bad and **badly.** (1) *Bad* is always correct as an adjective (*badly* is colloquial). "His conduct was *bad.*" "He feels *bad* [rather than *badly;* see Article **13b**]." (2) *Badly* is always correct as an adverb (*bad* is colloquial). Rather crude: "He did *bad* in the algebra exam." Better: "He did *badly*. . . ."

Balance. Colloquial when used in the sense of *remainder.*

Because. Not to be used for *the fact that.* "*The fact that* [not *because*] he is absent is no reason why we should not proceed."

Between. Ordinarily used of two persons or things, in distinction to *among,* which is used of more than two. But in certain collective relationships *among* does not convey the idea intended and *between* should be employed. Multiple contrast: "There are marked temperamental differences between Slavs, Teutons, and Latins." Each item considered severally in relation to each of the others: "Conferences between Ordway, Cantwell, and Leaman clarified all uncertainties as to their respective claims." Reciprocal action: "An alliance was effected between Germany, Italy, and Japan."

Blame on. Colloquial for *put the blame on* or *blame.* Faulty: "Don't blame it on me." Better: "Don't blame me."

Borned. A monstrosity for *born.* "I was born [not *borned*] in 1925."

Bursted. Dialectal. The past tense of *burst* is the same as the present.

Bust or **busted.** Inelegant or slang for *burst.* Right: "Yesterday the water pipe burst." "The bank failed."

But what. *That* is often preferable. "I do not doubt *that* [not *but what*] he is honest."

Can and **may.** *Can* means *to be able; may* means *to have permission. Can* for *may* has a certain colloquial standing.

Cannot help but. A confusion of *can but* and *cannot help*. "I can but believe you"; or "I cannot help believing you"; not "I cannot help but believe you."

Caused by. Not to be used to refer to a verb or to the diffused idea of a clause. Wrong: "He was disappointed caused by the lateness of the train." Right: "His disappointment was caused by the lateness of the train."

Claim. Means *to ask or demand as a right or due*. Colloquial for *maintain* or *assert*.

Complected. Dialectal. *Light-complexioned* and *dark-complexioned*, though correct, are long and awkward. Prefer *fair* and *dark*.

Considerable. Colloquial when used as an adverb. "He talked *considerably* [not *considerable*] about it." "He looks *considerably* [not *considerable*] better."

Could of. An illiterate form arising from slovenly pronunciation. Use *could have*. Avoid also *may of, must of, would of*.

Credible and **creditable.** *Credible* means *capable* or *worthy of belief; creditable* means *meritorious*.

Different than. *Different from* is correct. *Than* is a conjunction. The idea of separation implied in *different* calls for a preposition rather than a word of comparison.

Disremember. Not in good use.

Done. A gross error when used as the past tense of *do*, or as an adverb meaning *already*. "*I did it* [not *I done it*]." "I've *already* [not *done*] got my lessons."

Don't. A contraction for *do not;* never to be used for *does not*. The contraction for *does not* is *doesn't*.

Doubt that it won't. A double negative. "I *doubt that* the engine won't start" means, logically, "I *am not sure that* it *won't* start"; that is, "I *think that* probably it *will* start." If you really doubt, follow the verb *doubt* with a positive instead of a negative statement: "I doubt that the engine will start."

Dove. Colloquial for *dived.*

Drownded. Vulgar for *drowned.*

Due to. An adjective; in current use often employed as an adverb. Grammatically correct use (modifying a noun): "His refusal of the offer was due to his father's opposition." Still grammatically questionable (modifying a verb): "He refused the offer, due to his father's opposition." The traditional adverbial modifier is *because of*: "He refused the offer because of his father's opposition."

Eager. See Anxious.

Emigrate and immigrate. *Emigrate* means *to leave one country to seek residence in another; immigrate* means *to enter a country not one's own for the purpose of residing there.* The same man may *emigrate* from Europe and *immigrate* into the United States.

Enthuse. Colloquial. Not in good use in formal writing.

Etc. An abbreviation for the Latin *et cetera,* meaning *and other* [*things*]. Do not use unless the *other things* will come readily to the reader's mind. *Et* means *and;* therefore avoid *and etc.* Do not misspell the abbreviation by transposing *t* and *c.*
  Etc. Except at the end of a sentence, this abbreviation should be followed (as well as preceded) by a comma. "You will find stationery, etc., in the observation car."

Expect. Means *to look forward to.* Colloquial in the sense of *suppose* or *surmise.*

Fine. Use cautiously as an adjective, and not at all as an adverb. Seek a more exact word.

Fix. Overused and often abused. Choose a more exact word when you can.

Former. Means the first or first named of two. Not to be used when more than two have been named. The corresponding word is *latter*.

For to. Incorrect for *to*. "He made up his mind *to* [not *for to*] accept." "I want *you* [not *for you*] to listen carefully."

Funny. Colloquial for *strange, queer, odd*.

Gent. A vulgar abbreviation of *gentleman*.

Get. A verb of many uses and meanings. In formal discourse avoid the slang or colloquial ones, especially these: "I get it [understand it]," "The grapefruit juice got him [struck him] in the eye," "His enemies are out to get him [destroy him or kill him]," "Such things get me [irritate or disturb me]."

Get to. Dialectal in expresssions like "Ev didn't get to come" and "The batter bunted but the runner didn't get to get home." Say "Ev couldn't come" and "The batter bunted but the runner had no chance to get home."

Go, went. Avoid in slang or dialectal senses: "He didn't go [intend] to break the vase," "I can't go [endure] such conduct," "When he went [began or showed his intention] to tell us, something interrupted."

Good. An adjective, not an adverb. Wrong: "He did good in mathematics." Right: "He did well in mathematics." "He did good work in mathematics."

Got and have got. Overworked; often used needlessly. Redundant: "I have got to change those spark plugs." [Say: "I have to change..." or "I must change...."]

Gotten. An old form now usually replaced by *got* except in such expressions as *ill-gotten gains.*

Guess. Expresses conjecture. Preferably not used for *think, suppose,* or *expect* unless implying uncertainty.

Had of and **had have.** Illiterate. "I wish I *had known* [not *had of* or *had have known*] about it."

Had ought. Illiterate. "He *ought* [not *had ought*] to have resigned." "We *oughtn't* [not *hadn't ought*] to make this error."

Hanged and **hung.** *Hanged* is the correct past tense of *hang* in the sense *put to death, hanged on the gallows; hung* is the correct past tense for the general meaning *suspended.*

Hardly. Not to be used with a negative.

Healthy and **healthful.** *Healthy* means *having health; healthful* means *giving health.* "Milk is healthful." "The climate of Colorado is healthful." "The boy is healthy." In colloquial usage the distinction is not always observed.

Heighth. Improper spelling (and pronunciation) of *height.*

Hygienic and **sanitary.** Both words mean *pertaining to health. Hygienic* is used when the condition is a matter of personal habits or rules; *sanitary* is used when the condition is a matter of surroundings (water supply, food supply, sewage disposal, etc.) or the relations of numbers of people.

In. Often misused for *into.* "He jumped *into* [not *in*] the pond."

Infer and **imply.** *Infer* ordinarily means *to conclude from facts or reasoning. Imply* means *to express indirectly, to suggest.* "From what you say I infer that the dispute has been settled." "Your words imply that the dispute has been settled."

Instants and **instance.** *Instants* means *small portions of time;* *instance* means *an example.*

Intensives (too, so, such, that). Good writers do not ordinarily use *too, so,* or *such* by itself as an intensive. Instead they do one of three things: (1) omit the intensive altogether (probably the best treatment); (2) employ an intensive like *very, much, extremely,* or *indeed;* or (3) complete the thought of *too* with a following phrase, or the thought of *so* or *such* with a following *that* clause.

Informal: The story was too absurd. Coal whined so piteously. Wilberforce is such a fast walker.

Better (method 1 or 2): The story was absurd. Coal whined piteously. Wilberforce is an exceedingly fast walker.

Also better (method 3): The story was too absurd for belief. Coal whined so piteously that I let him in. Wilberforce is such a fast walker that he almost meets himself coming back.

That as an intensive is colloquial. Not good usage: "I was that tired." For the use of superlatives as intensives see **Superlatives.**

Irregardless. Never use. Say *regardless.*

It's. Means *it is;* not to be written for the possessive *its.*

Kind of. (*a*) Colloquial when used to modify adjectives or verbs. "He was *somewhat* [not *kind of*] lean." "She *half suspected* [not *kind of suspected*] what was going on." (*b*) When used with a noun it is not followed by *a.* "That *kind of man*"; not "That *kind of a man.*"

Lady. A genteelism in many uses. Prefer *woman* in such expressions as these: "A *woman* I know," "The *woman* in blue," "A *saleswoman* [not *saleslady, washlady*]."

Later and **latter.** *Later* means *more late*; latter means *the second in a series of two. The latter* is used in conjunction with the phrase *the former.*

Lead and **led.** *Led* is the past tense of the verb *to lead. Lead* is the present tense. The metal is spelled *lead* and pronounced *lĕd.*

Learn and **teach.** *Learn* means *to get knowledge of; teach* means *to give knowledge of* or *to.* "The instructor *teaches* [not *learns*] me physics." "He *learns* his lessons easily."

Leave and **let.** *Leave* means *to abandon; let* means *to permit.* "*Let* us [not *leave* us] face it."

Less and **fewer.** *Less* refers to quantity; *fewer* refers to number. "He has *fewer* [not *less*] friends than he had."

Let's us. This form crudely repeats the pronoun. The correct colloquial substitute for *let us* is *let's.* Especially avoid *Let's you and I.* "*Let's* [not *Let's you and I*] enter the contest."

Liable. See **Likely.**

Lie and **lay.** *Lay*, a transitive verb, means *to cause to lie.* "I lay the book on the table and it lies there." A source of confusion between the two words is that the past tense of *lie* is *lay*:

I lie down to sleep.	I lay the book on the table.
I lay there yesterday.	I laid it there yesterday.
I have lain here for hours.	I have laid it there many times.

Like, as, as if. *Like* is in good use as a preposition and may be followed by a noun; *as* is in good use as a conjunction and may be followed by a clause. The use of *like* as a conjunction is colloquial. Right: "He is tall like his father." "He is tall, as his father is." "It looks *as if* [not *like*] it's going to rain."

Likely, apt, and liable. *Likely* and *apt* merely predict (connect them with *likelihood*). *Liable* conveys the idea of harm or of being responsible (connect it with *liability*). "It is likely to be a pleasant day." "I am apt to stay longer than I should." "He is liable for damages."

Literally. Means *in actual fact, truly, not figuratively*. Do not use where you plainly do not mean it, as in the sentence "I was literally tickled to death."

Locate. Colloquial for *settle* or *establish oneself*.

Lose and loose. *Lose* means *to cease having; loose* as a verb means *to set free*, and as an adjective, *free, not bound*.

Lose out. Not used in formal writing. Say *lose*.

Lots of. A mercantile term which has a dubious colloquial standing. Not in good literary use for *many* or *much*.

Might of. A vulgarism for *might have*.

Most. Colloquial when used for *almost*. "*Almost* [not *most*] all."

Muchly. Wrong adverbial form. Say "*much* [not *muchly*] improved."

Neither. Used with *nor*, and not with *or*. "Neither the man whom his associates had suspected *nor* [not *or*] the one whom the police had arrested was the criminal." "She could neither paint a good picture *nor* [not *or*] play the violin well."

Nice. Means *delicate* or *precise* in the best literary usage. *Nice* is used informally to indicate general approval, but the best writers avoid this use. Approved usage: "He displayed nice judgment." "We had a *pleasant* [not *nice*] time."

Noplace. Wrong form of *no place*.

Not . . . no, not never, not hardly. In early English the double negative was in good use. In modern English it is commonly considered that "two negatives cancel each other" or make an affirmative. Thus *not nobody* now means *somebody*, and *not nowhere* suggests *somewhere*.

Nowhere near. Archaic and dialectal for *not nearly*.

Nowheres. Dialectal or vulgar.

O, Oh. *O* is ordinarily used with a noun in direct address; it is not separated from the noun by any marks of punctuation. *Oh* is ordinarily used as an interjection; it is followed by a comma or an exclamation point. *Oh* is sometimes used informally in direct address; it is followed by a comma. "Hear, O King, what thy servants would say." "Oh, he's falling!" "Oh, Sam, Jim wants you."

Of. Do not use for *have*. "He should *have* [not *of*] gone."

Off of. This expression needlessly contains two prepositions and repeats the idea of separation. Use *off* alone. "He jumped *off* [not *off of*] the platform."

O.K. (OK, okay, okey). Colloquial except when used in endorsing documents.

On account of. Do not use as a conjunction. "He is feeble *on account of his age* [not *on account of he is old*]."

One, one's; he, his. The interchange of *he* and *his* with *one* and *one's* is accepted American usage, especially in informal speech and writing. "One can only do his best." "One can only do one's best" is very formal. Also correct: "A person can only do his best."

Only. Place *only* where it cannot appear to modify the wrong word. Wrong: "He *only* spent ten dollars." Right: "He spent *only* ten dollars." Do not carelessly precede with *not*. Wrong: "He *isn't only* three years old." Right:

"He *is only* three years old." Do not use in place of *but*. Wrong: "I would like to go *only* I haven't time." Right: ". . . *but* I haven't time."

Ought to of. A vulgarism for *ought to have*.

Over with. Colloquial for *over*.

Party. Slang when used for *a person*, except in legal phrases.

Perfectly all right. *All right* carries the idea of absoluteness. Omit *perfectly*.

Phenomena. Plural. "It was an interesting *phenomenon* [not *phenomena*]."

Phone. A contraction not employed in formal writing. Say *telephone*.

Plenty. A noun; not in good use as an adjective or adverb. "He had *plenty of* [not *plenty*] resources." "He had *resources in plenty* [not *resources plenty*]." "It is *extremely* [not *plenty*] cold."

Practical and **practicable.** *Practical* means *not theoretical; practicable* means *capable of being put into practice*. "A practical man." "The arrangement is practicable."

Predominate and **predominant.** Do not substitute the verb form *predominate* for the adjective form *predominant*. "The *predominant* [not *predominate*] group favors these measures." "Factory workers *predominate* in this district."

Principal and **principle.** *Principal* as an adjective means *chief* or *leading; principle* as a noun means a *general truth* or *rule*. *Principal* as a noun means a *sum of money*, or the *chief official of a school*.

Proof and **evidence.** In a law court, *proof* is *evidence sufficient to establish a fact; evidence* is *whatever is brought forward in an attempt to establish a fact*. "The evidence against the prisoner was extensive but hardly proof of his guilt." In colloquial speech, *proof* is sometimes loosely used as a synonym for *evidence*.

Proposition. Means a *thing proposed*. Colloquial when used of an action, a commercial undertaking, or a commodity to be sold. Right: "I will make this *proposition;* he may accept it or not." "It is sure to be a paying *venture* [or *transaction* or *enterprise*, not *proposition*]."

Quiet and **quite.** *Quiet* is an adjective meaning *calm, not noisy; quite* is an adverb meaning *entirely*, or (in colloquial use) *to a large degree*.

Quite a. Colloquial in such expressions as *quite a while* and *quite a number*. Both colloquial and illogical in *quite a few* (= a few in a large degree).

Raise. Many persons feel that *rear* or *bring up* is preferable in speaking of children. "She *raised* sheep and *brought up* her seven children without help."

Rarely ever. Crude for *rarely, hardly ever*.

Real. Uncultivated, crude for *very* or *really*. "She was *very* [not *real*] intelligent." "He was *really* [not *real*] brave."

Remember of. Not to be used for *remember*.

Respectfully and **respectively.** *Respectfully* means *in a courteous manner; respectively* means *as pertaining to each*. "Yours *respectfully* [not *respectively*]." "He handed the check and the dun to Gray and Hodgins *respectively*."

Right smart and **right smart of.** Dialectal.

Rise and **raise.** *Rise* is an intransitive verb; *raise* is a transitive verb. "I rise to go home." "I raise vegetables." "I raise the stone from the ground."

Said. Meaning *before-mentioned, already referred to* is in good use in legal language only.

172

Same. No longer used as a pronoun except in legal documents. "He saw her drop the purse and restored *it* [not *the same*] to her."

Scarcely. Not to be used with a negative.

Seldom ever. Illiterate for *seldom, hardly ever.*

Shall and will. For use of these words see 12e(2) and c(1).

Sight. *A sight* or *a sight of* is colloquial for *many, much, a great deal of.* "A great many [not *a sight*] of them."

Sit and set. *Set* as a transitive verb means *to cause to sit.* "He *sets* the chair in the corner." "The chair always *sits* before the desk."

   Set as an intransitive verb has two special uses: "The sun *sets.*" "The hen *sets* till the eggs are hatched."

   The past tense and past participle of *set* are *set;* those of *sit* are *sat:*

I always set it in its place.	I sit down.
I set it in its place yesterday.	He sat in this very chair.
I have always set it just here.	A vase has always sat on the mantel.

So. Not incorrect, but loose, vague, and often unnecessary. (*a*) For the use of *so* as an intensive see **Intensives.** (*b*) The frequent use of *so* as a connective is a mark of amateurishness. *So* is an elastic word that covers a multitude of vague meanings. Language has need of such a word, and in many instances (especially when the relation between clauses is obvious and does not need to be pointed out) *so* serves well enough. Use it, but not as a substitute for more exact connectives. Beware of falling into the "so" habit.

Abuse of *so* as a vague coördinating connective: So I went to call on Mrs. Woods, and so she told me about Mrs. White's new gown; so then I missed the car, and so of course our supper is late. [Strike out every *so.*]

In expressing reason or result do not always begin with a main clause and follow it with a trailing *so* clause. It is better to strike out *so* and reduce the first clause to a phrase or a subordinate clause. Thus for the sentence "I was excited, so I missed the target" substitute one of the following:

> In my excitement I missed the target.
> Because I was excited I missed the target.
> Being excited, I missed the target.

In expressing degree or manner prefer the form *so ... that*:

> Right: I was so excited that I missed the target.

Some. Not to be used as an adverb. "She was *somewhat* [not *some*] better the next day." Wrong: "He studied some that night." Right: "He did some studying that night."

Someplace. Wrong form for *at some place*. Wrong: "They could land someplace or other." Right: "They could land at some place or other."

Some place. Colloquial when used as an adverb. Use *somewhere* or the adverbial phrase *in any place*.

Somewheres. Dialectal. Use *somewhere*.

Species. Has the same form in singular and plural. "He discovered a new *species* [not *specie*] of sunflower." *Specie* means *metal money*.

Stationary and **stationery.** *Stationary* is an adjective meaning *fixed; stationery* is a noun meaning *writing materials*.

Statue, stature, statute. *Statue* means *a carved or molded figure; stature* means *height; statute* means *a law*.

Such. (*a*) For the demonstrative use of *such* see **Intensives.** (*b*) To be completed by *that*, rather than by *so that*, when a result clause follows. "There was such a crowd *that* [not

174

so that] he did not find his friends." (*c*) To be completed by *as*, rather than by *that*, *who*, or *which*, when a relative clause follows. "I will accept such arrangements *as* [not *that*] may be made." "He called upon such soldiers *as* [not *who*] would volunteer for this service to step forward."

Superior than. Not in good use for *superior to*.

Superlatives. Should not be used as intensives. When they are used in making comparisons, the basis of the comparison should be supplied. Informal: "This is the best fudge!" "She is the cleverest cat!" Better: "This is delicious fudge!" "She is a clever cat [or *a remarkably clever cat*]!" Also better: "Of all the fudge I have ever tasted, this is the best." (See **Intensives.**)

Sure. Colloquial (sometimes slang) when used as an adverb. "It *surely* [not *sure*] was pleasant." In answer to the question "Will you go?" either *sure* or *surely* is correct, though *surely* is preferred. "[To be] sure." "[You may be] sure." "[I will] surely [go]."

Suspicion. A noun. Dialectal when used as a verb. "He *suspected* [not *suspicioned*] their motives."

Take and. Often unnecessary, sometimes crude. Redundant: "He took the ax and sharpened it." Better: "He sharpened the ax." Crude: "He took and nailed up the box." Better: "He nailed up the box."

Tend. In the sense *to look after*, takes a direct object without an interposed *to*. "The milliner's assistant *tends* [not *tends to*] the shop."

That. See **Intensives.**

That there. Illiterate for *that*. "I want *that* [not *that there*] box of berries."

Them. Not to be used as an adjective. *"Those* [not *them*] boys."

There were or **there was.** Do not use unnecessarily. Crude: "There were seventeen senators voted for the bill." Better: "Seventeen senators voted for the bill."

These kind (or **sort**) and **those kind** (or **sort**). Colloquial forms loosely used for *this kind, that kind. Kind* and *sort* are singular nouns and regularly take the singular adjectives *this, that*—not plural *these, those.* Right: "Why do you buy *this kind* of shoes?" "I hate *that sort* of trousers."

This. Do not use *this* so loosely and vaguely that the reader fails to see what word or idea is referred to (see **5**). Faulty: "The managers told him they would increase his salary if he would represent them in South America. He refused this." Better: "He refused this offer."

This here. Dialectal for *this.*

Those. Do not carelessly omit a relative clause after *those.* Faulty: "He is one of those talebearers." Right: "He is one of those talebearers whom everybody dislikes." [Or] "He is a talebearer."

Those kind, those sort. Ungrammatical. See **These kind.**

Thusly. Wrong adverbial form. Use *thus.*

Til, 'til, and **till.** *Til* is an improper form of *till* or *until.* *'Til,* though it may be defended as an abbreviation of *until,* is not accepted by good writers. Do not carelessly misuse *till* for *when.* "I had scarcely strapped on my skates *when* [not *till*] Henry fell through an air hole."

Too. See **Intensives.**

Transpire. Means *to give forth* or *to become known.* "The secret transpired." Careful writers object to the use of *transpire* for *occur*. "The sale of property *occurred* [not *transpired*] last Thursday."

Unique. Means *alone of its kind*, not *odd* or *unusual*.

United States. Ordinarily preceded by *the*. "The United States raised a large army." [Not "United States raised a large army."]

Up. Do not needlessly insert after such verbs as *end*, *rest*, *confess*, *settle*.

Used to could. Very crude. Say *used to be able to* or *once could*.

Very. Should be accompanied by *much* when used with the past participle. "He was *very much* [not *very*] pleased with his reception." "We were *much* [not *very*] inconvenienced by her visit."

Want to. Not to be used in the sense of *should*, *had better*. "You *should* [not *want to*] keep in good physical condition."

Way. Dialectal or colloquial when used for *away*. "*Away* [not *way*] below the average."

Ways. Colloquial for *way* in referring to distance. "A little *way* [not *ways*]."

When. (*a*) Not to be used for *that* in such a sentence as "It was in the afternoon that the races began." (*b*) A *when* clause, being adverbial, should not be used as a predicate noun. See 13c.

Where. (*a*) Not to be used for *that* in such a sentence as "I see in the paper that our team lost the game." (*b*) A *where* clause, being adverbial, should not be used as a predicate noun. See 13c.

Where at. Illiterate. "Where is he?" [Not "Where is he *at*?"]

Which. Do not use for *who* or *that* in referring to persons. "The friends *who* [not *which*] had loved him in his boyhood were still faithful to him."

Who. Do not use for *which* or *that* in referring to animals or things.

Will. For correct use of *shall* and *will* see 12e(2).

Win out. Not used in formal writing or speaking. Say *win*.

Woods. The singular form should ordinarily be preferred. "*A wood* [not *A woods*]."

Would have. Do not use for *had* in *if* clauses. "If you *had* [not *would have*] spoken boldly, he would have granted your request."

Would of. A vulgarism for *would have*.

Yourself. Intensive or reflexive; do not use when the personal pronoun will suffice. "You [not *Yourself*] and your family must come."

You was. Illiterate. Use *you were* in both singular and plural.

EXERCISE

X-19. Faulty Diction

Rewrite, correcting all faults of diction.

1. This is all the farther we can go until we get money for more gas.
2. The bottles of hair tonic were altogether on the shelf.
3. Don't blame it on me. You three were supposed to settle the thing between yourselves.
4. Being in college is a lot different than being in high school.
5. I expect you want me to pay my rent in advance.
6. The baby was so pretty. It's a shame it wasn't more healthful.
7. Leave the note lay there on the table so as he can find it easily.

8. Most all of us lost out financially by locating in the east part of town.
9. I have lots of proof the proposition will not pay off.
10. They set so stationery I suspicioned they might of been dummies.
11. If you want to keep in good shape, take and tend to a lot of horses way out in the country for a summer.
12. I used to could settle up my business with Roxwell in no time at all. With this here new man I'm very delayed every day.
13. This here car has lose bearings, and its apt to break down out nowheres.
14. I expect you to be already by eight o'clock.
15. She says she doesn't reckon as she wants to go anyplace tonight.
16. It could of been the light-complected girl, yet I can't help but believe she's honest.
17. He don't look like an emigrant to this country.
18. They had ought to have gotten their grades by now.
19. He has promised to learn me how to play golf, but I'd feel kind of silly practicing in front of a bunch of people.
20. There's not nowhere near as nice people here as they was back home.
21. Neither you or I has discovered who is the principle party behind the plot.
22. There were plenty men in the company, but the manager only let Carter do the buying, and he wasn't very practicable.
23. These kind of fish are a right smart tastier than that there specie, even though the later are sort of unique.
24. He was the kind of a writer which tells every detail of what transpires in a man's life.
25. If you would have waited til I phoned you, you could of bought tickets with Bill and myself.

Spelling

No one is able to spell all words on demand. But in formal writing every one must spell correctly even unusual words. You should own and have instant access to a dictionary. Though the dictionaries listed in Article **50b** are the most comprehensive, a good abridged volume will meet your normal spelling needs (see the list in Article **18a**).

Ready access to a dictionary, however, has one disadvantage to you in your spelling. You may depend upon the volume too much. The ideal course is to consult your dictionary every time you really need it, but to teach yourself to need it seldom. You can gain a large degree of independence from it by means of (*a*) careful observation and (*b*) a clear knowledge of certain rules.

SPELLING THROUGH OBSERVATION

20. Make a habit of observing the exact combination of letters in every ordinary word. Concentrate upon a few words at a time; fix their spelling in mind, review them often, make your mastery over them permanent.

HOW TO IMPROVE YOUR SPELLING THROUGH OBSERVATION

20a. Identify Your Errors Record in correct form the words you yourself habitually misspell. The list will be shorter than you think. It may comprise not more than twenty or thirty words. Unless you are extraordinarily deficient, it will certainly not comprise more than a hundred or a hundred and fifty. But these words trip you again and again. Your first task is to identify them—to hunt them out as enemies who are striking at you unrecognized.

20b. **Visualize Words** Make use of the eye in learning to spell. Teach yourself to look so carefully at written or typed words that a false spelling or misprint will stand out like a deformity. In lists of words you are learning to spell underscore or capitalize the troublesome letters, and thus bring to your aid the powerful reinforcement of vision.

In the following list note the italicized letters as indicating trouble spots. (Some of the difficulties are partly due to the indistinct sound given unaccented syllables.)

all right	defi*n*ite	incl*i*nation
*al*most	*de*scribed	maint*e*nance
ap*t*itude	di*v*ide	opp*o*rtunity
ch*o*sen	*etc.*	parli*a*ment
could *have*	excell*e*nt	pleas*a*nt

prep*a*ration	sac*ri*fice
prev*a*lent	sep*a*rate
privi*l*ege	*s*ure
rid*i*cule	T*ue*sday
*ri*diculous	vill*ai*n

(Spelling list: 25 words)

Attention to etymology and cognate forms can assist in the spelling of some of these words. Thus to remember the Latin *finis* precludes the use of *a* in *definite*; to remember *prepare* keeps *e* out of the second syllable of *preparation*; to remember *busy* makes *i* before *s* in *business* impossible. (But do not let kinships cause you to misspell such words as *pleasant, prevalent, pronunciation,* and *maintenance.*)

181

20c. **Study Pronunciation** Make yourself hear the exact
sound of words. Often misspelling results from heed-
less pronunciation. Listen to speakers who articulate carefully. Understand, so far as you can, why the particular
combination of letters is employed.*

(I) Do not omit sounds In the words of the following list
be sure to put in the italicized letters (sometimes omitted
because of faulty pronunciation):

can*d*idate	gener*a*lly	len*g*th	represen*t*ative
compliment*a*ry	going	li*a*ble	soph*o*more
consider*a*ble	gover*n*ment	liter*a*ture	temper*a*ment
cur*i*osity	hist*o*ry	quan*t*ity	
ever*y*body	lab*o*ratory	recogni*z*e	

(2) Do not add sounds

athletics	hindrance	momentous	rigmarole
casualty	identify	original	similar
disastrous	lightning	problem	suffrage
entrance	mischievous	remembrance	umbrella
grievous			

(3) Do not transpose sounds

cava*l*ry	hund*r*ed	*per*form	*pre*fer	*pre*scription
child*r*en	irre*lev*ant	*per*spiration	pre*jud*ice	trage*d*y

* Sound is not always a sufficient guide to spelling. Reformed or
simplified spelling attempts in certain words to have old spellings
replaced by new ones which conform to sound. Not all the recom-
mendations have won equal degrees of acceptance. Thus according to
Webster's New International Dictionary (Second Edition) the forms
quartet and *program* are preferred, *altho* and *catalog* are recognized
but not preferred, *enuf* and *thru* are recognized as of reformed standing only, and *thruout* and *alfabet* are not recognized at all. If you
employ simplified forms, you must employ them consistently.

(4) Note whether a consonant sound is given once or twice

dis-appoint	rec-om-mend	Brit-ish *
dis-satisfy	ac-com-modate	Bri-tan-nica *
de-fer	ac-cu-mulate	o-mis-sion
dif-fer	a-cross	com-mis-sion †

(*Six spelling lists: 80 words—including those in the second footnote on this page*)

As several items in the preceding list show, the ability to distinguish the main word from the prefix or suffix is further insurance of correct spelling. Other examples: *mis-apply, mis-spell, open-ness, civil-ize.*

(5) Distinguish between words of similar sound Master the spelling of words which have similarity in sound (and often in appearance) but are different in meaning. Make spelling conform to the sense intended.

accept, except	aloud, allowed
access, excess	altar, alter
advice, advise	angel, angle
affect, effect	aught, ought
all together, altogether	bearing, baring, barring
allusion, illusion	born, borne

* The shift in the accent accounts for the shift in the position of *t*.

† As pronunciation often affects spelling, so does spelling often affect pronunciation. Note these words:

    write   writing   written

Normally in a monosyllable or accented syllable which contains a single consonant preceded by a single vowel, the vowel is short:

    plan   let   rid   knot   occur

But adding a silent *e* to the syllable makes the vowel long:

    plane   complete   ride   note   cure

Doubling the consonant before a suffix makes the preceding vowel short:

    planned   letting   ridding   knotted   occurred

Not doubling the consonant before a suffix makes the preceding vowel long:

    planed   completing   riding   noted   cured

breath, breathe
by, buy
capital, capitol
censor, censure
clothes, cloths, close
coarse, course
complement, compliment
conscious, conscience
corps, corpse
council, counsel, consul
dairy, diary
deprecate, depreciate
device, devise
desert, dessert
dining room, dinning
dual, duel
formally, formerly
forth, fourth, forty
hear, here
heard, herd
hoping, hopping
imitate, intimate
ingenious, ingenuous
instance, instants
irrelevant, irreverent
its, it's
later, latter
lead, led
lessen, lesson
loath, loathe
loose, lose

new, knew
nineteenth, ninety, ninth
past, passed
peace, piece
perceive, pursue
plain, plane
precede, proceed, supersede
presence, presents
principal, principle
prophecy, prophesy
quiet, quite
red, read
respectfully, respectively
right, rite, write, playwright
seize, siege
sense, since
shone, shown
sight, site, cite
speak, speech
stationary, stationery
statue, stature, statute
steal, steel
than, then
there, their, they're
to, too, two
track, tract
waist, waste
weak, week
whole, hole
who's, whose
your, you're

(Spelling list: 160 words)

(6) Practice spelling by syllables * One of the surest ways
to learn a word both structurally and orthographically is
to spell it syllable by syllable, pronouncing after each syl-

---

* For the principles by which words may be divided into syllables,
see 55a(3). For writing compounds solid, separate, or with hyphens,
see 23, particularly the special word lists at the close.

lable the sound of that syllable and the sound of the entire word to that point. Example:

> i-n, in, in-
> c-o-m, com, incom-
> p-r-e, pre, incompre-
> h-e-n, hen, incomprehen-
> s-i, si, incomprehensi-
> b-i-l, bil, incomprehensibil-
> i, i, incomprehensibili-
> t-y, ty, incomprehensibility

20d. **Form Right Muscular Habits in Spelling** Never permit yourself knowingly to write an incorrect spelling of a word. Not only will the erroneous form impress the memory through the eye, but the manual act of arranging the letters falsely will do much to create a wrong habit. Right spelling may have mechanical help—proper muscular impulses—as well as the help of observation. You can teach yourself to spell, not only by eye and by ear, but by hand.

EXERCISE

X-20a.

Prepare for your instructor a corrected list of words which you have misspelled in your papers to the present time.

X-20b.

Copy the following words, underscoring the trouble spots of each. Copy also from the list in **20b** all the words which you are not sure you can spell correctly.

academic	despair	element	mathematics	sentiment
almighty	different	evidence	meant	superintendent
based	divine	existence	might *have*	used to
Britain	does	grammar	optimism	vengeance
coloring	doctor	humorous	pessimist	whether
criticism	dormitory	knowledge	politics	which
dealt	eighth	manual	positive	would *have*

(Spelling list: 35 words)

X-20c(1).

Copy the following words and underscore the letters (here italicized) which careless speakers do not sound. If you are prone to omit letters or syllables in spelling, copy also the list in **20c(1)**.

accident*a*lly	compe*t*itive	fur*t*her	natur*a*lly	satisfac*t*orily
acc*u*rate	ea*t*ing	hur*r*ying	person*a*lly	stric*t*ly
arithm*e*tic	ev*e*ry	iden*t*ity	phys*i*ology	su*r*prise
bu*r*st	fav*o*rite	in*t*eresting	preven*t*ative	us*u*ally
bus*i*ness	Feb*r*uary	lib*r*ary	re*a*lize	varie*t*y

(*Spelling list: 25 words*)

X-20c(4).

Copy the following words and divide each word into syllables at the italicized point. Test the correctness of your divisions by consulting a dictionary. If you are weak in deciding whether a consonant between syllables should be doubled, copy also the list in **20c(4)**.

ad*d*ress	begin	di*s*sipate	mi*s*spell	emba*r*rass
ad*o*pt	beg*g*ing	i*m*age	neces*s*ary	o*p*inion
at*t*ract	di*s*appear	i*mm*ediate	occa*s*ion	o*pp*ose
beco*m*ing	di*s*ease	mi*s*ery	occu*r*rence	pro*ff*er
ha*b*it	di*s*sent	mi*ss*ionary	assu*r*ance	professor

(*Spelling list: 25 words*)

X-20c(5).

Copy the following sentences, choosing from the parentheses the word which the meaning requires:

1. He has (lead, led) a busy life.
2. Of (coarse, course) we could scarcely (breath, breathe) when the (plain, plane) left the ground.
3. I (loath, loathe) a snake and all (its, it's) ways.
4. His (presence, presents) was unexpected, but our host (accepted, excepted) it pleasantly.
5. I am (hoping, hopping) you can tell me (who's, whose) (device, devise) it is.

RULES FOR SPELLING

21. **Learn and apply the most useful rules for spelling.** Many words (see the preceding article) must be mastered individually, with such aid as may be obtained from their sound, appearance, origin, kinships, etc. Other words may be mastered through the use of definite laws.

HOW TO IMPROVE YOUR SPELLING THROUGH THE APPLICATION OF RULES

Sure knowledge of a few rules will help you to spell whole troops of words. Though you will, of course, find exceptions to the rules, you will find few to **21a** and **21b.**

21a. Words in *ei* or *ie*

(1) Write *i* before *e*
When sounded as *ee*
Except after *c.*

After c	*After any other letter*
re*ce*ive, de*ce*itful	be*lie*ve, *fie*ndish
*ce*iling, incon*ce*ivable	*wie*ld, *thie*vish, retrie*ve*

Exceptions: *Neither financier seized either species of weird leisure.*

(2) Of *ei* or *ie* words those in which the sound is *ee* are the ones really difficult to spell. Those in which the sound is something else (especially *a*) usually have *e* first.

Regularly Spelled *a* Sounds	Other Regularly Spelled non-*ee* Sounds	Irregularly Spelled non-*ee* Sounds
n*ei*ghbor	h*ei*ght	fr*ie*nd
w*ei*gh	h*ei*r	s*ie*ve
fr*ei*ght	for*ei*gn	f*ie*ry
		tr*ie*s, etc.

(*Spelling lists: 25 words, the word "seize" being disregarded because it is listed in* **20c.**)

187

21b. Doubling a Final Consonant

(1) Words which double the final consonant In adding a suffix which begins with a vowel (as *ance, ed, ing*), double a final consonant if all three of the following conditions are fulfilled: (*a*) if the word is a monosyllable or has the accent on the last syllable, (*b*) if a single vowel precedes the consonant, and (*c*) if the consonant itself is single. (Summary of the test: **Accent, One, and One.**) *

Monosyllables (one vowel, one consonant):

bat-ted	clan-nish	get-ting
chum-my	bag-gage	

Accented final syllables (one vowel, one consonant):

begin-ning	control-led	unregret-ted
commit-tee	repel-lent	

(2) Words which do not double the final consonant Words which end in a vowel, or which do not meet the conditions of the Accent, One, and One test, do not double the consonant.

Monosyllables (other than one vowel, one consonant)	Accented Final Syllables (other than one vowel, one consonant)	Unaccented Final Syllables	Suffix Not Beginning with a Vowel
he*l*p-er	perfor*m*-ance	prohibit-ed	allot-*m*ent
go*a*d-ed	discla*i*m-er	murder-ous	spot-*l*ess
com[*e*]-ing	reli[for *y*]-able		

(*Spelling lists: 20 words*)

---

* Two special classes of words seem at first to violate the rule for doubling the final consonant:

1. Words like *quitting, quittance, quizzes, squatter, acquitted, equipped.* After *q, u* has the force of *w;* hence a word of this class contains only one real vowel in the accented syllable.
2. Words like *conference* (from *confer*), *inference* (from *infer*), *preferable* (from *prefer*), and *referee* and *referendum* (from *refer*). These derivatives shift the accent from the syllable which bears it in the source word.

21c. Dropping Final *e*

(1) In adding a suffix which begins with a vowel, drop final *e*.

guide, guidance
please, pleasure
force, forcible
white, whitish
confuse, confusion

desire, desirous
arrive, arrival
college, collegiate
use, using
lose, losing

hide, hiding
dislike, disliking
oblige, obliging
love, lovable
mistake, unmistakably

But before a suffix beginning with a vowel, *e* is retained in

dyeing
singeing
(to prevent
confusion
with *dying*
and *singing*)

peaceable
serviceable
noticeable

(to keep *c* or *g* from being
hard before *a* or *o*, as in
cable, *gable*, *cold*, *go*)

changeable
unmanageable
outrageous
advantageous

us[e]able (as a variant
  spelling)
unsaleable (as a variant)
eyeing (as a variant)
mileage (preferred
  spelling)
acreage   agreeing
hoeing   tingeing
shoeing

(2) In adding a suffix which begins with a consonant, retain
final *e*.

strange, strangeness
arrange, arrangement
entire, entirely
grace, graceless
revenge, revengeful

But before a suffix beginning with a consonant, *e* is dropped in

duly	ninth	acknowledgment
truly	awful	judgment (preferred
wholly	argument	American spelling)

(*Spelling lists: 45 words, the word "ninth" being disregarded because it is listed in* **20c.**)

21d. Changing Final *y* before a Suffix

(1) In adding a suffix which begins with any other letter than *i*, change a final *y* preceded by a consonant to *i*.

accompa*ny*, accompa*ni*ment	car*ry*, car*ri*age
cry, *cri*es, *cri*ed	symmet*ry*, symmet*ri*cal
come*dy*, come*di*es	stu*dy*, stu*di*ous (but stu*dy*ing)
ear*ly*, ear*li*er	de*fy*, de*fi*ance (but de*fy*ing)

(2) Do not change before a suffix a final *y* preceded by a vowel.

st*ay*, st*ay*s	vall*ey*, vall*ey*s	bu*oy*, bu*oy*ant
pr*ay*, pr*ay*ed	destr*oy*, destr*oy*s	enj*oy*, enj*oy*ment
b*oy*, b*oy*s	conv*ey*, conv*ey*ance	portr*ay*, portr*ay*al

Exceptions:

p*ay*, p*ai*d	s*ay*, s*ai*d	d*ay*, d*ai*ly
l*ay*, l*ai*d	sl*ay*, sl*ai*n	g*ay*, g*ai*ety (but *gayety* is also used)

(*Spelling lists: 25 words*)

21e. Forming Plurals In forming the plurals of nouns, employ the practices shown in the following items.

(1) Plurals of ordinary nouns Add *s* or *es*:

officer, officers	leaf, leaves	⎱ *f* changes to *v* for the
picnic, picnics	knife, knives	⎰ sake of euphony
sandwich, sandwiches		

(2) Plurals of nouns ending in *y* Treat like ordinary nouns unless the *y* is preceded by a consonant or by *u* sounded as *w*; in that case change *y* to *i* and add *es* (see **21d**):

ess*ay*, ess*ays*	al*ly*, al*lies*
monk*ey*, monk*eys*	soliloq*uy*, soliloq*uies*
la*dy*, la*dies*	

(3) Plurals of nouns ending in *o* Add *s* or *es*—always *s* if final *o* is preceded by a vowel.

Add *s* to these nouns:

canto	quarto
piano	dynamo
solo	Eskimo
silo	soprano

cameo ⎫	vowel
radio ⎬	preceding
trio ⎭	final *o*

Ad *es* to these nouns:

no	hero	potato	mosquito
echo	Negro	tomato	

Add either *s* or *es* to these nouns:

zero	motto	buffalo	volcano
cargo	banjo	memento	

(4) Nouns retaining old declensional plurals These exceptional nouns form their plurals (*a*) without a change, (*b*) by the addition of *en* (*ren* in *children*), or (*c*) by a change in the stem vowels:

deer, deer	brother, brethren	foot, feet
heathen, heathen(s)	(also *brothers*)	goose, geese
sheep, sheep	child, children	mouse, mice
swine, swine	ox, oxen	

191

(5) Plurals of foreign nouns

Nouns with foreign plurals only:

alumna, alumnae	datum, data
alumnus, alumni	[Mr.], Messrs. (Messieurs)
analysis, analyses	[Mrs.], Mmes. (Mesdames)
basis, bases	oasis, oases
chassis, chassis	parenthesis, parentheses
chateau, chateaux	phenomenon, phenomena
crisis, crises	thesis, theses

Nouns with both foreign and English plurals:

bureau, bureaux, bureaus
appendix, appendices, appendixes
candelabrum, candelabra, candelabrums *
criterion, criteria, criterions
focus, foci, focuses
formula, formulae, formulas
fungus, fungi, funguses
index, indices, indexes
medium, media, mediums
memorandum, memoranda, memorandums
nucleus, nuclei, nucleuses
radius, radii, radiuses
seraph, seraphim, seraphs
stratum, strata, stratums
syllabus, syllabi, syllabuses
tableau, tableaux, tableaus

(6) Plurals of compounds

Make the principal word plural by the usual method for that word. In a few instances make two members of the compound plural.

Make only the principal word plural:

sons-in-law	by-products	commanders in chief
passers-by	major-domos	

---

* The plural form *candelabra* is often used as a singular; from this singular a new plural, *candelabras,* has been evolved.

Exceptions:

stand-bys (verb + preposition) handfuls ⎫ felt as
cupfuls ⎬ single words

Make two members of the compound plural:

women-servants   gentlemen-farmers
*(Spelling lists: 85 words, only the foreign
plurals of the foreign words being counted.)*

(7) Plurals of letters, signs, figures, and words spoken of as words
Add *'s* to thwart ambiguity: Cross your *t's* and dot your
i's. [Note that *is* would be taken as a verb.] His *?'s* look like
8's, but not like *$'s*. Spell your *which's* correctly.

Add *s* to figures indicating rates of interest: Chesapeake
and Ohio 3s.

EXERCISE

X-21a. Words in *ei* or *ie*

1. Copy the 25 words listed in **21a**, underscoring *ei* or *ie*.
2. Copy the following words, inserting *ei* or *ie*:

rel . . . f	m . . . n	ap . . . ce
n . . . ce	conc . . . ted	y . . . ld
unbel . . . vable	sh . . . ld	shr . . . king
undec . . . ve	rec . . . pt	counterf . . . t
ach . . . vement	repr . . . ve	v . . . l

(Spelling list: 15 words)

X-21b. Doubling a Final Consonant

In accordance with the rule for doubling a final consonant

write the present participle *(in ing) of these words*	*write the past tense* *(in ed) of these words*
sin	acquit
shine	develop
pin	repeat
pine	benefit
stop	compel

write the word which belongs in the expression

an (ill-stared, ill-starred) lover
priests (robed, robbed) in black
(shaming, shamming) the devil
hills (sloping, slopping) down
a runner (striped, stripped) for the race

write the forms called for

the superlative of *brief*
the adjective of *system*
the noun of *fail*
the noun of *recur*
the verb of *fat*

(Spelling list: 20 words)

X-21c. Dropping Final *e*

In accordance with the rule for dropping final *e* add the ending

-*al* to *refuse*
-*ity* to *obscure*
-*able* to *recognize*
-*ing* to *judge*
-*ation* to *invite*

-*ful* to *taste*
-*ing* to *subdue*
-*ary* to *imagine*
-*ous* to *courage*
-*ic* to *hygiene*

(Spelling list: 10 words)

X-21d. Final *y* before a Suffix

Change each listed word in accordance with instructions in the parentheses:

apology   (Write the adjective)
copy   (Write the third person singular of the verb)
enemy   (Write the plural of the noun)
parley   (Write the plural of the noun)
reply   (Write the past tense of the verb)

(Spelling list: 5 words)

X-21e. Forming Plurals

Write the plural of

church
country
woman
colloquy
religion

(Spelling list: 5 words)

SPELLING LIST

22. To possess the skill expected of college freshmen, be able to spell correctly ninety per cent of the 605 words listed in Articles 20 and 21 and their exercises, and the 295 words listed in this article.* (The lists have been carefully compiled on the basis of the actual misspellings in college themes.)

absence	attacked	conferred	elementary
abstinence	attendance	conqueror	eligible
absurd	audience	continuous	eliminate
accustom	author	coolly	eminent
acquaintance	awaiting	couldn't	encouraging
actor	awkward	courteous	equipped
aeronautics		courtesy	especially
again	balance	crept	exaggerate
aggravate	barbarous	cruelty	exceed
already	before		exhaust
always	boundaries	debater	exhibiting
amateur	break	decide	exhilarate
among	brilliant	depth	expense
amount	built	descend	experience
analogous	burglar	description	explanation
annual	busy	desperate	extraordinary
anxiety		digging	factory
any	calendar	disadvantage	familiar
apparatus	can't	disagree	fascinate
apparent	cemetery	discipline	finally
appearance	certain	disillusion	football
appreciate	characteristic	disobedient	forfeit
appropriate	chauffeur	doesn't	frantically
aren't	choose	don't	fraternity
arising	civilize	drudgery	freshman (adj.)
around	column	dying	furniture
arouse	common		
article	comparative	early	gallant
ascend	concede	ecstasy	gambling

*For the correct form for writing additional compounds see the special word lists, **23e.**

195

gathered
gauge (or gage)
genealogy
goddess
governor
grandeur
guard
guess
guilty

half
harass
hasn't
haven't
having
herself
hesitancy
hoarse
huge
hypotheses

illegible
illiterate
immigration
imminent
impossible
incidentally
incredible
independence
infinite
influence
instead
intelligence
intentionally
interfere
irresistible
isn't
itself

license (or
  licence)

literal
logically
loneliness
lying

making
manufacturer
many
marriage
material
memorable
message
miniature
minutes
momentous
much
murmur
muscle
mysterious

nickel
none
nowadays

obstacle
occasionally
o'clock
offered
oneself
opened
openness
operate
oppressive
orally
organize
oriental
ourselves
overrun

parallel
paralysis

particularly
partner
pastime
peremptory
perform
perhaps
permanent
permissible
perseverance
persuade
pervade
physical
picnicking
pitiable
poem
poetry
poison
politician
possession
practically
prairie
preference
primitive
prisoner
probably
prodigy
prove
purchase
putting

quizzes

rapid
ready
really
recede
reference
regard
region
religious
repetition

reservoir
restaurant
rhetorical
rhythm

safety
scenery
schedule
science
secretary
seems
sergeant
several
severely
shan't
sincerely
slept
smooth
some
special
specifically
specimen
stopped
stories
strenuous
subtle
succeeds
successful
sugar
summarize
superintendent
suppose
supposition

tearing
temperature
tendency
therefore
thorough
tired
together

transferred	university	village	where
treasurer	unnamed	violent	wherever
trouble	unsophisticated		within
typical	until	warrant	without
tyranny		wasn't	won't
	vacancy	wearing	wouldn't
undoubtedly	valuable	weather	wrote
ungrammatical	very	Wednesday	
universally	vigilance	welfare	yourselves

COMPOUNDS

23. Make logical distinctions in writing compounds as single words, separate words, or hyphenated groups. When in doubt follow dictionary usage.

HOW TO DETERMINE THE PROPER FORM FOR A COMPOUND*

23a. Compounds Showing the Extent to Which Meanings Are Merged

(1) Write solid a compound in which the meanings of two (or more) words are thoroughly merged.

She stood to watch the *kickoff*. [We do not think of *a kick* and then of the direction *off*.]

(2) Use a hyphen to join the members of a compound (*a*) in which the meanings of the individual words are only partially merged or (*b*) in which confusion or misreading might result from writing the words either solid or separate.

This is sheer *make believe*. [Write *make-believe* to show partial merging of thought.]

He led the *runner up* to the judges' stand. [Write *runner-up* to prevent misreading.]

* For writing the plurals of compounds see **21e(6)**.

Did you ever see a *shoe polish* like this? [Write *shoe-polish* to prevent misreading.]

She could not afford to *recover* the chair. [Write *re-cover* to prevent misreading.]

In a *takeoff* just before the *fadeout* two clowns had a *setto* before a *leanto*. [Prevent confusing combinations of vowels by writing *take-off* and *fade-out*, of consonants by writing *set-to* and *lean-to*.]

(3) Write separate the members of a compound in which each word clearly maintains its separate identity.

They listened meekly as he read the *riot act*.

The *Missouri Compromise* averted a conflict.

The Chinese burn *joss sticks* for incense.

NOTE—The extent to which meanings in a compound are merged is often difficult to determine. As one of the hosts of examples in the dictionary, take these three compounds of *half*: half dollar, half-hour, halfpenny.

23b. Compounds Forming a Single Adjective

(1) Use hyphens to join words serving as a single adjective before a noun.

well-kept lawn	an up-to-date pressure cooker
so-called patriots	a let's-see-you-try tone of voice
an old-school politician	a thirty-dollar-a-week clerk
twentieth-century ideas	

But hyphens are not used within adjective compounds which are normally written solid.

a nondescript cur

Nor, ordinarily, is an adverb in *ly* joined with a hyphen to the adjective following.

brilliantly executed plays

(2) Omit the hyphens when the words follow the noun.

The lawn is well kept.
They are patriots, so called.
He is a politician of the old school.
Your ideas are twentieth century.
Our pressure cooker is strictly up to date.
His tone was "Let's see you try."
The clerk earns thirty dollars a week.

23c. **Compound Numbers—Cardinal and Ordinal** Use hyphens in compound numbers from twenty-one (twenty-first) to ninety-nine (ninety-ninth).

twenty-three	sixty-five	eighty-nine
Twenty-third Psalm	eighty-ninth paper	

Do not use hyphens in compounds of *hundred* (*hundredth*), *thousand* (*thousandth*), etc., when these numbers are used as nouns. Preferably do not use hyphens in such compounds when the numbers are used as adjectives.

NOUNS

one hundred	four hundred and one
twenty-three hundred	three million and seventy-two

ADJECTIVES

Ordinary form	*Permissible form*
the one hundredth page	the one-hundredth page
the four hundred and first bale of cotton	the four-hundred-and-first bale of cotton
the twenty-three thousandth machine	the twenty-three-thousandth machine
the three million and seventy-second paper bag	the three-million-and-seventy-second paper bag *

* For the use of figures in writing large numbers see **55b(2)**.

23d. Fractions as Compounds

(1) Hyphenate the two parts of a fraction only when the two parts are used as a single adjective before a noun.

   a *three-fourths* part   a *one-third* share

(2) A hyphen is not necessary when the parts are read separately as adjective plus noun.

   three fourths of my life   *one third* of his fortune
   thirty hundredths   *thirty-one hundredths*
   one thirty-second of an inch

23e. Special Lists of Compound Words

(1) Write these words solid:

almighty	wherever	foremost	(a) windup
almost	whenever	topmost	knockout
already	whoever	innermost	blowout
although	whichever		touchdown
altogether	whatever		
	whatsoever	childlike	
	however	fairylike	classroom
anybody		godlike	textbook
everybody		ladylike	underdog
nobody	myself	workmanlike	
somebody	yourself		superhuman
	herself	misgive	midwestern
anyhow	himself	misinform	
somehow	itself	misplace	counteract
	ourselves	misread	withhold
anything			
everything	overlook	upon	nowadays
nothing	overrun	into	tomorrow
something	overtake	within	
	overthrow	throughout	indeed
anywhere			someone
everywhere	outburst	thereupon	airport
nowhere	outcome	moreover	newsprint
somewhere	outcry	inasmuch	
	outdoor	nevertheless	selfsame

200

(2) Hyphenate these words:

self-confidence	ex-treasurer	re-cover (cover again) ⎫ *
self-educated	cure-all	re-create (create anew) ⎭
self-made, etc.		

all-American	pre-eminent ⎫	
anti-Masonic	anti-intellectual ⎬ †	
non-Aryan	doll-like ⎭	
pro-British		

(3) Write these words separate:

all right	in fact	side line	post card
no one	en route	some place	real estate
in order to	et cetera	high school	lieutenant colonel
in spite of	parcel post (or	post office	major general
	parcels post)		

(4) Write these words in any of the ways shown. Some of the
following words illustrate the tendency for compounds
to evolve from separate words to hyphenated words to solid
words. Webster's Dictionary gives each first spelling in our
list as preferred, but in general use such words as *coöperate, coördinate,* and *percent* are more commonly written as
one word.

today, to-day	basketball, basket ball
co-operate, coöperate, cooperate	onto, on to
co-ordinate, coördinate, coordinate	oneself, one's self
per cent, percent	vice-president, vice
	president

**(5) Write these words differently according to the part of
speech or the emphasis intended:**

awhile (adv.)	sometime (adv.)
(for) a while (noun)	(for) some time (noun)

* The same letters without a hyphen would form a different word.
† Hyphens in these words aid the eye by preventing a congestion
of like letters.

good-humored (adj.)
good humor (noun)

everyday (adj.)
every day (noun)

everyone (pronoun meaning *everybody, persons in general*)

every one (pronoun meaning *each person individually*)

anyone (pronoun meaning *any person*)

any one (pronoun meaning *a single person*)

EXERCISE

X-23a. Compounds Showing the Extent to Which Meanings Are Merged

Copy the following expressions; as the meaning requires, insert hyphens, leave unchanged, or write solid.

1. an old stand by
2. a snapper up of trifles
3. a grand duke and his grand daughter
4. an annoying show off
5. a pleasant mother in law
6. a throw back to ancestral faults
7. a delegate at large
8. a stop over in Chicago
9. a top floor apartment
10. the official stop watch
11. a cashier's check
12. ten dollar books [each costs ten dollars]
13. an over sight
14. a badminton shuttle cock
15. cast off clothes
16. a cash book
17. a honey bee
18. a home run
19. knee deep in work
20. a coat of mole skin

X-23b. Compounds Forming a Single Adjective

Copy the following expressions; as the term requires, insert hyphens, leave unchanged, or write solid.

1. an over rated motion picture
2. organizations which are tax exempt
3. a conscience stricken thief
4. over diligent officials
5. a holier than thou attitude
6. a death like stillness
7. a junior college student
8. a don't you believe it manner
9. a helio centric universe
10. roughly dressed fellows
11. lighter than air craft
12. three pieces of one inch pipe

13. a self confessed tax dodger
14. a custom built roadster
15. a one place monoplane
16. the hoped for position
17. a house that is well kept
18. a genius, self acknowledged
19. highly paid executives
20. salesmen who are over paid

X-23c, d. Compound Numbers and Fractions as Compounds

Copy the following expressions; as the terms require, insert hyphens or leave unchanged. If two forms are acceptable, list both and indicate which is ordinary usage.

1. two thirds of a cup
2. seventy fifth page
3. four and three thirty seconds
4. two times twenty five dollar bills makes two hundred dollars
5. nine tenths of the subscribers
6. forty two hundred
7. a seven eighths part
8. five million and twenty one
9. seventy two hundredths
10. the six hundred and second visitor

CAPITAL LETTERS

24. Capitalize (1) the first word in a sentence or in a line of "traditional" poetry, (2) all the important words in the title of an artistic work or of a periodical, and (3) proper names, the pronoun *I*, and the interjection *O*.

HOW TO DETERMINE WHEN CAPITALS ARE NEEDED

24a. Capitalization of First Words

Capitalize the first word of a sentence: The pilot reported his position to the tower.

Capitalize the first word of a title even if the word is an article: *A Journal of the Plague Year.* [For the capitalization of other words in a title see **24b**.]

Capitalize the first word of a quoted sentence: Our senator declared, "This appropriation is essential to the preservation of our forests."

Do not capitalize an indirect quotation: Our senator declared that this appropriation is essential to the preservation of our forests.

Do not capitalize a fragmentary quotation: Our senator declared that this appropriation is "essential to the preservation of our forests."

Capitalize the first word of a complete statement inserted in a formal way into a sentence: The problem is, Who will provide the necessary money?

Ordinarily capitalize a long statement following a colon: His committee made a favorable report: There was at this time enough money in the treasury to begin work on the new building.

Do not, ordinarily, capitalize a short, informal statement following a colon: The quarterback decided to take a chance: he called for a quick kick.

Capitalize the first word of each item in an outline: [See examples in **32c(1)** and **(2)**.]

Capitalize the first word in each line of "traditional" poetry:

> To him who, in the love of Nature, holds
> Communion with her visible forms, she speaks
> A various language. . . .

Do not capitalize words which a modernistic poet has written without capitals:

> A train's whistle is a magic carpet
> on which my imagination climbs
> and whirls across unthinkable spaces.

24b. **Capitalization of Important Words in Titles** All words except prepositions, conjunctions, and articles are usually regarded as important.

Capitalize (along with the first word) all important words in the titles of books: *The Cloister and the Hearth, Travels* *with a Donkey.* [Sometimes a long preposition or conjunction is regarded as important: Walter Pritchard Eaton's essay "On Being Cheerful Before Breakfast."] *

Capitalize the important words in the titles of plays: *All's Well That Ends Well.*

Capitalize the important words in the titles of periodicals: *Saturday Review of Literature, New York Herald-Tribune.*

Do not capitalize *the* or *magazine* (unless it is part of the title): the *Woman's Home Companion, Coronet* magazine. [But] *The Nation, Harper's Magazine.*

Capitalize the important words in the titles of articles, essays, poems, stories, and themes: "The Rôle of the Nurse in Public Health" [article], "Grace before Meat" [essay], "Song of Myself" [poem], "Murder by Moonlight" [story], "My Trip to the Yosemite" [theme].

Capitalize the important words in the titles of non-literary works of art: "The Laughing Cavalier" [portrait], "The Moonlight Sonata" [musical composition].

24c. Capitalization of Names

Capitalize individual identifying names: United States Senate, Democrat (a member of the political party), Harold, Shorty, Great Smoky Mountain National Park, Spain, Catholics, Methodists, Christian, Europe, God, Christ.†

Do not capitalize common or general names: dog, man, senate, democrat (one who believes in democracy), a national park.

Normally capitalize adjectives derived from proper names: *Spenserian* stanza; *Hitlerian* tactics.

Do not capitalize name-derived adjectives whose meanings have become generalized: *italic* type, *pullman* car, *pasteurized* milk.

---

* Capitalize also the words *Volume, Book, Part,* and *Chapter* (but not *page*): Parrington's *Main Currents in American Thought,* Volume I, Book III, Part II, Chapter 3, page 357.

† Usage is divided on capitalization of pronouns referring to the deity. Pronouns referring to pagan deities (Venus, Zeus, etc.) are not capitalized.

Capitalize the names of regions: the North, the East, the Orient. Do not capitalize points of the compass: turn west, a south wind.

Capitalize the names of days, months, etc.: Tuesday, February, Christmas, Easter, Memorial Day, Fourth of July, June tenth. Do not capitalize names of the seasons (unless they are personified): fall, spring, winter. [But] O wayward, fickle Spring!

Capitalize the names of races and languages (and adjectives derived from them): Indian, Japanese, Negro, Latin, English, French, Chinese junk, Caucasian race. Do not capitalize school studies (except languages): history, art, science, mathematics, biology, engineering, dramatics.

24d. Capitalization of General Terms Added to Names

Capitalize a general term used as a part of a place name: 523 West Thirty-seventh Street, Boulder City, Kern County, Worth Lake, Merrimac River, Red Mountain, Lake Elsinore, Mt. Everest, Point Barrow.*
Do not capitalize a general term not used as a part of a place name: a river west of town, a mountain behind the lake.

Capitalize a general term added to the name of an organization: Roosevelt School, the Baptist Church, the Santa Fe Railroad, the Standard Oil Company, the University Club, William and Mary College, the University of Wisconsin.†
Do not capitalize a general term not used as a part of the name of an organization (unless the term has specific reference): our high school, a church, a competing oil company, a service club, coeducational colleges. [But when such terms have specific reference they are usually capitalized] the Faculty, the College, the Freshman Class, the Home Office, the Board of Directors.

* Newspapers tend to use a small letter for the general term when it follows the place name: *Tenth avenue, Ozark mountains.* But they capitalize the general term when it comes first: *Lake Louise, Mt. Shasta.* Newspaper usage is permissible if it is followed consistently.

† Newspapers tend to use small letters for general terms even when those terms are added to the proper names of organizations or structures: *National Biscuit company, American Tennis club, Lyceum theater, Standhope building, Clifton's restaurant.*

Capitalize general words added to the proper name of a structure: the San Marcos Building, Moose's Department Store, the College Shop, Brooklyn Bridge, Apartment 3, Tudor Arms, the Cathay Theater, Stearns Wharf.*

Do not capitalize a general word not a part of a proper name: a new office building, a hat shop, an apartment house, a neighborhood theater, the fisherman's wharf.

24e. Capitalization of Titles of Persons

Capitalize a title that is used as part of the name: † Uncle Roy, Captain Lain, General Manager Witherspoon, Mr. Green, Dr. Carr, President Fox, the Reverend Mr. Hartwell, General Marshall.

Do not, in ordinary writing, capitalize a title used in an appositive construction: ** Atterby, president of the college; my cousin, Jane Clegg; John, my brother; Compton, the lawyer. [But in the address of a letter such titles are commonly capitalized] C. D. Orway, Principal, East Union High School; O. F. Johnson, President, City Transit Company.

Do not capitalize a title used in place of a name (except for an official of very high rank): the mayor, the chief of police, the general manager, the dean, the judge; [but] Justice of the Supreme Court, President of the United States.

24f. Capitalization of the Pronoun *I* and the Interjection *O*

Capitalize the pronoun *I*: Whenever I hear the bells I am reminded of my childhood.

Capitalize the interjection *O* (in direct address): Hear me, O mighty men of war and peace.

Do not capitalize the interjection *oh* (unless it begins a sentence or is to be especially emphasized): The audience responded with "oh's" and "ah's" of astonishment.

* See second note on page 206.
† Any word regularly capitalized should also be capitalized when it is abbreviated. See 55b(1).
** For the definition of *appositive* see 14. For *"merged"* appositives see 26a.

EXERCISE

X-24a. Capitalization of First Words

Copy, inserting capitals wherever they are needed. If the words in an item form a complete sentence, insert a period and capitalize properly. Do not capitalize an incomplete statement.

1. our delegate to the convention
2. the new traffic lights are effective in reducing accidents
3. Margaret shouted, "stop him! he forgot his brief case"
4. Henry said to forward the money to the escrow company
5. he was reading a well-known work by Housman, *a Shropshire Lad*
6. they hoped he would fulfil his promise to "give the best performance of my life"
7. the question they raised was, when would the new regulations go into effect?
8. "when you arrive in Mexico City go directly to the consul," he said, "where you will be given a letter of introduction"
9. she had only one choice: to comply with their demands
10. "you're a fool!" he shouted, "leave that switch alone!"

X-24b. Capitalization of Important Words in Titles

Copy, capitalizing all important words.

1. *The merchant of venice*
2. "How to read a book"
3. "The nutcracker suite"
4. *The atlantic monthly* magazine
5. "A conversation with an old sailor"

X-24c. Capitalization of Names

Copy, using capital letters for only those names which require capitalization.

1. He is pastor of the largest baptist church in dallas, texas.
2. As a member of the united states senate he traveled to europe to investigate the plight of the jews.
3. Life in the orient is difficult for the poorer chinese natives.
4. The fourth of july falls on a saturday this year.

5. My college course includes biology, latin, engineering, and english.

X-24d. Capitalization of General Terms Added to Names

Copy, properly capitalizing terms used as parts of names. State in parentheses whether you have employed formal or informal (newspaper) usage.

1. His address in Boulder city is 234 south Mackinaw street.
2. On their vacation they drove through the Ozark mountains, camping near a river.
3. After being graduated from Jefferson high school he went to work for the Rock Island railroad.
4. A new office building was erected next to the Strand theater.
5. While attending the university of Michigan she was elected secretary of the freshman class.

X-24e. Capitalization of Titles of Persons

Copy, properly capitalizing all titles of persons.

1. Nevertheless aunt Nettie quit her job when she married mr. Jamison.
2. The reverend dr. Whitman was noted for his inspiring sermons.
3. He was sent by general manager Holcomb to see doctor Pelley and R. M. Wilcox, director of the engineering school.
4. While still the mayor of a small town he had ambitions to become a justice of the supreme court.
5. Green was captain of the ship.

Punctuation

PRINCIPAL USES OF THE COMMA

One Comma to Separate (Article 25)
Two Commas to Enclose (Article 26)

ONE COMMA TO SEPARATE

25. Use one comma to separate
   a. main clauses joined by a coördinating conjunction
   b. items in a series
   c. misleading combinations of words.

Do not use a comma without a reason.

HOW TO USE THE SEPARATIVE COMMA

25a. Main Clauses Use a comma regularly between main clauses joined by one of the coördinating conjunctions (*and, or, but, for*).* If there is no conjunction use a semicolon.†

To fix the rule in mind, visualize the clauses as long dashes.

——————, and ————   ——————, but ————
——————, or ————   ——————, for ————
                 ——————; ————

---

* Coördinating conjunctions less frequently used are *nor, yet,* and *so.*
† For detailed treatment of the semicolon see **29b.**

(I) Regular punctuation of compound sentences

Main clauses joined by coördinating conjunctions:

Prices are going up, and the end is not in sight.
We can walk to the park, or Pete can drive us there.
The man earns plenty of money, but his wife spends it all.
Sue had been wise to wait, for her bus came promptly.

Main clauses not joined by coördinating conjunctions:

Bamboo wood requires no paint; it has a natural hard shell.
We heard a single sharp crash; then all was still.

Practice Comma or semicolon?

Copy the word before and the word after each space. Insert the proper mark of punctuation.

1. The barn was warm in winter   and we felt a drowsy pleasure in our morning work.
2. The barn was warm in winter   we enjoyed working there.
3. When it rains the mules get mired   and the marooned traveler must wait with what patience he can muster.
4. Is the vase earthenware   or has it the translucence of true porcelain?
5. We think of the Amazon basin as a jungle   but actually it contains vast areas of open prairie.
6. Keep your hand away from a freshly killed wasp   for it still has power to sting.
7. For a moment nothing happened   then with a deafening roar the engine started.
8. Some women vote as their consciences dictate   others have husbands.
9. At ground level one can hardly notice the pattern of a town   but from the air it stands out like a flower on a carpet.
10. Microfilming will make unnecessary the erection of large buildings to house books   for by the microfilm process a whole library can be condensed into the space now occupied by its card catalog. [Note that a long sentence may require only a single mark of punctuation.]

211

(2) Permissible variations

Between clauses complicated by internal commas a semicolon may be used: Mice got into the sugar, the flour, and the bacon; but they could not reach our matches, which we kept in a tin box.

Between short parallel clauses the comma may be omitted: We called and we shouted. She must eat or she will die. Tag whined and he howled. The winds blew and the rains came.

Between clauses closely connected in thought the comma may be omitted: The nut was missing from the shaft and the propeller was held in place only by its thrust against the water.

Experienced writers omit the comma if they feel that the meaning is better served without it. When the student omits a comma between main clauses he should note in the margin of his paper the exact reason for the omission.

(3) Warning Do not mistake a compound predicate (or other compound element) for a compound sentence. Ordinarily no comma is used with such elements; occasionally a comma is required for contrast or emphasis.

Regular usage with compound elements (no comma):

Predicates: Stay and help us.   Go or stay as you wish. A pilot must wear warm gloves or freeze his fingers. Captain Gray put on warm gloves and bundled up tightly.

Subjects: In Suez both the nights and the days were hot. Neither Helen nor I could rest.

Objects: You may bring me a cup of coffee or a pot of tea. With it serve sandwiches and cookies.

Modifiers: Before eight and after twelve Elizabeth is free. You'll find her either at the library or at home.

Compound elements separated for contrast:

Predicate: He tried to reach 25,000 feet, but failed.

Compound elements separated for emphasis:

Predicate: The rescue party encountered a howling blizzard, yet pushed on.

25b. Series *

Use a comma between the items of a series	unless they are linked by *and* or *or* throughout.
a crisp, cool morning	a cold and frosty morning
from Iowa, from Georgia	from Iowa or from Georgia
In the market we saw lettuce, cress, tomatoes.	a salad of lettuce and cress and tomatoes
We will wash, polish, and deliver your car.	We will wash and polish your car and deliver it.

(!) Adjectives are separated by commas if they are equals. Sometimes they are not equals. For example, in *an old gray fox* the word *gray* qualifies the noun in a special way; *old* modifies *gray fox*.

EQUALS	NOT EQUALS
a short, exciting chase	an exciting short⌒story
a ripe, juicy pear	a big Jonathan⌒apple
white, sun-splashed walls	an old stone⌒wall
sparkling, fun-loving eyes	dark⌒blue eyes
a tall, thin, awkward lad	a thin little⌒black⌒cat

(2) In a series having the form a, b, and c the final comma is frequently essential to prevent confusion.

Desserts included ice cream, pie, and cheese with crackers. [The final comma prevents linking *pie* and *cheese*.]

Randolph-Macon, William and Mary, and Washington and Lee are colleges in Virginia [exactly three colleges].

Split two plump fryers, dust lightly with pepper and salt, and brown in butter [three separate steps].

Some writers omit the comma before the connective unless it seems necessary for clearness. The safer usage is to insert it consistently.

---

* A series is a succession of elements of like grammatical form and rank—two or more words or word-groups harnessed like a team, doing the same work in a sentence. They may or may not be linked by connectives (*and, or, but, nor, yet*).

(3) Warning Do not place a comma before or after a series unless it is required by a definite rule.

Right [no comma before *Iran*]: He had traveled in strange lands like Iran, Bulgaria, Rumania.

Right [no comma after *lens*]: Printing, gunpowder, and the lens were inventions of the Renaissance period.

Right [rule for enclosing appositives—**26a**—requires the first and the last comma]: Gifts of clothing, particularly shoes, sweaters, and mittens, are always appreciated.

25c. **Misleading Combinations** Use a comma to separate words which might erroneously be read together.

Better still, recast the sentence.

Adverb mistaken for preposition: Outside the walls of the prison loomed dark and forbidding.

Insert a comma: Outside, the walls of the prison loomed dark and forbidding.

Verb wrongly compounded: Johnny picked up the paper wad that had nicked his ear and snapped it sidewise at Jim.

Insert a comma: . . . that had nicked his ear, and snapped . . . .

Verb with tendency to "grab" succeeding noun: Whenever she moved the house seemed to shake.

Insert a comma: Whenever she moved, the house . . . .

Verbal with tendency to "grab": Because Pat liked to fight the sergeant sent him on a dangerous mission.

Insert a comma: Because Pat liked to fight, the sergeant sent him on a dangerous mission.

Or recast: Because Pat was a good fighter the sergeant sent him on a dangerous mission.

Misapplied modifier: They found crabs and jellyfish and limpets clinging to the rocks.

Insert a comma: They found crabs and jellyfish, and limpets clinging to the rocks.

Or recast: They found crabs and jellyfish on the sand and limpets clinging to the rocks.

25d. Superfluous Commas Do not use a comma without a definite, adequate reason. Ordinarily, do not separate by a single comma a close grammatical sequence like subject-verb-object.* [You may, of course, use *two* commas to set off an interrupter (see **26**).]

(1) Basal parts Do NOT break the links between

subject and verb: How Tom won the race⌒is a mystery.
verb and object: He said [that]⌒he would go at once.
verb and complement: What he said was not⌒what he meant.
parts of a compound subject, verb, or object: † A farmer rises at dawn⌒and toils until sundown.

(2) Series Use a comma only between items, NOT

before a series: John studied⌒chemistry, geology, and biology.
or after a series: His knowledge of chemistry, geology, and biology⌒proved useful in the jungle.

(3) Connectives Place NO separative comma between

preposition and object: We saw no animal except⌒a lizard.
conjunction and following word, phrase, or clause:
  We use hydrocarbons, such as⌒methane and acetylene.
  Good dancing may attract a man, but⌒it takes good cooking to hold him.

(4) Close modifiers Place NO comma before or after a modifier which closely limits the word modified (see **26d**).

At the party everyone⌒but John⌒had a good time.
Skating is good exercise⌒for both children and adults.
[The prepositions *but* and *for* must not be mistaken for conjunctions.]

---

* A comma may occasionally be needed to prevent awkwardness: *Whatever is, is right.*
† Such parts may of course be separated by commas if they are in series. See **25b**. They may occasionally be separated for contrast or emphasis. See **25a (3)**.

EXERCISE

X-25a. Punctuation between Main Clauses

Copy each sentence. Underline the subject and verb of each main clause, and the coördinating conjunction if there is one. Insert the required mark of punctuation, if any.

1. Memphis differs from Portland and both differ from Chicago.
2. The creature must have been a rodent for its upper teeth protruded.
3. Are we to wait for the bus at the junction or will the driver pick us up farther on?
4. Lincoln opposed slavery but slavery he held to be a secondary issue.
5. His primary purpose was to preserve the Union and in that purpose he never faltered.
6. President Cleveland vetoed the first big pension bill thus he antagonized the Grand Army of the Republic.
7. Owls make noises resembling conversation the range of their vocabulary is remarkable.
8. The back door closed she could hear the click of the latch and the pad of his feet returning.
9. In slow filtration water flows through a thick bed of sand and is drained off through a layer of gravel.
10. Set the candle in a pan of water and light it then place an inverted jar over it.
11. In the theater or even in the movies bright new ideas come along to push out the bright old ideas but nothing ever changes in radio.
12. Gypsies are very exciting people and in the Balkans they have the same glamor that surrounds toreadors in Spain and movie stars in America.
13. The doctor revived the patient but sensitive brain tissues had been injured while the oxygen was cut off.
14. Cold weather does not exterminate grasshoppers for their eggs remain in the ground all winter and hatch in the spring.
15. The new governor dissolved the assembly almost immediately for daring to criticize His Majesty's government but the burgesses met next day at an inn.

X-25b. Items in a Series

Copy each sentence, inserting necessary commas.

1. For making furniture we use such woods as walnut mahogany maple oak.

2. At college I could not decide whether to major in mathematics or physics or chemistry.

3. Mosaics are pictures or designs made by embedding small pieces of colored tile opaque glass marble or similar materials in the surface of masonry.

4. Those who take principal rôles in the operetta must rehearse individually together and with the chorus.

5. We ordered lamb and mint sauce asparagus and hollandaise and hot biscuits and honey.

6. During their first weeks of practice the players grew restless quarrelsome dissatisfied. The morale of the team improved with the employment of a skillful young athletic trainer.

7. One after another the boats pull into swift water swing sidewise to take the waves and are rushed downstream.

8. Fill a test tube half full of water add two cc. of tartaric acid and stir the mixture with a glass rod.

9. In those days Carson City was a tough crowded unorganized boom town. Money came easily and went quickly.

10. Standard-voltage electric razor outlets steaming hot water and linen towels are featured in our men's lounge.

11. A girl can earn her way by working in an office by staying with children or by clerking in a store.

12. Substances made from plastics can be rigid or flexible opaque or clear dull or brightly colored molded or woven. Most plastics are light in weight and smooth in texture.

13. We must build pipelines raise the dam construct additional reservoirs. We must either obtain more water or abandon our homes and gardens.

14. Our guide proved to be the sort of mountaineer who can hike twenty miles prepare a supper of fried ham and corn pone and have energy left to spin yarns around the campfire.

15. Turn right at the large signboard which marks the city limits drive along Washington to Western and then turn left and drive two blocks.

X-25c. Misleading Combinations

First copy each sentence, inserting commas where they are needed. Then recast sentence 4 and one other.

1. Beyond the road wound steeply down toward a narrow bridge.
2. When they are caught young otters are easily tamed.
3. She served doughnuts and coffee and hot spiced cider from a punch bowl.
4. The new variety of corn will survive a drought which would destroy most grain and produce a crop besides.
5. Whenever I tried to study some history students would begin jabbering about the quiz they had just taken.

X-25d. Superfluous Commas

Write the number of each sentence and state why NO comma should be placed at each point marked ⌒.

1. The canyon of the Sur⌒is a good place to study geology.
2. Dr. Andrews believed⌒that the Gobi Desert is worth exploring.
3. It is apparent⌒that the control of the Mississippi River alone⌒requires the coöperation of twenty states.
4. We fried our trout over the campfire⌒and gulped them down, and then we considered whether to set up our tents⌒or climb to the top of the hill.
5. The strange creature appeared to be⌒heavily furred, a light gray-brown⌒in color, and about the size of a rat.
6. Successful farming requires the right combination of⌒climate, topography, and soil.
7. Among foods rich in vitamin B are the whole grain cereals, such as⌒rolled oats and unpolished rice.
8. A child needs not only playmates⌒but also close relatives; yet in the modern family neither brothers and sisters⌒nor aunts and uncles⌒are plentiful.
9. In the early thirties⌒the citizens of several Eastern winter sports areas formed⌒"ski patrols." [The quotation marks here set off words used in a special sense (see **28c**).]
10. They expected the boat to return in two days, but⌒the damaged propeller delayed it for two weeks. Every part of the boat⌒but the propeller⌒escaped harm.

TWO COMMAS TO ENCLOSE

26. Use two commas to enclose an interrupter or a loose modifier.* Elements to be enclosed include

    a. Appositives   **c.** Place and date completers
    b. Guide words   **d.** Nonrestrictive modifiers

HOW TO USE ENCLOSING COMMAS

26a. **Appositives** An appositive is a noun (often with modifiers) inserted to explain another noun. Regularly set off an appositive by commas before and after.

Dr. Hunt, *our family physician*, told me to eat big breakfasts.
My home state, *Minnesota*, has a large Scandinavian population.
The concert, *an informal event sponsored by the Music Department*, featured two of my favorite instruments, *the harp and the flute.* [When an interrupter ends a sentence an end mark replaces the second comma.]

An appositive which identifies very closely is not set off by commas. It may merge with the base noun to form a phrase which has the force of a single name: Peter the Hermit, Mary Queen of Scots, my friend John. It may be set off sufficiently by italics (**55c**) or by quotation marks (**28c**): the opera *Mignon*, the good ship *Rover*, the word *ain't*, the expression "you've had it."

An appositive may be thought of as a cut-down clause.

1. Dr. Hunt, [who is] our family physician, told me...
2. Dr. Hunt, [who is] a cheerful and tubby man, told me...
3. Dr. Hunt, [a] cheerful and tubby [man], told me... [or]
4. Dr. Hunt, [who is] cheerful and tubby, told me...
5. Dr. Hunt, [who is] nicknamed Tubby, told me...

* When a loose element comes at the beginning or end of a sentence only one comma is required.

Clause-cutting may leave modifiers instead of nouns. *Apposed adjectives* (examples 3 and 4) are regularly set off by commas. A past participle with an explanatory name (5) is set off unless it identifies a general term.

Loosely added: Saul, *later called Paul,* journeyed...

Built in to identify: A man *named Saul* journeyed...

26b. Guide Words Set off a conversational interrupter or a directive expression. Use two commas unless the interrupter comes at the beginning of the sentence, when one comma suffices. Necessary end marks may replace one comma or both.

(1) Speech Tags

"Our water supply," *the note said,* "is nearly gone."

Tom turned to Jean. "Are you ready?" *he asked.*

"Yes," *she answered.* "Let's start at once."

"But where," *Tom wondered,* "is my knapsack?"

Jean replied, "You hung it on that tree."

Do not set off speech tags from indirect discourse: Jean replied that he had hung it on a tree.

Do not set off a speech tag from a quotation woven into a sentence: He muttered "Rats" and pushed forward.

(2) Direct Address

You can see, *Nancy,* that it's raining.

All right, *Mr. Chairman.* I'll sit down.

Charlie, you and I must have a long talk.

(3) Interjections Responsive Expressions Echo Questions

Oh, the orchestra is playing.

Why, so it is. *Well,* let's dance.

Yes, I like banana cream pie.

You like it too, *don't you?*

(4) Directive Expressions
> They decided, *it seems*, to build some shelves.
> *First*, they bought a piece of plywood.
> They had not thought, *however*, of measuring. . . .

Many words and phrases may be used either as directives or as plain adverbs. The test: Does the expression qualify the sentence, or does it modify one word?

Set off a directive: Shall we, *then*, become the aggressors?
Do not set off an adverb: Trouble *then* began.

Expressions like *that is* and *for example* are directives.

That is CORRECTLY PUNCTUATED

as a simple directive: I attempt to understand the plan of a book. I try, *that is*, to outline as I read.

with an appositive or other interrupter: The season of indoor track meets—that is, the period from late January to the end of March—always seems too short to me.

when introducing a main clause: Cromwell was a dissenter; that is, he opposed the Church of England.

[A comma regularly follows the directive *that is*.]

For example, namely CORRECTLY PUNCTUATED

as a simple directive: This pen, for example, flows freely.

with an appositive: Many cities, for example Duluth and Omaha, follow our plan.

with an appositive (equally correct): Many cities—Duluth and Omaha, for example—follow our plan. [The dashes give emphasis.]

Only two presidents—namely, Wilson and Roosevelt—won my uncle's approval.

Such as CORRECTLY PUNCTUATED when introducing examples: He dislikes all kinds of highly flavored food, such as beans with chile, curries, Roquefort cheese.

[No comma separates *such as* from the example which follows it.]

221

26c. Place and Date Completers Set off each interrupter which explains place or time:

From Burlington, *Iowa,* my grandmother moved to Greeley, *Weld County, Colorado.* On June 2, *1898,* she boarded the train.

I wrote to the Rockefeller Foundation, *49 West Forty-ninth Street, New York 20, New York,* requesting a copy of the president's review for 1950.

Do not set off items that are woven in:

. . . the president's review *for 1950.* He wrote to Senator Johnson *at the Senate Office Building in Washington.*

Practice Appositives, Guide Words, Completers

Copy each sentence. Insert necessary commas. Identify each situation by an explanatory phrase. Example:

The pony, restless, tossed his head. apposed adjective

1. Mary Wright my roommate lives in Duluth.
2. Mary a good-natured girl never complains when I leave my clothes lying around. Helen prim and tidy picks them up.
3. The plane one of those huge transports that look as steady as the Rock of Gibraltar tilted and slid earthward.
4. "I'm not apt to wake up" said Joe "unless somebody blows a bugle."
5. It could be of course that Hardy is guilty. After all he did try to escape.
6. Our first assignment—that is reading three outside books—must be completed by Friday.
7. Our instructor it seems expects us to be on time. "If you come after eight" he said "you will find the door locked."
8. On Sunday March 2 an impartial report appeared in at least one newspaper the *Christian Science Monitor.*
9. Tickets for our next play *Ever Since Eve* will go on sale at the Campus Bookstore on Thursday morning February 16.
10. Your Uncle Stephen writes that his train will arrive in Wichita at 7:15 on the evening of March 16.

26d. **Loose (nonrestrictive) Modifiers** Use commas to set off a detachable word, phrase, or clause. The test is: Can this modifier be removed without distorting the main idea of the sentence?

(1) Adjectival modifiers (relative clauses, participial and prepositional phrases, adjectives following the noun)

Set off a modifier added to a proper name or a term already identified.

Do not set off a modifier used to identify or restrict a general term.

LOOSE (DETACHABLE)

Tom Lang, *who was married only last month,* has quarreled with his wife.

My neck, *which was stiff,* is all right now. [I have only one neck. The modifier is added, not essential.]

The murals, *which had been painted in fluorescent colors,* glowed in the dark. [All the murals glowed; all were fluorescent.]

The knife, [which was] *now loosely dangling,* no longer appeared sinister.

Watching closely, we saw the cell elongate.

My Antonia, by Willa Cather, is a good novel.

The driver, *angry,* shouted an insult.

BUILT-IN (RESTRICTIVE)

People *who are quarrelsome* should not marry. Dogs *that fight* are a nuisance.

The finger *that was hurt* is all right now. [The modifier is needed to point out *that particular* finger.]

The murals *which had been painted in fluorescent colors* glowed in the dark. [Only some glowed; others were not fluorescent.]

The knife *dangling from his belt* reminded us that he was a fighter.

Anyone *watching closely* could see the cell elongate.

Any novel *by Willa Cather* is worth reading.

The *angry* driver shouted an insult.

(2) Adverbial clauses

Set off (a) loosely inserted clauses beginning with *when, where, after;* (b) *though* or *while* clauses expressing concession; (c) clauses of reason with *as* or *since;* (d) clauses of result.

Do not set off close modifiers expressing (e) a particular time or place; (f) sole reason or sole condition; (g) degree or manner; (h) single purpose.

LOOSE

At the end of the first half, *when the score stood 34 to 7,* we left the game.

At Oak Lodge, *where the music is always excellent,* we stopped for dancing.

Though Tom had no money, he ordered dinner. [Tom had no money, but...]

I'll take lemon pie, *if you please.* [Loosely added]

While we found nobody in the house, we did discover a man hiding in the barn.

He gave up raising cattle, *as he found raising alligators more profitable.* [Reason]

Rocks crashed down, *so that* the tunneling was interrupted. [Result]

BUILT-IN

We left *when the score reached 34 to 7* [= at that particular time].

We like to go *where we can dance. Where we danced* the music was excellent.

Because I have no money I cannot eat. One cannot buy food *unless he has money.*

I'll take lemon pie *if you do.* [Sole condition]

One man stood guard *while the other two searched the house.* [Time]

He raised alligators as easily *as you might raise puppies.* [Degree]

They cleared away the rocks *so that the work could proceed.* [Purpose]

For clearness, set off a very long introductory clause even though it modifies closely: If a bottle of liquid containing the superfine abrasive used for the final polish is shaken, the suspended matter takes half a day to settle.

(3) Adverbial phrases and plain adverbs; absolute phrases

Set off loose *with* phrases, directive expressions, and absolute phrases.*

Do not set off ordinary prepositional phrases or simple adverbs.

LOOSE

The runners passed the stand again, *with Joe now well in the lead*. [The phrase qualifies the whole sentence.]

After all, you must admit that she did come quickly. [Directive—qualifies sentence.]

The tree fell, *fortunately*, when no one was near.

The day being cloudy, we used no color film. [Absolute.]

The experiment finished, we compared notes.

The child looked up, *her eyes wide with wonder*.

To make a long story short, we reached land.

BUILT-IN

I went *with Mary* to see the races. The others could not keep up *with Joe*.

After the party we came home. Call me *after five*. [Time—modifies the verb.]

The tree crashed *heavily* to earth. [Simple adverb.]

On a cloudy day color film does not register well.

At the end of the experiment we compared notes.

The child looked up *in wonder*.

At long last we reached the shore.

To prevent ambiguity or to secure emphasis, set off an introductory infinitive phrase of purpose: To mix an angel food cake, sift the flour with the sugar and cream of tartar four times, beat the egg whites until they are fluffy but not stiff, and fold in the dry ingredients.

Do not set off an infinitive phrase which is short and closely restrictive: To win votes you must make promises.

* An absolute phrase is an expression which, though attached to a sentence, is grammatically independent of it. The "nominative absolute" consists of a noun plus a participle: *The plan having failed*, we decided to employ a lawyer.

EXERCISE

X-26a, b, c. Setting Off Interrupters

Copy each sentence. Insert necessary commas and state the reason for each.

1. Stefansson the noted explorer conducts a program of arctic study at Dartmouth College Hanover New Hampshire.
2. The constant speed of light approximately 186,000 miles per second refers to light in empty space.
3. The speaker asked "Have we become entangled in a cycle of wars?" After a pause he went on "It is a grim question my friends but we must face it."
4. You can order a film called *Drafting Tips* from the Educational Film Library Association Room 1000 1600 Broadway New York City.
5. At eleven o'clock on the morning of June 10 1947 I boarded a plane for the journey from Bombay India to Cairo Egypt.
6. In Egypt the most advanced of the Arab states the death rate is higher than in India.
7. In rural areas as a matter of fact there is but one doctor to every 10,000 inhabitants.
8. What is it would you say that sets a girl off from others as being well dressed?
9. Why it's hard to tell. Some girls—Helen and Marjorie for example—spend very little, yet always look attractive.
10. For our vacation we decided to tour the southwest a part of the country unfamiliar to us.
11. In Santa Fe New Mexico we got into conversation with a trader named Sam Pickett.
12. He told us that wool rugs formerly an important product of the Navajos are no longer made in quantity.
13. Most of the grazing area—that is the region which furnished food for wool-bearing sheep—has become depleted.
14. "Do you suppose" I asked "that the fertility of the soil can be restored?"
15. "No I do not think that is possible" he answered. "Some other source of income must be found."

X-26d. Setting Off Loose (Nonrestrictive) Modifiers

Copy the sentences, inserting necessary commas. Some items require no punctuation.

(1) Adjectival modifiers

1. My sister Jane who is just recovering from tonsillitis has to stay indoors for a few days.
2. An allergic reaction to penicillin may occur in persons who have had athlete's foot.
3. On Eniwetok atoll which lies southwest of Wake Island in the central Pacific our government conducted experiments in nuclear fission.
4. Some islands [which have been] used for experiments in nuclear fission are no longer habitable.
5. All our sheets which had been hung on the clothesline were stolen. [Could this sentence be punctuated in two ways? What would be the difference in meaning?]
6. Sue dressed in a plaid skirt and a red jacket met us at the door. The girl dressed in gray was her cousin.
7. As a finale we had music by the entire orchestra. They played selections from the ballet *Gaîté Parisienne* by Offenbach.
8. The position which I hoped to secure was taken by a man who had worked for the same company in another town.
9. She pushed the hood back from her face which shone red not only from the firelight but also from the day's exposure to wind and sun.
10. My father who is an experienced golfer could hardly restrain a grin as I teed off.
11. He who will discipline himself can command life instead of petitioning it.
12. A swimmer caught in a rip tide often has a hard struggle to escape.
13. At the beach last summer my cousin Ray caught in a rip tide was nearly drowned before help could reach him.
14. When my roommate is sick he has the disposition of an alley cat that has been teased.
15. Tired of being teased the monkey snatched the banana and scampered away.

(2) Adverbial modifiers and absolute phrases

16. Pete came into church after the collection had been taken.
17. Roger arrived at 11:10 just after the choir had sung the opening hymn.
18. The Industrial Revolution entered a new phase when the gasoline engine came into use.
19. A new phase of the Industrial Revolution began in the eighties when the gasoline engine first came into use.
20. As each plane lost altitude it would begin to wobble and waver like a little boy walking a rail fence. [Time]
21. As cars and planes will not run without fuel we must conserve our dwindling oil supply. [Reason]
22. We placed our camera well back from the clearing so that the underbrush would hide it. Everything being in readiness we settled ourselves to wait until dusk when the deer always come down to drink.
23. Just as I bent to check my flash bulb I heard a splash. Peering through the dim light, I discerned antlers outlined against a bank on the other side of the stream.
24. I tripped the shutter. The buck, frightened by the flash, bounded away so that we got barely a glimpse of him before he disappeared.
25. Our timber lands having been despoiled we must now undertake an extensive program of reforestation.
26. My friend Samuel Robbins though he turned twenty-nine only last month has already composed two symphonies.
27. He was eighteen when he first came to work in the office a diploma clutched in his hand.
28. In Pennsylvania last year 557,000 tons of cinders were used to reduce the peril of travel over icy roads.
29. The new discoveries of iron ore in Quebec and Labrador promise the largest source of this vital raw material since the discovery of the Mesabi deposit in Minnesota.
30. The one thing that the alloy steels have in common is that they retain a good deal of toughness even after they have been hardened to the point where they might be expected to lose their valuable properties. [A long sentence may be so tightly woven as to require no punctuation.]

THE APOSTROPHE

27. Use the apostrophe in contractions and in the possessive case of nouns, but not in possessive pronouns.

27a. **Contractions** Use an apostrophe to mark the precise point in a contraction where a letter is omitted.

Right: doesn't   didn't   can't   don't   won't   aren't
        there's   he's   she'd   I'll   you're   they've

Right: I didn't know they'd be here at nine o'clock [o'clock = of the clock]. Let's decide who's going.

27b. **Possessive Pronouns** Do not use an apostrophe with a personal pronoun or with *whose*.*

Right: ours   yours   theirs   his   hers   its   whose

Distinguish between the possessive *its* (= belonging to it) and the contraction *it's* (= it is).

Right: The cat washes *its* face. *It's* an Angora cat.

Practice   Possessive Pronouns and Contractions

Copy the sentences, inserting necessary apostrophes only. Above each italicized word write *p* for *possessive* or *c* for *contraction*.

1. The man lost *his* dog. *Hes* looking everywhere.
2. The dog wants *its* master. *Its* a cocker spaniel.
3. *Whose* car is that? *Whos* coming with us?
4. This house must be *theirs*. Look! *Theres* Robert.
5. What is *your* name? *Youre* first on the list.
6. How far that little candle throws *its* beams!
7. I shall be ready when *its* time to go.
8. This picture is *ours*. That one is *hers*.
9. The room is mine. *Its* not *yours* any more.
10. The church with *its* tall spire stood before her.

* The indefinites *one's*, *other's*, etc., follow the rule for nouns.

27c. **Possessive Case of Nouns** Use an apostrophe to form the possessive case of a noun.

Nouns not ending in *s* add **'s**   man $+$ **'s** $=$ man**'s** suit

men $+$ **'s** $=$ men**'s** suits

Nouns ending in *s* add **'**   boys $+$ **'** $=$ boys**'** suits

HOW TO APPLY THE RULE

1. Find the base word by turning the possessive into an *of* phrase: boys' hats = hats *of boys.* [Base word, *boys*]

2. Add an apostrophe: boys**'**, ladies**'**, women**'**, children**'**.

3. If the base ends in *s* add nothing more; if not, add *s*.

two boys**'** suits   ladies**'** hats   the girls**'** dormitory
a boy**'s** coat   men**'s**, women**'s**, and children**'s** clothing

Practice Write correctly as possessives with apostrophes:

the homes *of students*	clubs *for women*	*lawyers* fees
pensions *for veterans*	work done *by a man*	a *doctors* son
the eyes *of a girl*	a *ladys* privilege	*babies* feet
the eyes *of girls*	*teachers* salaries	my *sisters* dress
the views *of parents*	my *brothers* noses	a *friends* house

(1) Possessives of proper names ending in s To a plural name add the apostrophe only. To a singular name either add the apostrophe only or (the commoner usage) add *'s.*

Right for plural names: The Smiths**'** house, the Burnses**'** dog, the Morrises**'** garden

Permissible for singular names: Keats**'** poems, Thomas**'** car, John Evans**'** uncle, Mr. Morris**'** garden

Preferable for singular names: Keats**'s** poems, Thomas**'s** car, John Evans**'s** uncle, Mr. Morris**'s** garden; BUT Jesus**'** work [*'s* is regularly added to monosyllables. It is added to other singular names unless the extra syllable would be hard to pronounce.]

Warning: Never split a name or other term with an apostrophe. Write *Dickens**'*** or *Dickens**'s** novels* (not *Dicken's*), *ladies**'** hats* (not *ladie's*).

(2) Complicated possessives

To show joint possession use the sign of the possessive with only the last name in the series:

Crawford and Blake's Music Store, Sam and Bill's father

To show separate possession use it with each name:

meet at Nancy's or Jean's house, Sam's and Bill's fathers

With compounds and phrases add the sign of the possessive to the last word:

her daughter-in-law's cooking, Joe the plumber's wrench, the dean of men's office, the mayor of Danville's car

The double possessive is correct in certain idioms:

I'll see you at Mary's [house]. It's just a habit of Jim's. that boy of Mr. Wilson's, a friend of my mother's

The apostrophe is frequently omitted in the names of organizations:

Citizens Advisory Committee, Municipal Taxpayers League West Side Boys Club, Farmers Mutual Insurance Company [Follow the form used by the individual organization.]

(3) Apostrophe or *of* phrase?

With idioms expressing time or measure regularly use the apostrophe:

the day's work, a year's training, two weeks' wages ten minutes' walk, a month's vacation [Time] a dollar's worth, two dollars' worth, five pounds' weight a ship's length, a stone's throw [Measure]

With other nouns naming inanimate objects show possession by *of*:

the style of the book [NOT the book's style], the management of the farm [NOT the farm's management]

To avoid a clumsy possessive use an *of* phrase:

the voice of one of my friends [NOT one of my friends' voice], the property of the Carbide and Carbon Chemicals Corporation

27d. **Plurals of Letters, Numbers, etc.** Form the plurals of
letters, numbers, and words spoken of as words by
adding *'s*. (Warning: never form a regular plural by adding
's.)

Right: Your *t's* look like *i's*. Some boys use too many *and's*.

EXERCISE

X-27a, b. Contractions and Possessive Pronouns

Rewrite, inserting necessary apostrophes. Place each precisely.

1. If its your dog you must know its name.
2. Isnt it too bad that Nancy cant come?
3. Heres one glove, but Ive mislaid its mate.
4. Dont you think its time to go? Lets be off.
5. I cant understand why they werent invited.
6. The bridge is theirs, and theres no other road.
7. It isnt likely that his figures will differ from hers.
8. Whos driving, and whose car is he taking?
9. Shouldnt those tires of yours be recapped?
10. Youre weakening your argument, arent you?

X-27c. Possessive Nouns

Copy the sentences. Insert apostrophes and state the reason
for each.

1. He has his fathers red hair and his mothers brown eyes.
2. Bobs brother won first place in the mens tennis singles.
3. The army junked two million dollars worth of planes.
4. In the Lewises garden we found ripe strawberries.
5. John Davis [s] note said that he had gone to Vincents.
6. Jim just paid a months rent to Douglas [s] aunt.
7. This radio of Charles [s] will not work.
8. We should invite both Toms and Marys friends.
9. I applied for a position at Simon and Schusters [one firm].
10. The president of the Girls Athletic Association has approved Sallys taking part in the tournament. [A noun or
pronoun which modifies a gerund takes the possessive case.]

QUOTATION MARKS

28. Use quotation marks to enclose quoted speech, borrowed material, terms used in a special sense, and minor titles.

HOW TO QUOTE

28a. **Speech and Dialog** Use quotation marks to enclose the exact words of a speaker. Quote all of what is said and only what is said. Indicate every change of speaker by a new paragraph (see also **35e**).

(1) Punctuation and paragraphing of dialog

Place quotation marks both before and after each speech.

When a quotation is broken by a speech tag use a separate set of quotation marks for each part:

> "That certainly was sudden," Matt remarked.

> "Somebody pinch me," Harvey muttered; "I don't know whether I'm dead or alive."

Set off each separate speech, not each sentence within a speech:

> Matt said, "You're alive, all right. You climbed out of that cockpit, didn't you? Say, what did you think about when you knew we were going to crash?"

Do not paragraph separately outside comment which accompanies or replaces a speech tag:

> Harvey stared at him. "All I could think," he answered finally, "was that none of us would live through this."

Set off a speech tag by commas unless some stronger mark would be used if the tag were omitted:

> "Get down from that seat," called the red-haired man, "before I shoot you down."

> "By whose order?" inquired Sam.

> "Never mind whose order," the man snapped. "Get down!"

> [A question mark or exclamation point follows the quotation directly. A period or semicolon follows the speech tag.]

233

(2) Special problems in the punctuation of quoted speech

Enclose a quotation within a quotation by single marks: *

> "One man said, 'I'm badly hurt,' " the driver reported.
>
> "I was awakened," the girl told us, "by a voice shouting 'Fire! Fire!' " [No comma is needed after *shouting* because the quoted word *fire* is woven into the sentence.]

Place commas and periods inside a closing quotation mark:

> "Every man," Ruth insisted, "is as lazy as he dares to be."

Place other marks inside if they apply to the quotation only, outside if they apply to the main sentence only:

> Someone asked, "Doesn't might make right?"
>
> Who shouted, "Might makes right"?

For a *quoted* question within a question ordinarily place the question mark inside the quotation marks:

> Who asked, "Doesn't might make right?"

Never use double end marks. When two different marks are involved retain only the stronger: I did not know how to answer the man who asked, "Doesn't might make right?"

(3) Direct vs. indirect quotation

Use quotation marks for direct quotations: The driver reported, "One man is badly injured." [the exact words of the speaker]

Use no quotation marks for indirect quotations: The driver reported that one man was badly injured. [An indirect quotation may of course be part of a direct quotation: The driver reported, "One man said that he was hurt."]

A direct quotation of part of a sentence may be introduced by *that*: The court referred to the principle that "all people stand equal before the bar of justice." [The words are those actually spoken.]

Wrong: He repeated that "he was fed up with his job." [Omit quotation marks; The words he spoke were, "I am fed up with my job."]

---

* It is permissible to use single marks for ordinary quotations, double marks for quotations within quotations.

28b. **Borrowed Matter** Use quotation marks to set off borrowed material—phrases, sentences, or paragraphs.

(1) Accuracy Quote word for word. If you omit words insert three dots . . . If the omission comes at the end of a sentence add a period. If quotation marks follow, place them after the end mark. If you insert words, as of explanation or summary, enclose them in brackets [ ].

On page 199 of the *1947 Britannica Book of the Year* this statement is made: "Efforts to protect children and youth from harmful labor . . . were again evident by 1946. . . ." The article continues, "World wide concern for the welfare of young workers appeared in the discussions at the International Labour conference . . . and . . . advances [in child protection] were made during the year in Great Britain, the British dominions and the United States."

If you quote part of a sentence enclose only the words actually quoted.

The article states that the conference recommended medical examinations "as a prerequisite for employment of minors under 18 in both industrial and nonindustrial occupations." [When a quoted passage is built into the sentence no comma precedes it.]

(2) Long quotations If you quote two or more paragraphs place quotation marks at the beginning of each and at the end of the last only.

"New techniques for using penicillin involved incorporation of the drug in lozenges . . . for infections of the throat and in sprays . . . for infections of the lungs.

"Tablets of penicillin were developed which could be taken by mouth in doses of 50,000 and 100,000 units. About three times the dosage is required when the drug is taken by mouth instead of by injection." *

* Morris Fishbein, "Medicine," *1947 Britannica Book of the Year*, Encyclopaedia Britannica, Inc.

In a term paper or similar work you may set off a long quotation simply by setting it in from both margins and single spacing, omitting quotation marks.

You need not use quotation marks for poetry, as the verse form sets it off.

28c. **Words Used in a Special Sense** Use quotation marks to set off a word or phrase given a special meaning. Do not set off terms in common use.

(1) Technical terms Set off terms newly coined or different in meaning from the everyday sense of the words. (In a paper set off such a term the first time it is used, not afterward.) Do not set off technical or scientific words which have come into common use.

Right (a new term): This radio station uses a recently developed beam-switching tube, the "Cyclophon."

Right (specialized use of common words): One type of antenna is the "clover leaf," a cluster of four curved elements.

Right (familiar technical terms): Broadcasting by frequency modulation has greatly improved reception.

(2) Slang Do not set off slang or dialectal words except when they are introduced abruptly into formal writing.

Incorrect: We put out "ads" that "knock 'em cold." [Apologizing by quotation marks does not make excessive use of slang acceptable. If you do use slang—in a letter to a close friend, for example—use it without apology.]

Correct informal usage: We put out ads with punch. [Colloquial expressions are not set off. They are appropriate in informal writing to give an effect of terseness and vigor.]

Correct formal usage. We put out striking advertisements. We try to catch the eye of the reader—to "wow" him. [In formal writing a slang expression may be introduced for emphasis. It would seem incongruous if it were not set off.]

236

(3) Warning Do not set off proverbial expressions or nick-names. Do not use quotation marks to label humor. Do not use them to emphasize a particular expression.

Right: His wits often went woolgathering. We called him Fuzz.

Right: The mule had a powerful chassis and non-skid feet.

Right: Do you enjoy living in the out-of-doors?

28d. **Titles** Use quotation marks to set off minor titles.

(1) Titles of minor parts Use italics for the name of a major work; use quotation marks to set off parts, such as poems or stories in a collection, articles in a magazine, chapters in a book.

Right: In Miss Millay's volume *The Buck in the Snow* I like best the title poem, "The Buck in the Snow".

Right: In the September *Atlantic* Stephen Potter writes on "Golfmanship: Or How to Win Without Actually Cheating."

Right: One chapter of *Language in Action* is called "The Little Man Who Wasn't There."

Right: The story appeared on page one of last evening's *New York Times* under the headline "Rail Strike Averted."

(2) Titles of minor works Use either quotation marks or italics for titles of works of art, short musical compositions, plays, motion pictures, radio programs.*

Right: Da Vinci's famous mural "The Last Supper" is painted on a wall which is crumbling away.

Right: My favorite among Stephen Foster's songs is "Jeanie with the Light Brown Hair."

Right: I have been listening to "The Chicago Roundtable."

Right: Laurence Olivier's film version of *King Henry V* attracted large audiences. [Quotation marks would be permissible. Italics are somewhat more common for plays.]

---

* In letters and other informal writing, titles may be set off simply by capitalizing the principal words. In typewritten letters titles are frequently written entirely in capitals.

EXERCISE

X-28a, b, c. Quotation Marks

Copy the passages, inserting necessary quotation marks.

1. What's the matter, Jim? inquired Pete. Have you a cold?
   Yes, I seem to have picked up a sniffle, answered Jim.
   Pete shook his head. Too bad you haven't pneumonia, he
   said, because they know what to do for that.

2. A voice called, Keep to the outside wall. The steps are not
   so narrow there. The words echoed strangely down the long
   passage.

3. In an article called Let Fly Downhill, published in *Harper's
   Magazine* for January, 1948, Eric Swenson says of skiing
   that it has progressed in twenty years from the status of a
   foreign foolishness to that of a national mania. [The sentence contains a quoted passage introduced by *that*.]

4. Roger told me that he went skiing last weekend.

5. I was deeply moved, Elaine said, when the minister began,
   Dearly beloved, we are gathered together   [Besides inserting quotation marks, indicate correctly by dots the
   omission of the rest of the sentence.]

6-8. [Besides adding quotation marks, place brackets around an
   inserted explanatory phrase. Also, place the correct number of dots in each blank space.]   Near the end of his
   third volume Gibbon says, This awful revolution the col-
   lapse of the Western Roman Empire may be usefully applied to the   instruction of the present age. He smugly
   describes the existing state of affairs (1780):   the prosperity of our own or the neighboring kingdoms may be
   alternately exalted or depressed; but these partial events
   cannot essentially injure our general state of happiness
   He concludes on a note of high optimism   Europe is secure from any future irruption of Barbarians

9. In the baseball game yesterday a southpaw, Slim Condon,
   pitched a sizzling no-hitter.

10. Chapter I of Masteller's helpful little volume, *How to
    Avoid Financial Tangles*, is called Elementary Property
    Problems.

OTHER MARKS

29. Learn the use of end marks and of the semicolon, the colon, dashes, parentheses, brackets.

HOW TO SEPARATE STATEMENTS

29a. **End Marks** End questions with question marks; end other sentences with periods or (occasionally) with exclamation points. (Use an exclamation point to express strong emotion; do not use it to emphasize trivial ideas or to label humor.)

Right: Where were you? What does it matter? Why bother?

Right: He asked where I was. [A statement, even though it includes an indirect question, is followed by a period.]

Right: Did he ask where I had gone? [An interrogative sentence, whether or not it includes an indirect question, is followed by a question mark.]

Right: Sit down. Have a drink. Tell me about your trip. [An imperative sentence is regularly followed by a period.]

Right: Halt! Don't turn! We have you covered. [A sharp command takes an exclamation point. A declarative sentence which follows it usually takes a period.]

Right: Oh, look! Oh! You startled me. [The exclamation point comes at the end unless *Oh* requires special emphasis.]

Right: Oh, run along. [For mild expressions no exclamation point is needed.]

Right: Yes. Surely. Of course. Great! When?
[Conversational bits are treated as sentences.]

Right: "Hit this one!" yelled the pitcher.
Where can we find the men? the money? the equipment?

[A question mark or an exclamation point used within a sentence replaces the expected comma.]

239

29b. **The Semicolon** Use a semicolon between main clauses not joined by *and, or, but, for* (see also **25a**).

The weeds must have been perennials; they were deeply rooted.

The jaws of the scoop swung open; out tumbled dirt and debris.

Slowly he lifted the blankets; slowly he let his feet slide down to the cold floor.

In France before the Revolution great misery and great injustice existed; nevertheless the ruling classes felt secure.

The FBI takes over where local law enforcement leaves off; that is, it pursues criminals across state borders.

(1) Use a semicolon between independent statements if they form a logical unit. Otherwise separate them by a period. Do not use a semicolon to set off a subordinate element.

Right: Three men and a boy sailed away; four men returned.

Right: The three men and the boy sailed away. They were to battle many a storm before they could return.

Wrong: On the whole, *Macbeth* was well acted; though the prophecies of the witches were not very clearly spoken.

Right: ... *Macbeth* was well acted, though the prophecies....

(2) Use a semicolon instead of a comma between main clauses joined by *and, or, but, for* if the clauses are complicated by internal commas.

A fluid coupling does the same work as a friction clutch; but the principle on which it operates, the use of centrifugal force, is entirely different.

You are an honest man, and I am your uncle; and that's two lies.

(3) Use semicolons to separate the items of a series complicated by internal commas.

For the enclosed six dollars please send me the following: one cross-cut saw, twenty-two-inch blade, at $1.50; one jack-plane at $1.50; and three half-inch chisels at $1.00.

29c. **The Colon** Use a colon to introduce a long or formal direct quotation, explanation, question, or example. Use a colon before a formal appositive series at the end of a statement. Do not use a colon before a list of items which are not appositives of an introductory term. Do not use a colon in an interrupted sentence.

Right (formal quotation): The author makes this unqualified statement: "The rivalry of the two systems is a permanent fact. We must use all our power to keep it within bounds."

Right (formal question): Here another problem arises: what will be the cost of generating power from uranium and thorium?

Right (formal explanation): The spy was playing a difficult game: he was trying to appear a coöperative member of the group and at the same time to ferret out its secrets.

Right (formal appositive series at the end of a statement): These prefabricated houses use four types of material: aluminum sections, small concrete slabs, large panels of foamed concrete, and asbestos sheeting.

Right (not an appositive series): Prefabricated houses must be made of materials which are easy to handle, such as aluminum, foamed concrete, asbestos.

Right (not an appositive series): These prefabricated houses are built of aluminum, concrete, and asbestos. [Warning: Place no comma after *of*. See **25d (2)**, **(3)**.]

Right (not an appositive series): The materials used in these houses are aluminum, concrete, and asbestos. [Place no comma after *are*. See **25b (3)**.]

Right (an appositive series in mid-sentence): Three specially selected men, Heath, Rogers, and Kimball, will go on duty at nine. [Rule **26a** for appositives requires commas before and after the series.]

Better: Three specially selected men—Heath, Rogers, and Kimball—will go on duty at nine. [The use of dashes prevents confusion.]

HOW TO SET OFF PARENTHETIC MATTER

29d. The Dash Use a single dash to denote hesitancy or breaking off. Use dashes in pairs to set off interrupters which are emphatic or complicated by commas. Make the dash twice as long as the hyphen.

Breaking off: The next morning—let's see, what happened then?

Hesitancy: I can hardly speak of—of that terrible time.

Emphatic interrupter: I wanted to see Alaska—father knew that —and here was my chance.

Emphatic interrupter: A Harvard man now serves on the *Radcliffe News*—as fashion editor, no less! [An end mark may replace the second dash.]

Emphatic appositive: One person—his old choirmaster—the great singer never forgot.

Appositive with *for instance, for example*: Some diseases—influenza, for example—are believed to be caused by viruses.

Appositive series: In the tar-pits naturalists find bones of animals now extinct—mammoths, giant wolves, saber-toothed tigers. [The dash is less formal than the colon.]

(1) Combination with other marks A dash is not used after a comma, colon, or semicolon. An element between dashes does not begin with a capital or close with a period. It may be followed by a question mark or an exclamation point.

Right: At last we arrived—no one knew how—at the camp.

Right: She fell asleep—would you believe it?—in the middle of the lecture.

(2) Warning The overuse of dashes is a mark of lazy and hurried writing.

Excessive use of dashes: We went to a show last night—a good show really—not the best I've seen lately but one of the best —a kind of musical phantasy.

Recast: We went to a good show last night, one of the best I've seen recently. It was a musical phantasy called. . . .

29e. Parentheses Use parentheses for enclosing figures slipped in to confirm a written number. Use parentheses for asides and for inserting explanatory matter or additional information.

Confirmer: I enclose five dollars ($5.00).

Aside: The program (they hope) will fill the theater.

Explanatory matter: The red algae (the color may be red, violet, or purple) are nearly all marine.

Extra information: The compositions of Cesar Franck (1822-1890) gave rise to storms of controversy in music circles.

Information needed at a particular point: Java has 800 persons per square mile (the U.S.A. has 45) and in another generation will have 1,400.

(1) Parentheses or dashes

Use parentheses to submerge information: Mr. Donaldson, the faculty adviser (who was held responsible even though he had not seen the article), was called before the Committee on Publications. [The parenthetic clauses merely explain why Mr. Donaldson was called.]

Use dashes to emphasize a point: Mr. Donaldson, the faculty adviser—he had not even seen the article, remember—was called before the Committee on Publications. [Emphasizing the parenthetic statement by dashes suggests that it was unfair for Mr. Donaldson to be called.]

(2) Combination with other marks
A sentence which contains a parenthesis is punctuated exactly as it would be without the parenthetic matter.

Right: The horse has evolved from a small, four-toed mammal (see Fig. 122); every stage in the process is traceable. [The mark of punctuation is placed *after* the second curve.]

Right: Among important composers of the early nineteenth century we must include Schubert (1797-1828), Mendelssohn 1809-1847), and Schumann (1810-1856). [The commas are placed where they would fall if the numerals were omitted.]

(3) Punctuation within parentheses An interruptive sentence within parentheses is not capitalized. No end mark follows it unless it is a question or an exclamation. A parenthetic sentence between two other sentences requires a capital and an end mark.

Right: We tramped for an hour (my feet were aching) before we rested.

Right: We tramped for an hour (how my feet ached!) before we rested.

Right: We tramped for an hour. (Why had I ever come?) Finally we stopped to rest.

29f. Brackets Use brackets to insert explanations, corrections, or omitted matter in the body of a quotation.

Pringle continues, "Generally speaking (it is, of course, a pretty wide generalization), one is aware of a certain failure of the creative spirit in the ruins of the Roman Empire. . . . Not only the conquerors but natives of the provinces [the people of Cyrene and Leptis] imitated classic forms." [The matter in parentheses was inserted by the original author, that in brackets by the person quoting.]

EXERCISE

X-29a. End Marks

Copy these sentences, supplying necessary periods, question marks, and exclamation points.

1. We were asked to explain what makes water hard
2. "Do you know what makes water hard" "Yes"
3. "Look Is that a signal" "Oh, I don't think so"
4. "Stop" the watchman shouted "Here comes a train"
5. What rattled the windows Was it gunfire an explosion an earthquake
6. Drive with care Slow down at intersections
7. "Oh What's that" "Don't move It's a rattler"
8. Oh, Martha What a shocking mistake
9. The waiter asked how many were in our party
10. "How many are in your party" the waiter asked

X-29b. The Semicolon

Copy the following sentences, supplying semicolons where they are required. Supply commas or periods between main clauses when they are appropriate. Capitalize where necessary.

1. The man must have been there a moment before his cigarette was still burning.
2. Some of the paintings were abstractionist in technique others were conventional.
3. Every year in this country erosion carries away half a million acres of topsoil that is, every twenty-four hours we lose the equivalent of two hundred farms.
4. The snow kept falling it covered the road two, six, ten inches deep.
5. A heavy snow had fallen during the night by ten o'clock next morning, however, the road was open.
6. There appeared to be no one in the office but a half-open file stood on the desk and chairs were stacked with papers.
7. The quality of a Hollywood actor's work is recognized only in the context of success for prizes are awarded only for rôles in popular pictures, never for a good piece of acting in a picture which has failed.
8. The port burst into activity trucks rumbled along the streets cranes and winches creaked loudspeakers blared orders to scurrying workmen.
9. The Department of Agriculture lists four grades for canned fruit: A, or Fancy B, or Choice Broken and Offgrade.
10. We observed three species of birds not often seen here: the scarlet tanager the Baltimore oriole, both male and female the tiny yellow warbler or wild canary.
11. James will never be elected for the progressives consider him too cautious and the conservatives regard him as a dangerous radical.
12. Ninety-nine per cent of obesity is the result of overeating one per cent is due to other causes.
13. The town sprawled beneath us, half hidden by the butte on which we stood beyond it stretched an endless plain.
14. Food went up fifty per cent textiles doubled in price.
15. Browne has promised to give us a concert only the date remains to be agreed upon.

X29c. The Colon

Copy the sentences, inserting colons as required.

1. I quote from Huxley "Indeed, the whole size and shape of bones is plastic. If a puppy is prevented from using its leg . . . after six months the bones of the unused limb will be only about half the length of those used to carry weight."

2. My favorite English comedies are *As You Like It, She Stoops to Conquer,* and *The Importance of Being Ernest.*

3. I have three favorites among English comedies Shakespeare's *As You Like It,* Goldsmith's *She Stoops to Conquer,* and Wilde's *The Importance of Being Ernest.*

4. Our modern world has witnessed the rise and decline of five great empires the Roman, the Chinese, the Arabian, the Mongolian, the British.

5. Two important questions to ask about a candidate for public office are these Is he intelligent? Is he honest?

X-29d, e. Dashes, Parentheses

Copy each sentence. Insert dashes or parentheses.

1. When the policeman pulled up beside us but why go into that?

2. Linnaeus 1707-1778 grouped all animals into six classes.

3. Hal dipped the daisies all four thousand of them in blue dye.

4. At our track meets held usually on Saturday afternoons we compete with teams from different parts of the state.

5. Students who had not found rooms I was one were told that they could not register for classes.

6. Even the richest fishing grounds the English Channel, for instance yield only one pound dry weight of fish per acre.

7. If other nations China, India, Russia have a great many people, shouldn't the United States increase its population?

8. No. A better plan who can doubt it is to take measures which will help other nations improve their standard of living.

9. A steel shortage would have existed even if war had not destroyed 18 million tons the figure commonly given.

10. We landed at the airport. Why do most airports have such an improvised look? It took us an hour to reach town.

PART TWO

LARGER ELEMENTS AND PROBLEMS

The Whole Composition

ANALYZING YOUR SUBJECT AND SHARPENING IT FOR A DEFINITE PURPOSE

30. Take a subject rich in interest (one on which you are well informed or one on which you want to be well informed). **Analyze and limit your subject. Determine your purpose and your controlling idea. Find a title.**

HOW TO FOCUS YOUR WRITING

30a. Limiting the Subject Think over your subject and choose one phase that you can develop with thoroughness. A broad subject tempts you to skim over the surface with generalities and abstractions. A limited subject helps you to dig deep, to write definitely and concretely.

You can limit in many ways. For example, the broad subject "Stage Design" might be limited by

Number:	Three principles of modern stage design
Kind:	Abstraction as a method in stage design
Part or aspect:	Color values in stage design
Purpose:	Stage design for the college theater
Time and place:	Innovations in American stage design during the last ten years.
Human element:	The work of Robert Edmond Jones

For a short paper limit the scope still further. Try beginning with *one, the best, the first, the most, my.*

The best method for a small stage
My biggest problem in stage design
The sets for our production of "Pinafore"
The most useful innovation in stage design

Caution: Limiting by space or time may not limit scope. Changing "The duties of the stage designer" to "The duties of the stage designer in America" does not limit the principles to be explained. "The chief duty of the stage designer" limits scope.

When you are given an abstract or general subject help yourself by thinking of concrete objects or specific events related to it. Suppose that you have a list of suggested subjects for a paper in psychology. One general subject is "Prejudices and Aversions." How can you limit it? Think of some experience of your own: "How I acquired an aversion to spinach." One personal experience would of course be too slight for a paper and would not give sufficient evidence from which to generalize; but it might suggest a suitably limited yet important subject, "How an aversion is acquired."

Follow a similar procedure for an abstract subject like "Democracy." Think of situations you have actually observed which cast light on the workings of democracy. Consider, for example, school social functions and organizations, campus politics, athletics. Formulate a limited subject suggested by your observations: "How group pressure influences voters," "Sport as an influence for social democracy," or possibly "Some undemocratic features of our student government" or "How one campus organization combats prejudice."

30b. **Determining Your Purpose and Your Controlling Idea**

Sharpen your limited subject to accomplish a specific purpose. Ask yourself, Who is my reader? What do I want to do with him? Entertain him? Inform him? Persuade him?

Determine your thesis or controlling idea. Ask yourself, Exactly what point do I wish to make? Express the idea in a single sentence.

Limited subject: The College Frolics

Purpose: to entertain Bill Brown in the infirmary

Controlling idea: The dress rehearsal last night was a riot of errors.

Purpose: to explain to an inexperienced committee how to work the lights for the show

Controlling idea: Making light properly support stage activities requires careful planning, thorough familiarity with the equipment, and alert attention to cues.

Purpose: to persuade a budget committee to approve a large expenditure for lights

Controlling idea: In the long run expenditure for lights is an economy, since lighting can obviate many changes of scene.

Your purpose may be to clarify a problem for yourself.

Purpose: to determine my fitness for a job as salesman

Controlling idea: Since I have made a study of sales technique and since I have a knack for persuading people to buy things I would probably succeed.

Your purpose may be to present an objective study—a common purpose in college work.

Purpose: to determine the desirability of sectioning students in school on the basis of I.Q. ratings

Controlling idea [reached after examination of material]: Sectioning on the basis of I.Q. has disadvantages which, in the view of many authorities, outweigh the advantages.

30c. Finding a Title Try to think of an exact and effective title, one that indicates accurately the nature and limits of the composition. If no good phrasing occurs to you immediately, formulate a working title. As you write you may think of a better one.

Title broad or vague: Do not write *Drawing* if your material is restricted to *The Wistful Characters of Abner Dean*.

Title incomplete: Do not write *Tin* when you can indicate the scope of your treatment by an added phrase: *Tin or Glass on the Pantry Shelf; Tin—the Master of Bolivia*.

Title deceptive: Do not write *How Sales May Be Increased* if your paper discusses rather *The Qualities of a Good Salesman*.

Title inappropriate: Do not write *Nuts to You* as the title of a serious article on *Industrial Uses of Peanuts*, or any title whose bearing on the subject is not eventually clear.

Title empty: Do not write as a title merely the subject of an assignment—*A Character Sketch, An Exposition, An Informal Essay*—but rather *Philosopher With a Broom, The Woodwinds for Color, Good Eating—an Oyster Roast*.

EXERCISE

X-30. Analyzing a Subject

Which subject in each group is most narrowly limited? For each broad subject write a different one-phase subject. For one of your one-phase subjects write a controlling idea and a title.

People	Financial problems
Teachers	Where my money goes
Professor White	A college student's budget
Tennis	Color
Duties of a linesman	Psychological effects of color
Sports	I dislike brown
Mountaineering	Restoring denuded areas
Climbing with ropes	Erosion
My worst moment	One experiment in reforestation

FINDING AND ORGANIZING MATERIAL

31. Find and arrange in a clear and effective order enough material to develop your subject thoroughly.

HOW TO COLLECT AND ARRANGE IDEAS

31a. **Finding Material** Get things to say before you begin to write, the substance you need to round out your ideas fully. Think out the hows and whys, the implications, uses, results; think what your reader needs to know. Start by jotting down your controlling idea and possible main points. Under these jot down definite facts, concrete illustrations, incidents, bits of dialog. Or begin with details and from them discover a controlling idea and main points. Jot items in any order as they occur to you; keep them flowing. Once you begin to jot you will find that one idea suggests another.

Suppose you have noticed a condition that needs a remedy. You might collect the material you have in your mind by some such jottings as these.* (Notice that the details are not yet sifted and ordered.)

Controlling idea: Several conditions contributing to the shortage of nurses for bedside care can be remedied.

Supporting material to be considered:

Possible causes of the shortage	Remedies
working conditions, pay	admit practical nurses?
training—time, expense	lower requirements?
requirements (find out)	shorten training?
appeal of other positions	raise pay?
non-academic squeezed out (example)	nurses' aides?
mistaken attitudes (example)	freedom?

* For writing based on research see **52.**

If your information is inadequate at any point, consult books and magazines (see **50**) or make a personal investigation. Take notes (see **51**) and combine the material with your jottings.

31 b. **Logical Division and Proportion** Sort your material into logical divisions, deciding what main points you need to cover your subject completely. Keep your main points few, so that you can be concrete and thorough. Assign space to each according to its importance to your purpose and controlling idea. Discard any material that is irrelevant or out of proper proportion.

Related topics brought together under main points:

Influences against choice of bedside nursing as a career
> Greater attraction in pay and working conditions of occupations other than nursing
> Greater freedom and prestige in other branches of the profession both inside and outside hospitals

Faults in requirements and training of nurses
> Mistaken selection by academic ability rather than by ability and interest in caring for the sick
> Disproportionate emphasis on study of science
> Excessive time and expense of training

Means of overcoming the shortage
> Improvement in pay, working conditions, and prestige
> Adjustment of standards to admit "born" nurses
> Development of a corps of nurses qualified and recognized by a special degree for bedside nursing only

(I) **Beginnings** Do not assign too much space to beginnings.
If you are discussing John Marshall's part in determining the rôle of the Supreme Court you will want little if any material on Marshall's previous career. On the other hand if you are analyzing your brother's psychological quirks you will want material on his early life.

(2) **Excess** If you find one division growing out of all proportion to others weigh it carefully. You can thin it down or build others up until points of equal importance receive approximately equal coverage. Or you can revise your original plan and devote your entire treatment to the part that has shown itself most vital.

(3) **Inadequacy** If you find one thin little topic with nowhere to go give it some thought. If it is unimportant, discard it. If it is important, either include it in one of your present divisions by broadening the classification or make it the basis of a new division by adding new material.

INSTRUMENTS OF THE ORCHESTRA

Strings
Woodwinds
Brasses
Percussion instruments
Piano

wind-machine?

[Broaden the last topic:
Instruments for special effects]

A CONDITIONING PROGRAM

Diet
   Kind and amount of food
   Time of meals
Exercise
   Practice for event
   Other activities
Rest and sleep

worry?

[Include in a new division:
   Mental discipline
      Attitude toward event
      General attitudes]

Practice Sorting Material

State a controlling idea for the following subject; group the related topics under three or four main points. Eliminate any irrelevant topics. Add any needed topics.

Subject: Keeping up the college plant

grounds	repairs	replacements	maids
laundry	janitors	gifts to library	utilities
buildings	cleaning	student labor	gardening

31c. **Logical and Effective Order** Arrange your divisions in an order suited to your subject, your reader's needs, and your purpose.

(1) Different orders are useful for different purposes.

Next-in-Time Order: Place first what happens first and later what happens later. This order is normal in narrative and often useful in exposition, particularly in explaining a process or a cause and its effect.

Next-in-Space Order: Place first what one would see or encounter first and proceed to what one would see next. This order is normal in description—near, middle, far; left, center, right; head, body, limbs.

Next-in-Importance Order: Place the most important matter first, the next in importance second, etc.—an order common in news stories, but undesirable in most writing.

Rise-in-Importance Order (Climax): Hold back the more important divisions of the subject until the end, or near the end —an order most useful in creating suspense or in building toward a strong conclusion.

Order of Likeness or Difference (Comparison): Treat first all the points about one idea and then the points about a similar or an opposed idea. Or treat one point about one idea, the same point about an opposing idea, another point about the first idea, the same point about its opposite, etc.

General-to-Particular Order: Give first a general idea or total impression and follow it with details, or proceed from details to the general idea. A variation is a Parts-to-Function order.

Simple-to-Complex or Familiar-to-Unfamiliar: Place first the easily understood or the well known.

(2) The subject itself may suggest the most effective order— next-in-time, next-in-space, parts-to-function.

PRESENTING A UNIT TO FIFTH GRADERS	A BOOSTER PUMP
1. Introducing the subject	1. Parts
2. Guiding class discussion	2. Operation
3. Fitting work to individual needs	3. Accomplishment

256

(3) Your reader's needs may decide the order. What does he
need to know first, next, last? Must he have the big idea
first for information or last for suspense or emphasis? Would
a comparison help him?

THE STUDENT CURRICULUM COMMITTEE
1. Purpose
2. Membership
3. Procedures

A NEW PROCESS
1. The familiar
2. The unfamiliar
3. Advantages

(4) Your purpose may decide the order. How can you take a
reader to the goal you want him to reach? (1) by beginning with a direct statement? (2) by withholding the
statement until the end?

Your purpose may be to show how a principle or an opinion applies to a particular instance, or how it operates under
certain conditions, or why you believe it to be true. The
natural method is to begin with a direct statement and follow
with supporting details.

Principle: Water seeks its own level.
Application: a siphon

Opinion: Most radio commercials are objectionable.
Examples: the repetitive, the intimate, the pseudo-scientific

You may wish to lead your reader to a possibly unwel-
come conclusion. To state your view at the beginning might
antagonize him. You therefore use the indirect method,
opening with no more than a hint and then giving him bit by
bit specific evidence. At the end you state your conclusion
as a clincher.

Opening: A particularly fine series of concerts is to be given
here, for which students can get reduced rates.
Support: names of artists, programs, benefits to be gained
Clincher: It's such a worth-while opportunity that I thought
you might raise my allowance to cover it.

You may wish to discover a solution—for example, in reasoning out a problem of conduct or of practical finance or a philosophical question. Not knowing the solution, you begin by stating the problem. You then write out specifically the factors involved, pro and con. At the end you may be able to state a conclusion.

Problem: Ought I to change roommates?

Analysis of present situation: sources of discord, possibility of adjustments

Analysis of possible results of change: effect on present roommate, relations with possible roommate, effect on work

Conclusion: ?

EXERCISE

X-31. Sorting and Ordering Material

a. Jot and proportion material for one of these subjects. Group details under a few main points.

What's wrong with college food   How to give up smoking
A character trait I dislike   First steps in teaching anyone
Don't dim those lights; polarize   to drive a car
Heating by radiation   A big difference between . . . .

b. For each of these subjects write down a definite purpose with a definite reader. Select two and plan the best order, tentatively listing main points under each and stating what order you have followed.

1. Making a blueprint
2. How radar operates
3. Presenting new foods to infants
4. May I go to Norway next summer?
5. My favorite spot in the library
6. The biggest problem in rural electrification
7. Which shall I be—an architect or a civil engineer?
8. How would Rosalind have behaved in Viola's place?
9. Budget blues—my ends don't meet
10. How a "law" of physics is derived

OUTLINING

32. Use an outline to secure clearness and force in writing. Use outlines to systematize and test your knowledge.*

Before building even a small house one must make a floor plan showing proportions, functions, relationships. Just so, one must plan before building a structure of ideas.

Outlining is a flexible process to be adapted to individual needs. For a short paper or an informal talk the outline may be merely a list of two or three main points in order.

BUDGETING FOR COLLEGE

1. Fixed expenditures: food, shelter, tuition, school supplies
2. Adjustable expenditures: clothing, recreation, personal goods and services

For complicated subjects the outline may be a complete chart of the material to be covered. Some sort of plan is essential if ideas are not to wander and backtrack and come to no conclusion.

Two procedures commonly used, alone or in combination, in developing outlines are explained below in detail. Try each procedure once; vary thereafter to suit special needs. Many individual adaptations are possible. Some experienced writers do parts of the planning and ordering in their heads; others work out every step on paper.

The time when an outline sets in final form will vary with the individual and with the occasion. As a rule it should be kept fluid until the actual writing of the paper begins. The main thing is to devise a procedure that helps you to select and arrange material so that a reader may easily follow your thought.

* For an outline used to test the organization of an article already written see 34b.

HOW TO DEVELOP AN OUTLINE

32a. Grouping Ideas for Clear Presentation—Working Up

1. Collect a quantity of material on your subject by jotting notes on a sheet of paper or on separate slips or cards (31a). Pin down every idea that occurs to you.

2. Study the collected material to find what items belong together. For each group of related items write a heading. If you have many headings discover three or four main heads that will cover them. Number the items or sort your cards to match the headings.

BUYING A USED CAR

compare prices—ads	1	evidence of accidents	2
bluebook ratings	1	history of car if possible	4
different makes	1	mileage	4
consult owners	1	road test—slow speeds	3
reliable dealers?	1	climbing performance	3
body type desired	1	even braking	3
price that can be met	1	check brake linings	2
check with mechanic	2, 3	figure costs of essential repairs	
compression, blow-by	2	into price of car	4
cracks in cylinder block	2	backlash, bucking, ping	3
vibration and noise	2, 3	evidence of previous repairs	2

Main Heads:

Preliminary consideration	1	Road test	3
Examination of standing car	2	Final assessment	4

3. Sharpen a controlling idea to accomplish a definite purpose with your material (30). Discard items that do not fit; add any necessary items (31b).

4. Decide on the most effective order for the main heads and for the items within each group (31c). Mark the order with numbers or letters.

5. Unless your notes are clear and your subject simple, make a fresh copy in outline form (32e).

32b. Dividing Ideas for Clear Presentation—Working Down

Instead of adding up lesser ideas to find main ideas one may break down main ideas to find supporting lesser ideas.

1. Sharpen your subject, decide on your purpose, formulate and write down your controlling idea.

2. Discover the big divisions of your subject, choosing the best basis of division for your purpose (**32d**). List main headings with several lines of space between. If your headings do not seem to cover the subject adequately, revise them or add more or narrow your subject. If you find that you have more than four or five main divisions, reconsider. Your basis of division may be faulty; you may have mistaken a subordinate idea for a main idea; your subject may have been insufficiently narrowed. Combine or cancel to reduce the number of main divisions.

3. Under each main head discover and write down the necessary subdivisions. First decide which main heads are most important. These you will subdivide most fully. Be sure the subheads cover the main heads adequately. Complicated subdivisions may require sub-subheads, but do not class mere details as subheads. If supporting details occur to you jot them down at the far edge of the paper in a line with the ideas they support. Do not, however, include them in your finished outline.

4. Discover the best order for the divisions and subdivisions, and number accordingly.

5. Put your outline into final form (**32e**).

Practice Developing an Outline

1. Choose a topic from **30** or **31** or from another course and *work up* to an outline (through the first four steps).

2. Choose another topic and *work down*.

32c. Types of Outlines

(1) Topic outlines Build a topic outline of headings, preferably nouns or their equivalent.

A Test for Potential Athletic Ability

1. Need for a test
2. The Sargent jump test
    a. Technique of the jump
    b. Computation and interpretation of the score
3. Placement of the testee

(2) Sentence outlines Build a sentence outline of complete
sentences, properly punctuated. Sentence outlines are
useful for subjects requiring careful analysis.

The Workings of Inflation and Deflation

I. Inflation and deflation result in the main from changes in
the ratio of money and credit to goods available.
  A. Prices rise when the proportion of money to goods in-
creases, whether from an increase in circulation or a
decrease in goods.
  B. Prices fall when the proportion decreases.
  C. Psychological and special economic factors also act.
II. Severe inflation brings hardship to many people.
  A. Those on fixed income must lower their standards.
  B. Wage earners suffer because wages lag behind prices.
  C. All classes are ruined by a runaway inflation.
III. Severe deflation brings hardship to many people.
  A. Debtors repay money of more worth than their debt.
  B. Manufacturers, merchants, and farmers suffer, because
returns fall faster than costs.
  C. All classes are damaged by continuing deflation.

(3) Paragraph outlines Build a paragraph outline of summarizing sentences, each giving the gist of one paragraph.
A paragraph outline is useful for digesting study material
and for testing a finished paper; see **34b(1)**. For planning, it is
inadequate; it does not show relationships.

32d. Logical Requirements of a Well-constructed Outline

(1) Accurate division Avoid overlapping classifications by keeping to one basis of division throughout each series of items. Try to find the most meaningful basis.

OVERLAPPING	ACCURATE	ACCURATE
MOZART'S WORKS	MOZART'S WORKS	MOZART'S WORKS
Early pieces	In childhood	Sonatas and symphonies
Sonatas	In youth	Operas
Operas in Italy	In maturity	Masses and oratorios
Church music		Other compositions

In writing from the first outline it would be hard to tell where to treat sonatas written at the age of seven or operas written in Vienna. The accurate outlines give clear guidance—one by *time*, the other by *form*.

Make the classification complete. Be sure that the main heads cover the subject completely; be sure that the subheads under each main head cover that head completely. At need revise or add subheads or narrow the group head.

INCOMPLETE	SUBHEADS REVISED	HEAD NARROWED
PLANTS	PLANTS	SHORT-LIVED PLANTS
1. Annuals	1. Short-lived plants	1. Annuals
2. Biennials	2. Perennials	2. Biennials

A catch-all head (*Other, Miscellaneous*) is sometimes added for completeness.

Do not use a lone subhead. Add a companion head or incorporate the idea in the group head.

Faulty: 1. Disadvantage
          a. Inferior strength

Right: HEAD ADDED   IDEA INCORPORATED
   1. Disadvantages   1. Disadvantage: inferior
      a. Inferior strength   strength
      b. Higher cost

(2) Logical coördination and subordination Do not write as a main topic what is logically a subtopic, or as a subtopic what is logically a main topic. Exclude details.

ILLOGICAL	LOGICAL
Uses of Magnesium	Uses of Magnesium
1. Peacetime uses	1. Peacetime uses
2. Garden tools	*a.* Industrial equipment
3. Industry	*b.* Domestic articles

(3) Appropriate length and complexity Keep main heads to a minimum—three to five. For a simple subject have only main divisions and perhaps subdivisions, but not sub-sub-divisions. For a complicated subject subdivide more fully, but not minutely. Every heading in your outline should be worth expanding in your treatment.

EXCESSIVELY DETAILED	SIMPLIFIED
Big Stream Water Project	Big Stream Water Project
I. Background	I. Background and history
A. Previous systems	A. Previous systems
1. Areas included	B. New water district
a. Farms	II. Plan of operation
(1) 6200	A. Irrigation layout
	1. Tunnels and siphons
	2. Pumping plants

(4) Meaningful headings Make your headings specific, not empty like "Introduction, Body, Conclusion." The "body" is in effect the composition and should have the entire outline devoted to it. Even headings like "Present conditions, Causes, Remedies," useful early as a rough guide, should be made specific as soon as possible:

Wide variations in educational opportunities
Main causes—economic inequality and sectionalism
Pros and cons of federal aid

32e. Formal Requirements of a Well-constructed Outline

(1) Parallel form Make headings of the same rank parallel in form. Do not shift from sentences to nouns to other forms. Prefer nouns or verbals of one kind.

HEADINGS NOT PARALLEL	HEADINGS PARALLEL
STATEHOOD FOR ALASKA	STATEHOOD FOR ALASKA
1. It has enough people.	1. Adequacy of population
2. Now subject to Congressional whim	2. Unsoundness of subjection to Congressional whim
3. To develop resources	3. Need for development

Mixed	*Infinitives*	*Gerunds*	*Nouns*
To discover	To discover	Discovering	Discovery
Invention	To invent	Inventing	Invention
Applying	To apply	Applying	Application

(2) Indention and symbols Show the relationships of ideas by using equal indention and like symbols for heads of equal value. Capitalize the first word of each head.

A LONG, COMPLICATED OUTLINE

I. ⎫
II. ⎭ Use Roman figures for the main heads, beginning each at the margin.

   A. ⎫
   B. ⎭ Use capital letters for the subheads, indenting as shown to make the main heads stand out.

      1. ⎫
      2. ⎭ Use Arabic figures for the sub-subheads, indenting to make the subheads stand out.

         a. ⎫
         b. ⎭ Use small letters for the next subdivision, indenting still further.

III. If a head runs over, indent its second line the same distance as the next lower division.

A SHORT, SIMPLE OUTLINE

1. ⎫
2. ⎭ Use Arabic figures for the main heads.

   a. ⎫
   b. ⎭ Use small letters for the subheads.

X-32. Constructing an Outline

1. Make these faulty outlines logical and formally correct.

SHAKESPEARE'S WORKS

1. Early work
2. Plays
3. The great tragedies
4. *Othello*
5. Poetry

EXTENDING THE NORTHERN RANGE OF CEREAL GRAINS

1. Main problem in northern latitudes
   a. Short growing season
2. Ways of speeding maturation
   a. Select quick-growing strains.
   b. Changes aided by X-rays and chemicals
3. Artificial acceleration by hormones, heated soils
4. Exposure of seed wheat to cold speeds maturation.
5. Economic factors

2. Prepare a topic outline for one of the following subjects or for one that interests you in another course; work up. Narrow or revise any subject to suit your needs.

An effective balance of qualities in a baseball team
Planning a cross-country trip
Three needed improvements in the architecture of houses
The present exhibit in the art gallery
The incidence and effects of malaria

3. Prepare a sentence outline for one of the following subjects or for one from another course; work down.

Exactly what is freedom of the press?
The changing functions of the Electoral College
The relation of physical science and philosophy
Mental hygiene is not psychiatry
The value to me of my history courses
Certain laws of dominant and recessive genes

DIRECT BEGINNING
ADEQUATE DEVELOPMENT
DECISIVE ENDING

33. Make the beginning direct and interesting. Develop your subject adequately in clear steps. End decisively.

33a. A Direct, Lively Beginning Drive toward the center of your problem or situation in your first sentence; submerge or eliminate incidental details and side issues. Stir your reader's curiosity. If possible begin concretely.

(1) Weak beginnings Do not begin with needless explanations or details. Do not write a general introduction. (In a long or complex article a preliminary explanation or formal introduction is occasionally desirable, but the need is infrequent in ordinary writing.) Do not make trite general statements before coming to your particular subject.

Needless explanation: During my freshman year I could not climb Mount Prospect because I had a job that left me no leisure for excursions. At the beginning of my second year my time was even more limited because I was trying to make left tackle. It was, therefore, not until last Saturday that my chance came. Four of us set out at sunrise.

Begin directly: At sunrise last Saturday four of us set out to climb Mount Prospect. [Necessary details of time and place can often be tucked into a beginning phrase.]

Unnecessary introduction: The importance of vacations has long been recognized. The word itself comes directly from the Latin, and we know that the Romans had country villas and lake resorts. In this paper I shall discuss the best place I know of for vacations.

Trite generalization: Many families are probably pondering the question of where to spend their vacations.

Simply begin: High in the Sierra runs the John Muir Trail.

267

Do not let your opening sentence depend on your title for its meaning. Make it tell its own story.

SECURITY FOR THE FARMER—A WILL-O'-THE-WISP

Dependent beginning: This problem has never been solved.

Make an independent beginning: How to place farming on a sound economic basis is a problem that has never been solved.

(2) Effective beginnings Gain interest by introducing your main problem or thesis in a way that raises questions in your reader's mind. Use one of the following devices.

Suggest *what*: Before I came to college I expected my education to do three things for me.

Suggest *how*: Our political system makes it difficult for most citizens to take an intelligent part in government.

Suggest *why*: Astronomers will not gaze at stars through the giant telescope at Palomar. [It acts as a camera.]

Gain interest by a striking statement, a direct question, a bit of dialog that forecasts your subject.

Make a striking statement: Experience has shown that ninety per cent of potential cripples would never become deformed if they received the right treatment at the right time.

Ask a direct question: You have eaten food that tasted like sawdust, but have you ever eaten sawdust that tasted like food?

Gain interest by an incident or anecdote that leads into your controlling idea. Prefer a real happening from your own observation or experience; an invented incident is likely to sound made up for the occasion.

Tell a simple incident: The other day I encountered three little boys playing with a wagon on which they had printed "City Morgue Wagon." "Tommy's the corpse," two of them shouted, "and we're taking him to the morgue." [Lead into your idea. Where had they heard of a morgue? Is unexplained death common? Or do radio mysteries and "comic" books build a strange world for our children?]

268

Made up: A man and his wife were driving home about midnight. They had both been drinking, and they did not see the little child crossing the street until it was too late. [Such an incident sounds artificial if it is not individualized.]

Recall an actual occasion: One afternoon in my hot-rod days I was out on a country road with a friend, testing our Suicide II on sharp turns. Dissatisfied with my puny efforts, Ken took over and stepped on the gas. We roared around a curve—and found the road blocked with cows, a boy trailing behind them. Ken jammed on the brakes and whipped the wheel over and we slewed through the barnyard gate, missing the boy by the thickness of his overalls. I saw the tube of the right front tire balloon out of the casing like a king-size chew of bubble gum. I saw the horse-trough go by.... [The next sentences in telling the outcome should lead into the main idea.]

Practice A Direct, Lively Beginning

1. Copy the sentence that really makes a beginning.

Hepzibah the Hamster

Almost everyone likes to keep pets. In my family we always had dogs and cats around, and my sister once had a pet lamb. I'm told that my grandmother as a girl in Australia kept a young kangaroo in the house. My acquaintance with hamsters began when one escaped from the room next door and dined on my best sweater. To make up for the damage her owner presented her to me, and my troubles really started.

2. Revise this beginning to make it direct and interesting.

Sanitary Requirements for Food Handlers

Americans travel a good deal, and every little stop on the highways has some sort of eating place. In cities and towns a great many people eat at least one meal a day at a restaurant or a lunch counter. Most cities and states have sanitary regulations and some kind of inspection, but probably every eating place in the country violates some principles of sanitation through the ignorance or slackness of those who handle food. Wise codes and enforceable ordinances have been devised, one of which is explained in this paper.

33b. A Well-proportioned Body Develop your main points
fully in plainly announced steps. Build up each part
with accurate and adequate concrete details, facts, examples,
reasons, proof, or whatever solid substance is required to
convey full meaning to your reader. Define, describe, enu-
merate, compare, illustrate, reason (see Methods of Development, **39**).

If you run dry look first of all for observed facts,
down-to-earth applications of what you are saying. Consider
too whether you have overlooked any vital opposing facts;
if so, qualify your statements to show *to what extent* and
how they are true. Take the reader's point of view; ask
yourself whether his natural questions are fully answered,
whether you have given him a lifelike picture. Resist the
temptation to fill out with mere words—weak repetitions
and generalities. Build honestly with the specific and the
concrete.

(1) The big idea Develop most fully the parts most important
to your controlling idea. Do not linger over minor points
so long that you must scant your big idea when you reach
it. For practice you may find it helpful to write the most
important part of some paper first and then to go back and
fill in the necessary introductory steps.

Saving What's Left

Controlling idea: Certain wilderness areas in this country should
be zoned in perpetuity, to be forever free from the sights,
sounds, and other manifestations of civilization.

1. Other areas exist for commercialized recreation. [Treat specifically but briefly.]
2. The wilderness has special virtues—historic, scientific, protective, recreational. [Treat adequately—about one-fourth
   of the paper.]
3. The main threats to the wilderness can be countered by
   positive action of the people. [Detail fully.]

270

Keeping an eye on an outline will help your sense of proportion. In a good outline your big idea will be most fully subdivided, and the lesser importance of preliminaries will be apparent. As you write you will try to cover each minor point in a sentence or two and to expand each major point to a paragraph or more.

Can Specialists Be Educated Men?

Controlling idea: How can a student acquire enough specialized training for a chosen career without sacrificing the values of a liberal education?

I. Values of a liberal education
    A. General knowledge   1 paragraph
    B. Understanding and judgment   2 paragraphs
    C. Social adjustment   ⎱   1 paragraph
    D. Other intangibles   ⎰

II. Interference by requirements for various careers
    A. Teaching   2 paragraphs
    B. Engineering   1 paragraph
    C. Bacteriological research   1 paragraph

III. Suggested means of solving the problem
    A. Interdepartmental correlations
        1. Explanation   2 paragraphs
        2. Advantages [make specific]   1 paragraph
        3. Disadvantages [make specific] 1 paragraph
    B. Survey courses
        [1, 2, 3, as above]   4 or 5 paragraphs
    C. Forum weeks: lectures, panel discussions
        [1, 2, 3, as above]   4 or 5 paragraphs
    D. Directed reading
        [1, 2, 3, as above]   1 or 2 paragraphs

IV. The best compromise   1 paragraph

Notice that division into topics is not identical with division into paragraphs. A topic may require more or less than a paragraph of treatment.

(2) Minor points Give enough space to minor points to en-
sure a reader's understanding of the subject.

For example, in writing about the improvements in radio
made possible by frequency modulation you will need to
give a little space to the difference between amplitude
modulation and frequency modulation, so that your reader
can understand the exact nature of the advances.

In narration, having begun as you should a little before
the main event, you may need to slip in some essential of
who, what, where, when, why, or *how* that cannot be
woven into the story without clogging the action. Put it
in concise form close to the beginning.

Phrase minor ideas in such a way that they do not over-
shadow the main topic.

Overshadowing: What does a prefabricated house really mean?
It means a house equipped with all the most recent devices for
simplified living, shipped in a number of packing boxes and
assembled on the site in a short time. The house must be
suitable for year round living in the temperate areas of the
United States and must include heating plant, refrigeration,
cooking facilities, hot and cold water, bathrooms. Prefabricated construction implies a structural system using frame sections and wood, building board, concrete, or metal panels
precut in a variety of standardized sizes.

Subordinate minor ideas: What does a prefabricated house really
mean? It means a house whose parts are built as units in a factory and merely assembled on the site. The factory provides
frame sections, together with panels of wood, building board,
concrete, or metal, precut and assembled in units in a variety
of standardized sizes. Commonly plumbing and wiring are included in such units. In addition a utility unit is supplied,
which contains a furnace, a water heater, and gas, oil, and
electrical connections. For assembly around this core are included kitchen, bathroom, and laundry fixtures. [The second
sentence states the main idea. The next two sentences treat
wall structures; the last two, utilities.]

(3) Clear relations Focus your development to make plain the bearing of each idea; do not merely throw scattered items in the general direction of your subject.

Unfocused ideas: The first point I want to emphasize is that football should be enjoyed—by the players and by the spectators. Play for fun, and forget the score. Make the game a contest of wits; try to outsmart the other team. Use all your plays, and don't be afraid to try something original. Remember, though, to do everything to the best of your ability and to operate as a team. [The clear lead in the first sentence is abandoned by the third.]

Focus on the main idea: The first point I want to emphasize is that football should be enjoyed—by the players and by the spectators. Play for fun, and forget the score. Enjoy the game as a contest of wits, your team trying to outsmart the other. Try original plays, whether they succeed or not. Put up a good fight, with your mind as well as your muscles. The crowd will like it.

(4) Clear leads Announce your steps clearly. Do not back into your topics. Do not throw out "false leads"; that is, do not appear to announce a topic that you do not follow up.

False lead: Differences between one individual and another make possible the division of labor. A high degree of difference may set an individual off from the group so far as to create a social problem. The study of genetics . . . [*division of labor* and *social problem* give false leads away from *differences*, the idea the writer was trying to use to introduce the topic *genetics*.]

Give a clear lead: The differences between human beings are many and varied. How can they be explained? The study of genetics. . . .

To transitions from point to point give as little space as you can without letting your reader lose his way. (For transitions between paragraphs see **34b**; for transitions within the paragraph see **37**.)

33c. A Decisive Ending As soon as you have said your say bring your writing to an effective close.

(1) Formal endings End a long paper with a brief summary or with an echo of your opening (slightly changed to show arrival at your announced destination) or with some other form of clincher.

Title: THIS HUNGRY WORLD

Opening sentence: Do you believe that food is winning the race with population?

Incomplete ending: Even the richest fishing grounds yield only about one pound of dry weight of fish per acre, and the amount of edible aquatic plants is strictly limited by the extent of shoal water. [The paper ends with a detail. The main subject is left in suspense.]

Complete by a brief summarizing paragraph: Even before the war two thirds of the people of the world were inadequately fed. At the present rate of increase the world will double its population in ninety years. But the fullest utilization of known resources on land and sea cannot do more than double our present food supply. Therefore only a rigorous limitation of population will mean enough food for all.

Or complete by an echo of the opening: Evidently at present rates of increase of food and population food is losing the race, and the world is growing steadily hungrier.

Or complete by a suggestion for action: Bringing food and population into balance requires widespread education and the higher standards of living that tend to lower birth rates. Let us make a beginning in this country by teaching the facts in our schools, in motion pictures, over the radio. When we here understand the problem we can work for its solution at home and abroad.

Or complete by a forward-looking conclusion: Since food production is unavoidably limited we must limit world population to match. By great wisdom and tremendous exertions we might bring the food and the population of the world into balance by 2100. Are we wise enough to make the effort?

(2) Informal endings End a short paper with a clincher, or simply stop. Cancel high-flown moralizings, tag-ends, and afterthoughts.

High flown: The expanding program of adult education is bringing new interests to men and women all over America who make up this great and glorious land. [Omit the *who* clause.]

Tag-ends: Even in the fog we knew we had hauled out on old Duck Rock. We were home. The next day we recovered the boat from the sand bar. Tom and I have often thought since of our narrow escape. But it probably taught us a lesson. We never forgot the spare oars again. [The last four sentences add nothing essential to the story. They should be omitted.]

Afterthoughts: I should have said that, in planning the wiring, the kitchen should have a circuit to itself. And so should any other room where a great many appliances will be used. [Include such points as an integral part of the composition in their proper place, or omit them.]

Practice   A Decisive Ending

Revise these endings to make them complete and decisive.

1. I landed hard, but safe. Since my experience I prefer the chest type of parachute pack, because it is the only kind that can be opened by hand if the mechanism should fail to operate. One is not bothered with wearing it while in flight. One can bail out with it just as fast as with the seat pack or the back pack. There are no other types that I know of.

2. What are we going to do about traffic-obstructing pedestrians? Legally nothing, but maybe some day people will have a little more consideration for the automobile driver. Or all cities may put in underpasses or overhead crosswalks.

EXERCISE

X-33. Developing a Subject

After outlining one of the subjects listed in **X-32** write a paper on it. Give due attention to proportioning and to making relationships clear. Compose an effective beginning and a decisive ending.

REVISING AND PROOFREADING

34. Revise your work for unity and completeness, clear organization and transition, effective presentation, and accurate form. Revise for one thing at a time.

Write your first draft quickly. Lay it aside for a day or two, so that you will see its faults from a reader's point of view when you resume work on it. Read one draft aloud, to disclose obscurity and monotony of diction or structure.

34a. **Unity, Completeness** Assure unity by narrowing, by disclaimer, by deletion, by addition.*

(1) Narrowing Make sure that the subject stated is no broader than the subject treated. Narrow any generalization to what your treatment actually supports.

Broad subject to be narrowed: As a teacher in junior high school I expect to make full use of audio-visual aids. [If the paper treats only *the motion picture as a tool of instruction* the term *audio-visual aids* promises too much and should be limited to *motion pictures.*]

Generalization to be narrowed: Second generation Americans look down on the country their parents came from. [Begin with *Sometimes* or *Some*; or specify—*whom I know.*]

(2) Disclaimer Acknowledge by a brief disclaimer any considerations vital to the subject that are not treated.

Disclaimer with explanation: Barring possible discoveries of oil and technical changes in our requirements, both of which are unpredictable, our oil supply will . . .

Disclaimer without explanation: Admittedly years of experience with people can give the soundest basis for judging character; still a young person can . . .

* For unity and completeness in the paragraph see **35a,** Adequate Paragraphs; **36a,** Limiting the Subject; **36c,** Focusing on the Main Idea.

(3) Deletion Check for proportion and relevance. Eliminate irrelevant ideas and phrasing that makes ideas seem irrelevant (see **42**).

Disproportion; irrelevance: The sprint is the young man's race —a dash at full speed over a relatively short course. In distance running a man must consider the shape of the course . . . the plans of his opponents . . . distribution of energy. . . . There is a good deal of discussion about permanent physiological effects of the longer distances. . . . For sprinting the primary qualification is. . . . [The digression into what the sprinter does *not* have to consider is out of proportion. A brief mention is enough, phrased to keep *sprinting* central and avoid the false lead into *distance running*.]

Reduce minor ideas: . . . over a relatively short course. Unlike distance running, wherein the runner must consider the course, the plans of his opponents, and a careful distribution of energy, the sprint requires chiefly the ability to hit and maintain top speed.

(4) Addition Make sure that major ideas are fully rounded out. Do not expect a single word or a single sentence to carry a major idea. Add supporting details and clinchers.

Inadequate development: Despite opinions to the contrary Prince Hal, to my mind, shows good breeding. At Eastcheap he makes himself common by running around with low companions, but his manners are more refined. He shows his honesty. . . . [Though the writer stresses *breeding*, he departs almost at once to *honesty*, giving his big idea only the doubtful support of *refined*.]

Add supporting details: Despite opinions to the contrary Prince Hal, to my mind, shows good breeding. For his own purposes he amuses himself with low companions from Eastcheap, but his speech, his manner, his point of view mark his quality. Furthermore only a well-bred man without condescension or snobbery could be accepted by such rogues in the way these accept him. Away from Eastcheap, at court or in the field, the prince's good breeding is plain in his poise, his graciousness, and his ability to command.

34b. Organization and Transition Assure coherence by straightforward order and clear transition.*

(1) Organization If the treatment backtracks or takes up the same point in two or three separate places, reassemble the material. Test your paper against an outline, either one written in advance of the first draft or one now drawn from the first draft. The following paragraph outline reveals faults in order in the paper from which it was drawn.

ADVANTAGES OF THE OPEN SHELF LIBRARY

1. Finding the best books for a particular purpose is easier with open shelves than with closed stacks.
2. Less advance information is needed.
3. Books may be readily compared for suitability and intrinsic value.
4. A variety of books on a particular topic is brought to notice.
5. Closed stacks are likely to reduce reading to those books directly assigned.
6. Less time is wasted and feelings of irritation and frustration are avoided.
7. The reader need not wait in line to present his call slip and to receive books that he may or may not want.
8. If a particular book is out the reader may substitute another without going back to the card catalog and waiting in line again.
9. The reader need not spend time in copying bibliographical data that may turn out to be useless.
10. If a particular book turns out to be inadequate the reader may substitute another without repeating the desk process.
11. Actual books offer more incentive to reading than the card catalog, just as living people are more stimulating than a list of names.
12. Bibliographies in books examined can help in finding other useful books on the same topic.

[Paragraphs 1, 6, and 11 show the big divisions of the subject: ease of selection, saving of time, incentive to reading. These

---

* For order and connection in the paragraph see **37**.

divisions are logical and arranged in a satisfactory order, though transposition of the first two might give a better lead into the third. The arrangement of the supporting paragraphs is less satisfactory. Under 1 the arrangement is passable. Under 6 a next-in-time order would be better: 9, 7, 8, 10 (the last two might be combined). Paragraph 12 belongs not to 11 but to 1; and 5, though not a perfect fit anywhere, might be worked in as a comment under 11.]

(2) Connection Connect every part to the whole; everything in the paper must belong to the controlling idea and must be shown to belong to it.* Notice in the following excerpt how repetition of key words and ideas at the beginning of each paragraph links the part to the whole.

Opening sentences of successive paragraphs:

"New England is the most closely knit group of states in the union. . . .

"This is not to say that the six New England states do not differ vividly among themselves. They do, as we shall see.

"Three qualifying points arise. One is that . . . the New England states only seldom express themselves in Washington with political unanimity. . . .

"Second, though the region may seem very closely tied and interlocked . . . there are some staggering disunities in such a simple matter as, for example, transportation. . . .

"Finally, from the point of view of geography and industrialization, there are two New Englands. . . ." †

Analysis of paragraphs to show repetition of key words and ideas:

¶1. New England . . . . closely knit
2. New England states . . . . differ
3. New England states . . . . seldom . . . unanimity
4. the region . . . . . . though tied . . disunities
5. [two] New Englands   two [New Englands]

* See **36d**, Relating the Paragraph to the Composition.
† John Gunther, *Inside U.S.A.*, Harper and Brothers.

(3) Transition Connect every part to the preceding part. Post each break or turn in thought. For extra clearness indicate continuation or restatement. Weigh the beginning and the end of the whole paper and then the beginning and the end of every paragraph.

Mark transitions by a word or two in the opening sentences of each paragraph, as in the extract above (*This is not to say, One, Second, Finally*), and by the repetition of phrases from preceding paragraphs. Show turns in thought by such signals as *although, on the other hand, a different view;* show gaps in time and place by *today, recently, some years later, in this country, elsewhere.* Signal other ideas at need.

Addition: besides, furthermore, in the second place, again
Cause or result: for this reason, on that account, therefore, consequently, under these conditions, as a result
Comparison: in the same way, similarly, likewise
Concession: naturally, of course, to be sure, although
Explanation: for example, in particular, more specifically
Repetition: in fact, in other words, obviously

Occasionally a transitional sentence is required; it is usually placed at the beginning of a paragraph.

Transition sentence needed:
   The veteran .... He .... He also .... His interests .... His vote .... From his point of view ....
   As a taxpayer .... As a householder .... As a parent .... [A signpost is needed at the beginning of the second paragraph to show change of direction: *So much for the veteran's point of view. But the veteran is also a civilian.*]

Whenever possible, make transitions clear by a natural sequence of thought and by parallel expression without obtrusive mechanical additions.*

* See **37b**, Parallelism; **37c**, Repetition, etc.; **37d**, Transitional Expressions.

34c. **Effective Presentation** Devote one reading to matters of sentence structure, style, and diction. Preferably read your paper aloud; your ear will help to detect roughnesses and inconsistencies.

Give attention to the following points:

Coherence (1-9, 42-44) Ask yourself repeatedly, Exactly what have I tried to say? Recast confusing passages. Rewrite careless sentences. Catch shifts in tense. Check reference and agreement.

Emphasis (48) and variety (16, 49) Distinguish between monotonous repetition and deliberate repetition to secure emphasis or to show connection.

Conciseness (15) Eliminate verbiage.

Accuracy and vitality of words (17) Replace vague abstractions with specific and concrete terms. Instead of mere links or weak passives, try to use active verbs that carry a full weight of meaning. Replace trite phrases with fresh expressions. Correct any lapses in diction (18 and 19).

Consistency of tone (45) and a smooth flow (47) Remove obstacles between your thought and the reader.

34d. **Accurate Form** Assure accurate form by reading the final copy carefully. Be alert to correct your known weaknesses—habitual errors in spelling, slips in grammatical form, careless omissions, excesses or confusions in punctuation, use of ampersand (&), inconsistent use of italics and quotation marks. If by a little care you attend to such details yourself, your papers need not be returned to you peppered with red marks and your instructor will be freed to give you help on the more important matters of content and organization.

Practice Accurate Form

Can you proofread accurately for details? Underscore the point or points of difference in each pair of items.

1. countries   counties   6. second hand   secondhand
2. parental   paternal   7. suggestive   suggestion
3. remodeled   remolded   8. reddish-yellow   reddish yellow
4. climatic   climactic   9. Macmillan   MacMillan
5. martial   marital   10. Barton and Burton Barton & Burton

    11. their fathers' books   their father's books
    12. rice, corn and wheat   rice, corn, and wheat
    13. Hill Brothers, Grocery   Hill Brothers' Grocery
    14. some time next week   sometime next week
    15. the New York *Times*   the *New York Times*

EXERCISE

X-34. Revising a Manuscript

Write a paper of three pages or longer on any subject assigned by your instructor. Lay the first draft aside for several days; then revise it. Read it over for one thing at a time: completeness, organization, effective presentation, accurate form. Note in the margin the kind of improvement needed at any particular point—deletion, transition, reference, punctuation, etc. Then rewrite, making the needed changes. Hand in both your original and your improved copies.

The Paragraph

A paragraph is a unit. All the sentences in a well-written paragraph center about a single main idea, a step or division in the thought of the whole composition.

DIVISION OF MATERIAL

35. In exposition make your paragraphs correspond to phases or aspects of the thought; in narration to shifts in time, place, or circumstance. In writing dialog begin a new paragraph for each change of speaker.

HOW TO DIVIDE EXPOSITORY MATERIAL

For a paper only a page in length narrow the subject and develop it in one or at most two unified paragraphs. In an expository article of several pages use a separate paragraph for each main division and for each phase of particularly important main divisions.* In a longer work such as a term paper use a separate paragraph for each important subdivision.

35a. Adequate Paragraphs in Exposition Begin a new paragraph for each major change of thought, but not for minor changes. Do not make a separate paragraph for a detail or for a part-idea. (Beware of one-sentence paragraphs!)

---

* For an example see **36b**, Separating Run-Together Paragraphs.

Suitable division of exposition to show stages:

THE DEVELOPMENT OF CHINESE WRITING

In Chinese writing there are still traceable a number of pictographs. A mouth was originally written as a hole . . . and is now squared. . . . The sun, originally a large circle with a dot in the center, has been converted into a crossed oblong. . . . By combining these pictographs a second order of ideas is expressed; for example, the pictograph for mouth combined with the pictograph for vapour expresses *words*.

From such combinations one passes to what are called ideograms: the sign for *words* and the sign for *tongue* combine to make *speech*; the sign for *roof* and the sign for *pig* make *home*. . . .

The Chinese soon discovered that pictographs and ideograms could be used to express other ideas different in meaning but having the same sound. Characters so used are called phonograms. . . .

[The last sentence of the first paragraph treats a minor phase and is therefore not separately paragraphed. The principal stages are the development of pictographs, of ideograms, and of phonograms.]*

(1) If a point is minor and its relation to the preceding paragraph is close, combine the two.

One adequate and one inadequate paragraph:

TRANSFERRING A DESIGN TO METAL

The craftsman in metal should draw the design of his project on paper and then transfer it to the metal that is to be worked. He can mark the design on the metal with a hard pencil, but such a mark is easily smudged with the fingers. Better, he can coat the metal with a dark layout stain and then trace around the design with a pencil or other sharp instrument, leaving a thin, bright line that will be easy to follow. If his design is an intricate one he can paste the paper to the metal and trace the outline by making small pricks through the paper.

* H. G. Wells, *The Outline of History*, The Macmillan Company [adapted].

If he wishes to cut a number of pieces of the same design the craftsman can gain time and accuracy by making a template or pattern out of cardboard or plywood and using this as a guide.

[Though there is a slight shift in thought, the second paragraph really describes a detail under "Transferring a Design."]

Improve by joining a minor point to a larger one:

The craftsman in metal should draw. . . . He can mark. . . . Better, he can coat. . . . If his design is intricate he can. . . . If he wishes to cut a number of pieces of the same design he can. . . .

(2) If a part-idea is important to the main subject expand it in a paragraph of its own.

One adequate and one undeveloped paragraph:

PHASES OF THE MECHANICAL REVOLUTION

In its initial phase the mechanical revolution was characterized by a great expansion in the use of steam. The exhaustion of the wood supply in England led to increased use of coal. From a simple engine designed for pumping out the coal mines Watt developed a steam engine which could be used for driving machinery. The first engines so employed were installed in British cotton mills beginning in 1785. After some years men discovered new uses for steam. The development of the locomotive and the steamship early in the nineteenth century revolutionized transportation.

A second phase in the mechanical revolution began with the application of electrical science to practical problems.

Improve by developing an important idea:

A second phase in the mechanical revolution began with the application of electrical science to practical problems. In 1835 the electric telegraph came into existence; in 1851 the first successful overseas cable was laid. In the nineteen-eighties Edison invented the incandescent lamp which made electric lighting possible. In that decade also the transmission of electrical power became a reality, so that electricity could be transformed into mechanical motion or heat or light far from its source.

35b. Convenient Paragraphs in Exposition Make each paragraph short enough to be readily grasped. If a topic has many details group them around two or three sub-centers—kinds, qualities, stages, cause-and-remedy, situation-and-example.

Material correctly divided for describing details:

Two Varieties of Ducks

Ducks and geese may be classed in either of two groups: surface feeders and divers. Surface feeding ducks have small feet which enable them to move around easily on dry ground; thus they often go ashore to find seeds of weeds and grains. Their small feet hinder them in swimming, and the maximum depth that they can dive is about three feet. They frequent shallow salt water, but they must have fresh water to drink. For these reasons large numbers of surface feeding ducks are attracted to the western part of Morro Bay, which consists of mud flats and winding channels.

The diving waterfowl have large webbed feet which give them tremendous swimming potentialities. They like to eat the sprouts and roots of vegetation that grows in pools twelve or fifteen feet deep. Seldom, if ever, do they stay on dry land, for their big awkward feet make it hard for them to move around. Diving waterfowl are, therefore, usually found in the deeper parts of the Bay.

[Separate grouping of the characteristics of the two varieties enables the reader to grasp the differences at once.]

Material correctly divided for giving directions:

Laying a Brick Walk

To build a brick walk, first mark the pathway to the desired width and cut the sides down vertically. The average size brick is about $2\frac{1}{4}$ inches thick; consequently the path should be dug at least $3\frac{1}{2}$ inches deep. This will allow $1\frac{1}{2}$ inches for a sand foundation, and the bricks will rest only a fraction of an inch above ground level. When you have made the excavation, roll or tamp the earth at the bottom of the path and make it as even as possible by adding or removing soil. After this add sand and level it.

Before you lay the bricks mark out your design on the sand; use a board or line to get each course straight. Follow your pattern, placing the bricks as close together as possible. After the bricks are laid, pour sand over the walk and sweep it into the joints. Finally, spray the walk with a garden hose, using the fine spray to pack the sand down.

[Separate treatment of the two stages, *preparing the path* and *laying the bricks*, helps the reader group and remember the many small points.]

35c. **Shorter-than-average Paragraphs in Exposition** Use extra-short paragraphs for special purposes.

(1) For summaries of complex subjects, use short paragraphs.

Material correctly divided for summarizing:

CRYSTALS AS VIBRATORS

Crystals vibrate steadily when they are attached to an alternating current. For this reason they can be used in broadcasting to control frequency. The rate of vibration depends upon the size and thickness of the piece of crystal used; for frequency control very thin wafers are used.

Each wafer of crystal has the ability to pick one frequency out of a current fluctuating at many frequencies. Because of this ability crystals are used in long-distance telephony to filter individual messages from the many carried together on a single cable.

Vibrating crystals have an additional property which has been put to practical use: at high frequencies they can be made to generate supersound, that is, sound beyond the reach of our ears. Such sound waves already are used by manufacturers to mix mayonnaise, peanut butter, and face cream. They are used extensively to spot hidden cracks and flaws in metal, plastic, and ceramic products. They may also be used as weapons—a use which has received much attention from writers of mystery stories and adventure strips.

Formerly, slicing natural quartz crystals was the only means of obtaining the thin wafers needed for processes using vibration. Recently, satisfactory crystals have been made in the laboratory.

(2) **For a transition** from one entire section of an article to another use a short paragraph.

Suitable transition from past to present:

DIFFERENT VIEWPOINTS IN PSYCHIATRY

Primitive man believed that his behavior was governed by powers outside himself . . . demons . . . possession. . . .

The contrasting viewpoint that all behavior, normal and abnormal, is a process of adaptation between physiologic needs and external circumstances seems to have been expressed first by the Greeks. Surprisingly modern are some of the concepts of Plato. . . . To Aristotle can be traced. . . .

Against this background of early theorizing we may examine the most important current concepts.

A few psychiatrists still hold that abnormal behavior is simply the result of physical disease or injury. A few others concern themselves with the role of the conscious mind. Most modern practitioners accept the strikingly different approach known as psychoanalysis. . . .

(3) **For light, informal essays** use short paragraphs.

Material suitably divided for light treatment:

The rules demand that wedding gifts must have a permanent quality—no canned goods, potables, pots of cheese-in-wine, or sweet-grass baskets. Divorce statistics are showy, but the assumption holds that the wedding present is necessarily for the ages.

The donor-to-be never docs learn who invented the rules, but his gift must be silver—sterling silver. Just as the Amsterdam diamond buyer can spot the imitation at forty paces, so can the wedding party identify plated ware even before the wrappings are off the package.

The smallest piece of silver which can qualify is a marmalade spoon. (A pickle fork is just a little too scrawny.) A seasoned donor could very well buy a gross or two of marmalade spoons and dispose of shopping risks once and for all. . . .*

* Charles W. Morton, "Accent on Living," *The Atlantic* (May, 1948).

HOW TO DIVIDE NARRATIVE MATERIAL

35d. **Paragraphing Narration** In relating a story begin a
new paragraph for each significant change in time,
place, action, point of view.

Suitable paragraphing to show a change in time:

All day our ship nosed her way among chunks of floating ice.
Snow fell in fitful gusts, blinding us and making our situation
perilous. We needed to reach the harbor mouth before a sudden
drop in temperature froze the floating ice into a solid mass; yet
if we hurried, we might run into an iceberg.

At about five o'clock the captain reported that another hour
should see us through. We could count on daylight—such as it
was—for a longer time than that. The temperature had not fallen.
We looked at each other, grinning in relief. And at just that
moment a shout came from the lookout, "Berg ahead!"

Suitable paragraphing to show a change in action:

Whenever I tried to ride Snort we had a brief battle. He
would hump up his back, toss his head, sometimes buck a little.
I would speak to him quietly, giving him a little leeway, but
keeping a firm rein. In a minute or two he would quiet down,
ready for the calf-roping.

In among the cattle we would glide. At a signal he would
pause, begin to push steadily, to press the chosen animal gently
toward the edge. Then with a sudden surge....

Suitable paragraphing to show a change in place and point of
view:

The freight train whistled and started with a jerk. From the
bushes beside the track a boy ran toward one of the boxcars.
As the crossing watchman started toward him the boy jumped
for the open door, landed on his stomach, and wriggled inside.

Benton, watching from the warehouse window, drew a deep
breath. He felt relieved that the boy had escaped, as glad almost
as though it had been himself....

35e. Paragraphing Dialog Indicate each change of speaker by beginning a new paragraph. Place explanatory or descriptive matter in the same paragraph with the speech to which it is most closely related.

Dialog correctly written:

"No-o-o. I don't believe it!" This was Hill, staring at the marks the plane had made in the snow.

"I'm going to church every Sunday if we ever get out of here," Harvey said.

Matt, bundled up in Folsom's overcoat, whistled softly. "Br-rother, what we missed!"

"Captain," Hill said, "you're a wizard. How did you do it?" Son said, "I didn't."

No one spoke. Then Matt, in his softly modulated Virginia accent, said, almost under his breath, "The Good Lord was with us."

Hill replied, "Yes, the Good Lord, Captain Tate, and twenty feet of snow to break the fall." *

Practice Paragraphing Dialog

Copy in correct form for dialog.

THE STOWAWAY

I was dizzy and my tongue and mouth were terribly dry. A man came up on deck. I went up to him and said, "Good evening." My voice sounded scratchy and it hurt my throat to talk. He glanced up and said, "Good evening," and walked away. I had thought surrendering would be easier than that. I followed the man, and when he stopped again, I said: "I'm a stowaway. Could you tell me where I can get a drink of water?" "You're the stowaway, are you?" he asked as calmly as if no ship was complete without one. "Yes," I said. "Can I get a drink of water?" "Where did you get on?" "Puntarenas. I'd like a drink. I'm terribly thirsty." †

* Marguerite Gaylord Tate, "Marooned in the Clouds," *The Atlantic Monthly* (February, 1948).

† Scott Seegers, "The Captain and the Stowaway," *Harper's Magazine* (April, 1948).

X-35. Division of Material

1. Rewrite the following material in two unified paragraphs.

CARE OF FILES

Like any other tool, a file needs care in storage. If files are thrown into a box with other tools the teeth are likely to be damaged. One good way to store files is to hang them in a rack such as that used for wood chisels and wood bits. Not only will this prevent the files from being injured but it will enable the user to find the particular file he needs without hunting.

Another good way to store files is to keep them in a large drawer with wooden partitions.

A file needs care in use. Files are rather brittle and should never be used to pry objects apart or for any job except filing.

A wire brush should be employed to remove bits of metal after a file has been used.

A file should be kept dry to avoid rust, as corrosion will dull the sharp edges of the teeth.

2. At what point would a natural division occur? Write the opening sentence of each paragraph.

THE ROOT SYSTEM OF A PLANT

The growing roots of a plant extend downward, deep into the soil, and are held firmly in place by the tiny pebbles, grains of sand, and particles of clay of which the soil is composed. A careful examination of a root system will show that it is composed of many long slender fibers. In the process of growth these have pushed their way through the soil, some extending outward. As each root grew, the delicate tip time and again met small pebbles or hard earth. These caused the root to turn so that after a while it became firmly entwined. Numerous rootlets branch from the root. An examination under a microscope of the tip of one of the thousands of delicate little rootlets will show that it is covered with a pointed cap. Just behind the cap on the root tip is a region covered with little hairlike growths called root hairs. The root hair is part of a living cell. Through its walls water and the minerals and air that are dissolved in water enter the plant from the soil.

291

UNITY IN THE PARAGRAPH

36. Build each paragraph around one central idea, one phase or aspect of a subject.

HOW TO MAKE EACH PARAGRAPH A UNIT

36a. **Limiting the Subject** Do not try to cover a large subject in a single paragraph.

Lack of unity due to excessive breadth of subject:

GLASS

Glass is one of our most important materials, and it is being used for an increasing number of products. Polished plate glass is in great demand for automobile windshields. By a new process both sides of the plates can be ground and polished at the same time. Another important product is optical glass, which has to be made with special care to prevent flaws. Another kind of glass is the heat-resistant type used for cooking utensils. There are not enough trained men to direct the development of new processes in glass manufacture.

Gain unity by narrowing the subject:

THE MANUFACTURE OF PLATE GLASS

The demand for polished plate glass to make automobile windshields has stimulated the development of methods that speed its manufacture. One new procedure permits grinding and polishing the glass on both sides at the same time. By the old method. . . . By the new. . . .

Or gain unity by sharpening and dividing the subject:

NEW METHODS IN GLASS-MAKING

Polished plate glass. . . . One new process. . . .
Optical glass . . . special care . . . recent refinements in grinding. . . .
Heat-resistant glass . . . ovenware . . . flameware. . . . By increasing the percentage of lead. . . .

36b. Separating Run-together Paragraphs Do not run together the treatment of two or more important and
clearly separate points.* Treat in separate paragraphs important steps in time, important parts, principal kinds or characteristics. Use separate paragraphs for each phase of a
particularly important division.

Lack of unity because paragraphs are run together:

Three principal forms of government developed in ancient
Greece. The first was monarchy. The earliest Greek city-states
were kingdoms. In some cities the ruling families maintained
their power for generations. Sparta, for example, had kings as
late as the sixth century B.C. Most of the Greek city-states,
however, had become aristocratic republics long before the sixth
century. Prominent families ruled more or less benevolently. As
new rich families rose to power they too became members of
the ruling class. A variation of this system of government by
the privileged few was the rule of individuals who gained influence for a time. These men, known as tyrants, usually came
to power on a wave of grievance against the existing rulers. A
third form of government that prevailed increasingly from the
sixth to the fourth century B.C. was known as democracy. . . .
[The major divisions are *monarchy, aristocracy, democracy.*]

Use separate paragraphs for major divisions:

Three principal forms of government developed in ancient
Greece. The first was monarchy. . . .
Most of the Greek city-states, however had become aristocratic republics long before the sixth century. . . . [Government
by tyrants, since it is a variation of aristocracy and is given only
two sentences, need not be paragraphed separately. If the writer
wished to emphasize it he could develop it at greater length and
make it a separate paragraph.]
A third form . . . was known as democracy. . . . [In the completed paper this third and most important form would probably be given several paragraphs.]

* See also **35**, Division of Material.

36c. **Focusing on the Main Idea** Do not mislead the reader
by beginning far from your actual topic. Do not confuse him by wandering from it after you have begun.

Lack of unity because of indirect beginning:

It seems that wherever there is a big problem a man sooner or
later appears who can solve it. This has happened many times in
the history of our country, not only in the political history but
in economics as well. For example, fifty years ago the South was
suffering because her single crop, cotton, had injured the fertility of the soil. Then along came George Washington Carver
with ideas about new uses for peanuts. . . .

Omit general remarks and focus on the central idea:

Fifty years ago the farmers of the South were becoming
poverty stricken because their single crop, cotton, had robbed
the soil of its fertility. A simple, earnest man, George Washington Carver of the agriculture department at Tuskegee Institute,
decided to attack the problem. His approach was twofold. He
taught the farmers. . . . He initiated research. . . .

Lack of unity because of wandering:

It is chiefly through his images that a poet reveals his likes
and dislikes, observations and interests. Shakespeare's images
centered around nature, animals, and birds, with emphasis upon
weather, plants, and gardening; about earthy, human examples
of the body in health and sickness; about indoor life, fire, light,
food and cooking. A writer tends to remain within a certain
range of images characteristic of him. Shakespeare and Marlowe
expressed themselves in quite different kinds of imagery. Marlowe used images drawn from books, especially the classics, and
from the sun, moon, planets and heavens, the latter group because his hobby was the study of astronomy.

[The actual topic is a comparison between the imagery of
Shakespeare and that of Marlowe. The first sentence makes a
permissible introduction. The third sentence interrupts by suggesting a new aspect of the subject. The fourth sentence tardily
announces the actual topic of the paragraph.]

Sort out the ideas:

It is chiefly through his images that a poet reveals his likes and dislikes, observations and interests. A comparison between Shakespeare's and Marlowe's imagery reveals great differences in background and personality. Shakespeare's images centered.... Marlowe, on the other hand, used....

A writer tends to remain within the range of images characteristic of him. Even in his use of classical source material Shakespeare introduced fresh, homely images from everyday life. For example,... Marlowe usually carried over the rich remote imagery of the original. An instance is found....

36d. Relating the Paragraph to the Composition Make clear the unity of each paragraph with the larger thought of the whole composition.

Relation of paragraph to subject not shown:

[The paragraph is from a composition on *Reasons Why the Indian Ceased to Resist the White Man*, and some of the reasons have already been stated.]

Buffaloes once ranged the prairie, thousands in a single herd. They were easy to hunt and they meant to the Indian what grain, pork, beef, and mutton meant to the white man. Then our government began the systematic slaughter of the buffaloes. The process was continued until the species was almost annihilated. [Only the underscored words give any indication of how the thought of the paragraph is connected with the general subject; and these words show the connection but dimly.]

Add definite evidence of relationship:

Another reason resistance ended was that buffaloes were destroyed. Buffaloes once ranged the prairie, thousands in a single herd. They were easy to hunt and they meant to the Indian what grain, pork, beef, and mutton meant to the white man. Then our government began the systematic slaughter of the buffaloes. The process was continued until the species was almost annihilated. When the Indian's meat supply was taken from him, his power of making war was gone.

EXERCISE

X-36. Unity in the Paragraph

1. List several topics suggested in the paragraph below. Sharpen the subject and write out possible opening sentences for two or three successive paragraphs.

AMERICAN POPULAR SONGS

American popular songs make a very interesting study. Some writers like Irving Berlin keep turning out successful songs for years, while other writers produce only one or two hits. The reasons for the success of a popular song are hard to analyze. Sometimes in the same season a very sentimental song and a very unemotional one will be equally popular. Songs of twenty years ago often make a hit when last year's songs seem out of date. The themes of many popular songs have been taken from classical music. Many popular songs appear first in musical comedies or motion pictures.

2. What two topics does the following paragraph treat? What sentences interrupt the discussion of the first topic? Sort out the material and rewrite it in two unified paragraphs.

PASSING ON THE HIGHWAY

To avoid the commonest kind of accident—the kind which results from careless passing—first fix in your mind the sort of situation in which passing is not safe. Never pass at excessive speed. Never pass on hills or curves or at road intersections. When you are sure that you have ample time and space drive up close behind the car ahead and sound your horn. Thus you warn the other motorist so that he will not turn out or try to pass the car in front of him. In many places a double line is used between lanes on sections of highway where passing is not safe. Never cross the double line. Never pass on a three-lane highway unless approaching traffic is far away. The second thing to fix in your mind is how to pass when it is safe. Swing out smoothly, well into the left-hand lane. Do not cut in too soon; allow more space than you think you will need. When a car is passing you, keep well to the right and do not increase your speed.

COHERENCE IN THE PARAGRAPH

37. Within a paragraph, arrange points in a clear order *
and knit them together by the use of parallelism, reference
words, and transitional expressions.

HOW TO MAKE EACH PARAGRAPH COHERENT

37a. **Order** Proceed from each point in a paragraph to the
one which logically comes next. Do not backtrack,
jump about, or change plan.

Lack of coherence because statements follow no clear order:

An interesting device has been developed to increase reading
speed. One girl developed a speed of 1416 words a minute, and
tests showed that her comprehension was almost 100 per cent.
She had thirty-three half-hour sessions of practice. The device,
called a tachistoscope, flashes numbers on a screen at speeds
ranging up to one one-hundredth of a second. It is a kind of
lantern. Students are asked to remember and repeat the numbers. Later, words are substituted.

[The second and third sentences jump ahead; a logical order
would be to describe *first* the device and *second* the results.]

Secure coherence by orderly arrangement:

An interesting device called a tachistoscope is being used
successfully to increase reading speed. The device, a kind of
lantern, flashes numbers on a screen at speeds ranging up to one
one-hundredth of a second. Students are asked to remember and
repeat the numbers. Later, words are substituted for the numbers. One girl, after thirty-three half-hour sessions, had developed such speed that she could read 1416 words a minute. Tests
showed that her comprehension of material read at this rate
was almost 100 per cent.

* For a table of kinds of order useful both within the paragraph
and in the whole composition, see 31c.

Lack of coherence because order of points is changed:

The teal, one of the prettiest little ducks we have, has a length of twelve to seventeen inches, a weight of ten to seventeen ounces, and a spread of twenty-two to twenty-five inches. The canvasback has a weight of two to three pounds, a length of twenty to twenty-four inches, and a spread of thirty-four to thirty-six inches. The widgeon, also called *baldpate* because of its head markings, has a length of eighteen to twenty inches, a spread of thirty to thirty-five inches, and a weight of one and one-half pounds.

[In making a comparison keep to the same order throughout. Here, for each bird give *weight, length,* and *spread* in the same order: The teal . . . ounces . . . inches . . . inches. The canvasback . . . pounds . . . inches . . . inches. The widgeon. . . .]

Practice   Orderly Arrangement

Rewrite each paragraph, arranging points in a clear order.

1. Leopold Auer, father of the modern school of violin playing, rejected Tchaikovsky's *Concerto in A Major* because he thought its technical difficulties were insurmountable. Later Adolf Brodsky played it at a concert in Vienna. Auer became one of its most brilliant performers after other violinists began to include it in their programs. Tschaikovsky had dedicated the concerto to him, but he returned the score to the composer.

2. Plastics fall into two general groups, the heat-resistant and the heat-sensitive. The heat-resistant kinds will not warp at high temperatures; they can even be put into boiling water; they will not flame or explode. They are not affected by cleaning fluids, and they do not break easily. They do not come in a very wide range of colors, however, or in clear form. The heat-sensitive plastics are light-weight, transparent, and multi-colored. They must not be boiled, and will even warp if you soak them in hot water. Some of them catch fire easily. They may be destroyed by cleaning fluids or other chemicals. Manufacturers have made them into fabrics, threads, and flexible films as well as into solid objects.

37b. **Parallelism** Use parallel sentence structure to show continuity or similarity of thought.*

Coherence impaired by shifts in sentence structure:

Renovating the upholstery of chairs, sofas, and settees is a task which can be undertaken satisfactorily by the home mechanic. A hammer, a screwdriver or an old chisel, pincers, an upholsterer's needle, and an appliance for stretching the webbing tightly are all the tools required. The necessary materials are burlap, webbing, a ball of good twine, and a package of ½-inch tacks. Buy the very best quality webbing, as the success of the work will largely depend upon its strength and durability. The twine should be real upholsterer's twine, and its life is lengthened if it is drawn across a lump of beeswax before use. The beeswax not only protects the twine from deterioration but discourages rust where the knots secure the springs.

Secure coherence by use of parallel structure for parallel ideas:

Renovating the upholstery of chairs, sofas, and settees is a task which can be undertaken satisfactorily by the home mechanic. The necessary tools are a hammer, a screwdriver or an old chisel, pincers, an upholsterer's needle, and an appliance for stretching the new webbing tightly. The necessary materials are burlap, webbing, a ball of good twine, and a package of ½-inch tacks. Buy the very best quality webbing, as the success of the work will largely depend upon its strength and durability. Get real upholsterer's twine, and draw it across a lump of beeswax before you use it. The beeswax not only protects the twine from deterioration but discourages rust where the knots secure the springs.

Parallelism with repetition of key word: necessary tools—necessary materials

Parallel sentence structure: Buy . . . webbing. . . . Get . . . twine and . . . draw it. . . .

* See also **8** and **48d(2)**.

37c. **Linking Devices** Link sentences by a skillful use of repetition and of synonyms, pronouns, correlatives.

Connection by repetition of key words:

The point of the minimum of restlessness always occurs early in the night. Though the greatest period of restlessness, or motility, follows immediately upon getting to bed, yet, after a period varying from fifteen to ninety minutes, that motility gradually decreases until a minimum for the entire night is reached. For boys the quietest hour of sleep is the second hour after they go to bed; for girls, strangely, it is the third hour. Are those hours, we may ask, absolutely quiet? No, but the quiet periods in these halcyon hours average as long as nearly seventeen minutes. They diminish steadily from that point, however, until in the ninth hour, the hour before rising, quiet periods average only about seven and a half minutes.*

Connection by use of synonyms:

Few car dealers have enough capital to assume the financial risks of making installment sales. When a dealer sells on credit, he usually turns over the time-payment contract to a finance company. This agency advances the money to pay the expenses of the transaction.

[Strained use of synonyms to avoid repetition is a fault. Skillful use of synonyms may enlarge the idea and prevent awkwardness.]

Connection by use of pronouns and correlatives:

One sort of ice, the sort which is picked up out of a cloud, is not too dangerous to a plane. It can damage the wings and clog the propeller blades; but it can be controlled with de-icers and alcohol pumps. Another sort, formed by freezing rain, can be extremely dangerous. It may sheath the whole plane with clear ice in a matter of minutes.

* Henry James Forman, *Our Movie Made Children*, The Macmillan Company. [Adapted]

37d. Transitional Expressions Use signals when they are needed to make clear a particular relationship in thought. Do not use so many that your work seems all knees and elbows. Try to make one thought lead naturally to another.

Incoherent because place and time are not marked:

We climbed to the top of Eagle Rock. We caught glimpses of faraway mountains and also of the Murdock River valley, which was heavily forested. The whole snow-covered range stretched out, peak after peak in a long line. We could see a road winding along beside the river and we even saw misty plains beyond.

Secure coherence by using signals:

Step by step we climbed Eagle Rock. At intervals we paused, glimpsing now far mountains at our left, now a forested valley at our right. At last we stepped out on to the level summit. Northward loomed the whole snow-tipped range, peak after peak. Southward lay the valley of the Murdock with road and stream winding out toward misty plains.

Awkward because transitional expressions are overused:

Radiant heat travels as light does, in waves. Also it travels in straight lines, as light does. However, it is changed to molecular heat when it strikes an object. For example, a sidewalk grows hot in the sun. A pan on a stove likewise is heated by radiation changed into molecular heat.

Recast to make signals unnecessary:

Radiant heat travels as light does, in waves which move in straight lines. When the rays strike an object the radiant energy is changed to molecular energy. A sidewalk grows hot in the sun; a pan on a stove is warmed by the radiant energy of the flame changed into molecular heat.

Practice Linking and Transitional Expressions

Copy linking and transitional words and phrases from each passage; connect them by dots. One passage uses transitional expressions awkwardly; rewrite it.

1. Bones show greater resistance to pressure than wood does. Human bones can stand compression up to 23,000 pounds per square inch before they snap—about twice the compressive strength of hickory.

2. In 1903 the sum spent for highways in states and their local units was about fifty million dollars. By 1941 the total annual expenditure had risen to more than one billion and three-quarters dollars, an increase of some three thousand per cent.

3. At the foot of the hill we stopped the car and climbed out. We arranged our knapsacks, ropes, and first-aid equipment and checked our carbide lamps; then we hiked up the slippery slope. At the cave mouth, where we paused to light our lamps, we could feel a chill draft. When we started in, it was like stepping from the street into an air-conditioned theater.

4. Many people object to radio commercials because they interrupt programs. However, the sponsors pay for the programs in order to get a chance to advertise, and therefore they cannot be expected to give up inserting commercials. Some sponsors, though, are beginning to realize that people are annoyed when the program seems to be just an excuse for advertising.

5. Until a few years ago the only way in which naturalists could obtain specimens of deep-water creatures was by lowering a net. The specimens were always dead when they reached the surface, and often mangled. Then Mr. Otis Borden invented an astonishing metal diving chamber called a Bathysphere. The globe is five feet in diameter—just large enough to hold two men. It has windows three inches thick made of fused quartz, the strongest transparent substance on earth. It is fitted with a tank containing forty gallons of oxygen, a number of scientific instruments, a first aid kit, apparatus to keep the air pure, and a telephone. In the Bathysphere observers have remained for long periods of time as far as a half mile below the surface of the sea.

BUILDING A PARAGRAPH

FOUNDATION SENTENCE AND TOPIC SENTENCE

38. To lay a firm foundation for a paragraph, give a clue to the central idea in the opening sentence. To make the idea unmistakably clear, state it precisely as a topic sentence.

In formal exposition most of the paragraphs have topic sentences. In narration and in informal exposition many paragraphs suggest rather than state the central idea.

Main idea stated as a topic sentence:

The mechanical tree planter combines the functions of plowing, trench-digging, and setting out seedlings. As the machine is pulled along by a tractor a wheel-shaped blade on the front cuts the sod. A plowshare fastened behind it makes a furrow. A second blade knifes roots to protect the trenching device, which then digs a trench four inches wide and eight inches deep. The workman, sitting in the rear, places each seedling in the trench. Two rubber packer wheels tamp the soil around it.

Main idea not stated, but suggested by choice of details:

He went out the door into the cold dawn. The mill was just east of the house and behind it he could see the first faint light of day bleaching the horizon. The great black smokestack of the mill stood against the morning sky, and the smoke which rose slowly out of it coiled into the upper sky and was lost in the lingering darkness. The lights in the mill were on but the workers had not yet come in and the massive brick building was as silent as the dark frosty earth about it. Ben felt the sting of the cold air on his face, he could see his breath come out like puffs of steam. He turned his coat collar up, rammed his left hand in his pocket, and limped off toward the mill.*

[All details suggest the *cold dominance* of the mill.]

* John Craig Stewart, "The Last Day," *The Atlantic Monthly* (February, 1948).

38a. **Formulating a Foundation Sentence** Do not begin a paragraph by making general or misleading statements. In the opening sentence either (1) introduce the topic, (2) state the topic, or (3) embody a detail which bears directly on the topic.

Topic obscured by preliminary general remarks:

Experts say that schools in the United States are failing to prepare students for family life. Some colleges offer courses about marriage, but fewer than ten per cent of the students take them. The course which our college gives in Preparation for Marriage has merit, but it is far from adequate.

Introduce the topic by a clearly preparatory statement:

In an effort to meet the growing demand for courses in family life our college offers Preparation for Marriage. This course, though it gives needed information, fails because. . . .
[The preliminary ideas are condensed to a phrase.]

Or introduce the topic by a transition sentence:

Topic of paragraph 1: the need for courses in family life
Transition sentence and beginning of paragraph 2:
The need is being met in some degree by our own college through a course called Preparation for Marriage. The course succeeds in. . . . It fails, however, to. . . .
[The preparatory ideas are first developed separately.]

Or state the topic directly:

The great fault of the course called Preparation for Marriage given by our college is that it emphasizes physical factors and neglects psychological ones.
[The foundation sentence is also a topic sentence.]

Or suggest the topic by a pertinent detail:

At the first meeting of our class in Preparation for Marriage the instructor remarked that the primary emphasis would necessarily be on physiology.
[The opening sentence *gives a clue* to the central idea, which might actually be *stated* in a summarizing sentence at the end of the paragraph.]

38b. **Formulating a Topic Sentence** When you state the central idea of a paragraph state it accurately. Be guided by your purpose. Give your idea the precise slant it needs to make a particular point at a particular place.

Topic sentences not clearly pointed:

ILLUSIONS ABOUT ALCOHOL

People commonly say that they use alcohol for one of three purposes: as a food, as a stimulant, or as a producer of warmth. It does act as a food of the fuel type. It is easily absorbed, as its molecules pass through the walls of the intestines without digesting. But it is an artificial food, and cannot be stored or used for body building. Besides, it contains less food than the fruit or grain from which it was made.

Alcohol also acts as a stimulant, after a fashion. It does make people brighten up, laugh and talk freely. The reason, however, is not direct stimulation of vital processes but the narcotizing of restraining influences. . . .

A warm feeling often results from drinking alcohol. This is an illusion, as the body temperature is not increased. The blood vessels of the skin are dilated, and a deceptive glow is experienced. Actually the body may be overcooled in the process. . . .

[The topic sentences do not slant toward the actual topic, *Illusions About Alcohol*; they suggest the *virtues* of alcohol.]

Topic sentences sharpened to show purpose:

People commonly say that they use alcohol for one of three purposes: as a food, as a stimulant, or as a producer of warmth. It does act as a somewhat inferior food of the fuel type, with, however, no value for body-building. Being easily absorbed, it is of some use when quick energy is needed. . . . But it is an artificial food. It cannot be stored. It. . . .

The effect of alcohol as a stimulant is deceptive. Actually it merely narcotizes restraining influences. There is no evidence that it stimulates vital processes. Instead. . . .

A somewhat similar illusion about alcohol is its warming effect. It makes one feel warm but does not produce any actual increase in body temperature. . . .

38c. Placing a Topic Sentence

(I) Introduction The topic sentence may be placed early, as a statement to be explained or proved or as a provocative idea to be explored. So placed, it reveals to the reader at once the nuclear idea around which details will gather.

Topic sentence early (a statement to be explained):

Conventional heating systems are expensive to operate. Radiant heating has not this disadvantage. In radiant heating hot water circulates through pipe coils buried in either floor, walls, or ceiling, turning these whole structures into heating panels. The panels do not primarily heat the air of the room; instead, they broadcast heat waves into it. Because there is no need to heat the air, the temperature of the water circulating in the coils can be kept low, with a resultant saving in fuel costs.

Topic sentence early (a proposition to be proved):

Modern society places an economic hindrance upon the reproduction of professional people. During the long period of university training required by most professions, young men and women of superior mental and physical ability can not afford to consider marriage. Frequently the ideal period of life for reproduction is spent in preparation to enter a profession. Young men and women of the professions are often thirty years old before they are economically able to support a family. . . .

Topic sentence early (an idea to be explored):

It is an extraordinary thing that the Greeks, with their lively and penetrating minds, never realized the possibilities of either microscope or telescope. They made no use of the lens. Yet they lived in a world in which glass had been known and had been made beautifully for hundreds of years; they had about them glass flasks and bottles, through which they must have caught glimpses of things distorted and enlarged. But science in Greece was pursued by philosophers in an aristocratic spirit, men who . . . were too proud to learn from . . . mere artisans. . . .*

* H. G. Wells, *The Outline of History*, The Macmillan Company.

(2) Conclusion The topic sentence may be placed late as a
   summary or a conclusion. So placed, it gives the writer
an opportunity for building toward a climax or for leading
up to an idea which might be rejected at the outset.

Topic sentence last (a conclusion):

   Wuthering Heights is an extraordinary book. It is a very bad
one. It is a very fine one. It is ugly. It has beauty. It is a terrible,
an agonizing, a passionate book. Some have thought it impossible
that a clergyman's daughter who led a retired, humdrum life and
knew few people and nothing of the world could have written
it. This seems to me absurd. *Wuthering Heights* is wildly ro-
mantic: now romanticism eschews the patient observation of
realism; it revels in the unbridled flight of the imagination and
indulges, sometimes with gusto, sometimes with gloom, in hor-
ror, mystery, fearful passions, and deeds of violence. It is an
escape from reality. Given Emily Brontë's character . . . and
fierce, repressed passions, . . . *Wuthering Heights* is just the
sort of book one would have expected her to write.*

(3) Sandwich Paragraph The topic sentence may be stated at
   the beginning and repeated in slightly different form at
the end. The "sandwich paragraph" emphasizes the main
idea. It also gives an effect of completeness.

Topic sentence first and last (sandwich paragraph):

   The true democrat is a person I admire. By democrat I do not
mean a member of a political party. Nor do I mean the mas-
querading snob who goes around "being nice to inferiors."
I mean the person who is sincerely interested in every human
being as an individual. For the true democrat no one is dis-
qualified by lack of social position, obvious charm, or clothes.
For him no freshman is so humble as to be beneath his notice;
no sophomore is so lofty as to be unworthy of his interest. The
true democrat greets everyone with sincere enthusiasm as if
to say, "I like you. You are interesting." I repeat, I admire the
true democrat.

   * W. Somerset Maugham, "The Ten Best Novels; Wuthering
Heights," *The Atlantic Monthly* (February, 1948).

EXERCISE

X-38. Foundation Sentence and Topic Sentence

For each paragraph: (1) Tell whether the opening sentence introduces the topic, states the topic, or embodies a detail. (2) Copy the topic sentence if there is one.

1. The student of modeling can easily make a flexible mold for use in the casting of decorative sculpture. Over his plaster figure he must apply first a layer of modeling clay, and then a thick plaster shell. When the shell hardens he must separate it from the figure, pull off the clay, replace the figure in the shell. Finally, he must pour into the space formerly occupied by the clay a mixture of latex and molders' glue. The material will soon set into a flexible solid that can be refilled at any time with statuary plaster.

2. A few years ago an English manufacturer, seeking the explanation of America's ability to produce an excellent car cheaply, made an interesting experiment. He obtained three American automobiles, all of the same "standardized" make, and gave them a long and racking tour over English highways. Workmen then took apart the three cars and threw the disjointed remains into a promiscuous heap. Every bolt, bar, gas-tank, motor, wheel, and tire was taken from its accustomed place and piled up, a hideous mass of rubbish. Workmen then painstakingly put together three cars from these disordered elements. Three chauffeurs jumped on these cars, and immediately started down the road and made a long journey just as before. The Englishman had learned the secret of American success with automobiles; the one word "standardization" explained the mystery.*

3. Look at a picture drawn by a child or a primitive person—a picture of a cat or of a snake, let us say. It may not be accurate as to details. It will certainly omit many features. But one quality it is almost certain to capture—the characteristic motion of the animal.

* J. Hendrick Burton, *The Age of Big Business*, Yale University Press.

BUILDING A PARAGRAPH

METHODS OF DEVELOPMENT

39. **Develop a paragraph by using concrete details, facts, reasons, etc., selected and arranged to accomplish your particular purpose.** Use any method or combination of methods you find helpful. Among the most useful are the enumerative method and the comparative method.

39a. **Enumeration** Make your thought clear by describing steps in a process, parts of a structure, qualities, kinds, reasons, causes, results, examples, details.

Enumeration of steps:

Roman roads were built with systematic care. The first step in making a Roman road was to dig down to solid ground and lay stones as large as a man could take in his hands. On these stones, smaller ones were pounded solidly with wooden beetles. On these, gravel or broken brick and pottery were laid. On main traveled roads, paving stones were laid over all, carefully fitted together, as level as a floor. Swamps required the additional precaution of driving piles for the foundation, and valleys or rivers were spanned by viaducts or bridges of masonry.

Enumeration of kinds:

There are three kinds of members in a termite colony. The first group, the reproductive termites, have wings which enable them to move about and to start new colonies. When they reach a new nest they shed their wings and disappear underground to lay eggs. They do not damage wood, but their presence indicates that destructive termites are also near. The second group, the soldiers, remain near the colony to guard it from other insects. They are often mistaken for white ants. The third group, the workers, do the actual damage. They provide food for the other members of the colony by eating wood from the inside, leaving only the outer shell. Because they remain in darkness, they can be discovered only by breaking into the wood. There they may be seen as blind white grub-like creatures.

Enumeration of points (as in forecasting or summarizing):

Three developments . . . can overcome many of the limitations of present-day agriculture. One is the chemical control of jungle growth, a key to the new croplands in the tropics. The second is "vernalization," a Russian-pioneered method of speeding up growth and thus adapting crops to the short growing season of the extreme north. Third—and potentially the most fruitful of all—is the manipulation of photosynthesis, the remarkable process by which plants manufacture food, as a means of radically raising yields on both new and old acres. . . .*

Enumeration of examples:

How can we explain the fact that some almost identical animals are found in widely different regions of the world? Why, for example, are tapirs found only in South America and Malaya? Why is one branch of the camel family, the camels themselves, found only in Asia and North Africa, while the other, the llamas and their kin, grows only in South America? Why are the lung-fish found only in Australia, tropical South America, and tropical Africa? Geology solves our riddle. Fossil remains of all three species show that they were once spread over most of the earth. The competition of more efficient creatures resulted in their extinction except in a few places peculiarly favorable to them.

Enumeration of concrete details:

He liked to go around with his grandfather to do the early chores, water the big horses when they came in hot and snorting from the field, go up into the great, dim, churchlike barnloft and pitch down dusty hay; and then he and his grandfather crossed the farm yard to the old rock house that lay golden and mellow in the evening light, washed their hands out in the kitchen in the cool soft water that came out amber-colored from the iron pump in the sink, and sat down to Grandma's supper of fried eggs, fried potatoes, bread and tea, and the little dish of brown, puckered apple pickles that she always put on the table.†

* Leonard Engel, "Crops by Magic," *Harper's Magazine* (March, 1948).

† Ruth Suckow, *The Folks*, Rinehart and Co., Inc.

Enumeration of stages:

Adventure for me has three stages. There is the first unshackled interval before starting, when my dreams are bounded by nothing, north, south, east, or west. There is the second interval when, footsore and insect-bitten, aching-backed and broken-spirited, I wish that I had never come. And then comes the third interval—and in this interval I know that such adventures are the caviar of my existence compared to which other events in my life are *Schwarzbrot*. In this interval the fantastic, the unreal, the magnificent, and the unimaginable, which might have occurred only to other people, are occurring really to me. And then I know that it is right that such things must be paid for in discomfort, discouragement, and weariness; I know it is right that they are not free.*

39b. Comparison Make your thought clear by using comparison or contrast. Give the points of similarity or difference between two objects or ideas.

Comparison to aid in discriminating:

The term *red-headed woodpecker* is sometimes applied indiscriminately to all woodpeckers with a touch of red on the crown. The true red-headed woodpecker has a red head, neck, and breast, a glossy blue-black tail and back, white rump and underparts. It nests in trees or telegraph poles. It feeds upon ants, larvae, and small fruits and berries. It is very pugnacious, and may often be seen chasing other birds of its own kind or of other kinds. The California woodpecker, a different species, has a red cap and white forehead, the back or upper parts tinged with green, white underparts and rump. Its nesting habits are the same as those of the red-headed woodpecker; its food is the same except that in addition it eats great numbers of acorns. It is gregarious rather than pugnacious; birds of this species may be heard constantly "talking" among themselves.

[Note that all points about one kind of bird are stated, then all points about the other. An equally valid method is to compare point by point.]

* Agnes Newton Keith, *Land Below the Wind*, Little, Brown and Company.

Comparison to aid in choosing:

Should we pay cash or buy on credit? [I] If a person pays cash, he reaps two advantages. [A] He pays a lower price. [B] He learns thrift, because every time he makes a purchase he sees the actual money leaving his hands. Rather than part with the money he will dispense with the article. Thus at the end of the year he not only has a fuller purse, but has made thrift a habit. [II] If a person buys on credit, though of course he buys more, his name comes to the attention of the proprietor of the store, who never waits on him personally and might never hear of him were his account not carried in the books. Thus if he buys at the right places, and makes prompt settlement at the end of the month, he forms valuable acquaintances and soon becomes known as a man to be trusted.

[The paragraph contrasts two main ideas, I and II. Under I two points of difference are enumerated.]

Comparison to aid in understanding:

In the lower part of the body are some big heavy bones shaped somewhat like a bowl. This bowl is balanced on the top of the legs, and holds most of the organs. If this bowl is balanced just right, the organs remain in place, the way they are meant to be, but if it is not balanced right, the contents are tipped so that they would come tumbling out if muscles intended for other work did not hold them in. This is hard on those muscles which have their own work to do, and if they are used to hold up things that should keep their own balance, sooner or later they give way, and there is a sad accident, or a general slump. Then instead of saying, "That foolish person always stood in the wrong position and of course his insides got out of place," we say, "Poor dear so-and-so has given out from overwork and has 'acute indigestion' or a 'floating kidney' or a 'bad liver.' How could it have happened?"

[After the comparison has served its purpose the paragraph is further developed by explaining a cause and its effect.]

The basic methods, enumeration and comparison, are not merely "ways of developing the paragraph." They are the ways of all thinking.

39c. **Other Methods** (special forms and combinations)

(I) A definition is a comparison. A logical definition names first the class to which an object or idea belongs and then the qualities which distinguish it (see also **41c**).

A marine is a soldier who serves on a vessel of war. Like the regular soldiers the marines are equipped and drilled for land battle. Like the regular soldiers they serve under military regulations rather than naval ones. Unlike the regular soldiers the marines spend the greater part of their time aboard ship. On land they serve rather as policemen than as fighters. . . .

(2) Elimination is a form of comparison which explains what a thing is not in order to show what it is.

Just what does constitute a libel published in a newspaper is often hard to determine. It is not criticism of the government or of governmental officials, for the Constitution provides for freedom of speech and of the press. It is not denunciation of political policies, for such denunciation is the normal procedure in every political campaign. It is not the printing of news that is false or only partially true, for errors are made unavoidably every day. Libel is the malicious defamation of a person, made public by writing, and tending to provoke him to anger or to expose him to public contempt or ridicule.

(3) Cause and effect is a form of enumeration which describes first a cause and then the results.

The development of oil fields in Venezuela has created an autophagous economy. Oil, a nonrenewable resource, is rapidly and surely being exhausted. For years the country has been content to float along on this golden tide, and has not even bothered to produce the crops, meat, and dairy products of which it is capable. The mass of people, receiving little benefit from the oil, have carried on subsistence agriculture, with the result that Venezuela is one of the most eroded countries in the hemisphere. . . .*

* William Vogt, "A Continent Slides to Ruin," *Harper's Magazine* (June, 1948).

(4) **Repetition** as a method means expressing an idea in different words or from different angles for clarity and emphasis. It is a rhetorical device often used in combination with enumeration or comparison.

Repetition with enumeration:

In the American ideology the struggle for existence, and the rivalry of nations for advantage, are held to be wrong, abnormal, and transitory. Our foreign policy throughout this period [1914-1948] has been dominated by the belief that the struggle does not exist, or that it can be avoided, or that it can be abolished. Because of this belief our aim has not been to regulate and to moderate and to compose the conflicts and the issues, to check and to balance the contending forces. Our aim has been either to abstain from the struggle, or to abolish the struggle immediately, or to conduct crusades against those nations that most actively continue the struggle.

Yet in the world as it actually is, the struggle is not abnormal, and it is perpetually renewed. Twice during this period we have sought to abstain from the struggle by declaring our neutrality. We have not been able to stay out of it. Twice we have conducted victorious crusades against the chief troublemaker, believing what was soon disproved by events: that if he could be eliminated, we would then have eliminated all troublemakers. Twice we have sought, by forming universal societies like the League of Nations and the United Nations, to abolish the struggle. They have not abolished the struggle.*

(5) **Combinations** Most paragraphs in ordinary writing combine several methods.

Combination of methods:

Two Kinds of Wealth

[Definition] We may define wealth broadly as that which satisfies human want. But we shall understand the term better if we divide it into the two kinds. [Enumeration] Wealth includes free goods and economic goods. [Contrast] Free goods,

---

* Walter Lippmann, "The Rivalry of Nations," *The Atlantic Monthly* (February, 1948).

as a rule, are found near at hand in abundance; but the most obvious characteristic of economic goods is scarcity. Free goods, being everywhere at man's disposal, are ordinarily to be had without expense or labor; but economic goods are obtained only at a cost in money and effort. [Enumeration of examples] Free goods include such things as fresh air, sunshine, and water. Economic goods include such things as food, fuel, and clothing. [Definition continued] Of course the division is not hard and fast. Free goods may be changed into economic goods by becoming rapidly scarcer. [Example] Standing timber, for instance, may come under the ownership or control of individuals, so that the supply is limited. [Contrasting example] That same timber in the form of the lumber in the houses of a deserted mining town may again become common property; but the likelihood of such reversion is rare, and [Definition continued] in general we may say that economic goods do not become free goods.

EXERCISE

X-39. Methods of Development

For each of the following paragraphs

1. Write the main idea in your own words.
2. Copy the topic sentence. (If the paragraph is a sandwich, copy both sentences.)
3. List the method or methods of development used.

1. When you are buying a motor boat consider exactly how you intend to use it. If you are going to do your boating on a river, pick a fairly fast boat that can buck the current when you travel upstream. It should have shallow draft to stay off river bars and flats, and its propeller and rudder should be protected against snags. If on the other hand you are going cruising in deep water, pick a boat with moderate speed, greater draft, and less freeboard (distance between water line and deck). High speed in open water isn't conducive to comfort. Within reasonable limits, the more draft your boat has, the more seaworthy it will be. And as windage is important on open water, the boat should have little freeboard.

2. The extent to which the Government may properly control the actions of private citizens and corporations is hotly contested—and will be so long as democracy endures. The authority of Government, carried to its extreme, is tyranny, or, as we now call it, dictatorship. The liberty of the citizen to do as he likes in his own affairs, carried to its extreme, is anarchy, or the breakdown of social order. Democratic liberty travels a narrow path between tyranny and anarchy. In the words of Daniel Webster, "Liberty exists in proportion to wholesome restraint." Our history is largely made up of the struggle to maintain enough but not too much restraint. That government is best which governs strongly enough to protect liberty and not so strongly as to destroy it.*

3. Cultivated plants tend to die out or to revert to their wild state because two principles of selection are in conflict. In natural selection the plants that are eliminated are those not fitted to their environment or not fitted to withstand competition, while in artificial selection the plants that are discarded are those thought to be least serviceable to mankind. Frequently, therefore, mutations (offspring markedly different from the parent plant) which are selected and thus preserved by man are very different from those selected and preserved by nature. For example, from the standpoint of man such a mutation as the seedless orange is desirable, but in nature it could not continue to exist, since the preservation of the species is best served by many seeds and a comparatively small amount of pulp. Likewise, from the standpoint of man plants having variegated leaves with white areas, resulting from a lack of chlorophyll, are desirable on account of their ornamental value. In nature variegated leaves would be eliminated, since the material used in constructing the white areas would be wasted so far as the chief function of the leaves is concerned. Thus many of our cultivated plants if left to themselves either die out or revert to their wild state.†

* David Cushman Coyle, "The American Way," *Harper's Magazine* (February, 1938).

† William H. Brown, *A Textbook of General Botany*, Ginn and Company [Adapted].

Clear Thinking

Writing may be grammatically correct and yet show serious faults in thinking. Before you can produce ideas of worth you must develop habits of accurate observation, careful evaluation, sound reasoning. Before you can communicate your ideas you must learn to use language with meticulous attention to its meaning.

Learn to observe (40a, 40b). Use firsthand sources to supplement and check information obtained from books. If you are to write a paper on "Habits of the Wood Rat" go out into the forest and watch a wood rat; describe exactly what you see. If you are to discuss some social or political theory, study its actual operation in a particular place. Check abstract statements by relating them to concrete objects or situations (see the prolog to 15-19, Diction).

Learn to seek information impartially (40a, 40b). If you are to write on some controversial subject do not be satisfied with discovering facts and opinions which support your own view. Find out what is to be said on the other side. By seeking complete understanding you lay a firm foundation for your conclusions.

Learn to discriminate. Know the difference between reliable and unreliable sources of information (40b, 50d). Distinguish important from unimportant ideas (43b). Learn to find matter which is relevant to your purpose and to discard that which is irrelevant (31, 33, 34a, 42a).

Learn to think logically (40b, 41).

Learn to use language with care (15, 17, 40c, 44).

REASONABLE STATEMENT

40. Base your statements on verifiable evidence and sound reasoning. Attend closely to the meanings of words.

HOW TO CORRECT FAULTS IN REASONING

Observe accurately; inquire impartially. Draw no conclusions not justified by the evidence. Test your statements for exaggeration, prejudice, hasty generalizations, unsound assumptions.

40a. Inaccurate Observation Do not be satisfied with approximations or distortions of the truth. Be precise in gathering information. State your findings in exact, specific terms.*

Foggy statement: A large percentage of our criminals come from the lower part of town.

Obtain the precise figures: Three districts in the lower part of town gave us thirty per cent of our juvenile delinquents during the first six months of last year. The other seventy per cent came from widely scattered areas.

Vague, extreme statement: Bartók's music is just a lot of noise.

Note specific points: Bartók uses dissonance, sudden changes of key, and other devices uncommon in classical music.

Sweeping exaggeration: Everybody needs sunglasses.

Qualify and restate in specific terms: People whose eyes are sensitive to light need sunglasses when they go to the beach, when they drive against glare, when they view outdoor games.

Distortion through ignorance or prejudice: Most doctors are humbugs. They hardly ever help a patient.

Look for information on both sides; state it specifically: Dr. Jones treated Helen for a year without helping her, but under Dr. Smith's care she improved.

* See also 17c.

40b. **Slips in Logic** Draw your inferences with care.

(I) Inadequate basis Make no generalizations based on inadequate evidence.

Generalization on flimsy evidence: Of the thousands of people I passed as I roamed about Boston, not one spoke to me. My experience proves that New Englanders are cold. [Only one way of testing cordiality is used here, and this one is valueless in large cities anywhere. No conclusion is justified.]

Large generalization from an insufficient number of instances: The Burke family were miserable in an apartment. So were the Eldreds. No one enjoys living in an apartment.

Draw a justifiable conclusion: Since my background and tastes are similar to those of these two families it is possible that I might not like living in an apartment either.

Sweeping generalization: The English are bullheaded.

Make an accurate, specific statement of fact: Winston Churchill had shown such firmness of purpose that some people considered him bullheaded.

Unfounded generalization: Increasingly, the state is providing social services of all kinds. I fear this social service state because I fear mediocrity. The people catered to by the social service state do not like to do their own thinking or to live their own lives. All they want is security, to be told what to do so they won't have to worry. [Such thinking in a vacuum often results from neglect of referents *—the actual John Smiths and Mary Browns about whom the writer is theorizing. Two grave errors occur here: (1) the writer lumps millions of people together and gives them all the same ideas and feelings: (2) he shows no evidence that John Smith has ever expressed such ideas or even acted as if he held them. He should have studied one aspect of social security in operation, interviewed real people, reported actual case histories. He should have recorded facts of all kinds, not merely those which supported his prejudices.]

* See the prolog to 15-19, Diction.

(2) Inaccurate basis Make no generalizations based on un-sound evidence.

Generalization from incompetent authority: American girls receive the wrong kind of education. My aunt, who has lived abroad all her life, has told me so repeatedly.

Qualify by assigning the opinion to the holder of it: According to my aunt, who has lived abroad all her life, American girls receive the wrong kind of education.

Inadequate support—the invented example: Summer camps develop honor and manhood. Let us take two boys, Edgar and Ralph. Edgar goes to a camp, and at the end of three months comes back an honest and upstanding youth. Ralph idles at home, and after three months is a sneak and a coward.

Qualify the generalization; use actual examples or give other support: Summer camps are intended to develop honor and manhood. Their activities. . . . The disciplinary system. . . . Trained counsellors. . . .

Disregard of a possible difference in conditions: Our industrial methods have made us prosperous. They would make any country prosperous.

Qualify the generalization: Other countries might benefit from the application of some of our methods. [Make the statement still more exact by specifying *what* methods *where.*]

Generalization based on inaccurate information and faulty inference: For one example of discrimination against women take what happened at San Francisco when the United Nations charter was being written. A little group of women lobbied faithfully for weeks to get a statement of belief in the equality of men and women into the charter. This example proves that there is discrimination against women, when they could not even get the word *sex* into the United Nations charter. [Both facts and conclusion are erroneous. In the charter the word *sex* does appear, as well as clauses protecting the rights of women. Omission of both, however, would not prove the existence of discrimination; the matter might well be considered irrelevant to the purpose of the charter.]
320

(3) Faulty assumptions Test your assumptions, giving special attention to "buried" assumptions. Do not assume that there are only two sides to every question—that if *A* is true *B* is false (or that *A* is all good and *B* is all bad). Both may be true; both may be false; both may be partially true. There may be a *C* or a *D* to consider.

Buried assumption: The front page of the *News-Press* is poor. About ninety-five per cent of it is devoted to national and international wire news, and there is no attempt to relate the wire news to local matters. [The conclusion—that the front page is poor—grows out of two buried assumptions: (1) that ninety-five per cent of a front page is too much space to devote to wire news and (2) that wire news should be related to local matters. Such assumptions should be made plausible, or the conclusions should be changed.]

Careless assumption that what follows is necessarily a result: The country adopted a high tariff and because of this prospered greatly. [Unless all other possible causes can be ruled out an effect cannot be assigned to one cause.]

State the facts and qualify the causal relation: The country adopted a high tariff, which may or may not have been a favorable influence in the period of prosperity that followed. [Or include other possible causes: An expanding economy.... New discoveries.... Peace....]

Disregard of alternate possibility: Our congressman did not secure the passage of the measure. Therefore he was only pretending that he wanted it passed. [He might have been unwillingly thwarted. Is there any evidence that he was merely pretending?]

Either prove the assumption or stop with the statement of fact: Our congressman did not secure passage of the measure.

Whole hog thinking: You say that Mary is flighty. It's a pity that you dislike her. [You have not said or even implied that you dislike Mary. You have mentioned only one quality, but the whole hog thinker accuses you of condemning Mary *in toto*.]

Faulty "either-or" thinking: If you are not for us, you are against us. [You may be indifferent to us. You may be for us in some respects, against us in others. You may never have heard of us.]

Investigate the implications: If you are not for us *we consider* that you are against us. [Or] If you are not for us you do not actively help us. Therefore you might as well be against us. [Even this is dubious. *Not helping* and *actively opposing* may be very different.]

(4) Other faults Avoid these common fallacies.

Faulty analogy: Since the darkest hour precedes the dawn, the fact that we are outclassed in the coming field meet makes us likely to win. [A superficial analogy does not strengthen a statement logically unsound.]

Find a closer analogy or make a simple statement: Since the favorite does not always win, our being outclassed in the coming field meet does not rule us out completely. [Or] We are outclassed, but we have not given up hope.

Faulty premise: Airplane travel is not safe. You will be safer to drive home with Jim. [Make sure of the facts before basing conclusions upon them.]

Begging the question (assuming in the major premise part of the material to be proved): The brutal game of football should be abolished. [Brutality is one of the points to be established or refuted. State each point separately with evidence to support it.]

Reasoning in a circle (an extreme form of begging the question): Written examinations should be abolished because there is cheating. We know there is cheating because cheating always accompanies written examinations. [The writer assumes a condition and then uses the assumption to prove that the condition exists.]

Reasoning beside the point: You must admit that civilization has progressed in the last few years when you think of the distance man has traveled from the cave. [The point at issue is progress in the last few years, not in man's whole career.]

40c. Word Slippage Do not let a word change meaning in one context. Slipped meanings cannot support logical thought, especially when the second meaning carries emotional connotations. Beware of slips from generic to specific, from abstract to concrete, or into nonsensical personifications.

Shifting the meaning of a word: Patton is a good coach, and most parents are glad to have their children influenced by a good man. [The first *good* refers to ability, the second to moral and social qualities.]

Give support for the second meaning, or omit it: Patton is a good coach and a man of fine character. Most parents are glad to have their children influenced by such a man. [Or] Patton is a good coach, and most parents are glad to have their children trained by an expert.

Slippage from abstract to concrete: Housing was one of the major issues of the campaign, because it had risen far beyond the price the average wage earner could afford. [The same word, or a word and the pronoun representing it, should not apply to *housing*, the problem, and *housing*, the shelter.]

Use a different word for the concrete sense: Housing was one of the major issues of the campaign, because dwellings of all kinds had risen in price far beyond what the average wage earner could afford.

Nonsensical personification: Smaller headlines would make the *Daily News* a more attractive paper. But the *Daily News* doesn't care what it looks like, so long as it sells. [The personification of a newspaper as an organ of opinion is common and acceptable: "*The Tribune* says...." "*The Times* condemns...." But personifying to the extent of endowing a paper with feelings about its physical appearance or its commercial success is absurd.]

Transfer the idea to the human beings involved: Smaller headlines would make the *Daily News* more attractive. But the publishers don't care what the *Daily News* looks like, so long as it sells.

Nonsensical personification: It cannot be said that science has failed, for it has amassed a great amount of useful information. But it has not made the best use of this information, because they have not related it to the living problems of man. Science should break down the barriers between specific studies and be made of practical use. [A vaguely personified *science* seems to include systematized knowledge, scientific method, scientists, specific scientific findings. Faulty reference emphasizes the slipperiness of the word in the mind of the writer.]

Distinguish the meanings and limit personification: It cannot be said that Science has failed, for a great amount of information has been amassed through scientific research. But this information has not been put to the best use, because it has not been related to the living problems of man. Scientists should break down the barriers between specific studies, correlate their findings, and put them to use.

Practice Word Slippage

Rewrite these passages to correct word slippage.

1. Some of us joined the Political Association but were disappointed, because all the discussions were entirely too political.
2. Charity is a major virtue, but several charities in our Community Chest last year disagreed so violently about how it should be administered that they pulled out of the Chest.
3. The modern concert suite differs from the classical in that its greatest desire is to exploit its contents—its story-telling possibilities or its mood—rather than its form.
4. In our world today we have capitalism and communism at each other's throats, each believing the other's ideas and methods unworkable.
5. Science could accomplish this; there is no reason it cannot if it will spend the time and effort on the study of human beings that it has on our material environment. Then Science could adjust the material and social environment for the maximum development of every individual.

EXERCISE

X-40. Slips in Logic

Rewrite each passage to make a reasonable statement.

1. The carpenters who worked on our garage took ten days to put in new joists and studding. No workman gives full value for his pay any more.

2. Fraternities are nothing but clubs for loafers. My brother, who never joined a fraternity, says so.

3. When a youth from the wealthier classes and one from the poorer classes are arrested it is a foregone conclusion which will suffer most.

4. Universal education and universal suffrage are false notions. With universal education the ones who are dull tend to pull the smart ones down to the semi-educated level. Universal suffrage has made people think they are entitled to equality in everything.

5. Unless you believe that employees should be at the mercy of employers you must approve of the closed shop.

6. You complain of certain injustices in this country. Why don't you go to some country that you'd like better?

7. The venom of the black widow spider is fifteen times as potent as the venom of a rattlesnake. [True] Therefore a black widow bite is more likely to be fatal than a rattlesnake bite. [False. Why? Consider relative quantities.]

8. The most satisfactory criterion of social desirability is, in my opinion, the ability of the individual to contribute to the family and to society. Persons mentally or physically incapable of earning a living, or doing the housework in the case of women, are by this criterion undesirable.

9. No thinking person could approve such an attitude on compulsory medical insurance.

10. A French author says that American writers are much more concerned about reviews and sales than European writers are. In fact he says that except for living expenses the serious writer over there cares only for the criticism of a small circle of friends. Such a comparison is ridiculous when one remembers the money poured into Europe by generous Americans. [What is the point at issue?]

CLASSIFICATION

4I. Complete ideas logically by accurate classification.

HOW TO BALANCE, COMPARE, AND DEFINE

Statements of equivalence, comparison, and definition all involve problems of classification—grouping or dividing ideas into classes or kinds. An idea thus grouped with another must be of the same logical class.

4Ia. **Logical Conformity** Make two ideas that are balanced against each other (A is B or $A = B$) of the same logical kind.* Make any grouping into classes logical.

(I) Unequal ideas Do not imply that a thing equals a part, attribute, or function of a thing.

Illogical: He liked to pore over some strange map, such as Africa. [A map is a *partial representation* of Africa.]

Change one of the terms to match the other: He liked to pore over a map of some strange region, such as Africa. [Or] He liked to pore over some strange map, such as Ptolemy's map of Africa [or *such as Ptolemy's of Africa.*]

Illogical: Endosmosis is the solvent moving from the less concentrated solution to the more concentrated. [Endosmosis is a process. It cannot equal a thing.]

Match a process with a process: Endosmosis is the movement of a solvent from the less concentrated solution to the more concentrated.

Illogical: His promotion was rapid, and soon he attained a vice-president.

Hold to one idea, the office or the officer: His promotion was rapid, and soon he attained a vice-presidency. [Or] . . . soon he became a vice-president.

* See also **8**, Parallelism.

(2) Confused aspects In giving information about a book, do not confuse the title with the contents or the book itself with its subject, scene, time, action, plot, or characters.

Illogical: Shakespeare's *Hamlet* occurs in Denmark. The drama takes several weeks. He speaks more lines than any other character in Shakespeare. [Distinguish *Hamlet* from Hamlet.]

Make your ideas fit logically: The scene of Shakespeare's *Hamlet* is the Danish court at Elsinore. The action covers a period of several weeks. The prince speaks more lines than any other character in Shakespeare.

(3) Incongruous series Make the items in a series alike in kind.

Unlike: Activities include dancing, horses, and the beach.
Reword: Activities include dancing, riding, and swimming.

Unlike things labeled as alike: Here are laboratories, machine shops, gardens, bookbinding material, carpentry, and various other occupations and trades that the monks can engage in. [The word *other* points to a list of *occupations* and *trades*, whereas some of the items indicate *places to work in* or *materials to work with*.]

Fit the sentence to items of one kind: Here are laboratories, machine shops, gardens, a book bindery, a carpenter shop, and various other places where the monks may work at almost any occupation or trade.

(4) Overlapping items Make the items of a series mutually exclusive.

Overlapping: For vitamin C you should eat oranges, lemons, and citrus fruits. [Oranges and lemons are citrus fruits.]

Make the third item exclusive by inserting *other*: You should eat oranges, lemons, and other citrus fruits.

Overlapping in part: For vitamin C you should eat oranges, lemons, tomatoes, and citrus fruits.

Recast and insert *other*: You should eat oranges, lemons, other citrus fruits, and tomatoes. [The insertion of *other* without reordering would label unlike things as alike.]

327

41b. **Logical Comparison** Do not compare a mere part or quality of a thing with the whole of another thing. In comparing an individual with a class reveal whether the individual belongs to the class.*

Illogical: The speed of an ostrich is better than a racehorse. [Speed, a quality, cannot balance racehorse, a whole.]

Insert a pronoun to balance the named quality: The speed of an ostrich is better than that of a racehorse. [Or] An ostrich is faster than a racehorse.

Illogical: Of course my opinion is worth less than a lawyer.

Use a possessive to indicate the ellipsis: My opinion is worth less than a lawyer's [opinion].

Illogical: Like all primitive races the pygmy women do the work.

Use the same word: Like all primitive women [or *Like the women of all primitive races*] the pygmy women do the work.

Illogical: The chance that two members of one family will carry the same undesirable gene is greater than two members of different families.

Recast: Two members of one family are more likely to carry the same undesirable gene than are two members of different families.

Self-contradictory: Chicago is larger than any city in Illinois. [Chicago belongs to the class *any city in Illinois*. Thus the sentence states that Chicago is larger than itself.]

With a comparative exclude the individual from the class: Chicago is larger than any other city in Illinois.

Self-contradictory: Chicago is the largest of any other city in Illinois. [The sentence states that Chicago is the largest member of a class to which it does not belong.]

With a superlative include the individual in the class: Chicago is the largest of all the cities in Illinois. [Or] Chicago is the largest city in Illinois.

* For incomplete comparisons see **2a**.

41c. Definition * Logical definition explains the meaning of a term by (1) naming the class to which the individual member belongs and (2) adding differentiae—characteristics that distinguish the member from other members of the class. Informal definition often explains the meaning of a term by a synonym or other substitute expression. Either sort of definition must classify logically.

1. Name the smallest class that will include the term to be defined.

Inadequate—class too broad: A table fork is something used to convey food to the mouth. [So is a cup, a spoon.]

Narrow the class: A table fork is a pronged implement used to convey food to the mouth.

2. Add essential differentiae—those that truly exclude other members of the class.

Incomplete: A newspaper is a printed sheet. [So is a magazine, a program, a handbill.]

Add differentiae: A newspaper is a printed sheet that gives reports of current happenings. It is published at regular intervals, usually daily.

Inadequate—differentiation incomplete: Forestry is the science and art of growing trees. [The definition fails to differentiate between forestry and other arts concerned with trees—arboriculture or orcharding, for example.]

Include all essential differentiae: Forestry is the science and art of managing a plant society of trees and shrubs in the wild.

3. Do not let the explanation depend for its meaning on a repetition of the term.

Uninforming: An archaeologist is a specialist in archaeology.

Use other words: An archaeologist is a specialist in the study of human life and customs of the remote past.

* See also 17c(4), and for extended definition see 39c.

4. Balance the term by the same part of speech. (Do not say that a noun equals an adjective or that something "is when" or "is where.")

Improperly balanced: Limpidity means clear, transparent.
Use a noun: Limpidity means clearness, transparency.

Improperly balanced: Splitting hairs is when one makes excessively fine distinctions.
Match a gerund with a gerund: Splitting hairs is the making of excessively fine distinctions.

5. Exclude emotional or moral judgments.

Biased: Capitalism is an economic system wherein free enterprise and private ownership of the means of production result in good living for all.

Biased: Capitalism is an economic system wherein the few live luxuriously at the expense of the many.

Define objectively; keep judgment separate: Capitalism is an economic system wherein resources and the means of production and distribution are privately owned and managed. [Pertinent facts and judgment may be added.] In theory, competition provides sufficient control; in practice, some government regulation has been found necessary. The system has to date produced a higher general standard of living than any other [this is opinion, not definition].

Practice Definition

1. Write an exact definition of *water* (exclude other liquids), *stocking* (exclude sock and shoe), *orthopedist*, *obscurity*, *property*, *sociology*, *tragedy*, *labor union*, *chasing rainbows*, *broadcasting*.

2. Rewrite these definitions, correcting any errors:

An alcoholic is a man who drinks [check class and differentiate].
The quantum theory is the theory of quanta.
An allegory is when a thing means something else.
Turbulence means violently agitated, riotous.
Socialism is a political and economic theory whose practice results in destruction of initiative, rewards, and hope.

EXERCISE

X-41. Classification

Rewrite to complete the ideas logically.

1. Seeds may be scattered by an explosive mechanism in the fruit. Common types of explosive dispersal are the squirting cucumber and the black acacia.
2. The harbor is decorative and is seldom used for freight distribution with the exception of a few lumber boats and sometimes as an unloading point for sheep.
3. So far the discussion has been the laws of motion.
4. Just as there are exercises for the parts of the body, so there are exercises for the ailments of the mind.
5. Fielding's *Tom Jones*, published in 1749, was a generous, soft-hearted, but weak young man.
6. Farming contributes the most deaths, factories next, construction workers next, and mining next.
7. Other uses to which the wharf is put are boat building, fishing equipment, and a restaurant near the end of the pier.
8. The idea of popular sovereignty led to the uprisings of the eighteenth century—the revolutions in America and France and a limited constitutional monarchy in England.
9. The three-quarter mile strip along the lake is thronged with summer visitors, bathers, and little children.
10. Psychology is valuable knowledge for all scientists, social scientists, philosophers, and those interested in humanity.

Rewrite to make the comparisons logical.

11. Naturally Thoreau's philosophy of life would differ from a college student.
12. Unlike most orchestras the strings are placed behind the woodwinds.
13. The hill section is reserved for the homes of the wealthy, and they make a bitter contrast to the poor housing conditions of the minority groups of the city.
14. Public schools progressed faster in Massachusetts than anywhere in the United States.
15. The insane have been the most barbarously treated of any other group of unfortunates.

PURPOSE, RELEVANCE

42. Unite all parts of a piece of writing around a central thought. Eliminate ideas and details not important for your purpose. Do not overload any passage.

HOW TO CORRECT IRRELEVANCE AND EXCESS

Effective writing demands singleness of purpose, in the whole and in the parts.* Each sentence and each paragraph should contribute to the controlling idea of the whole composition. In any passage minor points should either be brought into relationship with the main idea or be eliminated.

42a. Irrelevance Do not include in a sentence or passage a detail not obviously related to the main idea. Either omit the detail or show a connection. If the main idea is buried, dig it out.

Disturbing element: In explaining to a class the workings of a machine a valuable aid is a Transvue booklet. The booklets may be obtained from a firm in Milwaukee. The device consists of transparent sheets, each carrying a picture of one part. Closed, the booklet presents a picture of the machine as a whole. As the leaves are turned one part at a time is removed. [Omit the second sentence. If the information is needed introduce it later.]

Statements not obviously related: The gavotte was popular in the court of Louis XIV. It is a lively dance, something like a minuet, but less stately. It is named after a district in the Alps.

Subordinate one idea; omit another: The gavotte, popular in the court of Louis XIV, is a lively dance somewhat like a minuet, but less stately. [The central idea is the *nature* of the gavotte.]

* See 30 for the controlling idea and 36 for unity in the paragraph.

Details with no clear connecting idea: Starfish have arms radiating from a central body. The twenty ray starfish is orange and purple. Its rays come apart easily.

Unite the details by revealing a purpose: Every starfish has a central body with arms radiating from it. The twenty ray starfish may be identified by its orange and purple coloring and by the loose connection of its rays.

Main idea obscure: In a dictatorship too many people have to spend their time spying on other people. The leaders and other officials have to be protected by police. So do the government buildings and records. Slave labor is another thing that wastes manpower through inefficiency.

Dig out the main idea and relate the details to it: <u>A dictatorship is wasteful of manpower.</u> It must employ many persons as <u>police to guard the leader,</u> his officials, their offices and records. It uses slave labor, which is always inefficient.

42b. **Overloading** Do not try to tell too much; omit details which can be taken for granted. Do not overqualify.

Ask yourself: What *one thing* am I talking about? Then ask: What *one thing* am I saying about it?

Overloaded passage: Another loyalty was that of Dancy to his wife. This ended tragically, for when he escaped he went home to her and was caught and committed suicide rather than subject her to the futility of living in exile.

Eliminate minor details and rearrange: Another <u>loyalty</u>, that of Dancy to his wife, <u>ended tragically.</u> Rather than subject her to the futile life of an exile he committed suicide.

Overqualification: Until greater scientific knowledge is gained about man and until man himself is educated in the principles of genetics and eugenics, social betterment through these two fields will remain at more or less the standstill at which many people think it is now.

Go direct: Social betterment through eugenics and genetics <u>must</u> wait for <u>greater scientific</u> knowledge and more widespread education in these two subjects.

333

42c. **Repetitiousness** * Do not carelessly restate in a second expression an idea implicit in the first.

Repetition in different words: The entertainment facilities are limited, and for its size Centerville is sadly lacking in adequate places for diversion and amusement.

State the idea once: Centerville lacks adequate facilities for entertainment.

Unnecessary partial restatement: The survey is intended to bring out different points of view. Not everybody holds the same opinion. [The idea of the second sentence is too obvious to need emphasis.]

Omit the superfluous statement : The survey is intended to bring out different points of view.

Practice Repetitiousness

Rewrite to eliminate restatement.

1. The sizes of these flowers do not vary a great deal. They are all approximately the same.

2. State Street is the main business street of the city. It runs north and south for about sixteen blocks, from the river at one end to Hollister Avenue at the other. It contains most of the stores and offices.

3. Before we developed the films we shut the door of the dark-room tight to keep out every bit of light. Still the negatives were spoiled. We could not understand it, when we had been so careful to keep the film completely in the dark.

4. In sanding a piece of wood the correct motion is in the direction of the grain, with pressure on both forward and backward strokes. You will not get such good results if you try to work crosswise. Always work with the grain.

5. Senator Williams is a thoroughly honest man. He is completely straightforward in everything he does. Nobody has ever persuaded him to act in a dishonorable way.

---

* For needless repetition of an element see 16.

EXERCISE

X-42. Purpose, Relevance

Rewrite each passage to accomplish a single purpose.

1. To the right is the pier and lying at anchor are yachts, cat-boats, and motorboats belonging to various people.

2. The best way to acquire a tan without burning is to toast yourself evenly for a short time and then apply a protective lotion. Sunburn can do a lot of harm. You can safely increase the time of exposure from day to day.

3. As the coal car rumbled into the main passage, we bent over to keep our heads from bumping. This was the first time I had entered a mine. Our light split the darkness.

4. The Institute of Paper Chemistry designed an emergency house for fifty dollars' worth of material. It is 8 feet by 16 and can house a burned-out family of four. This house would be of great value in flood areas. The panel boards are made of waste papers cemented together.

5. Two thousand people spend their days toiling in that dingy building with the cracked windows across the river.

6. Lying by the ocean on the shore of a small bay that is eight miles wide at the mouth, Cape View has a harbor protected by a breakwater. This was built by the city.

7. While the program might help to build a better society it is one that can be carried out only with much work and great difficulty, if at all, except in certain cases.

8. Beethoven borrowed musical ideas from himself through the use of his sketchbook, in which he wrote down phrases as they occurred to him or as he remembered them, and through repetition of source motives.

9. It's a good thing for a paper to play down crime news to a certain extent. I think our paper's policy of never printing the names of first time juvenile delinquents is admirable, but I also think that a good crime should be written up but not smeared across the page.

10. It used to be that a child accepted the occupation of his father as his life work. Now many professions have developed, and there is a realization that the person best suited to a profession may not be the one who has a father in it.

335

ORDER AND RANK

43. Show the relationships between ideas by clear order and exact ranking.*

HOW TO PUT IDEAS IN PROPER RELATION

43a. **Natural Order** Place ideas in such sequence that relationships between them will be clear.

Confusing order: We decided to turn into a back road off the highway after traveling bumper to bumper all morning.

Put first things first: After traveling all morning bumper to bumper we decided to turn off the highway. . . .

Confusing order: A careless trainer may spoil a good colt. A good horse can never be made of a vicious colt. [Here the order of ideas is "Trainer . . . colt. Horse . . . colt."]

Turn one sentence end for end: A careless trainer may spoil a good colt. And a vicious colt can never be made into a good horse. [Now one idea leads into another: "Trainer . . . colt. Colt . . . horse."]

Mingled fact and opinion: Jefferson's defeat of Burr was fortunate for the country. Yet he won the presidency by only a narrow margin. Burr was not only an adventurer, but a traitor. [The statement of fact is sandwiched between two statements of opinion.]

Distinguish fact from opinion: Jefferson won the presidency by a narrow margin. His defeat of Burr was fortunate for the country. In the opinion of many authorities Burr was not only an adventurer, but a traitor.

Buried topic: Many men from our industrial arts department do not find desirable positions. College graduates do not always find employment readily. Many holders of the A.B. degree in arts and sciences are looking vainly for work. Even many young engineers lack jobs. [The badly placed general idea interrupts the flow.]

* See **31c, 34b,** and **37** for ordering of large elements.

Put the unifying idea in a prominent position: College graduates
do not always find employment readily. Many men. . . . Many
holders. . . . Even many young engineers. . . . [Or begin with
the illustrations, and place the unifying statement in the other
prominent position—the end.]

Confusing use of alternating ideas: Mountain flowers have more
appeal for me than tropical blooms. Tropical plants grow
rank with broad leaves and massive blossoms, but the alpine
plants are restrained and graceful, but storm-scarred and
toughened. The mat of delicate flowers lies above a gnarled
mass of fibres that are rooted firmly in the rock, but the roots
of tropical plants are spindly, scarcely developed. Their stems
are weak and slender, dissipated by luxury. Drawing an easy
living from rich soil, the plants of the tropics compete only
for space, but the mountain dwellers must not only fight
against drying wind and freezing cold but struggle for every
crumb of soil and drop of water.

Compare by wholes: Mountain flowers have more appeal for me
than tropical blooms. Tropical plants grow rank with broad
leaves and massive blossoms. Their roots are spindly, scarcely
developed, and their stems are weak and slender, dissipated
by luxury. Drawing an easy living from rich soil, the plants
of the tropics compete only for space. But alpine plants,
though scarred and toughened by storms, are restrained and
graceful. They spread a mat of delicate flowers over a gnarled
mass of fibres rooted firmly in the rock. Thus armored against
wind and cold, they struggle for every crumb of soil and drop
of water. [The writer says all he has to say about one subject, then uses *but* and proceeds to discuss the other. Note
that he could omit even the single *but* without confusion.]

Compare item by item, with parallel structure: Tropical plants
are rank, with broad leaves and massive blossoms. Alpine
plants are restrained and graceful, with delicate flowers.
Tropical plants have spindly roots and weak stems, alpine
plants a gnarled mass of fibres rooted firmly in the rock. Tropical plants, drawing an easy living from rich soil, compete only
for space. Alpine plants, fighting the elements, struggle for
every crumb of soil and drop of water. [Parallel structure
keeps contrasting thoughts clear without *buts*.]

337

43b. **Natural Ranking** Put each idea on its proper level; do not set down all ideas as equals.* Do not confuse the levels by misuse of connectives.

(1) Subordination of minor ideas

Failure to indicate comparative values: These buildings are often over a hundred years old. They are like shrines. The tribute of the community is hasty and commercial.

Build up one idea and subordinate the others: These buildings, often over a hundred years old, are like shrines to which the community pays a hasty and commercial tribute.

Dead level presentation of two ideas: The frog is a stupid animal and may be caught with a hook baited with red flannel. [Is the writer trying to tell us how to catch frogs or merely that frogs are stupid?]

Give importance to one idea: A frog, being a stupid animal, may be caught with a hook baited with red flannel [giving importance to *how to catch frogs*]. The willingness of a frog to bite at a hook baited with red flannel shows his stupidity [giving importance to *frogs are stupid*].

Exact relation doubtful: The spores of pine blister rust pass through an intermediate stage on the leaves of the wild currant. All wild currant bushes should be removed from the forest, and the remaining pines can be saved.

Show the precise relation: The spores of pine blister rust must pass through an intermediate stage on the leaves of the wild currant. Therefore the removal from the forest of all wild currant bushes could save the remaining pines from infection.

Importance reversed: One day I was running the dogs when I stepped on a snake. [Which is the more important event?]

Give importance to the big idea: One day when I was running the dogs, I stepped on a snake.

* See also **47a**, Tightening Sentence Structure, and **48a**, Emphasis Through Subordination.

(2) Accurate use of connectives

Subordination thwarted by unnecessary conjunction: Gerald went to bed, and leaving his work unfinished. [*And* here puts a participial phrase on an equality with the main clause.]

Omit the coördinating conjunction: Gerald went to bed, leaving his work unfinished.

Subordination thwarted by *and* with *which*: This is an important problem, and which we shall not find easy to solve.

Either coördinate the ideas or subordinate one correctly: This is an important problem and one which we shall not find easy to solve [coördinate]. This is an important problem, which we shall not find easy to solve [subordinate].

Subordination thwarted by *but*: Their chief opponent is Winter, a shrewd politician, but who is now less popular than he was. [*But* should join elements of the same kind.]

Use coördinate subordinate clauses: Their chief opponent is Winter, who is a shrewd politician, but who is now less popular than he was.

Miscoördination: I have written an essay giving my views on several matters about which there is considerable disagreement, but a reader might like to know what an ordinary student thinks about them. [The *but* idea should be coördinated with the subordinate *about which* idea, not with the main clause.]

Repeat the subordinating phrase in the *but* clause: I have written an essay giving my views on several matters about which there is room for considerable disagreement but about which a reader might like to know the opinion of an ordinary student.

Miscoördination: Shakespeare chose to decorate his poem not with jewels, needlework, or mythological figures, but he used little details of his own observation.

Subordinate the idea of the *but* clause by compounding it with a subordinate element: Shakespeare chose to decorate his poem not with jewels, needlework, or mythological figures but with little details of his own observation.

Misrelation through faulty division: These politicians are either ignorant or not concerned with the people's welfare. I don't know which, but if we knew more about the men we elect we could make better choices. [The thought of one sentence should not run over into a second which introduces a new idea.]

Join the related ideas and separate them from the new idea: These politicians are either ignorant or not concerned with the people's welfare; I don't know which. If we knew more about the men we elect we could make better choices.

EXERCISE

X-43a. Natural Order

Rewrite to secure clear order, making any necessary changes.

1. From August, 1944, when the program to fly whole blood to Europe was started, 150,000 pints reached the forward areas by March, 1945.

2. Emotional disturbance stimulates the adrenal glands, and the body is prepared for appropriate action by the glands.

3. A seedling which has begun its growth in the dark will grow faster and taller than a seedling grown in sunlight; however, the stronger and healthier seedling will be the one grown in sunlight.

4. Coöperatives are in general exempt from income taxes, provided they meet certain requirements. Objections by businessmen to such exemptions are not justifiable. The savings returned to members are not the same as profits from business. Coöperatives pay real estate, social security, and other taxes like any profit-making concern. Members must of course pay individual income taxes.

5. The heart can stand considerable strain, but it may be damaged by exertion after acute illness or extreme fatigue. But damage will not result from strenuous athletics if the body is trained to gradually increasing activity. But even in trained athletes the heart must have adequate rest before the next effort is made.

X-43b. Natural Ranking

Rewrite to place each idea on its proper level. Subordinate minor ideas. Use connectives accurately. Divide the material with care.

1. Greenvale has some small smokeless type industries. In general it is unproductive. The county is a major productive unit of the state.

2. Gandhi worked tirelessly for the freedom of India, and during his lifetime he was revered as a saint. [Either show a relation or cut the statements apart.]

3. In America we take all sorts of luxuries for granted, and all we have to do is put a nickel in a slot-machine and anything we want comes out, from peanuts to television.

4. We visited Nebraska last July and the crops were drying up.

5. The people were on their way to church, when suddenly the flood struck.

6. Members of these minority groups have little incentive to try for better jobs, and which they know will be refused.

7. I have had a little trouble with my schedule because I am taking a premedical course but I want to include subjects of general value.

8. The knowledge that chromosomes in germ cells are not affected by changes in body cells is invaluable to couples desiring children but either the father or the mother has been blinded, crippled, or made an invalid.

9. All the teachers in the Massachusetts colony had to be Puritans and frequently the minister of the town was the teacher. If the town had not provided a schoolhouse the classes met in his house.

10. I went to the hotel and Hoyt had not registered there. I was starting out the door when he suddenly rushed in.

COMPLETENESS, CONNECTION

44. Say what you mean. Insert any ideas necessary to show the connection between two thoughts or between two or more parts of one thought.

HOW TO CORRECT OBSCURITIES AND CONTRADICTIONS

44a. Half-expressed Ideas Do not halfway express an idea. Make sure that the reader gets your exact thought in full. Show the connection of ideas by smooth transition.

(I) Needed parts Resurrect buried ideas.

Half-expressed idea: When I think of Dr. Randall's book it is the specific examples.

Complete the thought: When I think of Dr. Randall's book I remember the specific examples as the most valuable part.

Incomplete: Haunted houses, in my opinion, is only a superstition.

Express the full thought: The belief that houses can be haunted is, in my opinion, only a superstition.

Buried idea: For two years there was no rain, and cattle died on the parched hillsides. This drought gave impetus to the agricultural development of the country. [Why? How?]

Insert needed information: For two years there was no rain, and cattle died on the parched hillsides. Seeing the danger of depending on an uncertain rainfall, the ranchers developed an irrigation system. A sure water supply gave impetus to the agricultural development of the country.

Buried idea: Many of the characters do small things to them but that are necessary to carry on the plot.

Expand the vital part: Many of the characters do things that seem trivial to them but that are actually important in forwarding the plot.

242

(2) Transitions Give guidance where a thought turns.*

Disconnected: This year many of the ducks coming from the bay taste fishy. Growing plants are lacking in their feeding grounds.

Insert a cause transition: This year many of the ducks coming from the bay taste fishy. Since ducks are vegetarians by choice a fishy taste indicates a lack of growing plants in their feeding grounds.

Disconnected: Americans were welcomed in Texas up to 1830, but then they were forbidden, as soon the Americans would rule Texas.

Insert cause and time transition: Americans were welcomed in Texas up to 1830, but thereafter Mexico, fearing they would gain power and rule Texas, forbade further immigration.

Disconnected: Towering above us was a giant gray rock. From its summit we looked across valleys and lesser ranges to the snowcapped peaks of the western wall.

Insert a place transition: Towering above us was a giant rock. We circled it and worked our way up. From its summit....

Disconnected: Noise can be more tiring than hard work. Last summer I worked in an airplane factory. [Such a gap in thought occurs oftenest between the first two sentences of a paper or of a paragraph.]

Insert a general-to-particular transition: Noise can be more tiring than hard work. This fact I verified by my own experience. Last summer I worked in an airplane factory.

Disconnected: In a school district all teachers should make it plain that they are willing to give help and advice to any pupil. Guidance should be available from trained counsellors.

Insert transition and explanation: In a school district all teachers should make it plain that they are willing to give help and advice to any pupil. In addition, guidance that is beyond the ability or time of the teachers should be available from trained counsellors.

* See **34** and **37** for transitions in larger elements.

44b. **Contradictions and Absurdities** Include any idea necessary to adjust contradictory ideas to each other. Do not allow conflicting ideas to carry your reader in two directions at once like a pair of unruly roller skates.

Contradictory: Delay the opening of your parachute and you will reach the ground safely.

Insert the missing idea: Delay the opening of your parachute long enough to avoid its being entangled in the plane and you will reach the ground safely.

Confusing: The commercialization of the public's interest in vitamins would lead people to believe that vitamin tablets, yeast, and other preparations are essential to health. Their value in correcting dietary faults, however, is considerable.

Insert the missing idea and needed qualification: The commercialization of the public's interest in vitamins would lead people to believe that vitamin tablets, yeast, and other preparations are essential to health. This belief is mistaken, although the value of some vitamin preparations in correcting certain dietary faults is considerable.

Contradictory: Too many come to school with interest in only one subject and lose interest in others. [Lose what they haven't?]

Qualify, and show time relationship: Too many on coming to school have a strong interest in only one subject and soon lose even a slight interest in others.

Topsy-turvy logic: Some people can better afford to pay for medical service than others, and for these the county has established a free hospital.

Turn the ideas the same way up: Some people can less well afford..., and for these...a free hospital.

Ambiguous negative: All of us couldn't go. [Or] We all couldn't go. [Could only some go, or could none go?]

For precision place the negative next to the word it modifies: Not all of us could go. [Some could] None [Not one] of us could go. [None could]

Inaccurate and contradictory: Like her larger neighbors Bloomton has a slum district on a smaller but identical scale. [How can a scale be both *smaller* and *identical?*]

Resolve the conflict by filling out the ideas: Like her larger neighbors Bloomton has a slum district. Though smaller in scale, it is equally squalid.

Confused statement of cause: A liquid travels up a straw by creating a suction.

Assign the cause to the proper agency: A liquid travels up a straw because atmospheric pressure forces the liquid into the low pressure area created by suction on the straw.

Absurd: The sponge fishermen obtain the sponges either by grappling for them with long hooked poles or by wearing diving suits and going directly to the ocean floor. [Obtain the sponges by wearing diving suits?]

Assign the modifier logically: The sponge fishermen obtain the sponges by grappling ... or by going down for them in diving suits directly to the ocean floor.

Roller skate sentence: He was defeated by only a few votes, but he seemed to take his defeat very cheerfully. [The *but* clause is logical after the discouraging *he was defeated* but not after the encouraging *only a few votes.*]

Follow out one idea at a time: He was defeated, but he seemed to take his defeat very cheerfully, perhaps because he had lost by only a few votes. [Or] He was defeated by only a few votes. Presumably he was disappointed, but he seemed to take his defeat very cheerfully.

Roller skate sentence: Although the *Courier* frankly admits that it is a pro-union paper it has more in common with the employers' associations than with the unions.

Develop one idea or the other (as determined by your purpose): Although the *Courier* calls itself a pro-union paper it has more in common with the employers' associations than with the unions. [Or] The *Courier* frankly admits that it is a pro-union paper; it is not so frank about other influences affecting it.

345

EXERCISE

X-44a. Half-expressed Ideas

Rewrite each passage, filling in missing ideas and necessary transitions. Add as many sentences as you need.

1. When we speak of inheriting brown hair and blue eyes it is the mechanism that produces brown hair and blue eyes.
2. Myths usually arise after the death of their hero. Strange stories were circulated about Roosevelt during his lifetime.
3. Since most of these people represented first generation wealth their children often were scattered and the estates were bought by others. [A lack of roots perhaps?]
4. While being pretty solidly middle class the people are inclined to be lenient with those of different faiths.
5. Along the Nile are five cataracts which interfere with travel although they are not like Niagara Falls.
6. Horace Mann took over the supervision of all public schools in Massachusetts. Churches wanted to continue their control, teachers could not see why they needed extra training, but the state refused to give Mann any assistance.
7. During the depression of the 1930's the merchants of the city were hard pressed. Herron's paper carried their advertising on the books until they were heavily in debt to him. This pressure of Herron's was so much resented that even now the businessmen feel little friendliness toward the paper. [What pressure? How did he use the debts?]
8. Where the ground is dry it is good to lie and look up at the cirrus clouds forming over the mountains and the beetles crawling through the grass-blade jungle.
9. As a psychology major I have a special interest in industrial psychology and aptitude tests. The Hale-Chalmers testing service near us on Bridge Street has grown tremendously in the last few years and is expanding at a rapid rate as contracts continue to pour in.
10. Federal aid to education should mean that the poorer sections of the country would receive enough to compensate for their poverty. These poorly trained students move to other sections of the country and lower the standards of the schools they enter.

X-44b. Contradictions and Absurdities

Make these sentences intelligible by adjusting the conflicting ideas.

1. When a seed has two cotyledons the food is in the cotyledons. If the cotyledons are both small the food will be in the endosperm.
2. Trips to the nearest town were often long and infrequent.
3. Eugenics and the atomic bomb are a threat to mankind, but the use of both promises untold good.
4. It is a book that may be read for years, but will lose its value progressively as its date of publication recedes.
5. Oppressive and repressive organizations make a mockery of the things that Jefferson, Lincoln, and Roosevelt tried to improve and correct.
6. The result is that by blowing through a straw the limewater turns milky in the presence of carbon dioxide.
7. There are three miles of beaches all of which are maintained by the park department and some by private owners.
8. That sickness and death are at times unnecessary and are preventable is well known.
9. Reading, although one learns from observation, is the first step toward knowledge.
10. Although many people have stolen, the delinquent is the one who is caught, and while the local police cannot be condemned for being too lax with the juvenile delinquent there is a tendency for the people to tolerate this condition.

Style

CONSISTENCY OF TONE AND IMAGERY

45. Adopt a style appropriate to your subject and your purpose, and use it consistently.

Style in a piece of writing as in a piece of wearing apparel should suit the occasion. For everyday use develop a simple, direct, natural manner of expression. Avoid technical or abstruse words and phrases, involved sentences, long and intricate paragraphs. Avoid also low colloquial expressions, primer sentences, childish rambling. Adapt your basic style to each occasion; make it at need a little more or a little less formal, strictly impersonal or definitely personal, serious or decidedly humorous. Maintain the tone that you have adopted.

Semi-formal, factual treatment of a subject (suitable in a serious paper): In 1910 the progressive wing of the Republican party rebelled against the conservatives. They drove Nelson Aldrich out of the Senate and combined with the Democrats to destroy the power of Joseph Cannon, Speaker of the House.

Livelier, less formal treatment of the same subject: "An insurgent," said Theodore Roosevelt, "is a progressive who is exceeding the speed limit." In 1910 the insurgent progressives got hold of the machinery of Congress and gave the throttle a yank. They drove Nelson Aldrich out of the Senate and teamed up with the Democrats to smash Joe Cannon's power in the house.*

* Roger Butterfield, *The American Past,* Simon and Schuster.

HOW TO SUSTAIN A PARTICULAR STYLE

45a. Consistency of Tone Do not change abruptly from a formal to an informal manner, or waver between the lofty and the commonplace.

Sudden change from semi-formal to markedly colloquial style: * Twice we have sought to avoid war by declaring our neutrality. We didn't make it stick.

Sustain the semi-formal style: Twice we have sought to avoid war by declaring our neutrality. We did not avoid it.

Sudden change from semi-formal to slangy style: Our newspaper should offer an equal amount of space to all candidates who wish to express their views. This playing favorites is phony. It sure louses up an election.

Sustain the semi-formal style: Our newspaper should offer an equal amount of space to all candidates who wish to express their views. By playing favorites the editor keeps us from making a democratic choice.

Or rewrite completely in a colloquial-to-slangy style (permissible in extremely informal writing): Our newspaper is a phony. It hands Joe Blow a two-column spread, pinches off Rube Ryan with two inches. Lightly, our editor tosses a monkey wrench into the gears of democracy.

Sudden descent from the lofty to the commonplace: † Under the leaves we discovered wild raspberries big as thimbles. They were rich and sweet to our taste. We had found a paradise in the wilderness! Of course the mosquitoes bothered us quite a bit.

Omit both the unnaturally lofty and the unnecessarily commonplace; add specific, pleasant details: . . . rich and sweet to our taste. Downstream we came upon a meadow gay with blue gentians.

---

* See also 18e.
† A sudden descent in style may be used deliberately for humorous effect. The device has been overworked on radio programs.

45b. **Connotation** Use words with connotations appropriate to the context.*

The denotation of a word is its literal meaning, its definition; the connotation is its suggested meaning, its appeal to emotion or imagination. Note the difference in the kind of feeling aroused by each of the paired words or phrases.

smile	mellow	bracing air	cookery queen	ran
smirk	rotten	cold wind	kitchen drudge	scurried

Effective use of connotation to show contrast:

It was just growing dusky as Laura shut their garden gates. A big dog ran by like a shadow. The road gleamed white, and down below in the hollow the little cottages were in deep shade. How quiet it seemed after the afternoon. Here she was going down the hill to somewhere where a man lay dead, and she couldn't realize it. Why couldn't she? She stopped a minute. And it seemed to her that kisses, voices, tinkling spoons, laughter, the smell of crushed grass were somehow inside her. She had no room for anything else. How strange! She looked up at the pale sky, and all she thought was, "Yes, it was the most successful party." † [In the first half of the paragraph the words *dusky, shadow, shade, quiet* lead to a tragic climax. In the second half Laura's still lingering mood of gaiety is carried by *tinkling spoons, laughter, the smell of crushed grass* to a different climax.]

Advertisers use connotation freely.

Mildly impressive: The finest trains in this country are built of B——— steel.

More effective: Every afternoon at 3:30 a California Zephyr in glittering stainless steel moves proudly out of Chicago. . . . [What words carry pleasing or impressive connotations?]

* For a treatment of faulty connotation see 17e.
† Reprinted from *Short Stories of Katherine Mansfield* by permission of Alfred A. Knopf, Inc. Copyright 1922, 1937, by Alfred A. Knopf, Inc.

45c. **Imagery** Use only such figures of speech and call up
only such images as go well with each other and
with the particular idea or picture. Avoid overworked figures and mixed images.

Overworked figure: The moon rose slowly. We gazed en-
tranced as the queen of the night ascended her throne.

Change to direct description: The moon rose slowly. We
watched it sharpen the world into lights and shadows.

Mixed image: The Republicans gained a foothold in the heart
of the cotton belt.

Retain a single clear image: The Republicans gained a foothold
in the South.

Mixed image: Swept together on a tide of strong emotion, these
two could not untwine themselves.

Retain one image or the other: Swept together on a tide of emotion, these two clung to each other. [Or] Bound by ties of
strong emotion, these two could not untwine themselves.

Revival of buried meaning: Rome is the outstanding example of
an empire that fell. [Ordinarily *outstanding* may not suggest
standing. But when joined with *fell*, it does.]

Use a neutral word: Rome is the most conspicuous example of
an empire that fell.

Intrusion of the literal into the figurative: Spring came scattering flowers, and there was rain a great per cent of the time.

Sustain the image: Spring came scattering flowers and rain.

Intrusion of figurative into the literal: Destroy these pests with
bait or spray before they get a strangle hold on your garden.

Eliminate the figure: Destroy these pests with bait or spray
before they ruin your garden.

Ludicrous suggestion of personification: Gradually the movement gained weight and led to the development of similar
societies in other countries.

Modify the image: Gradually the movement gained strength
enough to bring about the development. . . .

351

EXERCISE

X-45. Consistency of Tone and Imagery

Rewrite each passage in a single harmonious style. Eliminate mixed, overworked, and inappropriate figures.

1. In this poem Keats displays the pageantry of Greek mythology plus a good view of his own likes.

2. Industry promotes officials with technical competence instead of those who have skill in human relations. These dubs are the guys who foul up labor problems.

3. Nancy made a beautiful picture. She stood slim and straight as a reed, and her eyes shone like stars.

4. All these stumbling blocks keep people from climbing out of the ruts to which they are chained.

5. The sun sinking behind Mount Red Chief lighted up great masses of cloud. Over the ridges herds of horses grazed. There were donkeys, too; we heard one bray.

6. The hour you dreamed of is here. You stand alone in the moonlit garden, just you two. He folds your hand in his. Aren't you glad you thought of using Bergen's Hand Lotion?

7. When we delve into the relationship of heredity to human problems we must bring environment into the picture.

8. If two people contemplating marriage tried to foresee the possible causes of disharmony they would not get such rude jolts as quarrels cause when they erupt out of a blue sky.

9. The real Lincoln will probably never be known, for his picture is now so completely smothered under a patina of stained glass fiction and apocryphal rubbish that nobody knows where the truth ends and the myths begin.

10. Hay fever is one of these nasty ailments that get you no sympathy at all. Your friends either make poor jokes about your red nose or move rapidly away, suspecting that you have a cold. Actually, hay fever is not a disease, but an allergic symptom complex characterized by catarrhal inflammation of the mucous membranes. [Once you have taken a light tone sustain it. Do not go suddenly formal or technical.]

SIMPLICITY AND CONCRETENESS

46. Make statements precise rather than vague, simple rather than pretentious. Use concrete details freely.

HOW TO MAKE YOUR WRITING REAL

46a. Simplicity Use exact, specific terms (see 17). Avoid straining for effect. Avoid stilted language and jargon (see 18d).

Vague: Keep going the same direction. You can't miss it.
Be specific: Keep to the right. Turn at the first signal.

Flowery style: Shelley seems so captivated with his imaginative ascendancies to dazzling heights and vast spaces of the universe that it becomes the dominant, surging note of his mind no matter what he is describing.
Simplify: No matter what he is describing Shelley uses images which suggest dazzling heights and vast spaces.

Artificial, roundabout style: The author of this epistle attends an institution of learning not many miles distant from your campus.
Go direct: I am a student at a neighboring college. [Do not be afraid to use the first person.]

Formal statement of simple thought: The theory of relativity is difficult to understand. But experience has shown that a homely comparison may make baffling matters clear. Let us see therefore whether such a comparison will help us to grasp the theory in question.
Lighten and simplify: The theory of relativity is hard to understand. A homely comparison may make it clearer.

Passage stiff with jargon: It is the contention of this paper that perceptual variations can be scientifically apprehended in terms of appropriate metrics.
Speak plainly: I contend that variations in perception can be scientifically measured.

46b. **Concreteness** Make use of details which appeal to the senses. Relate abstract or general statements to concrete situations. (See also **17d.**)

No appeal to the senses: I liked to watch mother as she moved about the kitchen preparing our morning meal.
Use concrete details: I liked to lounge in the kitchen doorway, sniffing bacon and buckwheat cakes and watching mother's quick hands lift down the breakfast dishes.

Abstract statement: To achieve a better standard of living we must have all-out production.
Restate concretely: To achieve a better standard of living we must manufacture so many shoes and shirts and refrigerators that we can sell them at a price within the reach of the ordinary workingman.

General statement: Poor grades result from overcrowding.
Reinforce by a concrete example: In the house where I live four students are jammed into a single room. We can't walk around or shave or put on our shoes without bumping into each other. Concentrated study is impossible.

Passage which explains an idea by a concrete analogy:

It occurs to me that America looks on Europe as an air-observer looks on the earth below. He is near it—yes; he can see it spread out at his feet. Modern communication, transportation, science have brought him right on top of it; but he is insulated from it, by his power and freedom, by his mechanical and material genius, by the infinite resources at his ground base, which keeps him safe above it, at this great height, from which he can observe so well—and need feel so little. He is comfortable, well-fed, aloof, and superior. This is a terrible thing—the curious illusion of superiority bred by height; the illusion of being a god, that one has looking down on those pill-box houses, those pocket-handkerchief fields, those Noah's Ark animals, those ant-like human beings. The illusion of irresponsible power. One must never forget that Satan tempted Christ from a mountain top.*

*Anne Morrow Lindbergh, "Airliner to Europe," *Harper's Magazine* (September, 1948).

X46a. Simplicity

Rewrite each passage in a simple, direct style.

1. The marvelous perfection and the intrinsic excellence of Lincoln's Gettysburg Address as a masterpiece of English composition escaped even the ablest scholars of his day.
2. By honeyed expressions of endearment and artfully entwining caresses the gentle sex hold strong men in their power.
3. As the scientific age has progressed, emphasis has gradually been placed on the application of scientific method to that most important field, the study of mankind.
4. It is in general inadvisable for any person with heart disease to engage in the extreme exertion incident to strenuous sports like football, basketball, and hockey.
5. Certain personality variables predispose the individual toward adopting an ethnocentric ideology.

X46b. Concreteness

Rewrite or complete two passages, using concrete details.

1. On our way to Twin Lakes we passed through farming country. After lunch we began climbing the foothills. In mid-afternoon we reached the scenic part of our journey.
2. One place where I played as a child....
3. It's noisy where I work.
4. Diversification of holdings is an important principle of investment. [Use either an example or an analogy.]
5. One purpose of social conventions is to exclude outsiders.

Copy the following passage. Underline words and phrases which appeal to the senses.

The earth was warm under me, and warm as I crumbled it through my fingers. Queer little red bugs came out and moved in slow squadrons around me. Their backs were polished vermilion, with black spots. I kept as still as I could. Nothing happened. I did not expect anything to happen. I was something that lay under the sun and felt it, like the pumpkins, and I did not want to be anything more.*

* Willa Cather, *My Antonia*, Houghton Mifflin Company.

SMOOTHNESS

47. Fit the expression closely to the thought. Do not permit
     awkwardnesses of structure, movement, or sound to come
between the reader and the meaning.

HOW TO SECURE A SMOOTH FLOW OF IDEAS

47a. **Structure** Tighten your sentence structure. Place main
     ideas in main clauses; subordinate minor points. (See
43b, Natural Rank; **48a,** Emphasis Through Subordination.)

Stringy sentence: In Roman days there was nothing but human
     muscle to do all the work, and men had to lift all the stones
     or timbers by hand if something was to be built, and they even
     had to row the ships that carried cargo from port to port.

Tighten by reducing predication: In Roman days the muscles
     of men lifted the stones and timbers for building, rowed the
     great ships that carried cargo from port to port.

Sprawling sentence: Our beaches are protected by islands and
     the sand usually stays where it belongs, but sometimes the
     current from between the mainland and the islands sweeps
     it away and deposits it farther south.

Tighten by tucking in details as modifiers: Though our beaches
     are protected by islands, an occasional strong current in the
     channel sweeps a quantity of sand southward.

Loose structure: The Mexicans do not eat bread. They have
     plenty of corn, so they pound it up fine and make flat cakes
     out of it. These cakes are called tortillas.

Tighten by using an appositive: The tortilla, a flat cake made
     of finely pounded corn meal, serves the Mexicans as bread.

Bumpy effect: The cliffs at the edge of the antarctic sea are
     made of ice. Waves wash away the base. Clumps fall off and
     become icebergs. These icebergs have flat tops.

Combine into a single smooth sentence by using verbals:
     Undermined by the sea, great chunks of the ice-cliff break
     off to form the typical flat-topped antarctic icebergs.

356

Awkward piling up of nouns: The decline in the amount of immigration into our country is due to our sentiment against increase of population from foreign sources and the laws on the statute books of our government. [The sentence contains eleven nouns and only one verb—the colorless *is*.]

Use verbs: Immigration into our country has fallen off because we do not like to increase our population from foreign sources and have therefore passed restrictive laws. [The sentence contains five nouns, three main verbs, one infinitive.]

47b. Movement Secure forward movement within sentences and from one sentence to another. Make relationships plain.*

Awkward suspended construction: Why doesn't the Council find the reason for and the answer to these complaints?

Bring related parts together: Why doesn't the Council find out the reason for these complaints and the answer to them?

Overuse of subordination: A recent strike called by the Retail Clerks' Union of several grocery stores ended after it had nearly become a lockout by the strikers getting a ten cents an hour increase in wages.

Describe separate events in separate sentences: Recently the Retail Clerks' Union called a strike affecting several grocery stores. For a time the clerks were threatened with a lockout. Eventually they won a ten cents an hour increase in wages. [Note that throughout the passage the important subject is kept central: *Clerks' Union . . . clerks . . . they*.]

Inept use of subordination: The city ordinance prohibiting manufacturing to locate there because it might smoke up the city and ruin its reputation has kept industries away that ordinarily would spend money and create employment.

Use a compound predicate; rearrange subordinate clauses: Because factories create smoke the city by ordinance prohibits them and so deprives itself of the money and the opportunity for employment that industries would bring.

* Related treatments are Sentence Coherence, **9**; Coherence in the Paragraph, **37**; Overloading, **42b**, Order and Rank, **43**.

Material badly divided: The National Electrical Code specifies that a splice shall be "mechanically and electrically secure." This means, first of all, that the two wires should be joined so that they will not become loose and pull apart; and, secondly, that they should be cleaned thoroughly to offer as little resistance to the current as possible. After the splice has been made, use some material to insulate the splice.

Show relationship by accurate division and by using parallelism with repetition: The National Electrical Code specifies that a splice shall be "mechanically and electrically secure." For mechanical security the two wires must be so joined that they cannot pull apart. For electrical security the wires must be cleaned so that they will offer little resistance to the current, and the splice must be properly insulated.

47c. Sound Make your writing agreeable in sound and cadence. Guard against the repetition of a sound or a form at too close an interval. Avoid a broken rhythm.

Lazy repetition of words: For the first time in a long time the Players' Club is putting on a first rate production.

Replace with synonyms: For the first time in a long while the Players' Club is putting on a really fine production.

Awkward repetition of a syllable: We must realize that housing is a real problem.

Replace one word: We must realize that housing is a serious problem.

Awkward repetition of a sound with different spelling: The leafless trees stand out in sharp relief.

Replace one word: The bare trees stand out in sharp relief.

Unintentional rhyme: With the publication of the *Pickwick Papers* Dickens quickly became famous.

Reword: The *Pickwick Papers* brought Dickens immediate fame.

Disagreeable reiteration of a sound: The growing of grain for market gradually replaced grazing on the ranches.

Reword: The ranchers turned from pasturing cattle to planting grain.

358

Awkward repetition of gerund ending (*-ing*): Building a radio cabinet of your own will result in a considerable saving. Designing it is the first step. After measuring the units to be housed in the cabinet prepare working drawings to scale.

Reword: You can save money by building a radio cabinet of your own. To design such a cabinet, first measure the units to be housed. Then prepare working drawings.

Unnecessarily broken rhythm: Magnesium printing plates, the newspapers discovered, could, unlike copper and zinc plates, the kinds formerly used, be completely engraved in forty-five minutes.

Reorder to secure a flowing cadence: The newspapers discovered that magnesium plates, unlike the copper and zinc plates formerly used, could be completely engraved in forty-five minutes.

EXERCISE

X-47a. Tightening Sentence Structure

Rewrite each sentence. Place main ideas in main clauses. Reduce minor points to modifiers, appositives, verbals.

1. There are 140,000,000 rats in the United States, and they eat about 200,000,000 bushels of grain a year, and they also consume cheese, bacon, sugar, eggs, and other foods.

2. College courses in philosophy, sociology, ethics, and psychology are often destructive, for they do a lot of questioning and disproving and leave it to the student to reconstruct for himself, but he can't do this, because he has been taught simply to accept what he is told.

3. Members of a family often take trips together. Not all the money should be carried by one person. He might be robbed or get killed, and then nobody would have money, as the funds of a person who has died cannot be spent.

4. Concrete does not dry by the evaporation of water. A chemical change has to take place. This process takes about ten days. The forms should not be removed before then.

5. The principal measures necessary for the control of floods are the construction of dams and levees and a reduction in the amount of eroded land along watersheds. [Use verbs.]

X-47b. Securing Forward Movement

Bring related parts together. State important points separately. Arrange ideas in a clear, progressive order.

1. It is clear that one to gain knowledge and stimulate his thinking should read.
2. Care has to be taken in making optical glass to see that it does not become brittle or get air bubbles mixed in.
3. Shrubs grow even in deserts that are very sandy, especially near places where water seepage occurs, which often have a profusion of plants that make a bright picture in spring.
4. Since most flowers are arranged so that they cannot pollinate themselves there must be cross-pollination, that is, the transfer of pollen from the stamen of one plant to the stigma of another, which is usually carried on by the wind or by insects.
5. When a man marries there is no change concerning the separate property that was his before marriage or property that is given or bequeathed to him after he marries. He can also claim what he earns after marriage as separate property in most states, but some states have community property laws that provide that half of his earnings after marriage belong to his wife. [Use parallel structure.]

X-47c. Improving Sound and Rhythm

Make each passage agreeable in sound and cadence.

1. To drive a car through city traffic a driver must be trained to react instantly to any change.
2. From our seats in the balcony we got a good view of the revue.
3. When the snow goes our guests stack their skis and start fishing.
4. Medical science has advanced rapidly, and consequently the span of life has increased statistically by several years.
5. As for myself, I was determined, though my father tried to prevent it, to become a musician, since I played the saxophone so well.

EMPHASIS

48. Give each portion of your thought precisely the degree of emphasis it deserves.

HOW TO INDICATE RELATIVE VALUES

48a. **Emphasis Through Subordination** It is a mark of childish writing to make unnecessary separate statements, either as short choppy sentences or as clauses strung together by *and*. Eliminate excessive predication; subordinate and combine. [See also **47a** and **X47a**.]

(I) Subordinating details Express main ideas in main clauses, minor points as modifiers. Avoid upside-down subordination and oversubordination.

Too many main clauses: The witness answered all the questions. Everything he said was clear.

Reduce one clause to an adverb: The witness answered all the questions clearly.

Too many main clauses: They have a dining room in the building, and we can get hot lunches there.

Reduce one clause to a prepositional phrase: We can get hot lunches at a dining room in the building.

Excessive predication [series of short sentences]: Some species of birds are variable. Others are relatively constant. Wrens have many subspecies. Titmice and sparrows do too. The differences depend on where they live. Ducks show few variations. Some species of ducks have a wide geographical range. They are alike, though, wherever they are found.

Focus on the three main ideas: Some species of birds seem to have a greater capacity for variation than others. Wrens, titmice, and sparrows of different localities have developed into distinct subspecies. Ducks, on the other hand, show few variations even among those species which have a wide geographical range.

Excessive predication [ramshackle *and* sentence]: I was walking home and I heard a siren and then an ambulance raced by, and so I hurried to the corner, and just as I got there the attendants were lifting a woman on to a stretcher.

Emphasize main events; subordinate details of time and place: On my way home I heard a siren and saw an ambulance race by. When I reached the corner, attendants were just lifting a woman on to a stretcher.

Excessive predication [unnecessary pronoun-plus-verb]: The room was lighted only by a hearth fire. It looked shadowy and unreal.

Reduce one clause to a verbal phrase: The room, lighted only by a hearth fire, looked shadowy and unreal.

Emphasis thwarted by *and*: They began their perilous journey, and they had four horses.

Emphasize *perilous journey*: With four horses they began their perilous journey. [A prepositional phrase replaces a clause.]

Or emphasize *having the horses*: When they began their perilous journey, they had four horses. [A subordinate clause replaces a main clause.]

Upside-down subordination: An old man used to work for us who died yesterday.

Place the main idea in the main clause: An old man who used to work for us died yesterday.

Important point subordinated: Their exhibit was voted the best, taking the prize.

Place an important idea in a main clause: Voted the best, their exhibit took the prize.

Main verb subordinated: He has a manner which annoys me.

Eliminate unnecessary predication: His manner annoys me.

Oversubordination [house-that-Jack-built]: Sally is the girl who is leader of the chorus that is part of the show that is playing at the Jewel Theater.

Reduce predication; change some clauses to phrases: Sally leads the chorus in the show at the Jewel Theater.

(2) Eliminating unnecessary repetition Combine statements which are in part duplicates.

Unnecessary repetition of subject with *are* [primer style]: Rooms are marked on the floor. These rooms are about fourteen feet square.

Combine: The floor is marked off into rooms about fourteen feet square.

Unnecessary repetition of subject: We crossed the river slowly. Part of the time we waded and part of tthe time we swam.

Use verbals: Sometimes wading, sometimes swimming, we slowly crossed the river.

Unnecessary repetition of subject idea: The fog over the city is mixed with smoke. This mixture is called smog.

Combine, using a phrase and a clause: The mixture of fog and smoke which blankets the city is called smog.

Or for a different emphasis use verbals: A smoke-laden mist called smog blankets the city.

Unnecessary repetition through use of pronoun-plus-*is*: The next process is dubbing. This is the addition of the sound track to the film.

Use an appositive [informal definition]: The next process is dubbing, the addition of sound track to the film.

Unnecessary pronoun-plus-*is*: Kleinberg sits at the head of the table. He is president of the company.

Use an appositive [informal identification]: Kleinberg, the president of the company, sits at the head of the table.

Unnecessary pronoun-plus-verb: We looked at metal lamps with flexible stands. These came in both desk and floor types.

Use an appositive [informal explanation]: We looked at metal lamps with flexible stands, both desk and floor types.

Wordy duplication of ideas in subject and modifier: Ice blocks the highway for months. During the same period it prevents the use of the lake.

Use a compound predicate: For months ice blocks the highway and prevents the use of the lake.

48b. **Emphasis Through Separation** Write as separate statements ideas which, though related, are individually
important. Show by the degree of separation the exact
emphasis you intend.

Unemphatic: Motorists often find it convenient not to spend
their nights in hotels, and many of them sleep in auto courts.

Write the statements separately: Motorists often find it convenient not to spend their nights in hotels. Many of them
sleep in auto courts.

Unemphatic: Mosher leaped to the stage and shouted, "I will
never consent to that!" and he looked as if he meant what he
said. [Direct discourse is more forceful if separated from explanatory matter, particularly from that which follows.]

Make separate statements: Mosher leaped to the stage and
shouted, "I will never consent to that!" He looked as if he
meant what he said.

Straggling, unemphatic: We lived in Santa Fé for ten years,
and then my father died, so we moved to El Paso, Texas.
[There are three ideas: (1) ten years elapse; (2) a man dies;
(3) a family moves.]

Use separation and subordination to emphasize ideas 1 and 3:
We lived in Santa Fé for ten years. Upon the death of my
father the family moved to El Paso, Texas.

Or emphasize ideas 2 and 3: After we had lived in Santa Fé for
ten years, my father died. We then moved to El Paso, Texas.

Second idea unemphatic: Until 1941 our country remained
neutral, trying to reconcile the need for preparedness with
the comfort of peacetime living.

Fairly emphatic: Until 1941 our country remained neutral and
tried to reconcile the need for preparedness with the comfort of peacetime living.

Much more emphatic: Until 1941 our country remained neutral.
We kept trying to reconcile the need for preparedness with
the comfort of peacetime living.

48c. Emphasis Through Position

(1) Beginning and End To make a sentence or passage forceful, place the most important idea at the end; or place a
part at the beginning, a part at the end.*

Trailing prepositional phrase: I demand the release of the prisoners in the first place.

End strongly: In the first place, I demand the release of the
prisoners. [Placing an adverbial modifier early clears the way
for the main idea.]

Or begin and end strongly: I demand, in the first place, the
release of the prisoners. ["Tucking in" unimportant modifiers
gives the sentence a maximum of emphasis.]

Trailing participial phrase: The Congress voted to support the
President's foreign policy, putting aside party politics.

Emphasize *foreign policy*: Putting aside party politics, the Congress voted to support the President's foreign policy.

Or emphasize *Congress* and *the President—their united action*:
the foreign policy advocated by the President.

The Congress, putting aside party politics, voted to support
Trailing clause: The important thing is to begin promptly if a
person needs artificial respiration.

Emphasize the main point, *promptness*: If artificial respiration
is needed begin it promptly.

Trailing clauses with overcoördination: Some ranchers continued to graze their cattle on forest lands even after these
had become public property, and little was done to stop
them, though actually they were trespassing. [What ideas are
important? Why?]

Secure emphasis by rearrangement and separation: After the
creation of the forest reserve some ranchers continued to
graze their cattle on these public properties, actually in
trespass. Little was done to stop them.

* See also **38c(2)**, Topic Sentence Last, and **38c(3)**, The Sandwich
Paragraph.

(2) The periodic sentence To give your writing strength, use an occasional periodic sentence—that is, one in which most of the modifiers are placed early, so that the main idea is not completed until the end. To overcome a habit of writing stringy sentences, cultivate the semiperiodic sentence; place some modifiers (but not all) at the beginning or in midsentence.

Straggling sentence (unemphatic because of trailing modifiers): I saw two men fight a duel on a moonlit summer night a few years ago in a village in northern France.

Place all modifiers early: On a moonlit summer night a few years age, in a village in northern France, I saw two men fight a duel. [Employed now and then, the periodic sentence is desirable and effective. Employed through long passages, it makes writing stiff.]

Stringy sentence (poorly constructed, unemphatic): He takes the dealer's word then and there without stopping to ask questions, and he ought to know better.

Distribute modifiers: Though he ought to know better, he takes the dealer's word then and there, without stopping to ask questions.

Loose sentence (permissible but unemphatic): The Canadian summer was making the most of the time left for warm weather after a laggard spring and a cold June.

Place a modifier in midsentence: The Canadian summer, already shortened by a laggard spring and a cold June, was making the most of the time that was left.

Loose sentence: Only twenty-five to thirty per cent of the crude oil can be recovered from sands by present-day methods. [Most writing contains many loose sentences. For variety and emphasis, some should be made semiperiodic.]

Move modifiers forward: By present-day methods only twenty-five to thirty per cent of the crude oil in sands can be recovered.

(3) Order of climax To secure maximum emphasis arrange a series of details or ideas in the order of climax—the weakest first, the strongest last.

Weak series [anticlimax]: Gower put into his pocket five hundred dollars, a cigarette case, and a piece of bubble gum.

Place strongest point last: Gower put into his pocket a piece of bubble gum, a cigarette case, and five hundred dollars.

Weak sequence of ideas: We are threatened with disaster. Our difficulties are far greater than they were last season.

Reverse: Our difficulties are far greater than they were last season. In fact we are threatened with disaster.

Trailing clauses, anticlimactic arrangements of points: Mercury vapor liberates radiant energy when an electric current is passed through it. This energy takes the form of ultraviolet light, which is invisible but will make fluorescent material glow. Fluorescent lamps are made by coating a glass tube with fluorescent material and filling it with mercury vapor.

Emphasize *light, glow, lamp* (the climax): Mercury vapor through which an electric current is passing liberates radiant energy in the form of ultraviolet light. If the vapor is encased in a glass tube coated with fluorescent material, the light, though itself invisible, creates a diffused glow. Such a tube is called a fluorescent lamp.

Practice Emphasis Through Position

Rearrange to emphasize important ideas.

1. Portuguese is the official language of Brazil, let me add.
2. Meat prices soared to fantastic heights, stimulated by increased demand.
3. John Hobson saw a gleam of gold in the bottom of a pan which he had dipped in a mountain stream.
4. The treasurer had abruptly disappeared, together with thirty thousand-dollar bonds, seventeen hundred dollars in cash, and an antique Chinese vase.
5. The *Daily Star* offers you news of world events, the latest dope on sports, and all the popular comics.

48d. Emphasis Through Structure of Parts

(1) Active voice Use the strong active in preference to the weak passive voice. (See also **7d.**)

Weak passive voice: Your gift was appreciated by all of us.

Use the direct, forceful active voice: We appreciated your gift.

Passive voice: The train was seen speeding toward them. [The passive voice is especially objectionable when by failing to indicate the agent of the verb it unnecessarily mystifies the reader.]

For clarity, use the active voice: They saw the train speeding toward them.

Passive voice: A magnet can be used to retrieve screws and nuts that drop in inaccessible places.

For maximum emphasis use active voice and periodic sentence structure: To retrieve screws and nuts from inaccessible places, use a magnet.

(2) Parallelism Use parallel structure to set off two ideas as similar or opposite. (See also **8,** Parallelism, and **37b,** Parallelism in the Paragraph.)

Unemphatic: An American likes new ways of doing things, but an Englishman thinks that if something has always been done in a certain way he should go on doing it that way.

To sharpen the contrast use parallel structure: To an American the fact that something has always been done in a certain way is sufficient reason for changing it; to an Englishman that fact is sufficient reason for retaining it.

Weak and straggling: This paper, like many others, has some bad features, but in other ways it is good. The news articles are better than the editorials, which are feeble.

For balance use parallel structure: The paper is in some respects poor, in other respects good. The editorials are feeble, the news articles impressive. [Each sentence is now balanced within itself, and the two sentences balance each other.]

48e. **Emphasis Through Repetition** Repeat words or ideas which you desire to fix in the reader's mind.

Unemphatic: He works a great deal, but he seems never to get anywhere.

Emphasize by simple repetition: Work, work, work, all he does is work, and still he seems never to get anywhere.

Fairly emphatic: How did the general meet this new menace? He withdrew before it!

Strengthen by repeating the key idea with added meaning: How did the general meet this new menace? He withdrew to prepared positions. He executed a strategic retreat. In short, he ran away!

Weak: We hope that this shipment will reach you in good condition, and that you will favor us with other orders, which will be given prompt and courteous attention.

Use repetition with parallelism: We hope that this shipment will reach you in good condition. We believe that the quality of our goods will induce you to send us a second order. We assure you that such an order will receive prompt and courteous attention. [Here the repetition is not of a word or idea, but of an entire grammatical structure. Note the resolute march of the parallel expressions *We hope, We believe, We assure.*]

Practice Active Voice, Parallelism, Repetition

Make each passage more emphatic by improving the structure or by using repetition.

1. As we approached the house the blare of a radio was heard.
2. When wood is to be painted it should be rubbed with fine sandpaper first.
3. Some musicians give a mechanical performance, while the true spirit of a piece is conveyed by others.
4. The guns boomed several times.
5. David Copperfield seems thoroughly incompetent, for he allows himself to be robbed and cheated, and shows no understanding of women.

X-48. Emphasis

Rewrite each passage; emphasize main ideas.

1. We went trout fishing. We fished in Cherokee Creek. It was a pleasant afternoon.
2. A policeman was trudging down a street in the seedy part of town yesterday. Suddenly he stopped and stared.
3. Every girl will probably have to keep house at some time or other, so all girls should study household management.
4. A fantastic bird of ancient days laid eggs that weighed ten pounds. The bird is known in legend as the roc.
5. Private medical schools have been carrying on much of our research, and now they are short of funds.
6. I turned the flame higher, when the test tube cracked.
7. There are many difficulties in presenting drama by television, and one is that the actors have to learn their parts by heart and cannot read them as they do in radio.
8. We use up a tremendous amount of water in this country. We require about 100 gallons a day for each person, including what we use in industry and on farms.
9. A truck loaded with broken glass got out of control. It bounced against a rock wall. The glass was scattered for a mile, and many cars rushed into it and had blowouts.
10. The Australians imported rabbits. They hoped to get a cheap food supply. But the rabbits swept many areas bare of forage because they multiplied so fast.
11. Uranium is the material used in producing atomic energy. It is inserted in graphite bricks for storage.
12. Jane gave a dinner party last Tuesday. There were twelve of us. We went to the theatre afterward.
13. Dr. Nettler is one of my professors. He teaches sociology, and he is very stimulating. Every student in the school wants to join one of his classes.
14. I believe in free enterprise, but I do not believe that free enterprise includes the right to suppress competition.
15. The streets of the city are wide and tree-lined, and its twenty-five parks take up 227 acres and provide playgrounds for children and places of relaxation for adults.

VARIETY

49. Except when there is special reason to adhere to one pattern vary the structure of your sentences.

HOW TO VARY SENTENCE PATTERNS

49a. **Varied Beginnings** Occasionally place an adverbial modifier or a verbal before the subject. Occasionally transpose subject and verb. Except when the ideas are parallel, do not begin a succession of sentences with precisely the same construction.

Sentences on a dead level: Mrs. Benedict wrote a book on Indian mythology. She made six field trips to gather material. She usually traveled alone, but she sometimes took students with her.

Vary the beginnings: To gather material for her book on Indian mythology Mrs. Benedict made six field trips. Usually she traveled alone; occasionally she took students with her. [One sentence begins with an infinitive of purpose; two clauses begin with adverbs.]

Subject-and-verb always first: Elms are both beautiful and long-lived. They are loved by Americans more deeply than any other kind of tree. The Indians used them for council trees before the white men came. Our history tells of many individual elm trees which became famous as landmarks. Historic elms are found not only in New England but in all the eastern and midwestern states.

Change some beginnings: The elm, beautiful and long-lived, is perhaps the best loved of all our American trees. Before the coming of the white man elms were used by the Indians as council trees. During the colonial period and after, many individual elms became famous landmarks. Historic elms are found not only in New England but in all the eastern and midwestern states. [Do not place something before the subject in every sentence.]

371

49b. **Varied Lengths** Avoid a succession of short, choppy sentences. Avoid a series of compound sentences balanced in the middle like a seesaw. Break up involved sentences.

Unnecessarily choppy effect: This airline takes good care of its ships. We look after them the way people should look after their watches. Every plane goes through a preflight check. Then after fifty hours twenty-seven items are checked again. Then after 260 hours the auto pilot, air-speed indicator, and other devices are inspected and tested.

Vary the length by combining some sentences: This airline takes better care of its ships than many people do of their watches. Before each day's first take-off every plane is checked. After fifty hours. . . . After 260 hours. . . .

Seesaw effect: Ring was a sheep dog, and he tended the flock with his master. One day there came a deep snow, and the flock did not return. The men found the herder frozen stiff, and the dog stood shivering beside him.

Vary sentence length and pattern: Ring was a sheep dog who tended the flock with his master. One day there came a deep snow. When the flock failed to return, the men, uneasy, began a search. They found the herder frozen stiff; the dog stood shivering beside him.

Succession of long, involved sentences: One of the foremost figures of the Renaissance was Leonardo da Vinci. He was a versatile man, for besides painting pictures he became an engineer and scientist and designed an airplane, studied anatomy, and made discoveries in natural history, including the true nature of fossils. Another great figure was Galileo, because he dropped two unequal weights from a tower, proving that they fell at the same rate, and he also made a telescope and confirmed the view of Copernicus that the earth moves around the sun.

Break up into manageable portions: One of the foremost figures of the Renaissance, Leonardo da Vinci, showed remarkable versatility. Not only did he paint great pictures; he became an engineer and a scientist as well. He designed an airplane. . . .

49c. **Varied Types** Avoid overuse of any pattern. Beware
of too many main clauses; reduce some to subordinate clauses, prepositional phrases, appositives, verbals. Beware of a trailing style; introduce some periodic sentences.
Lighten flat-footed assertion by an occasional question.

Monotonous all-main-clause style: The natives of Borneo live
on rice. So do most Asiatics. They do not like tapioca or
other substitutes. They cannot raise enough for their needs,
so they have to depend on importing some from China.

Streamline: Like most Asiatics, the natives of Borneo live on
rice, which they prefer to tapioca or any other substitute.
Since they cannot raise enough rice for their needs, they
must depend on imports from China.

Monotonous main-clause-and-trailer style: Richardson may be
considered the father of the novel since he was the first
writer to analyze his characters psychologically. His first book
was *Pamela,* which was written in letter form. The story
seems a bit unrealistic to a modern reader because the heroine is always sitting down to write a letter.

Rearrange; use periodic and semiperiodic sentences: Because
he was the first story-writer to analyze his characters psychologically, Richardson is considered the father of the novel.
His first book, *Pamela,* was written in letter form. As the
heroine is always sitting down to write a letter, the story
seems a bit unrealistic to a modern reader.

Flatly assertive: Psychology tells us that human action stems
from self-interest. We may wonder about our own motives
and those of other people. Often the self-sacrificing people
really have a sort of neurotic selfishness, for what they pride
themselves on, selflessness, stems from a dissatisfaction with
themselves, which they try to lose by being kind to others.

Ask questions: When we learn from our courses in psychology
that human action stems from self-interest, we begin to wonder about our own motives and those of other people. Do
self-sacrificing people really possess a neurotic selfishness?
Do they act kindly toward others in order to lose a feeling
of dissatisfaction with themselves?

X-49. Variety

Rewrite each passage, varying sentence length and type. In some sentences place modifiers before the subject.

1. The republic of Czechoslovakia was created in 1918. It was made up of territories known in history as Bohemia, Moravia, and Slovakia. Bohemia had been an independent kingdom from 1198 to 1648.

2. The current trend in medicine is toward group practice. No one doctor can understand all kinds of ailments, so most doctors specialize. Then they join with others and in that way give their patients complete service.

3. The great blue whale is the largest living creature. In fact, it is the largest creature that ever lived. It has a very compact cylindrical shape. The dinosaurs were not so large. They merely had long tails, legs, and necks.

4-5. A student in this college needs a car. He needs it to get to classes. Living quarters are often far from the campus, and walking is out of the question. A man has to have a car to take girls out. They are used to riding, and they will hardly date anyone who has no car.

6. *Road to Survival* is a book about the dwindling food supply, and it is not optimistic. The author shows that land is being destroyed on every continent, and he thinks we are not doing enough to stop this waste.

7. Mrs. Ascot was forty-nine, but she looked older. Her face looked like a horse's face, and she had a slouching walk. She wore out-of-date clothes. Probably she never looked at herself in a mirror.

8. Children may not develop any artistic ability of their own if they are given ready-made pictures to color. They should feel free to let their imaginations run loose, since they enjoy color and design more than "telling a story."

9-10. A short circuit is the lowering of resistance between two wires that carry electric current, causing a large amount of current to flow for a short time. A fuse is installed in each circuit, and it stops the flow the second it gets overheated, but if a person is the cause of the short circuit the current can kill him before the flow stops.

Research

USE OF A LIBRARY

50. **Know how to use the resources of a library for reference and for research.** Learn to find books through the card catalog. Consult reference works both for information and for lists of sources. Make use of periodicals, particularly for information on current topics. Familiarize yourself with the plan and the rules of your particular library.

50a. **The Card Catalog** In most libraries each important book is represented by three cards in the catalog. All cards are placed in one alphabetic arrangement. To find a book by a given author, look for a card headed by his last name. If you know the title but not the author, look for a card headed by the first word of the title (omitting *a, an,* and *the*). If you are interested in a subject but are unfamiliar with books in the field, look under the subject itself; there you will find authors and titles listed. The last card under the subject may name related subject headings for you to consult.

To secure a volume, copy on the call slip
  1. The call number (printed in the upper left corner)
  2. The name of the author or editor
  3. The title of the book
  4. The volume number (if there is more than one volume)
Either present the call slip to an attendant or find the volume yourself.

Copy the call number accurately. Each letter, figure, and dot has a meaning. Most libraries use the Dewey Decimal System, which divides all printed matter into ten master groups. Each group is further divided and subdivided by tens. For example, 800 represents literature, 810 American literature, 817 American satire and humor. In 817 C59h, the call number for *Huckleberry Finn*, the C stands for the author, Clemens; the 59 means the number of the book in a list of his works; the *h* stands for the title.

These are the main groups of the Dewey Decimal System	000 General	500	Natural science
	100 Philosophy	600	Useful arts
	200 Religion	700	Fine arts
	300 Sociology	800	Literature
	400 Philology	900	History

50b. **Reference Works** Reference works are kept in the reference room of a library. Most of them stand on open shelves. A few you must obtain through an attendant.

Some reference works, such as dictionaries and yearbooks, supply information direct. Some list sources of information. Encyclopedias, in limited degree, do both. Hence an encyclopedia is often the best place to begin your investigation of a subject. To find material not treated in the main article on your subject, consult the index volume. To follow recent developments, consult the yearbooks issued to accompany the encyclopedias.

For the names of reference works which may help you with particular problems, consult *Mudge's Guide to Reference Books*. On the following page are listed some of the most useful reference works *

---

* For names of school dictionaries see **18a**. For finding information in a dictionary see **18b**.

ENCYCLOPEDIAS

Encyclopaedia Britannica, 14th ed., 1929. Yearbooks to date. Excellent in literature, art, history.

New International Encyclopedia, 1922. Less formal treatment of a wider range of subjects.

Encyclopedia Americana, 1945. Especially good in science, government, business, industry.

Encyclopedia of the Social Sciences, 1930.

DICTIONARIES, SYNONYMS, USAGE

Webster's New International Dictionary, 2nd ed., 1934.

New English Dictionary, 1933. An extended historical account of each word. Also called the *Oxford Dictionary.*

Crabb's English Synonyms, 1945.

Fowler's *Modern English Usage,* 1927.

Roget's *Thesaurus of English Words and Phrases,* 1944.

BIOGRAPHY

Who's Who in America, 1899 to date. Persons now living.

Who's Who, 1849 to date. British.

Dictionary of American Biography, 1928-1936. Persons not living.

Dictionary of National Biography, 1885-1900. British.

Webster's Biographical Dictionary, 1943. Living and dead.

LITERATURE, MUSIC

Cambridge History of English Literature, 1933.

Cambridge History of American Literature, 1933.

Literary History of the United States, 1948.

Gayley's *Classic Myths in English Literature and in Art,* 1911.

Bartlett's *Familiar Quotations,* 11th ed., 1946. Revised.

Grove's *Dictionary of Music and Musicians,* 1927-1928. Supplement 1940.

YEARBOOKS

The American Year Book, 1910 to date.

Statesman's Year Book, 1864 to date.

World Almanac, 1885 to date.

Statistical Abstract of the United States Government.

50c. **Periodicals** Current issues of periodicals are usually
displayed on magazine racks. Earlier issues will be
brought to you by the librarian.

Magazine articles are listed in various indexes. *The Readers' Guide to Periodical Literature* lists under author, title,
and subject all articles published since 1900 in about 200
American magazines. It gives references up to the preceding month. To obtain a particular article, copy on a call
slip the entire reference, including author and title of the
article; date, volume number, and pages of the magazine.
(An explanation of the abbreviations used will be found at
the front of each volume of the *Guide*. For clarity, you may
wish to fill out the abbreviations as you copy the reference.)
Present the slip to an attendant.

Indexes are available in many special fields other than
those named below.

INDEXES TO PERIODICALS

Readers' Guide to Periodical Literature, 1900 to date.
Poole's Index to Periodical Literature, 1802-1906.
International Index to Periodicals, 1907 to date.
Agricultural Index, 1913 to date.
Art Index, 1929 to date.
Dramatic Index, 1909-1946.
Education Index, 1929 to date.
Industrial Arts Index, 1913 to date.
New York Times Index, 1914 to date.
Public Affairs Information Service, 1905 to date.

50d. **Evaluating Books and Articles**

(1) Discovering material In seeking information on a particular subject, first compile a tentative bibliography. Look
for lists of sources in textbooks, in well-known works on
the subject, at the end of the treatment in an encyclopedia,
in indexes and guides.

Select titles which seem promising for your particular purpose, and copy on separate 3 x 5 or 4 x 6 inch cards the following data about each book or article: subject, author, title, facts of publication (place, publisher, date). Find out which books and articles are in your library; copy the call numbers on your cards.

(2) Judging material Gather the most promising books and articles. Examine each one closely to find out two things: whether it is an authoritative source, and whether it contains information precisely pertinent to your need.

In judging a book

1. *Note the author.* Is he a man of standing in his field? The title page may state his professional position. *Who's Who* will give details as to his training and background. In *The United States Catalog* you will find the titles of his published works. In other books on your subject you may run across opinions concerning him.

2. *Note the date.* For developments in science and other rapidly changing fields a recent date is important. For background information in any field an early work may be more authoritative.

3. *Look over the Table of Contents* to discover the scope, order, and manner of treatment. Note sections which may meet your particular need; copy the exact reference (chapter and page numbers) on your card.

4. *Try to grasp the point of view and the main ideas* by reading the preface; by reading a preview or a summarizing chapter if there is one; by looking for summarizing paragraphs at the beginnings or ends of chapters; by scanning section headings, running titles, boldface sentences.

5. *Consult the Index* to learn in detail what points are treated. Copy page references of points pertinent to your inquiry.

6. *Try to judge the actual worth of the material* by reading carefully the sections in which you are particularly interested. What do you consider to be the author's purpose? Is he defending a particular point of view, or is he presenting a factual, unbiased treatment? If he is defending a point of view, does he support his statements with facts? Does he consider adverse evidence? If he is presenting a factual study, does the work appear to be based on scholarly research?

In judging magazine articles

1. Prefer technical, scholarly, and serious publications. Do not rely on popular magazines.
2. Prefer long articles to fragmentary ones.
3. Prefer articles by known authorities.
4. Except for a special purpose such as a historical study prefer recent articles.

EXERCISE

X-50. Use of a Library

Follow directions. Write out the information.

1. From the card catalog get the title of a book on philosophy by John Dewey, first published in 1922.
2. From the card catalog learn the name of the author of *The Meaning of Relativity*, and the year in which the book was first published.
3. Find in the card catalog three books on *Petroleum*. For each, copy the information required for a call slip.
4. Copy from the *Readers' Guide* full reference information on three recent articles concerning the legal status of women in the United States.
5. Find the names of two books, two plays, and two articles dealing with racial prejudice which have appeared within the past ten years. For each, copy the information required to obtain it in your library.

6. What subject heads cognate to *Uranium* does the card catalog contain?

7. By what amount was the cost of living higher (or lower) four years ago than now?

8. Discover an important action concerning labor taken by one branch of the Federal Government in the past calendar year. Cite references in a periodical and in a yearbook.

9. Secure the following information concerning Alfred North Whitehead: date of birth and death; the field in which he wrote; titles and dates of publication of three of his books; professional positions held; opinions concerning him expressed by three competent persons (reviewers of his books or men writing in his field).

Choose one of the following:

10. Prepare bibliography cards (with page references) for two books, two magazine articles, and two newspaper articles which you might use in preparing a brief for the affirmative on the topic, *Should We Have World Federal Government Now?*

11. Prepare a tentative bibliography for a paper on *Freudian Psychoanalysis.* Include at least one encyclopedia article, three book references, and three articles in periodicals. Give volume and page numbers.

12. Find in three different books discussions of the fruit fly, *Drosophila,* with relation to its importance in the study of genetics. Copy full bibliographical data for each reference. State briefly on each card the scope and nature of the treatment.

13. Compile a bibliography of five or six items on *Furnishing a Small Apartment.* Include page numbers.

14. Compile a bibliography for a paper on *Two Phases of the Work of Stravinsky* (or another composer, or an artist or author).

15. Prepare bibliography cards for two books, two plays, and two poems you could use as source material if you were to write a dramatic essay on *Queen Elizabeth and Mary Queen of Scots: a study of conflicting personalities and their influence on English History.*

ASSIMILATION OF MATERIAL

51. To make material your own, read and take notes with discrimination; be able to paraphrase or summarize intelligently what you read or hear.

51a. Effective Reading Learn to do the kind of reading that requires creative activity on your part—the kind of reading in which you digest or assimilate the other person's ideas.

(1) Preview Take a preliminary survey of a book or an article to discover first the large goals and general plan and second the parts most important to you. Do not begin blindly at the beginning and plod through to the end; map the territory you are going to cover. Skim through the introduction or the first chapter for the author's announced purpose.

Example: I propose . . . to discuss the present state of philosophy in its human bearings. . . . such questions as: What is the distinctive purpose and business of philosophy anyway? How is it related to those concerns and issues which today stand out as the problems of men? *

From the table of contents or from chapter headings find out how the author approaches his subject, what points he thinks you need for full understanding. Consider what parts require most attention from you, either for following the author's reasoning or for furthering some purpose of your own.

For necessary clarification of any point glance at the beginning and end of a chapter to find announced topics or summaries.

---

* John Dewey, *Problems of Men*, Philosophical Library.

(2) Study In reading, run rapidly through easy or familiar material, noticing its slant and its connection with the general plan. Read intensively the difficult or unfamiliar.

Keep in mind the large goals of each chapter as you read; do not become immersed in detail. Pause for vistas and overviews. Try to anticipate the outcome of each chapter. Make a mental outline of the main points. Then you will know the goal of each division, know when you have made progress toward it, and know when you have reached it.

Relate what you read to your own experience. Try to think of instances and concrete applications. Give special thought to any new ideas that conflict with old; resolve the conflict or note it for further research.

51b. **Note-taking** Use notes to preserve the essentials of reading matter or lectures—in general the main points in rough outline form. Catch the vital matter.

(1) Notes in books In books of your own convert the printed matter into notes by underscoring the main points of chapters and paragraphs and by marginal marks or comment. Thus in effect you outline the material.

(2) Notes from lectures Note the name of the lecturer, subject, course, date. Write down headings. Omit preliminaries and minor details; try to give the gist of what is said. Leave space to go back and fill in.

(3) Notes from books To assemble material for a paper make notes on cards (3 x 5 or 4 x 6). For each book or article devote one card to complete bibliographical data; use these cards in compiling your list of sources [**52d(5)**].

Begin each new topic on a separate card, so that your material can be reorganized easily. Head each card with a label that will tell at a glance what it contains. Note the source briefly, always including the page number.

Make your notes brief, but sufficient to hold the idea without further reference to the original. Develop a system of abbreviations and shortcuts; identify a reference by a single word—author or title or a symbol designating the bibliography card on which you have recorded full data.

Record only what is essential. Look for facts and specific statements with a direct bearing on your subject.

Make your notes appropriate to the material and your purpose. A note may consist of

A single detail, such as a statistical item (and the authority for it)

> Walker p. 98
> World Pop. Est.
> by 1990 — 3 bill. +
> by 2040 — 4½ bill.

A brief outline of major points or of details pertaining to one point

> Dunlap p. 45
> Char. of Crowd Situ.
> 1. Common stimulation
> 2.   "   feeling & judgment
> 3.   "   activity

A summary, informal for a short passage or formal for a long passage or whole chapter (see 51d)

> Martin p. 293
> Miners' Safety Pleas
> Miners appealed to state Dept. of Mines, U.M.W.A., fed. CMA, Governor Green—Letters filed; no action.

A direct quotation of particularly telling phrases or vital matter (Quote exactly and indicate omissions; see 28b.)

> Baldwin p. 300
> Dangerous Thinking
> "When a people's minds accept the inevitability of war, war is inevitable."

A paraphrase is sometimes useful for preserving vital matter.

51c. **Paraphrasing** To paraphrase a passage give its complete meaning in other words. Paraphrase to make clear to yourself or to someone else a passage that is technical, or abstract, or in any way obscure. Paraphrase in adapting material from different sources to your own style; giving credit of course to the originator, you should learn to *weave in* borrowed ideas so that they go along naturally in meaning and in tone. You have not mastered an idea until you can present it in your own language.

Incongruous secondhand language: In experiments made to find out how well students recall material they feel strongly about, the results consistently buttress the conclusion that material which supports the subjects' attitudinal frame is retained better than material which controverts it.

Restate in your own words: In experiments made to find out how well students recall material they feel strongly about, the results support the theory that a person better remembers what he agrees with than what he disagrees with.

Practice paraphrasing different kinds of material. Translate from archaic language to modern, from technical to nontechnical, from formal to informal.

1. Put the idea of a passage into simple language.
2. Use as many words as you need—often more than the original; completeness, not compression, is the goal.
3. Do not add ideas that are not stated or implied in the original, but do not lose ideas that are implied.

Original: That oil is produced by geological forces acting generally through long intervals of time on the debris of aquatic organisms buried in the sediments is a belief held by most geologists.

Paraphrase: The theory accepted by most geologists about the formation of oil is that oil derives from the remains of water-dwelling animal and plant life. Deposited in silt, these remains have been acted on over a long period of time by pressures, heat, and movement within the earth.

385

51d. Summarizing To summarize a passage give the main points only, omitting details and nonvital matter.

(1) A summary may condense to a single sentence the meaning of each paragraph.

Original: Hammurabi was not the first king in the land of the Two Rivers who conceived the idea of written law. Fragments of very ancient Sumerian and Akkadian laws still survive.... There could have been no country of the ancient world where resort to writing for the purpose of consummating legal transactions was more common than in Babylonia. Almost every legal transaction was reduced to writing. ... The hard clay tablet seemed so final, certain, and imperishable! It is almost as if the land of cuneiform writing was destined to produce the first code. The originality of Hammurabi was to conceive the idea of an extensive popular codification of all the laws which were the prolific sources of dispute. All the laws which had been enacted before his time were written in Sumerian, which was the Latin of the land of the Two Rivers, and were deposited in the temple archives, where they were beyond the reach of the common people. Hammurabi wrote his laws in the everyday Akkadian speech and inscribed them on a pillar which was to stand in the temple courtyard where it might be read by all men. Thus would force and oppression be prevented. Thus would justice prevail. That this was his great contribution to legal technique Hammurabi tells us in the epilog of his Code, and it is worth repeating: "The oppressed who has a lawsuit shall come before my image as king of justice. He shall read the writing on my pillar, he shall perceive my precious words. The word of my pillar shall explain to him his cause, and he shall find his right." * [295 words]

Summary: Hammurabi's great contribution to legal technique was not the idea of written law but the idea of making knowledge of the law accessible to the people. [26 words]

* From William Seagle, *Men of Law from Hammurabi to Holmes.* By permission of The Macmillan Company, publishers.

(2) A **précis** (pronounced pray-see) is a kind of summary
that preserves the proportion and emphasis of the original
and to some extent the tone. It is a cutdown substitute for
the original passage and should be intelligible to those who
have not seen the original. A précis of several paragraphs
must be carefully linked to make a connected whole.

Précis of the passage on the preceding page: Hammurabi did not
originate the idea of written law. Laws older than Hammurabi
as well as business transactions and legal documents surviving
in cuneiform on the hard clay tablets of Babylonia suggest
the natural development of a code. Hammurabi's great idea
was to make law available to the people, to fetch it out of
the temple archives and out of the unfamiliar Sumerian language. By inscribing the laws in everyday Akkadian on a
pillar in the temple courtyard he intended that justice should
prevail, that the oppressed might read, understand his cause,
and find his right. [96 words—approximately one-third the
length of the original]

Précis continued: Yet the code of Hammurabi was archaic.
Babylonia, though great for its day, was a small country, its
economy based on agriculture, its famous commerce a relatively minor affair of donkey caravans and little boats. Clan
justice still survived, and even Hammurabi, the protector of
the weak, sanctioned practices that moderns would call cruel
and unenlightened. [164 word paragraph reduced to 56]

Test a précis on four points: thought, selection, flavor,
and expression.

Thought: Has the essence of the original been retained and
nothing read in that does not belong?

Selection: Are all the important points included and the
unimportant excluded?

Flavor: Have the tone and point of view of the original
been retained? Is the proportion similar?

Expression: Are the words well-chosen? the ideas coherent?
the necessary transitions skillfully made?

EXERCISE

X-51. Assimilating Material

Paraphrase passages 1 and 2. Then write a concise summary of 3 and of 4, and a précis of 4.

1. Americans cannot realize how many chances for mental improvement they lose by their inveterate habit of keeping up six conversations when there are twelve persons in the room.

2. The forest is the most effective agent for protecting soil from erosion because (1) the resistance of the soil to erosive action is increased by the roots of the trees which hold the soil firmly in place, and (2) at the same time the erosive force of the run-off is itself reduced because the rate of its flow is checked and its distribution over the surface equalized.

3. No good can come of emotional misjudgments about Leftists, the majority of whom are obviously of high moral character, and are dangerous only when their own sincerity makes them easy marks for Communist plots. Undoubtedly, there are such people as real Communists. They have a fanatic compulsion to destroy "bourgeois culture," known to us as democracy. They are opponents, whose tricks we hope to confound; they use the methods of underground warfare; but our own position is likely to be stronger if we avoid becoming blinded with moral indignation even about our enemies. Along with the Communist devotees travel those liberals who are simple enough to swallow the easier parts of the "party line," especially the part about letting Communists coöperate in liberal organizations. They just lack good judgment, and therefore should not be employed where they can unwittingly help in any plot engineered by their Communist friends. It is not morally wrong to be a typhoid carrier, though it is a good reason for being excluded from any room where things are cooking. Defense against dangers is most apt to succeed if the definition of the danger is reasonably accurate.*

* David Cushman Coyle, "Tolerance and Treason," *The Yale Review* (Spring, 1948). Copyright Yale University Press.

4. This [conformity to public opinion] is a social discipline, imposed on you, not by the state, not by governmental process of law, but by your fellows, by the organizations you belong to, by the corporations you work for, by the social group you live in. The Bill of Rights, and its application by the Court, is better understood, if we recognize that it does not forbid any of these social abridgments of your liberty. It forbids only governmental encroachments. Thus in the First Amendment it is Congress who shall 'make no law respecting an establishment of religion, or prohibiting the free exercise thereof; or abridging the freedom of speech, or of the press.' And the Fourteenth reads, 'nor shall any *State* deprive any person of life, liberty, or property, without due process of law; nor deny to any person within its jurisdiction the equal protection of the law.'

The Bill of Rights, then, protects you only in that clearing of freedom which you have already made for yourself in society and protects you there, not against the encroachments of the forest, but only against the forest rangers.

But what, as a matter of fact, does that mean? Government in a democracy, the democratic process, does not usually act on its own initiative. A totalitarian state, which has arrogated to itself the whole discipline, social as well as legal, is different. A democracy acts at the instance of interest groups. So what the Bill of Rights does, and pretty much all it does, is prevent a dominant or temporarily powerful group, whether a majority or a minority is beside the point, from enlisting the aid of government against you. What a private group can do to discipline you, using only social processes, is a matter between you and it.

The democratic process, you see, demands a great deal of self-reliance from the individual. Freedom in a democracy is not given you, or even guaranteed to you, by the state. All that you get is what you get for yourself, and all that the democratic process guarantees to you is that the state will not help anyone take it away from you.*

* Charles P. Curtis, Jr., *Lions Under the Throne*, Houghton Mifflin Company.

THE WRITING OF A TERM PAPER

52. Choose a topic that interests you and that you can grasp. Study the best authorities you can find on the subject, balancing different opinions. Think out your conclusions, organize your material, and present it clearly in proper form with due credit for all borrowed ideas.

52a. Preliminary Plan Take plenty of time for planning.

(1) Limiting the topic For adequate coverage in the usual term paper of twelve to thirty pages the topic must not be too broad. Though the treatment need not be exhaustive (except in graduate work) the paper must deal adequately with every important phase of the announced subject.

Either search out a topic already narrow or work your way down from a broad topic to a narrow one by approaching it in a particular way or from a special point of view (see also **30**). Jot down all the aspects that occur to you or that you run across in books. Gain a general view from an encyclopedia or similar source. Then limit your topic until you can treat your major points specifically and concretely, with examples.

In making your plan, be governed somewhat by the availability of source material. Suppose you are narrowing down from "The Effects of War on Civilians" to "The Biological Implications of War in the Atomic Age." Are you likely to find adequate and authoritative material in your college library? If not, have you time and facilities for obtaining it from somewhere else? Failing both, you will be wise to shift to some other aspect. It is disheartening to work out a glamorous plan only to be stopped dead when you try to carry it out.

390

(2) Plotting the course Prepare a rough outline to guide your research. Do not consider such an outline final; change it as often as improvements occur to you. New information will suggest additions and reproportionings.

Decide what areas should receive most attention in your reading, either for their intrinsic importance or for filling gaps in your knowledge. Decide whether your treatment would benefit from research other than reading—field studies or interviews, for example—and at what point in your research program such additions would be most fruitful. Make a list of key words that will help in finding pertinent books; include points requiring clarification.

52b. Study of Sources A term paper is not to be spun out of your own head. It is not to be taken slavishly from a single source. It is not to be a hodgepodge of undigested matter from several sources. It is to be a unified, coherent product of (1) your study and comparison of a number of sources (anywhere from three to fifteen) and (2) your independent thinking on the evidence, the theories, and the issues.

(1) Preliminary bibliography After the preliminary planning, your next step is to find (1) what the best authorities are and (2) whether they are available. For the method of finding the best authorities see **50b, c, d**. For discovering the resources of your library consult the card catalog (see **50a**). Whenever possible use primary sources as well as secondary. That is, use matter that was actually concerned in the event you are discussing: the authenticated words of a participant, eyewitness accounts, the actual document in question, inscriptions, objects, or persons involved; these are primary. Secondary sources are interpretations by outsiders: hearsay accounts, biographies (except when embodying firsthand material), and historical and critical estimates.

You will probably save time in the end by making a complete reference card for each promising title you find in the card catalog. Note the call number and all the identifying matter you will need for your bibliography (see **52d**). Later when you examine the book itself add a brief estimate of its scope and value. Thus you can return to it or avoid it without duplicating your work. If a book is out when you first apply you can note the circumstance and look for it again without recourse to the catalog. If you find material by browsing make a note of any books you have examined and discarded. As you read you can note on the card for a given book the chapter, section, or pages you have used.

(2) Collecting and filing material Once you begin you may be tempted to read matter not strictly germane to your subject. Keep on your charted course by (1) bearing your exact topic in mind, (2) taking advantage of tables of contents, indexes, and summaries at the beginnings and ends of chapters to find pertinent material, and (3) skipping unrelated matter.

Take notes selectively to fit your general plan. Be sure that each note is legible at first writing; copying is sheer waste of time. (See **51** for kinds of notes.)

File your notes every day by topics rather than by sources. Be sure to include notes on any field study or interview you may have conducted. The order of your files may be alphabetical, but a better order is a topical arrangement to match your outline. Guide cards for the main divisions will help. As your outline changes and comes closer to its final form you can rearrange your note file to match. You will thus have a constant check on the proportion of your reading, whereby you can easily avoid duplication and fill in any gaps.

52c. Organization and Development of Material Clear organization in a term paper is vital. All your material must serve one clear purpose. Therefore before beginning to write, review your notes and decide whether they fit your original purpose or suggest some modification.

(1) Ordering With a definite purpose clearly in mind—a problem to solve or an uncertainty to clarify—organize your note cards. Decide on a good order for your major topics, pushing the cards around until you are satisfied that you have found the most effective. Similarly arrange the minor topics under each major topic in the most effective order. Discard odds and ends. Do any necessary additional reading.

You may find it useful at this point to make a formal outline crystallizing the planned order. The outline may be included in your paper as a table of contents.

(2) Writing—the first draft You may begin to write with a brief introduction, announcing the scope and purpose of the paper and giving any essential background. Or you may prefer to begin directly with your first pile of notes and later write such introduction as you (or your instructor) may consider necessary. The introduction need not be set apart and labeled (unless your instructor requires it); a direct beginning can weave in any needed information and be more interesting than a formal preface.

Write your way through the piles, looking far enough ahead of your immediate card to insure continuity and blend. Clarify any unfamiliar or difficult terminology. For each main division formulate a specific question; answer it by presenting and analyzing evidence from your various sources. Make the whole build toward a definite conclusion.

393

Give credit for each idea as you work it in. A marginal jotting of source and page is enough in your first draft. In the final draft you will put the matter into formal footnotes (see **52d**).

Proportion your writing wisely. Ordinarily the second half of a paper treats more important ideas than the first. Therefore deal with the early parts as concisely as possible, and leave yourself time, space, and energy to do justice to your big ideas.

Give special attention to transitions. In presenting material from more than one source show the connection. If two authorities agree, say so. If they disagree or agree only in part, say so. Keep your reader constantly informed of the direction of your thought.

End with a summing up, an announcement of findings, a definitely stated conclusion, temperately expressed. The beginning and the conclusion should show what the paper attempts and what it accomplishes.

Revise (see **34**) and put your paper into final form.

52d. **Final Form, Indication of Sources** Make sure that your paper is correct in form. An elaborate term paper may have five parts:

   title page
   table of contents
   text (with footnotes)
   appendix or appendices (if needed)
   bibliography or bibliographies

The simplest term paper requires two:

   text
   bibliography

Include all the parts required by your instructor.

(1) The title page should give the title of the paper (centered), your name, the name of the course, and the date.

(2) The table of contents should list (with page references) the main divisions of the subject, the more important subdivisions (indented under their covering head), the appendix (if any), and the bibliography. The working outline revised to fit the final treatment can serve as a table of contents.

(3) The text, as described in **52c,** should present a survey of the material read and the results of the writer's independent thinking.

Footnotes Careful discrimination between borrowed material and the writer's own ideas requires accurate crediting of the source of every quotation and citation. Though acknowledgment can be worked into the text, precise information is better given in a footnote. Footnotes enable the reader to verify citations easily, to supplement the information given in the paper, and to place the responsibility for a statement on its originator.

Footnotes may also be used to add original comment or detail that might distort the text.

Reference to footnotes is best made by a number placed slightly above the writing line at the end of the citation or quotation. The numbers may run consecutively throughout the paper or begin at 1 for each page. The number is repeated at the beginning of the footnote. (In a research paper, asterisks * and similar symbols are less desirable than numbers.)

Footnote form offers several options, but the form chosen should be followed consistently. The forms here shown are acceptable in most colleges.

The first reference to a source should include

FOR A BOOK

the author's name (first name or initials first), the title (underlined), the volume (if there is more than one), and the page

Example: Arnold J. Toynbee, A Study of History, Vol. I, p. 5.

FOR AN ENCYCLOPEDIA

the author of the article (if given), the title of the article (in quotation marks), the name of the encyclopedia (underlined), the edition, the volume, and the page

Example: William McDougall, "Trance," Encyclopaedia Britannica, 14th ed., Vol. 22, p. 403.

FOR A MAGAZINE ARTICLE

the author's name, the title of the article (in quotation marks), the name of the magazine (underlined), the volume, the date (in parentheses), and the page

Example: William Vogt, "A Continent Slides to Ruin," Harper's Magazine, CXCVI (June, 1948), p. 481.

FOR A BULLETIN, PAMPHLET, RECORD

the sponsoring body, the name of the bulletin (underlined), the date, and the page

Example: U. S. Department of the Interior Grazing Service, The Act of June 23, 1938 (commonly known as the Pierce Act), 1940, p. 5.

FOR SECONDHAND MATERIAL

the original source, the quoting source

Example: Lodilla Ambrose, "A Study of College Libraries," Library Journal, XVIII (April, 1893), quoted in Bennet H. Branscomb, Teaching With Books, p. 34.

FOR AN INTERVIEW OR LECTURE

the name of the authority, his title or pertinent qualifications, the occasion, and the date

Example: Harold S. Norman, President, Florida Citrus Canners Coöperative, interview on labor policy, March 17, 1949.

If for any reason no bibliography is included, the first reference to a work must include the facts of publication, as shown in the discussion of the bibliography, **52d(5)**.

Later references to the same source use a short form.

Examples: Toynbee, Vol. I, p. 230.
Vogt, Harper's, p. 482.

If more than one work by the same author is used, distinguishing titles must be given.

If a reference to the same work follows its predecessor without an intervening footnote it requires only the word *ibid* (= the same) and the page reference. If a footnote intervenes, the new reference gives the author's surname, the abbreviation *op. cit.* (= in the work cited), and the page. A reference to the same page of the same work need give only the author's surname and the abbreviation *loc. cit.* (= in the place cited). A passage drawn from several different places in the same work may be footnoted *passim* (= here and there).

Other abbreviations often used in footnotes are the following: *cf.* (= compare), *p* (= page), *pp.* (= pages), *vol.* (= volume), *[sic]* (= thus, erroneous or peculiar matter just quoted in an exact reproduction of the original).

Footnotes are usually inserted (in single-space typing) at the bottom of the page, separated from the text by a horizontal line. In matter to be published, footnotes are inserted in the text immediately after the passage referred to and separated from the text by lines drawn above and below.

(4) An appendix, usually placed before the bibliography, may include tables, charts, or other illustrative matter and interesting sidelights or additions which would overload the text or which are not strictly relevant to the study.

(5) The bibliography, alphabetically arranged, should give complete identifying data for all the sources actually used (omitting works consulted but not drawn from). Periodicals may be listed separately or included with books. Primary sources may be distinguished from secondary sources. The bibliography does not include personal interviews; these are credited in the text or footnotes.

Each entry should include three parts: the author's name, the title, and the facts of publication. (Where only a part of a work is used page references should be added.) Each of the three major parts must follow a prescribed form.

Regularly begin each item with the name of the author or authors, surname first. A book by more than one author is alphabetized by the first author given on the title page. Anonymous works may be alphabetized by *Anonymous* or by the title. When the author is not given, an article from an encyclopedia may be alphabetized by the first important word in the title of the article. Articles from a composite work, a series or a symposium, may be alphabetized by the author of the individual article. Unsigned newspaper articles may be alphabetized by the name of the paper.

Second, give the full title of the work, underlined for a book, enclosed in quotation marks for an article. For translations add the name of the translator.

For articles add the title (underlined) of the larger work— the magazine, the encyclopedia (and its edition), the collection (and its editor or editors).

Last, give for books the place of publication, the name of the publisher, and the date. For a part of a book give the pages. For periodicals, encyclopedias, and collections, give the volume number, the date, and the pages. (For illustrations see the bibliography at the end of the Specimen Term Paper, **53**.)

398

53. A SPECIMEN TERM PAPER

UNCHAINING
OUR
STATE GOVERNMENT

You cannot tie a man's hands for
evil and leave them free for good.
Theodore Roosevelt

Malcolm R. Peattie
and
Donald H. Pflueger
Government 105
January, 1948

UNCHAINING OUR STATE GOVERNMENT

Introduction: Constitutional Problems

When the constitution of a state is soundly constructed, the state government runs efficiently and responds promptly to the will of the people. Most of our state constitutions are not so constructed. A number of states are still operating under untouched constitutions more than seventy-five years old.[1] A few have made complete revisions. A few are now in various stages of the process of revision. A few have tried to revise and failed. But, according to one experienced observer, "instead of improving the frame of government to attract the best men and permit them to serve the state efficiently, the typical state has taken the defeatist road of multiplying constitutional limitations in the vain attempt to keep bad men from doing too much harm."[2]

Here perhaps is the root of our constitutional difficulties. In the same way that we often vote against one man rather than for another so we shape our constitutions against a specific evil rather than for a general good. Times change and evils change and we amend further, but the old weapons of bygone fights lie buried in the constitution. From sheer mass the task of persuading the people that the old safeguards are unnecessary becomes increasingly difficult.

---

1. Thomas J. Herbert, "Can the States Do the Job?" *State Government*, XX (August, 1947), p. 218.
2. J.E.B., "The Manacled State," *National Municipal Review*, XXXVI (March, 1947), p. 123.

Why is it so hard to revise a constitution? Apart from the difficulty of the work itself the fundamental reason is that the people are not aware of the problem. "It takes a lot of doing and the vital need is to inform the people thoroughly on what is wrong with the old one." [1] With this in mind we are devoting this paper to a study of the constitution of our own state, California; of how it grew; and of the steps now being taken toward revision. We shall also at some points compare it with the *Model State Constitution*, prepared by the National Municipal League.

The *Model State Constitution* sets up a government organization with two major objectives—to provide desired services efficiently and economically and to give the people effective control. Its cardinal principle is that responsibility must be definitely placed and that therefore authority must be given commensurate with responsibility. To this end it provides that at the state level the only elected officials shall be a unicameral legislature, the governor, and the chief justice. Each thus becomes responsible for an entire branch of the government. All subordinate officers are appointed by and accountable to their respective heads. This simplification, though it removes some officials from direct reach of the people, actually makes popular control more effective; the public knows exactly where to place responsibility. To lighten the work of the legislature and to bring local affairs closer to the people, the Model Constitution allocates broad powers to local units. To enable the people to legislate at need, it establishes the initiative and the referendum. Throughout, it places emphasis on broad principles and structural outlines, on enabling rather than on restricting. The *Model State Constitution* empowers; it does not legislate. It is brief and easily understood.

From errors in theory, from historical circumstances, from public ignorance, and occasionally from deliberate malpractice, most state constitutions fall far short of such a standard. California's is no exception.

---

1. Charlton F. Chute, "How to Get a New Constitution," *National Municipal Review*, XXXVI (March, 1947), p. 124.

Constitutional History of California

The California constitutions of 1849 and 1879 reflected the turbulent times in which they were born. On the eve of the Mexican War California was a remote and neglected province of Mexico, a plum ready to drop as soon as the United States shook the tree. A country of rich rancheros, many of whom were Americans, it was governed only vaguely by Mexico. Actual government followed the alcalde system, a simple rule by local men of influence. Labor was supplied by Indians; each rancho was self-sufficient; and the capital, Monterey, existed chiefly for the social life of the aristocracy.

At the end of the war, a temporary military government was set up over the "conquered" province, and victors and vanquished sat down to wait for Congress to establish California as a part of the Union. But Congress was preoccupied, and took no action. Dissatisfaction grew as increasing numbers of settlers poured into California, bringing American ideas of law and government. Then in the winter of 1848-49 Marshall's discovery of gold on the American River became known in the East, and with the spring the wagon trains and ships started west. The sudden influx of new citizens made totally inadequate the paper military government that was haphazardly maintaining old Mexican laws.[1] Eventually in the summer of 1849 a constitutional convention was called by Governor Riley at Monterey.

Bringing their blankets, forty-eight delegates assembled. Only seven were California born.[2] The rest were in the main recently arrived Americans from the mining counties—originally merchants, farmers, lawyers, engineers, bankers, physicians, and printers, now goldminers.[3] These quite overwhelmed the conservative rancheros of the south, and cast the mold of northern dominance that has chafed Southern California ever since.

---

1. Josiah Royce, *California, passim.*
2. *Ibid,* p. 260.
3. Hubert Howe Bancroft, *The History of California,* Vol. VI, p. 288.

This first constitutional convention, working without even an enabling act from the United States Congress, completed its final draft in six weeks. The delegates copied largely from the constitutions of New York and Iowa, without inquiring too closely into possible defects. They wanted a document which would be accepted by Congress, and they didn't worry about any rough edges it might have. It was approved by the people, and in 1850 California elected two senators, Gwin and Fremont, and sent them to Washington with the new state constitution, where they secured its approval.

California thus came into the union without ever having been a territory, too preoccupied with gold to be serious about its own government. This does not mean, however, that the constitution was an unworthy document.[1] The members of the convention were for the most part men of vision, young, patriotic, and determined to have law and order. The first governor, Peter Burnett, was an able administrator.

The constitution was based on a sharp division of powers, short terms, and checks and balances residing in the hands of the people. It held with little change until 1862. Then the accumulated abuses of a dozen years brought on a flood of amendments, nineteen of them designed to improve the judiciary.[2]

In the boom times of the 50's California was a hectic whirl of land-grabs, gambling, paper cities and paper millions, and various forms of vice and corruption. The first legislature was called "the legislature of a thousand drinks" from its hobnobbing with lobbyists.[3] Women made up only eight per cent

---

1. Royce speaks of the Constitution of 1879 as a change for the worse. *Op. cit.*, p. 270.

2. Though Crouch and McHenry (*California Government: Politics and Administration*, p. 14) state that only three amendments were adopted between 1849 and 1879, the text of the constitution published by the California State Senate gives thirty-one *verbatim*, all but two being adopted in one year, 1862.

3. Bancroft, *op. cit.*, Vol. VI, p. 311.

of the population and in the mining countries only two per cent.[1] In San Francisco between 1848 and 1856 there were over a thousand murders and only one conviction.[2] The swift justice of the miners' tribunals had given way to the uncertainties of the official courts, which were often corrupt, always slow, and generally negligent of the public welfare. For a long period in 1856, for example, the Supreme Court did not sit because one justice was out of the state, one was in effect in jail—"confined" by the Vigilance Committee, and the third was vacationing (or perhaps hiding) at some springs.[3] To correct judicial shortcomings and to clarify procedure, the law-abiding elements pushed through the amendments of 1862.

As the rich gold strikes came to an end and the people of the state turned from the life of the mining camps to more orderly pursuits numerous defects in the state government began to appear. In San Francisco hoodlums terrorizing racial minorities and threatening law and order were put down by citizens' committees of vigilantes, setting a dangerous precedent. Depression following the Civil War brought distress and unrest. Farmers united against the railroads and other great corporations. Popular dissatisfaction was crystallized in the formation of the "Sandlot" or "Workingmen's" party, headed by Dennis Kearney, an Irish rabble-rouser, who centered his attacks on the railroads and their use of cheap Chinese labor. It was chiefly due to the agitation of Kearney's party that the moderate and conservative elements in the state legislature called for a constitutional revision in 1877. In 1879 this convention met at San Francisco. Present were 152 delegates, including fifty-seven of the Workingmen's Party, seventy-eight non-partisans, eleven Republicans, and ten Democrats.[4]

---

1. Charles Edward Chapman, "California," *Encyclopaedia Britannica*, 14th ed., Vol. IV, p. 288.
2. John Gunther, *Inside U.S.A.*, p. 10.
3. Bancroft, *op. cit.*, Vol. VIII, p. 225.
4. Crouch and McHenry, *op. cit.*, p. 15.

The convention was not as sensational an event as had been anticipated, despite the presence of the Irish laborites. Twenty-three committees went to work, and soon completed a revision.

The result was a curious mixture of progressive and reactionary provisions. Much matter was included that today would be considered statutory and many fences were erected against the peculiar evils of the time. The new constitution dealt at great length with the details of government, specifically limiting the power of the legislature. It forbade special legislation on dozens of subjects by name. Lobbying was made a felony. Tax regulations aimed at the great corporations were written in. Careful restrictions were placed on the disposal of public lands. The judicial branch was completely reorganized and minutely prescribed for. And the unfortunate Chinese received a whole article, designed to remove them from the California scene.[1] Where the constitution of 1849 was perhaps too loose in some respects, the constitution of 1879 was by modern standards much too tight. And the rusty chains of yesterday bind our government now.

The new constitution was adopted by the voters early in 1879, and went into effect on July 4th of that year.

The Constitution of 1879

When we examine the 1879 constitution, under which we are now living, we find a long and complicated document that practically defies analysis. With the amendments which have been added, it has become so formidable that comparatively few Californians have ever read it in its entirety. Children are graduated from our public schools without knowledge of it. Certainly this is one of several grounds for demanding a less cumbersome fundamental law.

Perhaps the worst evil of a balky and detailed constitution is the burden placed on the legislature and the electorate. In countless matters the legislature cannot act until the people move. Details must be constantly piled on details. In the last two decades an average of twenty amendments have been presented to the voters at each general election.

---

1. *Ibid.*, p. 17: "Most of the prohibitions and restrictions [on the Chinese] were subsequently declared invalid."

Just how long is California's constitution? As published by the California State Senate in 1945 it covers two hundred seventeen pages and totals more than 72,000 words—almost ten times the length of the Federal Constitution or the Model State Constitution. The original document as it appeared in 1879 contained some 16,000 words, the difference being due to the 256 amendments added since 1879. In view of these appalling figures it becomes apparent that only a sketchy analysis and summary of the constitution can be given here. Since the amendments have been written directly into the text of the constitution it is virtually impossible to separate the original document as it was created in 1879, or rather revised in 1879, from the present one. Special mention will be given to the most important amendments as they fit into the entire picture. Briefly, then, here is an analysis of our state constitution.

Unlike the rest of the document the preamble is terse and well worth remembering. "We, the People of the State of California, grateful to Almighty God for our freedom, in order to secure and perpetuate its blessings, do establish this constitution." [1]

The first article, containing twenty-five effective sections, is a declaration of our basic rights. Lacking the pithy elegance of the federal Bill of Rights it manages to say many of the same things. The basic freedoms and rights are included in this article, but are presented in a hodgepodge fashion. For example, the section dealing with liberty of speech and of the press, perhaps the most basic of all freedoms, does not occur until the ninth section. Intervening is a lengthy section dealing with the pleading of guilt before a magistrate and the yearly calling of a county grand jury, a relic no doubt of earlier troubles. An excerpt from Section 13½ explains why California school children know little about the "basic rights" as provided by the first article of their state constitution: "The State, or any of its cities or counties, may acquire by gift, purchase or condemnation, lands for establishing, laying out, widening, enlarging, extending, and maintaining memorial grounds, streets, squares, parkways and reservations in about and along and leading to

---

1. The preamble is the same as that of 1849 with the addition of the words *and perpetuate*.

any or all of the same, providing land so acquired shall be limited to parcels lying wholly or in part within a distance not to exceed one hundred fifty feet from the closest boundary of such public works or improvements; provided, that when parcels which lie only partially within said limit of one hundred fifty feet only such portions may be acquired which do not exceed two hundred feet from said closest boundary. . . ." California had no Jefferson.

Section 25, dear to the hearts of many Californians on the first of May each year, guarantees the right to fish in California waters.

The second article, with six sections, deals with the right of suffrage. Section 2½, an amendment adopted in 1908, establishes the primary election system of California. California was a pioneer in this movement.

The third article, Distribution of Powers, is unique for its brevity. The entire article is shorter than Section 25⅝ of the fourth article. This third article is derived from the 1849 con-stitution and provides for the distribution of powers into the three departments of government, legislative, executive, and judicial.

In sharp contrast to the third article, the fourth, which pertains to the Legislative Department, contains 37 sections which are long, detailed, and undoubtedly confusing even to many legislators. Everything from the kitchen sink to grandma's slippers is found here. Because we have not space for a complete analysis we shall mention only some of the more significant or more ridiculous sections.

Among the most important matters treated in the first section are the initiative and referendum. These two progressive instruments of government are a study in themselves.

Among the ridiculous features is the numbering system. The casual reader, perhaps a trifle sleepy by the time he gets well into the fourth article, suddenly is startled to find that he is seeing double when he runs across two sections both of which are numbered "1a." The first section 1a deals with the effective dates of legislation passed by the fiftieth session of the legislature in 1933, while the second section 1a states that all bureaus of the state must submit budgets and claims to the state controller.

The second section provides for biennial sessions of the legislature with the provision for extraordinary sessions called by the governor. The split session, whereby the legislature convenes and introduces bills, recesses for a minimum of thirty days, and reconvenes for further debate and voting, is also included.

Scattered among the important provisions of the article are sections whose rich variety of major and minor subjects typifies the confusion of the whole document and the intrusion of matter that belongs in the statutes, not in the constitution. No hint of logic appears in the choice or arrangement of material.

Section 22, unbelievably long-winded, provides among other things for the financing of the Panama-Pacific International Exposition held in San Francisco in 1915. Section 24 has an interesting echo of the 1849 constitution—a provision that all official writings shall be published only in the English language.[1] Section 25 lists a total of thirty-three items on which local or special laws cannot be passed, *e.g.*, granting of divorces, etc. Section 25a creates the California Horse Racing Board, while Section 25½ sets up a five-member Fish and Game Commission. Section 25⅝ (it's truly amazing how sections are divided into *a*, *b*, *c*'s, and fractions) assures California fishermen that all license fees and fines go into a fishing and game fund to be used exclusively for natural life preservation. Section 25¾ regulates wrestling and boxing matches; Section 26 prohibits lotteries and bucketing. Section 31a, a product of the cow-county legislators, assures cattle ranchers that if the state kills off their livestock as a preventive measure for disease control they will be promptly reimbursed. Once again the casual reader thinks he sees double, and does, as there are two sections 31b and likewise two sections 31d. The second section 31b authorizes the city of Escondido to hold stock in a mutual water company. Section 35 makes lobbying a felony, but this section has practically been laughed out of the constitution—by the lobbyists themselves. One need only look at some of the other sections of this same article to see more of the unsubtle workings of an omnipotent and omnipresent lobby.

---

1. The constitution of 1849 provided for publication in English and Spanish.

From the foregoing it can readily be seen that the fourth article of our state constitution is nothing less than unadulterated chaos. How did it get that way? First of all, the constitutional convention of 1879 was determined to restrict the powers of the legislature in every possible way. The inadequacies of the 1849 constitution in financial matters became a particular issue when this fourth article was discussed and written in 1879. Much of its detail resulted from attempts to break the octopus hold of the railroads on the state and on the legislature.[1]

Structurally malformed from the beginning, this article is all too typical of the constitution as a whole. The actions of succeeding legislatures, pushed and pulled by the lobby, and the frantic efforts of the electorate by means of the initiative, have only added more deadwood to the toppling structure.

[The analysis continues article by article, but for lack of space only excerpts are given here.]

. . . .

Section 12 [of Article 13, Revenue and Taxation], adopted in 1924 and probably unfamiliar to the majority of the present California electorate, reads as follows: "The Legislature shall provide for the levy and collection of an annual educational poll tax of not less than five dollars on every male inhabitant of this State over twenty-one and under fifty years of age, except persons holding an honorable discharge or discharged under honorable circumstances from the army, navy or marine corps of the United States, persons who pay a real or personal property tax amounting to at least five dollars per annum, paupers, idiots, insane persons and imbeciles. Said tax shall be paid into the State school fund." To the knowledge of the authors this section has never been enforced at the polls; by its very nature it would seem virtually impossible to enforce.

. . . .

The eighteenth article, Amending and Revising the Constitution, sandwiched between an article dealing with homestead

---

1. That hold was not broken until 1910, and even today the largest private landowner in California is the Southern Pacific. Gunther, *op. cit., passim.*

exemptions and the one directed at the Chinese problem of the 70's, contains only two sections, but is a vital part of the constitution. Section 1 states that when both houses of the legislature pass with a two-thirds majority any proposed amendment to the constitution said amendment must appear on the ballot at the next election. A simple majority given by the electorate is required to make such amendment a part of the constitution. The second section provides for constitutional revision when two thirds of both houses recommend a constitutional convention and the electorate at the next general election gives approval. It is strange indeed that this article which deals exclusively with constitutional amendment and revision makes no reference to the powers of the people to amend their constitution by means of the initiative.

· · · · · · ·

Article twenty, Miscellaneous, lives up to its name. One of its twenty-two sections forbids dueling and prescribes penalties! Most of the matter contained here should be dropped or transferred to the statutes. Its few points of constitutional concern should be placed elsewhere in the constitution.

· · · · · · ·

Article twenty-five is non-existent. The authors of this paper are at a total loss to explain the phenomenon, but this omission of an article makes the organization and balance of our constitution all the more incredible and fantastic.

The Road to Good Government

In any attempted revision we must face first the problem of separating the constitution from the statutes. About all that can be called "constitutional" in our document is the bill of rights, the definition and division of the triform government, the mechanics of legislation and suffrage, and certain miscellaneous provisions pertaining to the self-executing character of the constitution, amending process, and so forth. The remainder, generally speaking, has no place in a constitution. Many provisions are controversial matters incorporated in the constitution by interested groups to keep them safe from court rejection on the ground of unconstitutionality. The removal of this flotsam must be our first task.

Even after scraping off the mass of legal barnacles, we shall find that the ship of state is far from ready to meet the strains of the coming years. The rigging is tangled; the sails are bound by hampering restrictions. The crew doesn't trust the captain. The passengers, who select the crew, don't trust either. Even when the passengers have decided where to go, it is doubtful that a straight course will be set. The independent boards act as supercargos, taking orders from no one except themselves. The old ship still floats, but it is hardly seaworthy. It needs a thorough overhauling in every part.

In the executive branch, we find that the governor has a group of subordinate department heads elected by the people. They are often men who are opposed to his policies and aspire to succeed him. Many of the boards which he nominally heads are controlled by other executives, the legislature, or independent and ex officio leaders whose appointments are out of his hands. The process of administration is interfered with by the legislature. Buck-passing is the inevitable result. The governor lacks the authority to carry out a concrete program of administration in his own way.

The bicameral legislature may well be accused of too much politicking and too little legislation. Much of its inefficiency is accounted for by its clumsy organization. Some is undoubtedly due to constitutional provisions obliging the legislature to deal in detail with matters belonging properly to local units. The rest can be laid to its constant interference with matters outside its logical jurisdiction; the too great ease with which the buck can be passed to the electorate on just those questions which the voters send their representatives to Sacramento to decide; the quality of the members.

It is generally conceded that the representatives in the legislature do not meet often enough, or receive adequate compensation, to qualify as full-time legislators. We must forget the theory that government is a part-time job which any intelligent man can handle. The only lawmakers on full-time, adequate pay in Sacramento are the lobbyists.

In the matter of apportionment it is sufficient to say that the unbalance of popular representation in both houses is comparable to the "rotten borough" system as it existed in England about 1800.

The Judiciary has received a bad mauling at the hands of the legislature. Between 1879 and 1942 the article governing it was amended fifty-two times. Yet its structure in some respects is still archaic. For example, the present distribution of superior courts by counties finds the single judge in little Alpine county trying perhaps two cases a year and the fifty judges in Los Angeles county serving constantly but frequently finding themselves years behind in their work.

In revising the constitution, perhaps the hardest problem will be that of arousing and informing the public. The voters have on several occasions rejected proposals to revise the constitution which almost none of them have read. Many are fearful of losing their "constitutional rights" in some mysterious way. Others vote "no" on anything they don't understand. Still others feel that the constitution is satisfactory so long as conditions are not unbearable. Most feel that any faults it might have can be corrected by amendments and still more amendments. Oddly enough, however, when in 1934 the electorate voted for calling a convention, the legislature failed to provide the necessary machinery and appropriation—apparently because of fear of radical sentiments of the times.

First Steps Toward Revision

In 1947, through the efforts of Assemblyman Alfred W. Robertson of Santa Barbara and other supporters of constitutional revision, the legislature set up a joint committee to consider revision of the constitution.[1] The committee, composed of ten assemblymen appointed by the Speaker of the Assembly and ten senators appointed by the Chairman of the Senate Committee on Rules, was given a $50,000 budget and permission to work at any time until the end of the 1949 general session. It was empowered to draw on the aid of any local groups interested in good government—a power little used to this date. It was also empowered to appoint an advisory committee of 176 members.

---

1. A proposal for a constitutional convention had passed the assembly but had been defeated in the senate, possibly a reflection of the battle between rural interests preponderant in the senate and urban in the assembly.

The legislators met, called a convention, and sent out invitations to advisory delegates. The list of advisory delegates is a curious one. It includes many lobbyists and others representing interested groups. In issuing invitations to the convention the legislative committee asked these advisers to state what subcommittees they wished to serve on. This, in the opinion of many liberals, amounted to an invitation to pressure groups to help shape the new constitution or drag back the old one to conform to their own interests. To the unsophisticated observer it seems rather like sending a rabbit to carry lettuce. Will any real improvement be made by such a group?

Among the advisory members business, agricultural, and transportation interests were well represented; if labor unions were represented their delegates did not make their presence known. The membership was well supplied with noted legal talent. All the leading California universities sent representatives. The advisory committee tended in geographical distribution to correspond to population; fifty-eight of the 176 were from Los Angeles.

On October 29, 1947, in the historic Lobero Theatre in Santa Barbara, the convention was formally opened with the swearing in of the members and an address by Governor Warren (not present) delivered by Lieutenant-Governor Knight. In his address Warren urged a form of government directly responsive to the needs of the people. He urged a strong state government that accepts full responsibility and does not depend on the federal government.

The next speaker, the Honorable Justin Miller, president of the National Association of Broadcasters, former federal judge, and dean of two law schools, recommended among other things the removal of excessive restrictions on the governor and the legislature and the consolidation of responsibility in the executive branch.

After Miller's speech the theater was cleared and the twenty-man legislative committee met to adopt its rules and appoint the membership of its subcommittees, a purely formal move, since last-minute adjustments of membership on the subcommittees had been made at the reception for delegates given that afternoon in a local restaurant, between members of the legislative and advisory committees.

On the following day several speakers, including two former governors, addressed a meeting of these two committees. Their proposals were on the whole in accord with modern theories of government. Former Governor Culbert L. Olson recommended sweeping changes, particularly reapportionment. "Sixty-five per cent of the population elect only three senators while the remaining 35 per cent elect the remainder," he said. He proposed a unicameral legislature with staggered four-year terms at salaries of not less than $6,000 annually. The present two-house system, he said, is dangerous in that each house depends on the other to study bills carefully, resulting in the passage of many "joker clauses". A unicameral body besides avoiding duplication of effort would be less costly, since fewer members would do the work.

That afternoon the ten subcommittees met in open session to start their deliberations. The work of the convention was then turned over to them.

The sharpest criticism in the press was leveled at the composition of the subcommittees. Herbert L. Phillips, noted commentator, wrote in his column appearing in the *Sacramento Bee* on November 7 the following observation:

Approximately 40 lobbyists and professional representatives of special interests usually in Sacramento when the Legislature meets have been appointed to the subcommittees of the special Senate-Assembly Interim Committee which is trying to rewrite the state constitution. There are ten of them, for instance, on the thirty-one member subcommittee on "fundamental rights." There are 17 on the 56 member subcommittee selected to deal with the legislative department. And there are 21, or nearly half the subcommitte total, on the 45-member subcommittee on taxation and revenue.

The subcommittee lists reached Sacramento today from Santa Barbara where the Joint Committee on Constitutional Revision held its first major meeting a few days ago. Along with it came private comments from various northern political figures in attendance, who said they could not remember an occasion when so many lobbyists were assembled except at actual sessions of the legislature in Sacramento.[1] Very few major special interests in California, they reported, were unrepresented.

---

1. There are 294 registered lobbyists in Sacramento.

It was to be expected, of course, that all interested groups and corporations would have an eye on the proceedings, since the plan for revision of the Constitution of 1879 affects the entire state and all walks of life. But selection of special interest legislative advocates and business representatives as actual members of the subcommittees ... came as something of a surprise. ...

On the same subject Edward Kennedy, noted AP correspondent and managing editor of the *Santa Barbara News-Press*, stated in an interview with the authors that while "everyone is represented here except the people," the chances for a new constitution, at first hopeful, had become increasingly worse with the arrival of these paid delegates, and on the opening of the meeting, seemed almost hopeless.

Certain controversial issues may well deadlock these subcommittees, or the whole convention. In attempting a fresh approach to the constitution, rather than a mere shortening of the old document, the convention runs the risk of failing to accomplish anything at all.

Still, the improbable may be accomplished; a sound constitution may be produced. And then will come the last and most difficult hurdle—gaining popular approval. In 1849 the whole people demanded a constitution. In 1879 large new groups of people demanded a new constitution. Who speaks for the people in 1949? A few progressive legislators know that we must unchain our government. A few editors comment. A few teachers discuss the question. From the citizenry—silence. But as an editorial in the *Santa Barbara News-Press* remarked, "Assemblyman Robertson and his fellow legislators have started something ... that cannot be forgotten—or covered up like an embarrassing question no one should have asked." [1]

Conclusion: Recommendations

The authors of this paper have not touched on many of the problems of government bordering on the constitution, hoping that a clean-cut, broad new constitution will serve as a point of departure for reforms in these borderline areas. Such areas include the condition of political parties, voting, apportionment programs, and the general political atmosphere of the state.

---

1. *Santa Barbara News-Press*, October 29, 1947.

Keeping in mind, however, that a constitution and its resulting political system are only what the people make of them, the authors recommend:

1. A total revision of the present constitution—mere simplification, obviously, is not likely to be satisfactory.

2. A strong, unified executive branch, with a definite chain of command, to be headed and controlled exclusively by the governor, who is to be the only elected state executive officer.

3. A unicameral legislature of about one hundred members elected on a basis of two members from districts of equal population, without regard to county or other local governmental boundaries, the districts to be redefined with shifts in population at frequent and regular intervals, the members to be chosen for two-year overlapping terms, and to receive the same compensation that persons of comparable experience, ability, and knowledge receive in the professions or business.

4. A simplified and greatly expanded judiciary, somewhat removed from too-close legislative control by constitutional checks, with power to clean its own house by means of a judicial council as outlined in the Model State Constitution.

5. Elimination of independent boards. These boards are no more immune to political log-rolling and frustrated action than any other branch; they are removed from executive assistance and control; and to some extent they usurp the powers of the legislative and judicial branches. This fourth branch of government tends to be bureaucratic and undemocratic. It undermines the triform basis of our government. Worst of all, it is becoming further and further removed from popular control.

6. Security of the constitution from too easy amendment, but at the same time the installation of a permanent Legislative Constitutional Committee to consider all matters concerning revision or amendment. The requirement of a higher proportion of votes for passage of initiative and referendum measures having to do with amendment.

We believe that a constitution clearly stating these principles and actively protecting the fundamental rights of the people will unchain California's government.

BIBLIOGRAPHY

BANCROFT, HUBERT HOWE. *A History of California from 1542-1890.* San Francisco: The History Company, 1890, Vols. VI, VII.

BROMAGE, ARTHUR W. "Simplifying State's Business," *National Municipal Review,* XXXVI (March, 1947), pp. 131-136.

BUCK, A. E. *The Reorganization of State Governments in the United States.* New York: published for The National Municipal League by Columbia University Press, 1938.

CARPENTER, WILLIAM SEAL, and STAFFORD, PAUL TUTT. *State and Local Government in the United States.* New York: F. S. Crofts & Co., 1936.

CHAPMAN, CHARLES EDWARD, "California," *Encyclopaedia Britannica,* 14th ed. Chicago, 1939, Vol. IV, pp. 589-597.

CHUTE, CHARLTON F. "How to Get a New Constitution," *National Municipal Review,* XXXVI (March, 1947), pp. 124-130.

Constitution of the State of California. Sacramento: California State Senate, 1933, 1945.

CROUCH, WINSTON W., and MCHENRY, DEAN E. *California Government: Politics and Administration.* Berkeley: University of California Press, 1945.

DAHL, ROBERT A. "The Science of Public Administration: Three Problems," *Public Administration Review,* VII (Winter, 1947), pp. 1-11.

GUNTHER, JOHN. *Inside U. S. A.* New York: Harper & Brothers, 1947, pp. 1-63.

HARRIS, JOSEPH P. "Modernizing the Legislature," *National Municipal Review,* XXXVI (March, 1947), pp. 142-146.

HERBERT, THOMAS J. "Can the States Do the Job?" *State Government,* XX (August, 1947), pp. 215-218.

J. E. B. "The Manacled State," *National Municipal Review,* XXXVI (March, 1947), p. 123.

MACDONALD, AUSTIN F. *American State Government and Administration,* 3rd ed. New York: Thomas Y. Crowell Company, 1946.

MASON, PAUL. *Constitutional History of California.* Sacramento: California State Senate, 1945.

Model State Constitution, A., 4th ed., New York: The National Municipal League, 1945.

PHILLIPS, HERBERT L. "Politics in Review," *Sacramento Bee,* Nov. 7, 1947.

ROYCE, JOSIAH. *California from the Conquest of 1848 to the Second Vigilante Committee in San Francisco.* Boston: Houghton Mifflin Company, 1894.

Santa Barbara News-Press, Oct. 29, 1947.

Letters and Manuscript

LETTERS

54. See that your letters are clearly written, correct in form, specific and genuine in substance.

54a. **Business Letters** Write or type on one side of a sheet 8½ x 11 inches. Balance material on the page. Maintain uniform margins at least one inch wide. Either indent paragraphs an inch or a half inch, or use straight block (unindented) form.

(1) Heading and inside address In the upper right-hand corner give your full address and the date. Below it and at the left margin give the name and the full address of the person or firm to whom the letter is written. Make the heading and the inside address consistent in form. Do not abbreviate short words or omit *street* or *avenue*. Do not abbreviate the date.

(2) Greeting Place the greeting at the left margin, a little below the inside address. Use a greeting suited to the degree of formality of the letter.

Correct for an acquaintance
Dear Miss Smith: Dear Mrs. Jones: Dear Mr. Johnson:
More formal   My dear Mr. Johnson: My dear Mrs. Jones:
Correct for a person or persons unknown to you
  Dear Sir: Dear Madam: Gentlemen:
  Ladies (or Mesdames):
More formal   My dear Sir: *Most formal*   Sir: Madam:

CORRECT HEADING, INSIDE ADDRESS, AND GREETING

Block form (common for typewritten letters)

```
                    5043 Drexel Boulevard
                    Chicago 15, Illinois
                    July 6, 1953

Libbey-Owens-Ford Glass Company
1458 Nicholas Building
Toledo 3, Ohio

Gentlemen:
```

Indented form, open punctuation

```
                    106 East Race Street
                      Red Oak, Iowa
                        June 18, 1951

Mrs. Morey P. Page
  Post Office Box 385
    Carlsbad, New Mexico

Dear Mrs. Page:
```

Indented form, closed punctuation (now seldom used)

```
                    1433 Woodward Avenue,
                      Lakewood 7, Ohio,
                        October 24, 1950.

Mr. D. A. Forbes,
  3315 Centennial Boulevard,
    Nashville 8, Tennessee.

Dear Mr. Forbes:
```

(3) Content: plan Group your ideas logically. Do not scatter information. A letter applying for a position might consist of three paragraphs: Personal qualifications (age, health, education, etc.); Experience (nature of positions, dates, etc.); References (names, business or profession, exact street address). Finish one group of ideas before passing to the next.

(4) Content: language Make direct, specific, complete statements. Do not omit pronouns or write a telegraphic style. Use *I* if you need it. Avoid jargon and slang.

Roundabout: I am writing to say that I hope you will consider my application for a job in your store.

Direct: I apply for a position as clerk at the cosmetics counter in your drugstore.

Faulty telegraphic style: Yours of the 21st received, and in reply would say your order was filled and shipped next day.

Improved: We filled your order and sent the consignment by American Railway Express, charges collect, on March 22.

Stilted avoidance of *I*: Enclosed please find 10 cents, for which send me Bulletin 58.

Natural, clear: I enclose ten cents, for which please send me Bulletin 58.

Jargon: Received yours of the 3rd instant, and beg to advise I will send payment in full on August 1, as per contract.

Simple, specific: I have your request for payment of $19.75. By the terms of our contract the payment is due August 1. I will send it by money order on that date.

Unnecessary slang: We'll get on the job with your request for a catalog as soon as the printer comes across with some more copies. Our aim is to give A-1 service, as our ad stated.

Dignified, definite: Thank you for requesting a copy of our spring catalog. We will mail you one in about a week. Our first printing is exhausted.

(5) The close and the signature Begin the closing phrase in midline below the body of the letter; follow it by a comma. Handwrite the signature below and to the right of the close; type the name under it if the signature is hard to read. (A married woman signs her own name and writes or types her married name under it in parentheses.)

Use a close consistent in tone with the greeting.

Dear Mr. (Miss, Mrs.) Brown:	Yours sincerely, Sincerely yours,
Dear Sir (Madam): or Gentlemen: Ladies:	Yours truly, Very truly yours,
Sir: Madam: (used for officials)	Respectfully yours,

Note that only the first word of the close is capitalized.

Avoid old-fashioned expressions like *I am, I remain, As ever.* Avoid the weak closing participle: *Hoping to hear from you soon..., Wishing you..., Thanking you....*

Weak: Hoping you can give me some further
    information, I remain
                Yours truly,

                Florence Mitchell
                (Mrs. John B. Mitchell)

Improved: I shall be grateful for any
    further information you can give me.
                Yours truly,

                Florence Mitchell
                (Mrs. John B. Mitchell)

Titles and degrees such as *Mr., Dr., M.D., Ph.D.* are not used with a signature. (*Miss*) for an unmarried woman is permissible, but unnecessary.

Titles indicating office or position may be written below the signature if they are needed as explanation.

Wrong: Yours sincerely,
      Allen Jenkins, M.D.

Right: Yours sincerely,
      Allen Jenkins

Right: Yours truly,
      Ellen Weil
      Secretary to Dean Briggs

Right: Yours truly,
      James Ross
      Treasurer

No punctuation follows the signature.

(6) The outside address Use the same form (block or indented) used for the inside address. Ordinarily write city and state on separate lines. Be accurate in the use of names and titles.

Inaccurate: Monsanto Co.

Correct: Monsanto Chemical Company [Write a corporation name as it appears on the firm's letterhead.]

Right for a married woman or a widow: Mrs. George Turner

Right for a married business or professional woman: Mrs. Grace Turner, Dr. Helen C. Barnes.

Wrong: Mrs. Dr. Jenkins, Mrs. Professor Ward [A married woman does not acquire her husband's title.]

Right: Mrs. John Jenkins, Mrs. Arthur Ward

Wrong: Dr. A. Bruce Steele, M.D.

Right: Dr. A. Bruce Steele, or A. Bruce Steele, M.D.

Wrong: Reverend Beecher

Right: The Reverend Charles K. Beecher

Right: Senator Hubert H. Humphrey, The Honorable George A. Outland [a member of the House of Representatives]

MODEL BUSINESS LETTER

379 Valley Road
Montclair, New Jersey
May 14, 1940

Carl Griffith, Manager
The Acme Garage
11 Orange Road
Montclair, New Jersey

Dear Sir:

I apply for a position as mechanic's assistant in your garage. I am nineteen years
old and in good physical condition. On June
6 I shall complete my first year of study at
Stevens Institute of Technology, Hoboken;
after that date I can begin work immediately.

I have had practical experience in garage
work. For two years I have made a special
study of auto mechanics, in and out of
school. I worked last summer in Taylor and
Brown's Service Station. In addition, I
have become familiar with tools in my work-
shop at home, so that I both know and like
machinery.

For statements as to my character and
ability consult
Mr. Eugene M. Brown, of Taylor and Brown's
    Service Station (Montclair 22141)
Mr. George Knight, a lawyer, 115 Grove
    Street, (Montclair 03195)
Mr. Louis Vieth, a banker, 256 Upper Moun-
    tain Avenue (Montclair 03122)
Ralph W. Holt, Principal of Montclair High
    School (Montclair 32876)

Very truly yours,

Howard Rolfe

Block Form

R. E. Stearns
512 Chapel Hill Street
Durham, N. C.

Mr. Donald Kemp

3314 Salem Street

Baltimore 9

Maryland

Indented Form

Elizabeth Davis
Route 1, Box 238
Burlington, Vermont

Doubleday & Company, Inc.

14 West 49th Street

New York 26

New York

424

54b. Personal Letters

Write personal letters clearly and without crowding, on paper of good quality. Use matching envelopes.

(1) Form Place your address and the date either at the upper right or at the left below the signature. In letters to friends you may omit your correspondent's full name and address. Use a greeting, close, and signature suited to the degree of acquaintance. Place a comma after the greeting.

(2) Content Organize your material about a few centers; do not try to "tell everything." Consider your reader's interests. Respond first to whatever he has written you; then select from your own recent experiences and thoughts those which will appeal to him.

Avoid both stiffness and excessive informality. Use personal incidents, lively details, humor; do not use trite or wildly exaggerated language.

Unnecessarily stiff: I am starting this letter now, but I don't intend to finish until I hear from you, which I trust will be in the near future.

Interesting, natural: Who knows? Perhaps before I finish this letter the postman will bring one from you.

Forced humor: Was sure you'd committed suicide, but your letter finally got here, though it's as hard to decipher as a black cat on a dark night, hah hah! I mainly got the idea that you are going to summer school, and taking something or other from a *darling* man. Honey, I wouldn't like him. I'm off men, as off as a run pair of nylons.

Pleasant, genuine: Exactly what your letter says will remain your secret; the handwriting is inscrutable. Your first paragraph *seems* to tell me that you are going to summer school; that you like your teacher of science, (p)sychology, or something beginning with *s*; and that you think I would like him. You are wrong; I would not! I am bitter on the subject of men.

54c. Social Notes

(1) Informal Notes In writing a note of thanks or of con-
gratulation, a letter of condolence, etc., you may begin
directly with the greeting.

Avoid the use of trite expressions; say something definite
and sincere.

Trite; vague: Thank you very much for sending me a copy of
The American Past. I'm sure I'll enjoy it. The pictures look
fascinating.

Genuine, specific: Last evening I sat down with *The American
Past* at eight o'clock and did not put it away until a half hour
after midnight. By a happy combination of authentic cartoons
and pictures with terse, brightly written text Butterfield casts
sharp light on our social and political history. A page I particularly enjoyed....

Trite: I can't tell you how grieved I was to learn of your great
loss. Please accept my sincere sympathy. If there is anything
I can do....

Natural: Everyone who knew your father must share your grief.
His warm friendliness always brought good cheer. I remember
a particularly kind thing he once did for me....

A BREAD-AND-BUTTER NOTE

Dear Mrs. Marvin,

Sally was right. You do possess a remarkable understanding of the young. I keep remembering your unper-
turbed greeting when we routed you out of bed at one
A.M.; your enthusiasm over our party; your friendly help
with all our problems, from making ribbon sandwiches to
dressing for the Formal. My weekend was not just a holiday; it was an occasion.

Most gratefully,

Nan Ross

Oberlin, Ohio
March 20, 1952

---

(2) Formal Notes Use the third person (avoiding *I*, *my*, *me*, *you*, *your*) for a formal invitation, announcement, or reply. Give it no heading, greeting, closing phrase, or signature. Spell out every word except the street number and the abbreviations *Mr.*, *Mrs.*, *Dr.* In acceptances or regrets follow the same form as the invitation, repeating the day and the hour to avoid misunderstanding.

FORMAL INVITATION

Mr. and Mrs. Clarence King
request the company of
Mr. Charles Eliot
at dinner on Friday, the tenth of May,
at six o'clock
514 Poplar Avenue

FORMAL REPLY

Mr. Charles Eliot accepts with pleasure
the kind invitation of Mr. and Mrs. King
to dinner on Friday, the tenth of May,
at six o'clock.

[A formal reply is always written in the present tense]

EXERCISE

X-54. Letters

Rewrite each passage in direct, natural language.

1. Received your letter in regard to the book "Manual of Engineering Specifications," also your check, and in reply will say that I am mailing you a copy of the book under separate cover. Please return same within ten days.

2. The darnedest thing happened yesterday. You know I told you Ann fixed me up a date for the Formal with her cute cousin, who has been dying to meet me. Well, what did my brother do but breeze in last night with his roommate and introduce *him* as my date for the Formal. Was I burned up! Quick like a bunny I pulled a Houdini and went into a huddle with Ann....

Write out in correct form, fully punctuated, each numbered passage below, just as it would appear in a letter. Insert one horizontal row of dots in place of the body of the letter. Write the first heading in block form, the second in indented form with open punctuation, the others in the form you yourself prefer. Do not mix forms.

3. 2146 Stone Street Falls City Nebraska November 11 1951 Mr. H. C. Anderson Secretary-Manager Commerce and Industry Commission 263 State Capitol Cheyenne Wyoming Dear Sir Yours truly Samuel Roberts

4. 128 North Belmont Avenue Wichita 8 Kansas April 12 1952 Dear Aunt Martha Affectionately yours Maud Carter

5. 2062 East 175th Street Seattle Washington February 17 1950 Miss Margaret Welch Vice-principal John Burroughs High School 800 South McCadden Place Los Angeles 5 California My dear Miss Welch Sincerely yours June English Mrs. Arthur D. English

6. 1321 Enfield Road Apartment 2 Austin Texas May 6 1951 Dear Kathy Love Pete

7. 4241 Greenwood Drive Des Moines 12 Iowa May 22 1953 G. & C. Merriam Company Publishers Springfield 2 Massachusetts Gentlemen Yours truly Helen Thomson Reference Librarian Des Moines Public Library

8. 614 South Fifth Street Ironton Ohio The Honorable Thomas A. Jenkins House Office Building Washington D.C. Sir Respectfully yours Walter Moss

9. Randolph-Macon Woman's College Lynchburg Virginia September 28 1950 The Reverend Edwin M. Clark 4182 Watkins Avenue Bethesda Maryland Dear Sir Respectfully yours Anne Riley Chairman Students' Interfaith Committee

10. University of the South Sewanee Tennessee Miss Emily S. Jones Executive Secretary Educational Film Library Association, Inc. Suite 1000 1600 Broadway New York 19, N. Y. Very truly yours Ronald Wood

MANUSCRIPT AND MECHANICS

55. **Make your manuscript correct, attractive, and consistent.**
In all college papers either type or write in ink on white paper 8½ x 11 inches. Use one side only. Unless otherwise instructed, fold the written paper vertically and place on the outside your name, the course name and section number, the subject of your paper, and the date.

55a. Arranging Material on the Page

(1) The title Center the title on the page. Capitalize the first word and all other words except prepositions, conjunctions, and articles. Do not place a period after a title; use a question mark or exclamation point if it is appropriate. Do not underscore a title. Do not place it in quotation marks unless it is a quotation.

(2) Spacing Indent the first line of each paragraph about one inch. Keep uniform margins; divide words at the ends of syllables if necessary to avoid ragged holes at the right. Leave a space after a word and a double space after a sentence. In typewriting, use double spacing between lines except in footnotes and in quoted passages made to stand by themselves on the page. In handwritten pages, leave room between successive lines.

(3) Handwriting; deletion and insertion Write a clear, legible hand, uncrowded and unsprawling. Connect all the letters of a word. Take pains to keep capitals and small letters from looking alike. Form *a, o, u, n, e, i* properly. Write out *and* horizontally. Avoid unnecessary flourishes and curlicues. Dot your *i*'s and cross your *t*'s, not with circles or long eccentric strokes, but simply and naturally. Form the letters of proper names with care. Make your signature legible.

To cancel a word, draw through it a horizontal line. Never use parentheses to indicate deletion. Never hand in a page made unsightly by deletions and erasures; if more than two or three erasures occur copy your material.

To supply omitted words, write them above the line and show the place by inserting a caret ($_\wedge$) below the line.

(4) Syllabication Divide words between syllables only. Two consonants at the junction of syllables are separated except when they are equivalent to a single letter. A single consonant at the junction of two syllables usually goes with the second unless the vowel in the first is short and stressed. A prefix or suffix is regularly set off regardless of other rules.

Correct division (two or more consonants):

quar-ter remem-ber sur-prise ath-letic
univer-sity plan-ning dif-ferent com-mit-tee

Inseparable combinations:
fa-*sh*ion au-*th*entic so*ph*-omore ba*ch*-elor

Correct division (one consonant):

pre-ju-dice inti-mate be-lieved criti-cism
busi-ness ceme-tery elimi-nate mainte-nance

After a short stressed vowel:
pos'-itive gov'-ernment mag'-azine priv'-ilege

Correct division (prefix or suffix):

de-scribe dis-charge dis-appoint pro-fessor
market-able fright-ened study-ing myth-ology
de-part-ment ex-ist-ence photo-graph-ic

Never divide a monosyllable. Avoid separating one or two letters from the rest of the word.

Correct (monosyllables and short syllables):

through (not *thr-ough*) eliminate (not *e-liminate*)
rhythm (not *rhy-thm*) achieve-ment (not *a-chievement*)
dipped (not *dip-ped*) orig-inal (not *o-riginal*)
clothes (not *clo-thes*) busy (not *bus-y*)

55b. Using Abbreviations and Numbers

(I) Abbreviations In ordinary writing use few abbreviations.
Spell out titles such as *Professor, President, Secretary, Captain, General, Senator.* You may use the abbreviations *Messrs., Mrs., Mmes.* (Mesdames), *Dr., St.* (Saint), before proper names and *Jr., Sr., D.D., LL.D.,* etc., after proper names. Place a period after each such abbreviation.

Spell out Christian names unless initials are used instead: Charles, Robert, William. If you use initials place a period after each: D. C. Heath, Charles A. Sumter.

Write out the name of an agency or organization the first time you mention it in an article. After that use initials if they are commonly understood: Interstate Commerce Commission (ICC or I.C.C.); Society for the Prevention of Cruelty to Animals (SPCA or S.P.C.A.); Associated Press (AP); Tennessee Valley Authority (TVA); United Nations Economic, Social, and Cultural Organization (UNESCO). Periods are often omitted after such initials.

Spell out names of months, of days, of states, of countries: January, Wednesday, Christmas, Massachusetts, the United States.

Spell out *Street, Avenue, Building, Railroad, Fort, Mountain, Company, Brothers, Manufacturing,* etc.

Spell out words like *volume, chapter, page, history, mathematics, chemistry, department.*

Spell out names of weights and measures (except in statistics): pound, foot, centimeter, miles per hour.

Write *and* (not &). Write *in the morning, in the afternoon* (not *in the a.m., this p.m.*). Use *B.C., A.D.* when necessary to avoid confusion. Use *No.* or *$* before numerals when appropriate.

(2) Numbers Write out numbers which you can express in a few words.* Use figures for complex numbers and complicated sums of money, and for dates, hours (when followed by *a.m.* or *p.m.*), street addresses, telephone numbers, page references. Do not use a figure at the beginning of a sentence.

Right: The box weighs two hundred pounds.
     Xerxes had an army of three million men.
     I enclose seventy-five cents.
     He owed twelve hundred dollars.
     Grandfather Toland is eighty-seven years old.
     The train is due at a quarter past three.

Right: The farm comprised 3,262 acres.
     In 1930 the population of Kansas City, Missouri, was 399,746.
     He earned $437 while attending school.
     The cost of the improvement was $1,940.25.
     The plane landed at 10:00 a.m.

Make a series of numbers uniform; use figures rather than words.

Right: The frame is 2¼ inches wide and 1 inch thick. Two of the pieces are 18 inches long, the other 20¾ inches.

Except in legal or commercial writing, do not follow written numbers by confirmatory figures in parentheses. When you do use such figures make sure that they confirm the right elements.

Objectionable: We had six (6) guests.
Right: We had six guests.

Wrong: The bill is for seventeen ($17) dollars.
Permissible: The bill is for seventeen dollars ($17).

Wrong: The bill is for seventeen dollars (17).
Permissible: The bill is for seventeen (17) dollars.

* For the writing of compound numbers see **23c** and **23d**.

55c. Using Italics

(1) Quoted titles Use italics (indicated by underscoring) for the quoted titles of books and periodicals.*

Right: In *Democracy, The Threshold of Freedom,* Gosnell appraises the actual operation of the suffrage and of representative government.

Right: I subscribe to the *Atlantic, Harper's Magazine,* and the *New York Times* [or New York *Times*].

Use either italics or quotation marks for quoted titles of plays, musical compositions, works of art, motion pictures, radio programs.†

Right: Surely everybody admires *Macbeth.* [The italics show that the writer means *Macbeth* the play, not Macbeth the man.]

(2) Foreign words Italicize foreign words which are still thought of as foreign.

Right: A shout announced the coming of the *enfant terrible.*

Right: Usually a play begins *in medias res.*

(3) Words or letters as such Italicize words or letters made the subject of reference or comment.

Right: The word *so* is faded and colorless from constant use.

Right: The *t* in *often* is not pronounced.

(4) Words requiring emphasis Italicize a word or passage which requires great emphasis. Avoid overuse of italics.

(5) Names of ships Italicize the names of ships.

Right: The *Lurline* will sail at four o'clock.

---

* In letters and other very informal writing, titles may be set off simply by capitalizing the principal words. In typewritten letters titles are often written entirely in capitals.

† For additional examples see **28d(2).**

55d. **Acknowledging Sources** If you borrow a passage, a sentence, or even an idea, acknowledge your indebtedness.

(1) **Direct quotations** Regularly set off quoted prose passages by quotation marks. (For a detailed treatment see **28b.**)

(2) **Reference to sources** Ordinarily, give credit in the body of your composition for borrowed ideas or passages. If you use many sources, list them at the end of your paper and acknowledge your indebtedness for individual excerpts or ideas either in the composition or in footnotes.*

Textual acknowledgment of an idea:

The shallow analysis of the individual in the common expression "unchangeable human nature" has been exposed by John Dewey in his book *Individualism Old and New*. He maintains that human nature is not like the "given" in a theorem of geometry, but is dependent on environment.

55e. **Correction, Improvement** Revise all written work before you hand it in.† Correct your papers as soon as they are returned. Follow the method your instructor requires. He may ask that you make corrections on the back of the preceding page opposite the original errors. He may ask you to rewrite faulty sentences or passages or to rewrite the entire paper. When you are asked to rewrite, hand in the old version with the new. Never erase the instructor's signs or comments.

A figure I (or Ia, Ib) written in the margin of your paper means "Read Article I (or Section Ia, Ib) in the handbook and revise your sentence in the light of it." When an X follows the number, you are to study the article or section and write the exercise at the close.

---

* For discussion and illustration of the use of footnotes see **52d(3).**
† For a detailed treatment of Revision see **34.**

Symbols often used by instructors are listed below:

awk or k = awkward		√ =	error. Find it. Correct it.
cap = use a capital		¶ =	begin a new paragraph
lc = lower case	no	¶ =	no new paragraph
or no cap = use a small letter		∧ =	something omitted here
coh = incoherent		δ =	delete, take out
d = diction faulty	tr or	∽ =	transpose
gr = grammar faulty		? =	Who? What? Why?
p = punctuation faulty			Something is uncer-
sp = misspelling			tain, incomplete, or
ss = sentence sense			questionable here.

Keep all written work until the end of the year. When you have a conference with your instructor, take your work with you.

EXERCISE

X-55. Manuscript Rewrite the following passage, correcting errors in syllabication, the use of abbreviations, the use of italics, and the acknowledgment of sources. (There are ten errors.)

It is the frantic behavior of the mob that E D Martin objects to in his book The Behavior of Crowds. In his view, the social problem today is that numbers, not values, count. The individual is permitted neither to know nor to belong to himself. The social harmony, he says, is menac-ed by a great no. of cliques and parties, from the nation crowd down to the smallest sect. Prof. Martin offers a sugg-estion for the cure of crowd thinking by educ. means. In his foreword he writes, it is sufficient for my purpose merely to point out that the humanist way of thinking may provide us with just the educational method which will break up the logical forms in which the crowd mind entrenches itself.

INDEX

Individual items included in the Glossary of Faulty Diction are not listed in the Index. They may be found on pages 160-178.

The numbers refer to pages.

(37)

ANALYTICAL CHART

THE SENTENCE AND ITS PARTS

THE COMPLETE SENTENCE		**1** **Fragments Wrongly Used as Sentences** a. Complete Statement Test b. Grammar Test for Wholeness c. Phrases and Clauses d. Other Types of Fragments e. Permissible Fragments
THE CLEAR SENTENCE	**5** **Reference of Pronouns** a. No Antecedent b. False or Feeble Antecedent c. Ambiguous Reference	**6** **Dangling Modifiers** a. Modifier Beginning a Sentence b. Modifier Ending a Sentence c. Permissible Modifiers of the Whole Sentence
GRAMMAR	**10** **Case** a. Nominative Case b. Objective Case c. Possessive Case	**11** **Agreement in Number, Gender, and Person** a. Subject and Verb b. Pronoun and Antecedent
DICTION	**15** **Conciseness** a. Deadwood and Circumlocution b. Impersonal Constructions c. Passive Constructions	**16** **Repetition** a. Ungrammatical Repetition b. Tautology c. Awkward or Needless Repetition d. Necessary Repetition
SPELLING	**20** **Spelling through Observation** a. Identify Your Errors b. Visualize Words c. Study Pronunciations d. Form Right Muscular Habits	**21** **Rules for Spelling** a. Words in **ei** or **ie** b. Doubling a Final Consonant c. Dropping a Final **e** d. Changing Final **y** before a Suffix e. Forming Plurals
PUNCTUATION	**25** **One Comma to Separate** a. Main Clauses with a Conjunction b. Items in a Series c. Misleading Combinations d. Superfluous Commas	**26** **Two Commas to Enclose** a. Appositives b. Guide Words c. Place and Date Completers d. Loose Modifiers (nonrestrictive)

THE SENTENCE AND ITS PARTS

2
Omission of Necessary Words
a. Illogical Constructions (General)
b. Illogical Constructions (Double Capacity)
c. Misleading Constructions
d. Faulty Idiom
e. Permissible Incomplete Constructions

3
The Run-Together Sentence
a. Comma Splice
b. Telescoped Sentences

4
The Tacked-Together Sentence

7
Unnecessary Shift
a. Number
b. Tense
c. Subject
d. Voice
e. Mood
f. Point of View
g. Sentence Plan

8
Parallelism
a. Shift in Part of Speech
b. Shift Involving Larger Sentence Elements
c. Careless Use of Correlatives
d. Failure to Repeat Words
e. Misuse of Parallelism

9
Sentence Coherence
a. Related Elements Not Kept Together
b. Unrelated Elements Joined
c. Straggling Modifiers

12
Tone and Time
a. Indicative and Imperative Moods
b. Subjunctive Mood
c. Modal Auxiliaries (Potential Mood)
d. The Six Tenses
e. Formation of Tenses
f. Expression of Simple Time
g. Time with Reference to Basic Present
h. Reference to Basic Past
i. Reference to Basic Future
j. Progressive Forms, etc., in Time Relations
k. Anomalies

13
Substituted Forms and Elements
a. Adjectives Misused as Adverbs
b. Adverbs Misused as Adjectives
c. Other Forms and Elements Wrongly Substituted

14
Terms of Grammar

17
Exactness
a. Misused Specific Terms
b. Trite Expressions
c. General Terms
d. Abstract Terms
e. Faulty Connotation
f. Faulty Expression of Relationship

18
Good Use
a. Selecting a Dictionary
b. Finding Information in a Dictionary
c. Faulty Idioms
d. Technical Words, Jargon
e. Colloquial Terms
f. Slang
g. Illiterate or Ungrammatical Forms
h. Euphemisms; Genteelisms

19
Glossary of Faulty Diction

22
Spelling List

23
Compounds
a. Merging of Meanings
b. Compounds Forming a Single Adjective
c. Compound Numbers
d. Fractions as Compounds
e. Special Lists

24
Capital Letters
a. First Words
b. Important Words in Titles
c. Names
d. General Terms Added to Names
e. Titles of Persons
f. Pronoun I and Interjection O

27
The Apostrophe
a. Contractions
b. Non-use with Possessive Pronouns
c. Possessive Case of Nouns
d. Plurals of Numbers, etc.

28
Quotation Marks
a. Speech, Dialog
b. Borrowed Matter
c. Words Used in a Special Sense
d. Minor Titles

29
Other Marks
a. End Marks
b. The Semicolon
c. The Colon
d. Dashes
e. Parentheses
f. Brackets

THE WHOLE COMPOSITION	**30** **Analyzing Your Subject and Sharpening It** a. Limiting the Subject b. Determining Purpose and Controlling Idea c. Finding a Title	**31** **Finding Material and Organizing It** a. Finding Material b. Logical Division and Proportion c. Logical and Effective Order
THE PARAGRAPH	**35** **Division of Material** a. Adequate Paragraphs in Exposition b. Convenient Paragraphs in Exposition c. Short Paragraphs for Special Purposes d. Paragraphing Narration e. Paragraphing Dialog	**36** **Unity** a. Limiting the Subject b. Separating Run-together Paragraphs c. Focusing on the Main Idea d. Relating the Paragraph to the Composition
CLEAR THINKING	**40** **Reasonable Statement** a. Inaccurate Observation b. Slips in Logic c. Word Slippage	**41** **Classification** a. Logical Conformity b. Logical Comparison c. Definition
STYLE	**45** **Consistency of Tone and Imagery** a. Tone b. Connotation c. Imagery	**46** **Simplicity and Concreteness** a. Simplicity b. Concreteness
RESEARCH	**50** **Use of a Library** a. The Card Catalog b. Reference Works c. Periodicals d. Evaluating Books and Articles	**51** **Assimilation of Material** a. Effective Reading b. Note-taking c. Paraphrasing d. Summarizing
LETTERS AND MANUSCRIPT	**54** **Letters** a. Business Letters b. Personal Letters c. Social Notes	**55** **Manuscript, Mechanics, Correction** a. Arranging Material on the Page b. Using Abbreviations and Numbers c. Using Italics d. Acknowledging Sources e. Correction, Improvement